GENDER AND POLITICAL COMMUNICATION IN AMERICA

LEXINGTON STUDIES IN POLITICAL COMMUNICATION
Series Editor: Robert E. Denton, Jr.,
Virginia Polytechnic Institute and State University

This series encourages focused work examining the role and function of communication in the realm of politics including campaigns and elections, media, and political institutions.

TITLES IN SERIES:

GENDER AND POLITICAL COMMUNICATION IN AMERICA

Rhetoric, Representation, and Display

Janis L. Edwards

LEXINGTON BOOKS

A division of

ROWMAN & LITTLEFIELD PUBLISHERS, INC.

Lanham • Boulder • New York • Toronto •Plymouth, UK

Published by Lexington Books
A division of Rowman & Littlefield Publishers, Inc.
A wholly owned subsidiary of The Rowman & Littlefield Publishing Group, Inc.
4501 Forbes Boulevard, Suite 200, Lanham, Maryland 20706
http://www.lexingtonbooks.com

Estover Road, Plymouth PL6 7PY, United Kingdom

British Library Cataloguing in Publication Information Available

Library of Congress Cataloging-in-Publication Data
Gender and political communication in America : rhetoric, representation, and
display / [edited by] Janis L. Edwards.
    p. cm. — (Lexington studies in political communication)
  Includes bibliographical references and index.
  ISBN 978-0-7391-3107-7 (cloth : alk. paper) — ISBN 978-0-7391-3108-4 (pbk. : alk.
paper) — ISBN 978-0-7391-3109-1 (electronic)
  1. Communication in politics—Sex differences—United States. 2. Women
politicians—United States—Language. 3. Rhetoric—Political aspects—United States.
I. Edwards, Janis L., 1949–
  JA85.2.U6G46 2009
  320.97301'4—dc22   2009016009

∞ ™ The paper used in this publication meets the minimum requirements of
American National Standard for Information Sciences—Permanence of Paper
for Printed Library Materials, ANSI/NISO Z39.48-1992.
Printed in the United States of America

CONTENTS

CONTENTS

ACKNOWLEDGMENTS

No book is compiled in a vacuum. Many individuals helped to bring this collection of scholarship to fruition. First, I must thank Lexington series editor Robert E. Denton Jr. for his support for this project, among many others under his direction, that have helped put communication studies scholars "on the map" of political research. I might never have started down this road of inquiry if Jane Blankenship had not shared her enthusiasm about women in politics twenty years ago with her students and collaborators. I was also inspired in the conception of this book by the rich work of other scholars working from a rhetorical perspective, who have contributed their insights to the study of men, women, and gender dynamics in politics and society.

Dan Waterman's assistance in the early visualization of this project was crucial, as was the support and advice of Kathleen Kendall and Mary Kahl. The contributors to the volume have been unfailingly enthusiastic and cooperative through a process that cannot be characterized as leisurely. Teresa Bergman and Lisa Burns were my valued cheerleaders at key moments.

I must gratefully acknowledge Western Illinois University for providing the grant funds that led to my own initial study of the campaign films of Hillary Clinton and Elizabeth Dole, and the many comments from students, colleagues, and reviewers that helped me develop my specific contributions for this volume. Appreciation goes to Marsha Houston and Jason

Black, my colleagues at Alabama, for their special interest, discussions, and support. Marilee Urban accomplished early and important work on manuscript preparation. Lexington editors Matthew McAdam and Joseph Parry answered my many questions during the preparation and editing process with patience and good humor.

Finally, I must thank my many graduate and undergraduate students who have, since 1997, shared with me the adventure of studying political communication through a gendered lens. They have kept me on my toes and motivated me to constantly renew and update my thoughts and research on this important topic. Particular thanks go to the student members of our 2008 "PalinWatch" project at the University of Alabama for asking important and challenging questions, and for discovering some answers in the process. Their useful observations on recent political events translated into an increased commitment to this book's completion in the midst of the unusually compelling election events of 2008.

INTRODUCTION

Politics as a Gendered Space

Janis L. Edwards

Politics in the United States of America has always been intertwined with gender. Not only are gender norms and expectations deeply embedded in the institutions and procedures of society and public affairs but, as Kann argues, masculinity was injected into the rhetoric of early American citizenship through a "grammar of manhood" adopted in the discourse of the Founding Fathers.[1] The expectations of manhood that were woven into the national fabric of assumptions about political leadership and citizenship, and the consequences of those constructions, continue to define contemporary political practice in significant ways. The historic exclusion and marginalization of women from full and representative participation in the democratic process may be the most obvious linkage between gender and politics to some, but gender is inserted into and implicated in national politics in other ways both profound and subtle. Real-world events and academic interest in the continuing challenges and changes effected by various feminisms ensure that the subject of gender and political communication remains salient.

In response to recognition of politics as a gendered space, the academic fields of women's studies and political science began to merge interest over the topic of women's roles in institutional political structures, inspired primarily by events that propelled women into elective leadership and advocacy roles. The project of women's studies and its associations with the fields of political science and, eventually, political communication also demanded examination of women's historic position in the political sphere, a position which has been characterized by unique constraints, based on deeply entrenched views about gender differences in society, and marked by significant contestation.

Although women's involvement in the formulation of national social policy has been in evidence since the first wave women's rights movement more than a century ago, and while women had campaigned for or assumed leadership roles at national levels prior to the passage of women's suffrage in 1920, the story of women's paths to institutional political power remains characterized by novelty and tokenism, as it has for decades. The first women to serve in Congress typically were seated as replacements for their deceased husbands, or as placeholders for subsequent men candidates. With the historic underrepresentation of women in American political affairs, initial political science and political communication research into women and politics tended to follow the now well-worn path of "difference studies" that outlined the contours of gender-based differences through empirical research methods, but also treated women as "deviants" in the political sphere. Knowing what those gender-based differences *mean*—their construction and implications—is a project assumed more recently by rhetorical scholars.

Although the social science perspective on gender and political communication, developed by both political scientists and communication scholars, has effectively formulated a "coherent sub-field"[2] of gender studies, the project of this book is to acknowledge the contributions of rhetorical and critical scholarship to the study of gendered American politics, and encourage further development of this aspect of political communication research. The rhetorical perspective on political communication and gender was initially grounded in the rhetorical tradition, with its focus on speakers and speeches, but as that tradition has expanded, so has the scope of rhetorical and critical scholarship in politics and other topics.

The major initial work that expressed the rhetorical perspective on gender and politics centered on recoveries of the "lost voices" of women in American history who spoke on behalf of suffrage and other reform movements, or who dared to aspire to lead through their words and deeds. Working within a rhetorical tradition centering on oratory, scholars identified and assessed women public speakers from the nineteenth and early twentieth centuries,[3] most of whom spoke outside the established institutions of electoral politics and governance. Additionally, scholars turned their attention to the rhetorical dynamics and advocacy of the second wave of feminism as a movement, including in these studies a widening range of non-oratorical rhetorical expression[4] that responded to the methods of social protest employed in the 1960s and 1970s. From a disciplinary interest in social movements, rhetorical history, and subaltern voices, communication scholars began to address other questions of gendered politics in a more contemporary vein. As Beasley has noted, "the second wave occurred at the right time and asked the right questions in the right places from the 1970s to 1990s to prompt interest in research on gender and political communication."[5] From a critical-humanistic perspective this research took additional inspiration from the changing dynamics of rhetorical studies, which were expanding from the traditional study of the orator situated in a historical context to include analysis of rhetorical constructions of image and character accomplished through mediated forms and rhetorical homologies. While historical studies of women speakers have been both appropriate and important to the understanding of women's place in politics, increased attention to contemporary political figures, especially Hillary Clinton, prompted social scientists and rhetorical-critical scholars to begin to "speak to each other across methodological and epistemological divides"[6] and to make more diverse contributions to the study of gender dynamics in politics. By this time, particularly within the last two decades, rhetoricians and other critical-cultural scholars also began to investigate *masculinities* as political and cultural constructs, adding an important dimension to the scholarly focus on women in their roles as voters, candidates, spouses, appointees, and advocates.

While such intellectual efforts should be recognized and honored, their progress has been uneven. Political communication has developed into a vibrant and energetic area of inquiry within the communication discipline, but its linkages to gender issues have been eclipsed to some extent by the foundational work of political scientists. Until recently, I struggled to locate pedagogical material for my courses in gender and electoral politics that reflected the rhetorical standpoint from which I teach. Part of the reason for the belated emergence and prominence of communication studies (and especially rhetorical) work in gender and politics may lie in the fact that early gender studies in the communication discipline focused primarily on interpersonal and organizational contexts. Until the 2006 publication of Dow and Wood's text, *The SAGE Handbook of Gender and Communication*, no general textbook on communication and gender seriously addressed gender dynamics in the political sphere, or incorporated a substantial rhetorical perspective. Further, with their focus on the recovery of early feminist discourses, traditional rhetorical scholars only later began to train their critical lenses more consistently on the rhetoric of contemporary female politicians. Important rhetorical investigations of gender as a component in political communication emerged in the mid-1990s, following the lead of Kathleen Jamieson's influential book, *Beyond the Double Bind: Women and Leadership*,[7] and enlarging on the concept of the "feminine style" in political discourse.[8]

While more scholars in communication studies are addressing issues of gender and politics from a rhetorical, critical, and media studies perspective, their work often remains marginalized by a failure to confront the range of issues incorporated in the twin terms of "gender" and "political," even within political communication research. For example, the *Handbook of Political Communication*,[9] intended as an overview of the field, contains only one chapter that covers women as candidates and voters, while masculinity or other issues that bring together gender and politics are otherwise absent from the discussion. Scholarship in gender and political communication that is grounded in rhetorical and other critical or qualitative theories has blossomed in recent years, but still lacks the recognition enjoyed by political science scholarship as a cohesive area of research, in part because few books treat the topic holistically. Recent books by communication scholars interrogate gender (women) and politics through a prescribed role,[10] a specified context[11] or a methodological lens.[12] But, to date, there has been no volume of scholarly work on gender and political communication that adopts a comprehensive approach to the topic and deploys the critical frameworks of rhetorical, critical cultural, and media studies in its inquiry. *Gender and Political Communication in America: Rhetoric, Representation, and Display* is intended to fill this vacancy and to draw attention to the emerging contributions to the study of women and men in political contexts that are realized through critical methodologies, often building on established empirical studies to expand the scope of this important scholarly area.

The contributors to this volume share a concern for the *symbolic and rhetorical* constructs and functions of gender in the words, actions, representations, or performances of political leaders and other personae, as compared to the study of statistically measured effects of gender on political institutions, or the study of male-female difference as a political phenomenon.

We share with our social science colleagues the assumption that gender is a socially constructed phenomenon, and a recognition that *sex* and *gender* can be slippery terms. As rhetorical, critical cultural, or media scholars, we recognize that gender is performed and displayed, as opposed to being "something located within individuals."[13] Thus, our focus is primarily on how political communication constitutes gender through self-presentation and representation. We are scholars concerned with men and women as actors and voices on the public stage—performing and displaying roles as candidates, leaders, spouses, and media commentators—and with how the media represents those image constructions. Due to the importance of cultural identity as a generative factor in political symbolism, and given the unique historical dynamics of U.S. electoral politics, this collection of studies focuses on political communication in a national, rather than an international, context.

This book was nearing editorial completion during the 2008 presidential campaign. When our work began, we could not have predicted the specific issues and personae relative to gender that would emerge as the campaign progressed, although we knew that gender would remain deeply salient in American electoral politics. Although chapter authors do not deal directly with the gendered nature of voters in this volume, the practical recognition of women as a significant segment of voters, and the prominence of female leaders in the current national scene, assure the contributors that gender will remain a concern in politics for some time to come. However, new perspectives must emerge to take into account the advances of women, the exigencies of issues, and the growing challenge to a prevailing liberal feminist perspective on politics by conservatives such as George W. Bush and Sarah Palin, who have exploited gender issues for strategic gain.[14] As for the 2008 campaign, it is directly addressed in Erica Falk's study of Hillary Clinton's 2008 announcement discourse, and readers will find considerable relevance to the 2008 campaign in other chapters.

People rarely conceptualize gender without the recognition that factors such as race and class are intertwined with gender in the larger issue of identity. Race was clearly a factor in 2008, with the nomination and subsequent election of Barack Obama as the first African American president, as was gender in the female frame, with the prominence of both Hillary Clinton and Sarah Palin as candidates. But race was also implicated in the cultural references to whiteness that emerged in Palin's discourse, as was class in critiques of Palin's image, and in Obama's "celebrity." These themes and others that relate to candidate roles and expectations are echoed in *Gender and Political Communication in America* in several ways.

Hillary Clinton's 2008 campaign incorporated themes and controversies that have followed the Clintons for years. Janette Kenner Muir and Anita Taylor look to the political and marital partnership of Bill and Hillary Clinton as a marker of gender dynamics, in the ways that their roles mesh, contrast, and are interpreted. The authors' examination of the Clintons lays bare the basic distinctions between traditional male and female roles in society and politics, and leads the collection of essays.

Paul Achter and Teresa Bergman take up matters of race and its intersection with gender in their examinations of past presidential candidates of color. Achter considers race's intersections with masculinity through the example of Jesse Jackson, a former presidential candidate. Bergman examines the case of Shirley Chisolm, another African American presidential candidate, using her image in a biographical documentary film as text. Class is at issue in Sheree' Keith's analysis of the rhetoric of working women in the suffrage movement, a movement often characterized by its upper middle-class leadership. Sexual orientation also inserts itself as an issue in Christina Standerfer's analysis of Arkansas pol Kathy Webb, and in Jimmie Manning and Cady Short-Thompson's theoretical reconsideration of gendered terms and political bodies.

Sarah Palin's campaign as the Republican vice presidential nominee also highlighted the ways in which conservatives have recently appropriated the imagery and discourse of liberal feminism to serve their partisan interests. Stephen Klien and Margaret Farrar delve into the new conservative voice of prominent commentator Ann Coulter.

Societal expectations of women's domestic roles often intercede in public perceptions of female leadership when the woman involved is the mother of young children. Readers will find echoes of controversies over Palin's status as mother of an infant in Wendy Atkins-Sayre's case study of another new mother, Governor Jane Swift. And, as Hillary Clinton's 2008 presidential bid demonstrates, expectations of women's traditional domestic roles also are problematic for first ladies and for female candidates whose highest public recognition comes from their roles as political spouses. Kim Reiser and Janis Edwards explore those contradictions in different ways in the political campaign messages of Elizabeth Dole and Hillary Clinton. These contradictions are also inherent in press representations of first ladies as outlined by Lisa Burns.

As of this writing, Hillary Clinton has recently been confirmed as President Obama's secretary of state. Heather Aldridge Bart and Heidi Hamilton's examination of Clinton's female predecessors in that position provide a framework for continued analysis of women appointees in international affairs, an area of politics traditionally more often associated with masculine interests and proclivities.

The term *rhetoric* is used broadly to characterize the critical and text-based nature of the work in this volume. While some authors may include quantification in their methodologies, the terms *rhetoric, representation,* and *display* encompass a number of specific critical concerns and strategies evident in this collection. Several authors, including Klien and Farrar, Keith, and Reiser, employ the theory of feminine style to shape or augment their studies of women's discourse. Klien and Farrar further employ the rhetorical concept of genre in their study of the diatribe. Edwards, in her analysis of masculinity in political cartoons, highlights the rhetorical trope of metaphor. Bart and Hamilton undertake their study of the rhetoric of Madeleine Albright and Condoleeza Rice by applying discourse analysis within a framework of feminist international relations theory. Bergman, Edwards, Burns, and Falk critically consider issues of representation in film and journalism, and how gender is constituted and negotiated through those representations.

A more critical cultural approach is adopted in studies by Manning and Short-Thompson and Atkins-Sayre that focus on the body in politics, as well as Achtor's study of masculinity in a racial context.

The essays collected in *Gender and Political Communication in America* are intended to provide a glimpse at the rich range of possibilities that rhetorical and critical scholars pursue when looking at issues of gender and politics. We hope that *Gender and Political Communication in America* will help provide a basis for understanding the varied dynamics of gender in electoral politics and policymaking, and signal the importance of drawing from a range of perspectives to understand both gender's role in shaping political communication activities and the role of political communication in constituting our visions of gender and society.

NOTES

1. Mark E. Kann, *A Republic of Men: The American Founders, Gendered Language, and Patriarchal Politics* (New York: New York University Press, 1998), 30.

2. Francis Mackay, "Gender and Political Representation in the UK: The State of the Discipline." *British Journal of Politics & International Relations* 6, no. 1 (Winter 2004): 99–120. Also placing women and politics into mainstream political science research are Sarah Childs and Mona Lena Krook, "Gender and Politics: The State of the Art." *Politics* 26, no. 1 (February 2006): 18–28, and the longstanding U.S. journal, *Women & Politics*.

3. Work established in the rhetorical tradition includes, notably, Karlyn Kohrs Campbell's *Man Cannot Speak for Her: A Critical Study of Early Feminist Rhetoric* (Westport, Conn.: Praeger, 1989); *Man Cannot Speak for Her: Key Texts of the Early Feminists* (Westport, Conn.: Praeger 1989); *Women Public Speakers in the United States, 1800–1925: A Bio-Critical Sourcebook* (Westport, Conn.: Greenwood,

1993); and *Women Public Speakers in the United States, 1925–1993: A Bio-Critical Sourcebook* (Westport, Conn. Greenwood Press, 1994); Sandra J. Sarkela, Susan Mallon Ross, and Margaret A. Lowe's *From Megaphones to Microphones: Speeches of American Women, 1920–1960* (Westport, Conn.: Praeger, 2003); Molly A. Mayhead and Brenda DeVore Marshall's *Women's Political Discourse: A Twentieth Century Perspective* (Lanham, Md.: Rowman & Littlefield, 2005); and Sue Zaeske, *Signatures of Citizenship: Petitionaing, AntiSlavery, and Women's Political Identity*. (Chapel Hill: University of North Carolina Press, 2003).

4. For examples of rhetorical attention to the second wave women's movement see Brenda Robinson Hancock, "Affirmation by Negation in the Women's Liberation Movement." *Quarterly Journal of Speech* 58, no. 3 (October 1972): 264–71, and Karlyn Kohrs Campbell, "The Rhetoric of Women's Liberation: An Oxymoron." *Quarterly Journal of Speech*, 59, no. 1 (February 1973): 74–86. For a study of non-oratorical feminist rhetoric see Sonja K. Foss, "Judy Chicago's *Dinner Party*: Empowerment of Women's Voice in Visual Art." *Women Communicating: Studies of Women's Talk*, ed. Barbara Bate and Anita Taylor. (Norwood, N.J.: Ablex, 1988), 9–26.

5. Vanessa Beasley, "Gender in Political Communication Research: The Problem with Having No Name," in *The SAGE Handbook of Gender and Communication*, ed. Bonnie J. Dow and Julia T. Wood (Thousand Oaks, Calif.: SAGE Publications, 2006), 201–14.

6. Beasley, "Gender in Political Communication Research," 209.

7. Kathleen Jamieson, *Beyond the Double Bind: Women and Leadership* (New York: Oxford University Press, 1995).

8. The concept of "feminine style" was developed by Kathleen Jamieson in *Eloquence in An Electronic Age* (New York: Oxford University Press, 1988) and Karlyn Kohrs Campbell in *Man Cannot Speak for Her*. Its critical development includes Bonnie J. Dow and Mari Bohr Tonn, "Feminine Style and Political Judgment in the Rhetoric of Ann Richards." *Quarterly Journal of Speech* 79, no. 3 (August 1993): 286–303, and Jane Blankenship and Deborah A. Robson, "The 'Feminine Style' in Political Discourse: An Exploratory Essay." *Communication Quarterly* 43, no. 3 (Summer 1995): 353–66.

9. Lynda Lee Kaid, ed., *Handbook of Political Communication Research* (Mahwah, N.J.: Lawrence Erlbaum Associates, 2004).

10. For example, Molly Wertheimer, ed., *Inventing a Voice: The Rhetoric of First Ladies of the Twentieth Century* (Lanham, Md.: Rowman & Littlefield, 2004), and Erika Falk, *Women for President: Media Bias in Eight Campaigns* (Urbana/Champaign: University of Illinois Press, 2007).

11. Media is the prevailing context in Annabelle Sreberny and Liesbet van Zoonen, *Gender, Politics, and Communication* (Cresskill, N.J.: Hampton Press, 1996).

12. Karrin Vasby Anderson and Kristina Horn Sheeler, *Governing Codes: Gender, Metaphor, and Political Identity* (Lanham, Md.: Rowman & Littlefield, 2005).

13. Victoria Pruin DeFrancisco and Catherine Helen Palczewski, *Communicating Gender Diversity: A Critical Approach* (Los Angeles: SAGE Publications, 2007), xiv.

14. For a discussion of Bush's role in reinscribing gendered politics see Michaele L. Ferguson and Lori Jo Marso, eds., *W Stands for Women: How the George W. Bush Presidency Shaped a New Politics of Gender* (Durham, N.C.: Duke University Press, 2007).

NAVIGATING GENDER COMPLEXITIES

Hillary and Bill Clinton as a Political Team

Janette Kenner Muir and Anita Taylor

In the history of American politics there has never been a married political couple quite like Bill and Hillary Clinton. Each highly successful as political campaigners and leaders, their ability to work together as a team speaks to the Clintons' many successes during their political careers. As individuals, each Clinton has an innate ability to adapt and respond to various situations and be highly successful in garnering public support. However, as a couple, the influence and challenges the Clintons have experienced are far greater and worth exploring in light of the complexities inherent in managing individual political aspirations. By exploring the idea of Bill and Hillary Clinton[1] as a gendered political team we gain a more complete picture of the complexities faced when navigating career goals as a married couple, while also attempting to forge individual political pathways. Throughout their political careers the Clintons have made choices, together and individually, that provide lessons for all dual-career couples who attempt to manage the public versus private demands of life.

Using the Clintons as a case study, specifically considering their rhetorical actions, we focus on two fundamental propositions: First, the Clintons' communication must be seen as that of a team, not just two individuals acting, sometimes, in concert. This, of course, makes them inexplicable to one viewing their communication from the viewpoint of the individual rhetor working in isolation. Second, the Clintons enact gender, both as individuals and as a couple, in ways that push the boundaries of gender expectations in their cultural and social milieu.

MARITAL RELATIONSHIPS AND PRESIDENTIAL POLITICS

When serving in public life, a solid marriage and strong family support are essential aspects to a thriving career. For most successful politicians someone behind the scenes (a wife or partner) manages the home life, attends political events, and advocates for the political leader as needed. Nowhere is this support more explicit than in presidential politics, where public and private lives intersect in such pronounced ways and the symbolic implications of these roles are so powerful. Much has been written elsewhere on presidential spouses and the roles they have played while serving as first ladies.[2] First lady scholarship reminds us about the ever increasing expectations of this position and the ways women, throughout American history, have participated in this informal governance. Similar to royal families, the first lady serves as hostess, policy advisor, activist and ambassador, to name just a few services, and while many expectations for this position have changed in the last twenty years, traditional perceptions still run deep for many people.[3]

Of particular consideration in this essay is the marital partnership present in presidential careers and the ways in which gendered expectations and political demands shape this partnership. Writing about the rhetorical presidency as a "two-person career," Campbell describes the institutional demands placed on the married couple that preclude "a traditional public-private spousal division of labor" and require cooperative efforts in order to be successful.[4] These expectations build the First Ladyship role as a symbolic ideal or culture type, difficult to fully understand and often under great scrutiny. Campbell notes:

> In political terms, her every word is scrutinized in the belief that she is a reliable sign of the values or underlying belief of her husband. Accordingly, she becomes a lightening rod for discontent with his administration or opposition to its stands on particular issues.[5]

Despite the intense scrutiny and discomfiture this position often entails, its power is significant. Parry-Giles and Blair offer the view that "the first lady pulpit can act as a site for the performance of archetypal femininity; it can also function as a location of feminist advancement that challenges gender stereotypes, expanding women's political space."[6]

Hillary Rodham Clinton's specific power in the White House and her political work prior to winning the presidency with her husband is noteworthy in this context. Describing Clinton as a type of "Rorschach test" for illustrating the "binds that tie women in the public sphere,"[7] Kathleen Jamieson identifies a "complex interplay" between Hillary, "the labels through which she was viewed by reporters, columnists, supporters, and antagonists" and in turn, "the residues of the complex and sometimes contradictory expectations" that inform these encounters.[8] Volumes have been written about Clinton and the rhetorical choices she has made throughout her political life, her specific role in the White House and subsequent work as an elected senator. What have not been considered as directly are the difficulties of navigating gender complexities when successful, married couples attempt to work together in public life. As will be illustrated in this essay, the Clintons are a powerful, political team that has weathered multiple challenges and still maintained a great deal of popularity and good will with many Americans. There is much to be learned by considering their lives, and their marital relationship, through a gendered lens.

GENDER COMPLEXITIES AND
THE CLINTON POLITICAL TEAM

When viewed as a married political team, several issues surface regarding the concept of gender and how it is performed in various political settings. As a foundation for the arguments we will make about the Clintons' political successes and challenges, some clarity of definitions and theoretical background is useful. Noted elsewhere throughout this volume is the idea that gender denotes quite varied concepts. Commonly a distinction is made between sex—the supposedly biologically fixed entities of male and female, two categories believed not to be fuzzy—and gender, an obviously complex category consisting of social psychological and cultural differentiations between women (as a group) and men (as a group).[9] Moving beyond this widespread definition we know that gender is (genders are) many faceted entities with no single element (facet) being gender and other elements merely modifiers.

Reconceptualizing Gender

A number of elements or facets about gender should be noted. First, although the term "sex" is usually applied in reference to physical characteristics of individuals, "gender" has also been used in reference to individual characteristics. In a more typical sense genders are constructions of social and cultural groups. They are institutions, consisting as all such entities do of boundaries, rules (prescriptions, proscriptions, built-in penalties and rewards) barriers and channeled interactions.[10] This conception differs from a common use of the term "social construction"[11] that involves individual gender identities and practices being built through social interaction. Hence, gender in political communication is, in part, a matter of where the politics are occurring and the gender rules of that social-cultural milieu.

Second, it is important to understand that gender is created in interaction (communication among individuals) and is to a great extent a matter of relationships more than the characteristics of individuals.[12] Applying that concept to political communication compels recognition that rhetors and their audience(s) engage in the co-creation of what gender will mean as they communicate. That is, of course, not a simple analysis. To complicate the issue even farther, the analyst who hopes to understand either of the Clintons as individual political rhetors must recognize that they have engaged in a lifetime of co-creating their own gender relationship. And they have done so over a thirty-plus-year career during which the social-cultural institution of gender is shifting. As with all social-cultural change, some members of these groups change more rapidly than others. In many ways the Clintons, both as a team and as individuals, have been among the early adopters of the new cultural rules involving gender, as have some of their audiences, while others have accommodated these new rules more slowly.

Recognizing the role of interaction among communicators in establishing and maintaining genders leads to looking in a different way at the interactions among rhetors and audience(s). Most rhetorical scholars recognize that speaker/message/audience influences are multiple and multidirectional. Few such analyses of political rhetors, however, have attended to speaker teams rather than to individual speakers. Hillary and Bill Clinton require a more multilayered kind of analysis, because they have seen themselves as a team of equals almost from the time they became a political couple.

A third challenge to scholars attempting to better understand the Clintons as a political team is in noting the perceptual shift from the traditional view of gender as individual characteristics and behaviors, whether the characteristics are thought of as created by biology or social interaction.

Our perspective is built on recognition that gender does in part consist of those individual characteristics and behaviors; but, only in part. To fully understand how gender is implicated in the relationships built between the Clintons and their receivers, analysts must consider other elements of gender as well (i.e., the social-cultural structures and the interaction relationships). Moreover, in doing so the analytical perspective has to be sufficiently wide to include structures of the society in which the interactions take place.

Feminist Theory as Frame

Feminist theory provides the perspective necessary to understand the Clintons as a political team, not merely as two remarkable individuals, and certainly not as the traditional political couple where a wife provides the support and aura of legitimate domesticity needed for the husband to mount the pinnacle of success (pun intended). Lorber notes how the social and political structures of Western culture are more than gendered structures. Rather, the structures themselves form a facet of genders. Every culture has sets of rules pertaining to gender that frame, constrain and shape lives, so that individuals who live and achieve within the structures do so within the strictures of the culture's rules.[13]

In cultures that are patriarchal, gender is fundamental to cultural rules. Patriarchies (literally, rule of the fathers) structure lives and expectations to put males in charge. Leadership arrangements in patriarchal systems create the following outcomes: There is a ruler, who is male (or male-identified). Women are present in service roles (wives, clerks, consorts, housekeepers, nannies, occasionally as advisers). But service roles, like labor creating products for use, not sale, are not culturally valued as leadership work, hence socially invisible. Executives strategize (plan, organize, gather resources) and implement—or give instructions for others to implement. Effective leadership also requires attracting and motivating followers, fostering cooperation, maintaining effective climate, and so on—that is, the care and feeding of relationships. But none of that kind of work gets identified and valorized as essential to being a leader. Even when the relational skills are recognized as valuable they are considered less so than the executive tasks.

Patriarchal societies structure the caring and support tasks as women's work and either do not pay for it (the wife) or, when it must be hired (secretarial and janitorial services), pay less than they do for managers, accountants or technicians. Hence, even when the ruling person is physically female, she rules as would a "real" male, and she is often legitimated primarily by her relationship to a male, as in inherited roles. As that supposedly is a not a characteristic of democracies, the "inheritances" of offices by widows of politicians must be legitimated by an election. But few voters are fooled and indeed choose the successor because of her relationship to the deceased male. In the United States, with its strict rules of succession to the presidency such inheritance has never occurred in the top executive office although it not uncommonly happens among legislative representatives and state executive offices. Significantly, when women do achieve executive positions "on their own," their leadership often displays distinctly masculine characteristics.[14]

Another aspect of feminist analysis relevant to our discussion of the Clintons as a political team focuses on the tendency to locate leadership in individuals. Hardman, then Taylor and Hardman, revealed the strong proclivity for English thinkers to rank, and when presented with a comparison between one and more than one to choose one. Hardman's analysis draws on the relationships between language and thought processes. Here we direct attention to the same preference for one in leadership structures, whether in political or other institutional settings. Such structures often preclude recognizing the reality of shared leadership in executive roles, demonstrated perhaps most clearly by the uproar that initially met the Clintons at even the hint of a "co-presidency." The political structure, like most other institutions of our culture, recognizes one president, one CEO, that is, one leader. The system permits selection of one executive—in spite of widespread acknowledgement that never does only one person carry out the tasks of the position. All the rest are "staff"; they are helpers or advisers, underlings to whom the anointed chief executive officer gives instructions and allocates responsibilities. This perspective ignores the two-way flow of influence in any working pair; authority is not shared, it may be delegated, but never shared. Yet, for the political couple, the very nature of this delegation is problematic as it ignores the power exerted through the marital relationship and the indirect and intimate influence that suggests a "subtle intrusion of the private into the public, political sphere."[15]

While on its face such a system might appear not to be gendered, in fact it is inherently so given how executive tasks are structured. Executive tasks are strategic planning, logical analysis of factual data, marshalling resources needed to accomplish the plans, direction of organizational activities. Each of these tasks is male identified. And the entire system rests on a view of gender that suggests anything male identified cannot also be female identified.[16] The underlying mindset takes as a given that if something is male, it cannot also be female; if it is feminine, it cannot also be masculine. This mindset allows there to be two and only two genders and sees them as mutually exclusive. Moreover, the system co-identifies what is male or male identified as standard (the default leader or executive) form by which all else is judged; it is the preferred form, at least in all those aspects having to do with leadership in public roles, whether those be positions in government or business.

Framing the Clintons

Previous analyses of Hillary and Bill Clinton as leaders have considered them as individuals and/or a "couple," but, to our knowledge, no previous scholarship in assessing their work or lives has rejected the frame of individual person as leader. We propose to do that, recognizing the enormous difficulty in doing so. Sandra Bem has provided a helpful metaphor as we consider the task. She suggests that it is useful to think of genders as cognitive schemata and to recognize that cultures have prevailing cognitive perspectives about gender just as do individuals. Using the metaphor of lens she argues that U.S. culture is built on three such gender schemata: androcentrism, gender polarization and biological essentialism. Her argument is useful in doing this analysis because it reminds us that what we see depends to a very large extent on what filter or screen we are looking through. We propose to work with a lens that sees the Clintons as a team, albeit like any set of human relationships a team that is always in process and evolving. To extend the metaphor, we also propose to use both a wide-angle and a macro lens. We aim to see both the rhetorical team and the audience milieu in which the team is encased and with which it must always interact, and to examine some of those interactions in depth. Given that we are considering a team life that stretches from Arkansas in the early 1970s to the presidential primary campaign of 2008, we will not attempt to be comprehensive. We will, instead, select moments that demonstrate the team in formation and the challenges faced as negotiated gender roles and expectations intertwine with political careers.

HIGHLIGHTING A GENDERED POLITICAL TEAM

Since their initial meeting at Yale Law School, and in their subsequent courtship and marriage, the Clintons have shared an ambition for politics and public service. Several authors told the story of how they built their marriage, raised their daughter Chelsea, and forged a political life together.[17] This section identifies several highlights through the Clintons' political career that help to illustrate the ways they have worked together as a team and navigated gender expectations along the way.

Defining Moments: The *60 Minutes* Interview

In 1991, Bill Clinton declared his candidacy for president amid several challenges to his ability to lead, particularly due to his perceived inexperience and his alleged indiscretions with other women. To respond to these concerns, Hillary actively supported her husband through the electoral process, serving as his political advisor and strategist. As criticism was lobbed against Bill, many people believe that it was Hillary's support and style that kept him going in the race.[18]

One of the critical incidents in the 1992 campaign that illustrates this political partnership was captured in a *60 Minutes* interview on CBS television, conducted by Steve Kroft and described in numerous essays about Hillary Clinton as a defining moment.[19] The interview provided insight into the Clintons' relationship and political campaign goals. This interview was important because Bill worked to strengthen his credibility to be president; Hillary worked to assert his qualifications to be president and demonstrate her overall support for their relationship.

Hillary's performance during this interview pointed to gender characteristics that went against the grain of general cultural expectations, and revealed important information about how this political team functions. This interview helped to bolster Bill's campaign when Hillary claimed to love and respect her husband, and to also know his foibles. She recognized what they had been through together, and declared "if that's not enough for people, then heck, don't vote for him."[20] Kroft later remarked how Hillary was clearly in charge of the interview. She knew how to handle the issue, and her response closed off concerns about Bill's weaknesses, ultimately helping to save his candidacy.[21]

The interview revealed interesting contrasts between Hillary and Bill. Jamieson notes that media reports following this program described Hillary as tougher, more disciplined and analytical than Bill.[22] She appeared the most aware of the consequences of her behavior and political choices. Bill seemed more nervous, Hillary more disciplined.

These contrasts were evident throughout the campaign, showing both strategic difference and complimentarity. Bill demonstrated stronger speaking skills; Hillary knew more about strategic planning. Jamieson includes an *Los Angeles Times* quote that aptly captures the blending of this couple's relationship: "An Arkansas political columnist once melded their names into 'Billary Clinton' with good reason. . . . They are complimentary, a political and marital team; if they were a law firm, she would be the litigator, he the mediator."[23]

Hillary was a politically savvy partner who was also a wife who understood what it would take to get her husband elected as president. The role she played in the campaign received mixed reviews from voters, journalists and academics alike.[24] The political couple introduced themselves as a partnership—billing their marriage as the opportunity to get two leaders for the price of one. Media pundits pondered the implications of a "co-presidency" and terms such as "Billary," "HillBill," and "Clinton-Clinton" emerged, blending these two distinct personalities into a complex gendered image. The "twofers" claim set well with some parts of the electoral audience; other voters had trouble with it. The idea of a co-presidency directly confronts the thought patter of singular as preferred, executive as unitary. Many reporters struggled with how to write about HRC as political candidate's wife.[25]

Advocating Policy: Health Care Reform

Much has been written about the Clintons and their time in the White House. We know that Hillary, an activist first lady, was often compared to former First Lady Eleanor Roosevelt, one of her heroes. She was actively involved in policy issues, and she specifically took on the issue of health care, speaking at several House hearings. She traveled around the world as an ambassador for her husband and for the country, often making two to three speeches a day, especially on children's rights and women's roles.

During her time as a first lady, some observers saw Hillary as taking on too much and exhibiting a larger stake to the presidential power than had been true for past presidential wives. Violating traditional expectations of what a first lady should be, Clinton earned labels such as the "boss's wife from hell," and "a symbol of hard-edged feminist,"[26] and she was generally criticized for being too influential behind the scenes.[27]

Hillary's role in health care reform provides a useful example of how the Clintons behaved as a political couple, yet their actions were interpreted as two individuals. Consider the story: Bill appoints Hillary to manage the health care policy issue; she does all the public listening and delegating on the issue. Hillary and her "advisers" construct a massive, unwieldy bureaucracy. In the end, it was characterized as Hillary's plan and seemed helpless in the face of counterattacks exploring suspicions that the plan would actually take away medical privileges. Her proclivity to secrecy and failure to compromise were also heavily criticized. The "received wisdom" of contemporary observers was that *her* failure in this case led *him* to decide thereafter to approach reform piecemeal, for example, welfare reform (seen as repudiation of much of *her* prior work, not to mention her handling of the health care reform effort), with *his* turn in this (and subsequent) cases being primarily *his* turn with her out of sight nursing wounds from *her* failure.

Commentators and the public were largely convinced that she "bowed" or was "pushed" out of policy formulation thereafter; rarely did anyone think of it as a jointly drawn decision to turn the spotlight away from her. The action in this case mirrored their behavior after his gubernatorial defeat in Arkansas, leading to his subsequent reelection and later *his* use of *her* to craft education reform in the state—which was the model they had used in the health care reform matter.[28]

Handling Indiscretions: The Lewinsky Affair

Though the health care initiative failed on Capitol Hill, the Clinton presidency resulted in many noteworthy achievements. During these eight years, the United States experienced extended economic well being and relatively peaceful relationships with other countries than at any other time in recent history. The country experienced low unemployment, low inflation, dropping crime rates and the second termed ended with a balanced budget.[29] The dark spot of this presidency involved Bill's sexual involvement with a young White House intern that eventually led to his impeachment by the House of Representatives and a public apology to the nation.

How the Clintons handled the Lewinsky exposure and the subsequent reactions to both Bill and Hillary symbolize how this political team functions. To begin, consider the public and pundit construction of the event. Hillary is portrayed as devastated by the betrayal. She had thought that his peccadilloes were behind them. The "betrayal" is interpreted in the context of a traditional couple: He's defiled the marriage bed—again—in spite of previous vows to reform.

Seeing the Clintons, in this instance, as a traditional couple with traditional marital difficulties caused by an errant spouse, ignores the "reality" of their relationship over the previous decades. Consider an alternative construction of this indiscretion. Yes, Hillary is "devastated"; she's absolutely furious. Anger (which she has fairly often demonstrated) does temporarily immobilize. She's furious because Bill has possibly dealt a fatal blow to their (note, not his) presidency.[30] This alternative view is, of course, our "take" on events, but this is true for all other constructions as well, and it is not one without considerable support. The Clintons *always* (like every other human being) are face making and do so in view of their take on what the "public" will accept.

Over their political careers, despite numerous claims about Bill's extra-marital relationships, Hillary largely deflected these concerns and showed support through difficult times. The typical response was to wonder how she could ever forgive her husband for his sexual antics. Often while campaigning, Hillary (and at times, Chelsea) was pressed to respond to questions about her marriage and the various problems that had surfaced throughout the years. In every case, the response was that these are private issues and family matters. While this response did not assuage some public and media interests in this topic, it did serve to mute the discussion.

Building Political Coalitions: A First Lady for President

After several successful years in the Senate, on January 20, 2007, Hillary Clinton announced her new Presidential Exploratory Committee Web site, stating, "I'm in. And I'm in to win." Declaring her bid for U.S. president, through a Web site videocam, she called for a conversation about the future of the country. "I'm going to take this conversation directly to the people of America, and I'm starting by inviting all of you to join me in a series of Web chats over the next few days."[31] Viewed early on by many as the political frontrunner of the Democratic Party due to her fund-raising skills and name recognition, she attempted to claim that position, applying her drive and ambition to winning the election. In this sense, a role reversal occurs as Bill Clinton now becomes the supportive spouse of a viable political candidate.

The level to which Hillary Clinton was scrutinized during the 2008 presidential primary campaign is significant. While every serious presidential candidate had at least one Web site devoted to their campaign, some had several. But, in the case of Hillary Clinton, there were several "I hate Hillary" Web sites and numerous Internet blog discussions that continually raised issues about her campaign and her ability to lead the country. Pre-primary election analyses analyzed her character and continually compared her personality against the personality traits of her opponents, particularly Barack Obama,[32] arguing that Clinton's focus on competence would give her a leading edge in the 2008 campaign.

Hillary Clinton's campaign was hard fought, and she refused to give up, even when political pundits sounded her political death knell.[33] As many people encouraged her to step aside and let Obama claim the mantle as the Democratic nominee, she refused to back down, explaining how she was "fighting" for hardworking families who supported her.[34]

She fights for all those who have never given up on her. She declares herself a champion for those optimistic Americans who need her support. The language she interweaves in many of her messages combines the notion of a fighter with an empathizer who cares about the suffering that many Americans are experiencing, especially with the economy and health care.

As Hillary ran for president, there was much talk about the role Bill would play in the campaign.[35] During her senatorial races, Bill seemed to remain mostly separate as Hillary attempted to forge her own identity. Once Hillary's presidential campaign began, Bill stayed out of public view at first, helping and advising as needed. Once he emerged, there were moments when Bill's "help" seemed counterproductive. He became a lightening rod for negative criticism. Lots of speculation arose about the couple's relationship and its impact on her ability to get elected and the role Bill would play, should Hillary win the election. Once Hillary left the race, talk about her vice presidential chances were shadowed by concerns of what to do about Bill.[36]

One of Bill's primary roles in Hillary's campaign bid was to provide a strong critical voice that minimized Barack Obama's experience and complained about the press coverage Hillary received. Obama himself observed that he had to run against two formidable candidates in the Clintons. Cartoonists took this idea and visually depicted it in striking ways. Bill was often drawn as a large, imposing figure (a wrestler, a basketball or football player) next to a diminished image of Hillary. He was depicted as an attack dog, a mudslinger, a fire-breathing dragon, and an AK-47. In each of these cases, the cartoonist's view was that Bill handled the dirty work of Obama attacks while Hillary supported from the sidelines.

Some pundits noted that the campaign's inability to keep Bill Clinton in line and on message did his wife more harm than good.[37] Finally, after much speculation about when she would withdraw from the race, it was Bill, at a South Dakota gathering, who spoke first about the end of her campaign, at least three days before Hillary officially endorsed Obama:

> I want to say also that this may be the last day I'm ever involved in a campaign of this kind . . . I thought I was out of politics, till Hillary decided to run. But it has been one of the greatest honors of my life to go around and campaign for her for president.[38]

Whether this speech served as a "trial balloon" for Hillary's subsequent withdrawal announcement, a sincere reflection on *his* love of campaigning and respect for Hillary, or simply a lack of awareness that it was *her* right to make the first statements to the public, it is an incident that clearly speaks to the challenges of intertwining relationships and political life.

This example illustrates how little the Clintons seemed to work together during the 2008 primaries, a departure from previous styles of campaigning. Indeed, in the case of this national campaign, the Clintons many times showed an absence of "teamwork." What happened to the team as the primary season progressed? Perhaps part of the issue was the continual negotiation of how the team worked. Previously Bill was always the public face—now he was "the public face" again. But, this time he had to learn a whole new role that made this face look very different. *They* had to learn new roles, and in turn, develop a whole new dynamic for working together.

OBSERVATIONS ON GENDERED RELATIONSHIPS AND POLITICAL COMMUNICATION

We draw from these explorations of Hillary and Bill Clinton a number of noteworthy points regarding gendering in the Clintons' political constructions. Specifically, the importance of cultural boundaries and the challenge of married political teams are worth discussing here.

Gender: Informed by Relationships, Shaped by Cultural Boundaries

Over three decades in public life, Bill and Hillary Clinton managed to navigate gender expectations and build political careers that are, at times, both stunning and bewildering. As a political team, the Clintons developed an impressive resume and will, most likely, continue to do so as they consider next steps following Hillary's 2008 presidential bid. Their lives and rhetorical choices remind us that gender is an evolving process, informed by communication interactions among individuals and their audiences.

Traditional gender expectations based on the Clintons' marital relationship and the cultural milieu of the times were often confounded when Bill and Hillary behaved in ways that violated these expectations. Essentially the Clintons were living gender in new ways by blending characteristics and challenging cultural norms. A "blend" results when people mix traditional expectations for gender; for example, Bill is overtly and publicly warm and caring and focused on building relationships with audiences, while Hillary is cool, reserved and logical with a ten-point plan to solve problems. The blend is even more complete when one interacts with the individuals more fully and "sees" that the cool, rational, reserved Hillary is also warm, compassionate and has a belly laugh that fills the room, and one also sees the warm, caring, hugging Bill arguing strenuously for the ten-point plan to solve problems or bursting with anger at an aide who did not perform as Bill expected.

Clearly many of the rhetorical choices made by the Clintons are directly informed by their upbringing, the situations in which they engage, and the intersections of relational expectations. From childhood, Hillary lived in a Chicago suburb, was encouraged to speak her mind, to pursue education, to build a firm religious foundation.[39] There never seemed to be any question that she would have a successful career and do something that made a difference and challenged traditional expectations in the political sphere. She grew up in a setting where she could thrive and evolve into a strong, independent and principled woman. Bill grew up in Arkansas experiencing a strong mother, an alcoholic stepfather, and supportive grandparents. He credited his inspiration to enter politics to a poignant moment when, as a young man, he shook hands with President John F. Kennedy. Both Clintons lived formative years in the 1950s and 1960s. The two started from different places, with different kinds of support and encouragement; the Clintons embraced their environments and spirit of the times to compose their lives individually, together and as a political entity.

Marital Teams and Politics: A Zero-Sum Game

The Clintons' relationship, bound by marriage and forged by politics, displays several difficulties in navigating gender within the context of a married team. Looking at the Clintons' political lives over several decades, we are reminded of the challenges married couples face when having to work toward similar career goals. Jamieson sees these challenges as a "zero-sum game" where one person inevitably is expected to be better or stronger. The prevailing perception of marital partners is that "marriage can't be a win-win partnership."[40] Scrutiny of the Clintons by politicians, pundits, journalists and typical Americans offers a blatant reminder of the difficulty of approaching politics in this marital relationship, and suggests, as Jamieson notes, "that they both could not be comparably effective."[41]

These perspectives were echoed by many in the 2008 presidential campaign when political pundits and politicians attacked (and much of the
public bought the arguments) Hillary's claim of being experienced by saying she didn't have any "real" experience except that of failure in the health
care matter. George Will expressed this widely held sentiment when he
dismissed Hillary as simply a housewife watching for eight years (except
with regard to the health care issue). Reflecting on her experience (or lack
thereof) Will writes, "Clinton, having risen politically in her husband's orbit,
is a moon shining with reflected light."[42] A similar notion was mentioned
during an interview with Ted Sorenson on WAMU's *Diane Rehm Show*
where he was asked to comment on the presidential scene. Sorenson lauded
the political acumen of Obama and McCain and dismissed Hillary because
she ran "pretty much on the wings of much lingering affection for Bill."[43]

These perceptions underscore the zero-sum idea reminding us of the
challenges many dual career couples face when they marry and pursue similar journeys. Despite the fact that each person is strong in their own right,
there is always the perception by some that one is only successful because
of the other. In the case of the Clintons, this married political team reveals
a lifetime of leaving little to chance and continually jockeying for position.
In the early years of their marriage, Hillary made gendered choices to enable Bill's political success.[44] Hillary's decision to shift her own professional
identity and career to help her husband revealed an ability to respond to
the trappings of traditional gender expectations in order to achieve one's
larger goals. She followed Bill to Arkansas to focus on his political career,
and she adopted the last name of Clinton only after negative reactions experienced during Bill's first run as Arkansas governor. These choices meant
that she gave up her Washington career path to adopt the lifestyle necessary
for the spouse of a public servant, with her public identity defined by her
husband's. While Bill pursued public service and university teaching, Hillary practiced law and became the primary earner in the family. Despite her
success, Hillary experienced significant criticism for keeping her own name
and giving motherhood and career equal footing.

On the other hand, Bill always thought of Hillary as having a central
role in his administration and political life. She was by his side during
his presidential campaigns, directly engaged in policy issues while in the
White House (even setting up an office in the West Wing). Bill was the
orator who could connect with audiences and find ways to "feel their pain."
Consistently throughout his campaigns and during his time as president,
Bill's warm and compassionate disposition and his "down home" way of

talking tended to put people at ease and create lasting bonds. His Town Hall meetings were highlights of his political campaigns, inviting people in a sort of folksy manner to directly ask him questions and tell him what was wrong with the country. Based on Clinton's success with this style of debate, the town hall format is now commonly used during presidential elections, bringing regular citizens into public debate. Bill also has a great ability to connect with his audiences. He tells stories, plays a saxophone in public, jokes about his eating habits and talks about how much he loves and respects his family. Even when various charges were leveled against him regarding financial dealings and womanizing, very few of these charges were ultimately able to stick and Clinton came to be known as "Slick Willie" in many Republican circles.

Hillary's more reserved and steely demeanor, on the other hand, has often been interpreted as cold and calculating. She has been criticized as lacking a sense of humor and defended by those who argue that humor has no relevance for a woman in politics. In her presidential campaign she tried to lighten her image by making some light-hearted jokes and her videos appeared on the Web site YouTube (intentionally and unintentionally). In New Hampshire, an emotional moment came when in a small gathering a sympathetic questioner asked her directly how she was holding up through the rigors of the campaign schedule. Hillary's teary-eyed response was criticized by some as being "too emotional," others suggested this was a moment that underscored her humanity, and yet others claimed it was a calculated attempt at enhancing her self-image.[45]

On election night culminating the New Hampshire primary race, Hillary declared in her victory speech that "I listened to you and in the process I found my own voice."[46] Given her leadership over the years this declaration was in some ways perplexing, but it underscored the challenge needed to bring her candidacy to the national level. As she continued to campaign throughout the country, she did find her voice, her own way of speaking to millions of people about why she had qualifications for the presidency. With Bill and Chelsea by her side, as leaders in her political team, Hillary forged a path that no other woman had managed to do in the history of American politics.

FINAL WORDS

Clearly people feel a great deal of emotional intensity about Bill and Hillary Clinton. While many report strong dislike for the Clintons, they remain highly popular figures, each enjoying widespread public support throughout the country. As a team, they built a life-long career navigating the complexities of gender and providing new ways to think about men and women together in politics, a story that doubtless has not ended as of this writing. In this way they have been important pioneers in enlarging the political landscape. May others be willing to follow in their footsteps.

NOTES

1. For simplicity and clarity we will refer to the Clintons by their first names in the remainder of this chapter.

2. An excellent example of First Ladyship work can be found in the work edited by Molly Wertheimer, *Inventing a Voice: The Rhetoric of American First Ladies of the Twentieth Century* (Lanham, Md.: Rowman & Littlefield Publishers Inc., 2004).

3. As will be discussed later in this chapter, these perceptions played a part, to some degree, in perceptions of Hillary Clinton's ability to be president and her perceived lack of experience to run.

4. Karlyn Kohrs Campbell, "The Rhetorical Presidency: A Two-Person Career," *Beyond the Rhetorical Presidency*, ed. Martin J. Medhurst (College Station, Tex.: Texas A&M University Press, 1996), 180.

5. Campbell, 181.

6. Shawn J. Parry-Giles and Diane M Blair, "The Rise of the Rhetorical First Lady: Politics, Gender Ideology, and Women's Voice." *Rhetoric & Public Affairs* 5, no. 4. (Winter 2002): 565-600.

7. Kathleen Jamieson, *Beyond the Double Bind: Women and Leadership* (New York: Oxford University Press), 22.

8. Jamieson, 23.

9. Much academic debate focuses on the efforts to achieve clarity about definitions and operationalizations of gender, a concept now widely included in scholarship although still regularly confounded in most studies with the variable of sex. Recent useful publications attempting to summarize the variety of approaches include Dow & Wood, deFrancisco & Palcewski, Krolokke, and Sorensen. Almost always, and sometimes explicitly, ideas of what gender "is" involve attention to difference—whether the differences are found in behavior, personal characteristics, biology, groups or interactions. Social scientific studies have focused on differences between women and men as a group, although recently differences within each of the two groups have gained some attention. Critical, historical, and qualitative work in the social sciences has for a much longer time attended to issues that extend well beyond differences between women and men.

10. Such a definition is used primarily in sociology, a field from which many communication analysts take data while downplaying its institutional focus due to our emphasis on individuals and their interactions. Lorber may be the first widely read sociologist to articulate this perspective to feminist theorists outside her field; gender as social institution is a core concept in the discipline. See, for example, the mission statement of the official publication of Sociologists for Women in Society: *Gender & Society* focuses on the social and structural study of gender as a basic principle of the social order and as a primary social category. Connell (2000, 2005) expanded the perspective to focus on differences among men. These moves in gender and feminist studies were essential in moving the scholarship from near exclusive attention to how women differed from men, or on differences based on race, sexual orientation or culture among women.

11. Commonly, in communication studies, gender as a social construction has referred to the development of gender identities and role related behaviors through the process of social interaction, a scholarship focus with roots in personal construct theory of George Kelly (most recently articulated in his 1991 publication) that in turn relied heavily on phenomenological theories and symbolic interactionism.

12. Among the most influential shifts in conceptualizing gender in communication studies have been the insights about communication as performance. Sources of these insights applied to gender include Judith Butler, whose work could be thought of as channeling Foucault and has been brought into communication studies by many scholars. So many scholars have usefully contributed to this development that to name even the most influential would be a very long list. Work directing these developments specifically to gender issues include Kristen Langellier (1989, 1993, and others) and Leslie Baxter (1996 and many others). The supreme value added by all these scholars has been recognition that human performances involve both communication and gender and both inevitably involve interactions. Hence the conclusion that both are built in, and thus inhere within, some kind of relationship.

13. Judith Lorber, *Gender Inequality: Feminist Theories and Politics* (Los Angeles: Roxbury, 1998).

14. Margaret W. Matlin, *The Psychology of Women*, 3rd ed. (Ft. Worth, Tex.: Harcourt Brace, 1996) in her chapter on "Women and Work" reviews a considerable amount of research and concludes, "In general, the women who work in a stereotypically masculine occupation are similar to the men in that area" (p. 276). A similar point is made in the chapter "Managerial Women: Yesterday and Today" (9–25) in Margaret Foegen Karsten, *Management and Gender: Issues and Attitudes* (Westport, Conn.: Praeger, 1994). The same argument is developed by Robin Tolmach Lakoff in *Talking Power: The Politics of Language* (New York: Basic Books, 1990), esp. in the chapter "Why Can't a Woman be Less Like a Man?" It is true, of course, that some people argue that when alternative management styles seemed obvious and successful (Japanese Theory Y, e.g., team theory), possibly reflecting "women's ways," they were renamed and stripped of feminine associations. The

fundamental point, that executive and leadership functions (rationality, planning, data-driven decision making, risk taking, aggressive—read assertive for women—interpersonal style, competitive drive, etc.) have almost a perfect correlation with characteristics we think of as masculine and nearly a zero correlation with what are thought of as feminine—it doesn't matter whether the characteristic appears in a woman or a man.

15. Karlyn Kohrs Campbell, "The Rhetorical Presidency," 81.

16. Kessler and McKenna were among the first to clearly articulate the statement that our culture insists on two, and only two, unchanging and opposite genders. See, for example, *Gender: An Ethnomethodological Approach* (Chicago: University of Chicago Press, 1978, 1985). Numerous other disciplinary perspectives have also added to the literature on cultural dichotomies. See, for example, Deborah Tannen's work on public dialogue and entrenched gender roles, *The Argument Culture: Changing the Way We Argue and Debate* (London: Virago Press, 1998), or Michael Kimmel's excellent synopsis of the visible signs of gender in *The Gendered Society*, 2nd ed. (New York: Oxford University Press, 2004). From a rhetorical perspective, Celeste Condit's discussion of the complexities of gender dichotomies and the need to recast the gendering of rhetoric along the lines of diversity is also useful to this discussion, see "In Praise of Eloquent Diversity: Gender and Rhetoric as Public Persuasion," *Women's Studies in Communication* 20, no. 3 (Fall 1997): 91–116.

17. See, for example, Roger Morris, *Partners in Power: The Clintons & Their America* (New York: Henry Holt, 1996); Sally Bedell Smith's *For Love of Politics: Bill and Hillary Clinton—the White House Years* (New York: Random House, 2007); Christopher Anerson, *Bill and Hillary: The Marriage* (New York: Morrow, 1999); or Joyce Milton, *The First Partner: Hillary Rodham Clinton* (New York: Wm Morrow, 1999).

18. See Patrick S. Halley, *On the Road with Hillary: A Behind-the-Scenes Look at the Journey from Arkansas to the U.S. Senate* (New York: Viking, 2002).

19. See, for example, Burrell's discussion.

20. *60 Minutes*, 1992.

21. See Anne F. Mattina, "Hillary Rodham Clinton: Using Her Vital Voice," in *Inventing a Voice: The Rhetoric of American First Ladies of the Twentieth Century*, ed. Molly Meijer Wertheimer (Lanham, Md.: Rowman & Littlefield Publishers Inc., 2004), 423.

22. Kathleen Jamieson, *The Double Bind*, 35.

23. *Los Angeles Times* as quoted by Jamieson, *The Double Bind*, 36.

24. See, for example, the critique offer by Patricia A. Sullivan and Lynn H. Turner regarding the problems with Hillary's strategy of confrontation and accommodation in *From the Margins to the Center: Contemporary Women and Political Communication* (Westport, Conn.: Praeger Series in Political Communication, 1996).

25. For useful discussions about media coverage and Hillary Clinton, see Sullivan and Turner, *From the Margins*, 70–74; and Kathleen Jamieson, *The Double Bind*, 35–36.

26. Shawn Parry-Giles and Diane Blair, "The Rise of the Rhetorical First Lady," 567.

27. Janette Kenner Muir and Lisa Benitez, "Redefining the Role of the First Lady: The Rhetoric of Hillary Rodham Clinton," in *A Midterm Assessment of the Clinton Presidency*, ed. Robert Denton and Rachel Holloway (New York: Praeger, 1996), 139.

28. See, for example, the Mattina, Halley or Milton biographies supporting this claim.

29. "Biography of William J. Clinton." The White House. <http://www.whitehouse .gov/history/presidents/bc42.html.> (9 July 2007).

30. While this is an alternate interpretation offered by the authors, research supports this perspective. See Morris, Smith, Anderson cited above for more description of the Clinton relationship.

31. Hillary Clinton, "Announcement Speech." 20 January 2007, <http:// blog.4president.org/2008/hillary_clinton/index.html.> (5 May 2007).

32. Rich Lowry, "The World of Hillary Hatred," *Time*, 19 November 2007, 51.

33. Dana Milbank, "Still After the Holy Grail," *Washington Post*, 20 May 2008, A3.

34. Hillary Clinton, jmuir@gmu.edu "Why I'm In," 14 May 2008, personalized mass email (14 May 2008).

35. Interestingly, there has been little speculation about the potential role of Sarah Palin's husband, as of this writing (which occurs during the campaign), perhaps due, in part, to the difference between the presidential and vice presidential roles.

36. See, for example, Peter Nicholas's speculations in the *Los Angeles Times*, June 4, 2008 edition "Dream ticket? Clinton willing, but some see nightmare," Part A: Pg. 14, and his follow up essay, "Campaign '08: Race For The White House" *Los Angeles Times*, July 12, 2008, Saturday Home Edition, where he reports Obama's acknowledgement that Hillary was on his VP list, but Bill's potential role could be a difficult issue.

37. Chris Cillizza, "What Went Wrong for Clinton? *The Fix*. washingtonpost. com. 5 June 2008. Retrieved from the world wide web, http://blog.washingtonpost. com/thefix/2008/06/what_happened_the_clinton_defe.html?nav=rss_blog (14 June 2008).

38. "Bill Clinton Hints at End to Wife's Campaign," reports by both ABC and NBC synopsized on Newsmax.com. Retrieved 6/14/2008 from the world wide web, http://www.newsmax.com/insidecover/Bill_Clinton_hillary/2008/06/02/100847. html.

39. Mattina, 422-425; Muir and Benitez, 137-140.

40. Kathleen Jamieson, *The Double Bind*, 35.

41. Jamieson, 36.

42. George Will, *Washington Post* (6 June 2008): A19

43. *Diane Rehm Show*, interview with Ted Sorenson.

44. Gendered choices made by Hillary Clinton were especially evident in the changes that took place in her appearance. In the 1992 campaign, Hillary was known for her headbands. After winning the election, Hillary's clothes and hair styles reflected more of a sophisticated image befitting a "First Lady."

45. Robert Novak, "The Clintons' One-Two Punch" *Washington Post*, January 10, 2008, A21. Novak noted that, "with that background, Sen. Clinton's lachrymose complaint in New Hampshire on Monday that 'this is very personal for me' was widely compared to Muskie's crying jab in Manchester thirty-six years ago, which began his downfall. But whereas Muskie's tears were involuntary, only the naïve can believe Clinton was not artfully playing for sympathy from her sisters. . . ." About the same time, Robin Givhan, also in *Washington Post* January 8, 2008, C1, wrote an essay that essentially said the tears were real but also said: "It's no great leap to wonder whether that cracking in her voice yesterday had been self-consciously conjured up. Clinton got teary-eyed? Really? The disbelief might be cynical, but not unreasonable."

46. Quoted by Jon Meacham, "Letting Hillary be Hillary," *Newsweek*, 21 January 2008, p. 32.

2

WOMEN WHO SPOKE
FOR THEMSELVES

Working Women, Suffrage, and the
Construction of Women's Rhetorical Style

Shereé Keith

This essay seeks to understand the public-speaking style of working women and those women who stood up for their rights at the turn of the twentieth century by examining the interaction between gender and public communication through the concept of feminine style in political discourse.

FEMININE COMMUNICATION STYLE THEORY

According to Karlyn Kohrs Campbell, the feminine communication style contains a specific form of speaking. This style consists of both form and content but in this essay I will be specifically focusing on form, or the way that the rhetoric is constructed in terms of elements like tone, appeals, evidence and structure.[1] Campbell tells us that the feminine communication style contains a form in which

> personal experience is tested against the pronouncement of male authorities (who can be used for making accusations and indictments that would be impermissible from a woman) . . . The tone tends to be personal and somewhat tentative, rather than objective or authoritative. The persona tends to be traditionally feminine, like that of teacher, mediator, or layperson, rather than that of expert, leader, preacher, or judge. Strategically, women who use this style will seek ways to reconcile femininity with the traditional "masculinity" of

public discourse. A "womanly" speaker tends to plead, to appeal to the senti-
ments of the audience, to "court" the audience by being "seductive."[2]

Campbell comes to these conclusions after analyzing women speaking at
the turn of the twentieth century.[3]

Bonnie Dow and Mari Boor Tonn further expand on feminine style in
their 1993 study of Ann Richards' campaign rhetoric. They state that someone who uses this style acknowledges the audience through inclusive pronouns and encourages the audience to draw their own conclusions from the
examples the speaker offers, often in the form of personal anecdotes. This
kind of style is oriented toward connecting and maintaining a relationship
between the speaker and the audience by encouraging audience participation via elements like concrete examples. Dow and Boor Tonn explain:

> For example, when criticizing Ronald Reagan's handling of questions about
> the Iran-Contra affair, she compares his responses to those given by her chil-
> dren: "And when we get our questions asked, or there's a leak, or an investiga-
> tion, the only answer we get is 'I don't know' or 'I forgot.' But you wouldn't
> accept an answer like that from your children. I wouldn't. Don't tell me 'you
> don't know' or 'you forgot.'"[4]

The audience can easily relate to the experience of trying to get answers
out of a child, because that is an everyday experience. Relating this kind of
familiarity to something they have no direct experience with—questioning
Reagan about foreign policy—allows Richards to make a personal and vivid
connection with her audience. This kind of logic—taking small, concrete
examples about her experiences and using them to demonstrate a larger
claim about the office of the president—is a good example of the feminine
communication style in action.

Jane Blankenship and Deborah Robson discuss the characteristics they
see as part of feminine style. They state that political judgments are based
on "concrete, lived experience" and that someone using a feminine style
values "inclusivity and the relational nature of being" while this person con-
ceptualizes "the power of public office as a capacity to 'get things done' and
to empower others."[5] Inclusivity, relationships and empowerment of others
are part of the feminine style for Blankenship and Robson.

In her book *Eloquence in an Electronic Age* Kathleen Hall Jamieson
echoes these claims about feminine communication. In her discussion of
women who were historically involved in politics she says "women [were]
more inclined to personal speech . . . [women] also were ill disposed to
hostile verbs, aggressive behavior, and clear refutative postures . . . women

favor a nuturant, incorporative style."[6] Ultimately, Jamieson contends that the feminine style alone is not powerful enough for women. She argues that to be successful in the public sphere a female rhetor must be able to negotiate both masculine and feminine communication styles.

A more masculine speaking style differs in many ways. One way it is different is the type of reasoning used. Deductive reasoning, or arguing from laws, rules or widely accepted principles is a marker of masculine style, as opposed to inductive reasoning or arguing from observation. According to Dow and Boor Tonn masculine style is also abstract, hierarchical, dominating and oriented toward problem solving. Impersonal and formal forms of evidence are used, as well as abstract reasoning and a linear mode of reasoning. As noted in Campbell's quotation above, this language is objective and authoritative. The speaker employing masculine style would take on the persona of an expert, leader, preacher or judge. "At the turn of the century the general, mainly masculine, speaking style was characterized by florid language, personification, and allusions to literary, biblical, and historical materials."[7] Someone using a traditionally masculine style would approach "the audience as inferiors to be told what is right or to be led." [8]

Theories about women's public address originated out of the discussion of women speaking at the turn of the twentieth century, although they have been largely applied to contemporary case studies. Typically the women studied have been upper-class white women who fought for various causes like suffrage, abolitionism and temperance, or were more recent political actors. In the rest of this essay I will focus on working-class women who, I believe, change the way that we should look at gender and public communication.

WORKING WOMEN AND SUFFRAGE

At the turn of the twentieth century there were several reasons why a woman would find herself in a position as a waitress, sales clerk, or maid: The new industrial economy paid men too little to support a family; women eschewed or postponed family life and motherhood; and women had desires for education and professional careers or for big city adventures after a rural home life. Whatever the reasons that compelled a woman to take a wage-earning job at this time in America, they often received disapproval from other participants in society. Many conservative, reform-minded women who did not recognize these reasons as viable often sought to make it possible for women to take back their "rightful" place in the home instead of giving them tangible assistance in gaining rights in the workplace.

Being a working woman was often a harsh path to follow. Historian Kathy Peiss notes that women's "average earnings were one-half of those received by men in their employments. In New York factories in the early 1910s, 56 percent of the female labor force earned under $8.00 a week . . . the majority of women in retail stores earned under $7.50," at a time when nine or ten dollars per week was the minimum required for basic survival. These conditions resulted in the founding of aid organizations for these women in cities like New York.[9] Such reform organizations were not set up to help women get higher salaries but to aid female wageworkers in maintaining proper feminine virtues while they engaged in work for economic reasons.[10] Organizations like Travelers' Aid and the Working Girls' Club were set up to help women develop work habits that maintained their femininity, a femininity that had been defined according to domestic expressions of womanhood. Thus, working women presented a conundrum.

Single working women were especially seen as courting trouble and were thought to be prey to all sorts of immoralities. Conservative, upper-class reformers at the turn of the twentieth century felt working women threatened to "undermine the family by their personal moral laxity: they might have un-chaperoned contacts with men, spend money profligately, dress immodestly, or use profane language, as well as indulge in sexual liaisons."[11] The ultimate solution to the problem was to help prepare working women for marriage. Kessler-Harris states that reformers like Grace Dodge, a wealthy and religious woman, believed that marriage would ultimately solve both the working woman's problem as well as the working man's. She felt that by taking women out of the workforce there would be fewer workers and the man's wages would go up, better enabling him to support his family, thereby resolving two social problems.

However, since the task of taking every woman out of the workforce was not economically viable, then the next best thing was to aid them in dealing with the cause of their "downfall." Grace Dodge stated that the aim of her first society for working women was "that by associating together, wives, mothers and homemakers should be developed, [and] that the tone of womanhood be raised."[12] The reformers wanted to help females who had to work, but they wanted to help them on their own terms with the hopes of achieving the ultimate goal of leading women back into their traditional position in the family.

Consequently, reformers defined as proper labor for women jobs that would reinforce "values appropriate to future home life: gentility, neatness, morality, cleanliness."[13] (A job as a domestic servant, even though it paid very little, was seen as acceptable under this definition because it prepared a woman for domestic life.) In an attempt to protect their virtues, reformers like Dodge set up places where working women could live with other women away from men.[14] Often in these situations young women would be provided with lessons on cooking and sewing in preparation for married life. The home was the ultimate concern for reformers who placed a premium on the place of the woman in relation to the family, directing their aid in these terms. This goal of fortifying the home did not always benefit working women.

PROTECTIONISM AND SUFFRAGE FOR WOMEN

Organizations like the New York Working Woman's Protective Union (established in 1868), the Working Girl's Society of New York and the Women's Educational and Industrial Union (founded by Dr. Harriet Clisby for Boston-area workers)[15] were places where "the lessons of thrift and self-reliance through cooperative endeavor could be absorbed, where girls might learn useful household skills, and where good taste and morality could be discussed and absorbed."[16] Kessler-Harris and other scholars note that this path to reform that many middle- and upper-class women took did not always work well for the working class and in the end caused problems for women workers and their economic positions. Middle- to upper-class reformers who focused on working women's lives in terms of something such as moral reform were not in sync with workers who saw that improvements in their lives could better come from economic reform. Workers' strategies of petitions and strikes scared many of the middle- and upper-class reformers. Often, reformers' husbands or fathers owned the factories where women worked, so their family's livelihood was at stake. Conservative reformers also saw collective bargaining as leading to a communist-socialist way of thinking, instead of each man or woman standing on his or her own merit. These leanings were unacceptable in a capitalist society that had benefited their own families. Since economic reform at this time came at a price that was untenable for upper-class society there was another way that reformers sought to help working women: protectionist legislation.

Protective legislation included benefits like shorter workdays, hours of the day that employees could not work and also covered some conditions under which women could not work; for instance, there were particular jobs that were supposedly too dangerous for women to occupy. The height of protective legislation occurred between the years of 1910 and the early 1920s. For example, *Muller v Oregon* (1908) is the case that first allowed the restriction of hours for women working.

> What were the consequences of framing this legislation as something that helps working women keep their traditional role in the family? Lehrer writes that protective legislation set up a kind of protected status for women which appeared to be responding to their special needs as working women but which did so by leaving the major premises about women's position intact. In other words, these laws did not challenge the traditional assumption that woman's place was properly, or at least primarily, in the home, but rather reinforced it.[17]

Reformers sought to ameliorate the often miserable situations within the workforce; however, this help had the effect of situating women more definitively within the home.

Another relationship that was complicated for women workers was their connection to suffrage. Voting enfranchisement for women was complicated by perceptions of the "proper" role of women in society. The maternal or Victorian methods and attitudes of the reformers contributed to the absence of working women from the suffrage campaign for a time, even though it held potential benefits to women of all classes. Some of the specific divisions between the wealthier suffragists and women workers eventually helped spur the movement to success.

As the suffrage movement progressed into the twentieth century, the moral edge that the movement took up became more and more apparent. Progressives "endorsed a battery of electoral reforms and believed that all social problems could be solved by legislation. Women's suffrage meshed right into the progressive scheme."[18] During this period, suffragists put less emphasis on the equality and justice that the vote would bring to women, and they put more emphasis on the special qualities women would bring to the polls. They appealed to the middle-class stereotypes of women that were prevalent in society and in doing so appealed "both to middle-class men's views of women and to women's views about themselves."[19] This is most evident in the reasoning that antisuffragists used to try to keep women from the vote and how suffragists answered these claims.

The antisuffragists' strongest argument was the negative effect that the vote would have on women. They argued that women belonged in the home and that the vote of a woman was irrelevant, because women would not exercise a voice independent from that of their husbands. Antisuffragists believed that the vote and civic involvement would cause women to abandon their domestic duties, threatening the home as an institution. Traditionalists argued that women "were physically, mentally, and emotionally incapable of duties associated with the vote" because they were too emotional, prone to hysteria, too mild in nature, too pure and moral and not logical enough to carry out the duties of the vote.[20] These antisuffragists did not want women to have the vote for the harm that it would bring to women. They argued that women's role in charity work and their indirect influence over men were all that was necessary for women to affect society.

Suffragists argued in return that these special qualities that women possessed would bring reforms to the electoral process and would outweigh the less desirable (foreign-born) and less competent (uneducated) vote of some males. These claims allowed the suffragists to "[transform] the image of the suffrage movement from a threatening, challenging group into a wise, compassionate, and service-orientated one. The woman voter would not be the destroyer of home, family and society but their protector,"[21] expanding on her devotion to family-oriented charities.

In spite of nineteenth-century alliances with abolitionists, suffragists were not afraid to dip into the well of racist and anti-immigrant arguments to justify a vote for women over "undesirables" who already possessed voting rights. These "undesirables" also included other women. Elizabeth Cady Stanton (1815–1902), writing toward the end of her life in an 1897 essay, is famous for suggesting that the suffrage movement incorporate an educational restriction into its demand for the vote. She says that the "greatest block in the way of woman's enfranchisement today is doubling the ignorant vote" and an "educational qualification would answer this objection."[22]

This kind of restriction, if it ever became a law, would likely have a negative impact on working women of the time. In order to appease skeptics of female enfranchisement, and perhaps assuage their own racist and classist sensibilities, some of the more affluent suffragists tried to figure out how to deal with lower classes in the female population. Eleanor Flexner argues that ultimately these misgivings about the working class of women "could only do (suffragists) injury, since the immigrant, like any other voter, must be won to their cause."[23] Understandings about what was proper or desirable in a woman served to come between reformers who longed for the vote and a group of women who, by their sheer numbers, could help them get it.

Working women were also unsure of any benefit they would see from the vote. For working women, who got paid less than half of what men got paid, who were often found working in sweatshops, and who rarely had any personal dignity within the workplace or the promise of job tenure, equal rights was about more than getting the vote. For them "equality also meant better pay for their labor, security from fire and machine hazards or the unwanted attention of the foreman, and a chance to get home to their domestic tasks before complete exhaustion had overtaken them."[24] The vote was not being promoted as something that would give women a voice in their job situations, causing the idea of equality framed as suffrage to seem remote and unreal. The practical aspect of suffrage was not readily apparent to female wageworkers and the practical aspects of female wageworker's lives were not wholly apparent to middle-class suffrage supporters.

The organizing tactics of the movement also kept suffragists ideologically separated from working women. Flexner argues that working women felt out of place in the tearooms in which suffrage business was often conducted. The class positions of working women did not afford them the luxury of tearooms nor did their work and family obligations allow them free time. Moreover, many suffragists had no desire to include working women in their discussions. Dubois says of suffragists that at "parlor meetings in the homes of wealthy women, they tried to strike a genteel note."[25] Working women were not invited to these places nor would they have likely been comfortable if they had been included.

Eventually, suffragists reached out to working women. One such reformer was Harriot Stanton Blatch, the daughter of Elizabeth Cady Stanton. Blatch disapproved of her mother's call for an educational requirement and instead sought to get working women active in the fight for the vote. She argued that "the proletariat, whether able to read or not, can give a more valuable opinion upon such a question, for example, as the housing of the poor."[26] In an 1898 address to the National American Woman Suffrage Association Convention written by Blatch and Florence Kelley, they state, "No one needs all the powers of the fullest citizenship more urgently than the wage-earning woman, and from two different points of view—that of actual money wages and that of her wider needs as a human being and a member of the community."[27] Because of Blatch's influence, and others like her, the suffragists made some nontraditional moves that defied the notion of the proper role of women and aided in ultimately succeeding in their goal. In her bid to convince working women that the vote would ultimately help them gain economic control of their own lives, she began to utilize tactics that would take the campaign for suffrage into the streets. Blatch and others saw militant tactics, such as protests and marches, as a good way to garner attention and as something that would appeal to groups of women who were already in the public in a nontraditional way, such as working women. According to Dubois

> Gilded Age suffragists themselves accepted the Victorian convention that re-
> spectable women did not court public attention. The Equality League's [the
> organization Blatch formed] emphasis on the importance of paid labor for
> women of all classes struck at the heart of that convention. Blatch understood
> "the value of publicity or rather the harm of the lack of it." She encouraged
> open-air meetings and trolley car campaigns because they generated much
> publicity, which no longer held the conventional horror for her followers.[28]

Blatch made a concerted effort to abandon the former ideologies that had alienated workers from the suffrage movement and to challenge "existing standards of femininity."[29] This aspect of the fight for working women's rights adds another layer of complexity to this analysis. Women such as Blatch and Kelley were white women from the upper hierarchy of society who contested the traditional expectations for women at the time. When they spoke about and to working women it seems improbable that they would use a traditional feminine style in order to make claims about the need for rights for these women. These women were anything but traditional at this time and using a traditional style for communication about and to them would not make their speeches effective.

WORKING WOMEN AND RHETORIC

Working women in the nineteenth and early twentieth centuries did not fit the socially accepted norm of domestic femininity. Many working women, in fact, believed that their situation was natural and desirable for women. Eliza Turner, a suffragist and writer, states that in

> these days, when most girls have ideas of their own, she who stays in a home
> where she is not sufficiently needed to make her feel she pays her way, is
> apt to be discontented, restless, suffering a sense of humiliation; in a word,
> unhappy. The writer has known . . . many cases of this kind, where the sense
> of independence, even coupled with hard work, has changed the worker into
> a happy instead of a miserable woman.[30]

Mary Livermore, a feminist editor and educator, derided the prevailing feminine model, calling the "superfluous women" who hasten to wash their reputations of the taint of "strong-mindedness;" whose intellects are "accidents of the body," and, "like the candles inside Chinese lanterns, are of use only to light up, and show off to advantage, the pretty devices outside." They are superfluous women, who are so indifferent to duty, so lacking in high principle, so devoid of tender feeling, that they are capable of accepting any man in marriage—an octogenarian, an imbecile, a debauchee—if his establishment, his equipage, and bank-account are satisfactory.[31]

These women have demonstrated their ire with traditional assumptions about women. In fact, the traditional place for women, within a marriage and family, was called into question by women concerned for workers. Working women also questioned the traditional assumptions about the nature or needs of women. Marguerite Mooers Marshall, a worker who was concerned about protective legislation and its role in reinforcing traditional notions about women, wrote to the Women's Trade Union League about her concerns. She stated, "Why is it that the National Women's Trade Union League chooses to assume, the *typical anti-suffragist, anti-feminist* attitude—i.e., that women must 'be protected' . . . for their own welfare and that of the race?"[32]

The process of trying to protect women reinforced very traditional beliefs about who women are as human beings and as workers. These testimonials have demonstrated the unhappiness that some women saw as associated with sanctioned feminine gender roles. Both working women and women who spoke on their behalf felt that work and public activity made women stronger and happier. Instead of courting the audience's beliefs about its members, as a rhetor using a more feminine communication style would, these women speak out against tradition in a bold and confident way, more aligned with masculine communication.

Despite the espoused value of work in the lives of women, activist Eva McDonald-Valesh noted that women were still "held strictly accountable to the absurd social code which sets up one standard of morality for men and another for women. In addition . . . the ballot is still withheld, so that she has no voice in shaping legislation which may affect her condition."[33] McDonald-Valesh sought to point out the anomalies associated with women workers' relationship with working men. Anna Dickinson, a suffragist and abolitionist lecturer, stated that what women want is the "chance to do well-paid, as well as ill-paid work, and to have an opportunity to earn $50 or $500 a week, as well as a few cents."[34] She continued,

We are told that home is the sphere in which God placed woman. Well, grant it. What shall we do with those who have no homes, and those whose homes are the homes of brutality and vice? If the Almighty has invested woman with genius, it is not for man to limit its sphere. It is arrogating the purposes of the Infinite to fix the boundaries of intellect, be it male or female.[35]

Scholars identify the feminine communication style as one that portrays a personal and tentative tone, as opposed to one that is abstract and authoritative. Rhetors like Dickinson and McDonald-Valesh had strong ideas about women's lives. The tone for these women is not at all tentative. Rather, they employed an authoritative tone and aggressive stance to sum up the problematic situation for women at the time. When fighting for a nontraditional role for women in the public sphere, it does not make sense that the traditional feminine style would be used by women advocating for the status of workers. In this case, not only does the speaker's background matter in determining a speaking style but also the issue being addressed. It would not be very convincing to use a timid or "seductive" speaking style when you are trying to convince your audience to support roles for women that are neither timid nor seductive.

Not only is the tone in the rhetoric supporting women's rights more masculine than feminine, but the use of broad statements (another masculine trait), in this case about the nature of work, humanity and the position of women, is prevalent in this rhetoric. The masculine speaking style includes making claims using laws, rules or widely accepted principles as starting places to frame a persuasive argument. Working women and advocates did not appeal to localized beliefs about women; rather, in order to change the situation of women, they appealed to larger bodies of proof, such as general rules or ideas about their civilization and human relations. For example, suffragist Dickinson made claims about the nature of the human race. She stated, in relation to the social practices that keep men and women in different spheres, that "it is not good for one person to do the thinking of another, of one conscience to carry the responsibilities of another conscience, of one life to attend to the work of another life."[36] Core beliefs about human nature were starting points for Dickinson in her statements on the necessity of a public life for women. In this same vein, in order to support the idea that work is not something novel for women, Mary Livermore declared that "women have always been toilers from a time of coincident with the beginning of history, and, undoubtedly, anterior to that."[37] The historical ordering of humanity is used to show that the current situation of women is in line with the earliest women and not just a current whim. Lucy A. Warner, a working woman, declared, "Working men are not lacking in natural ability. Neither are working women. There is no copyright on brains. God is no respecter of persons, and so, to us working girls, He has entrusted one, two, and, to some, even five talents."[38] In these instances, broad claims about the nature of humanity, women, and problems affecting women are used in order to demonstrate that there are larger laws at work than those created by the current society. Broad claims are more characteristic of masculine style.

Feminine style highlights women's anecdotal experience, but in one instance of worker rhetoric, claims based on the experiences of a few (presumably capable) women were denied as adequate representations of women's experiences, since women varied in their abilities and training.[39] Instead, McDonald-Valesh demonstrated that inductive reasoning some- times provides false information about the true situation of women in the workforce. For her the "general rule" that women's labor was "both cheap and plentiful, and that she is less apt to rebel against bad conditions than man"[40] was a key point from which to argue for support for public roles for women. These "rules" support and guide this author's rhetoric about women and their role in the workplace, not a few examples about women who have found public life more welcoming. Broad, sweeping generaliza- tions about the nature of human beings, the workplace, and the potential of women were used to prove that women can, and perhaps should, do something different than fulfill conventional gender roles. This marker of style is more masculine than feminine, which is logical given the belief these rhetors have about traditional feminine roles.

Not only do the rhetors I have discussed point out the general condition of working women, they also provide solutions to the problems encoun- tered by women. In a speech to the Knights of Labor, L. M. Barry, a laborer and the leader of the Woman's Department within the Knights, states that she hopes "every Knight of Labor in Pennsylvania will give support to the bill which I have prepared and presented at the session of the coming State Legislature for the establishment of a Factory Inspector law."[41] The audi- ence is approached as one that should support the plan of action pointed out by this rhetor. She does not come to her audience lightly, with timidity or seduction in mind, as someone who uses the feminine communication style might do. Instead, Barry is confident about her explanation of the problems facing women in the workforce and she has come up with a solu- tion the audience should back. This confidence and problem-solving orien- tation are markers of the masculine communication style.

To demonstrate further, Harriot Stanton Blatch and Florence Kelley, both suffragists and labor activists, presented their audience with a solution to the problems plaguing working women. They argued that the situation

of working women was "untenable, and there can be no pause in the agita-
tion for full political power and responsibility until these are granted to all
women of the nation."[42] Warner tells us that the solution to lack of education among working women could be solved by giving "us the time and opportunity to use [their brains]."[43] These statements are given as commands
for their audience to follow. Women like Stanton Blatch, Kelley, Barry and
others quoted here set themselves up as leaders for working women to follow. They used a linear form of argument, a masculine communication style
characteristic, as they identified the problems for working women and the
strategies to deal those issues. These rhetors took charge of the situation
in order to give their audiences a chance at fighting to change their lives
for the better. They spoke as assertive leaders who expect to be followed.
They could not be timid and expect the circumstances of working women
to change. The supposed inherent timidity, tentativeness, or the privacy of
women is what allowed employers to take advantage of workers. Aggressive
speaking and insistence on solving their problems became a more militant
strategy to argue for better treatment.

The women I have quoted in this essay also employed characteristics of
the general masculine speaking style that was prevalent at the turn of the
century. As Campbell notes, allusions to historical and biblical materials are
common features of masculine rhetoric of the time, and these topics also
appear throughout the rhetoric in favor of working women's rights.[44] Lucy
Warner used such allusions in the following statement:

> Dear sisters, we who work in shop and store and factory, and in countless
> homes all over the United States, if it is because we work that people look
> down on us, then let us pray that the Lord will change their opinion, and go
> quietly about our business, for, among the "nobility of labor" there is an illus-
> trious company, at whose head stands the Carpenter of Nazareth, by Whom
> labor was forever glorified.[45]

The use of historical and biblical references in support of working women
as part of suffrage concerns are deployed as proof that suffrage activities are
sanctioned by larger ideologies or beliefs about human nature than those
currently dominating society.

Localized examples and personal experiences do not serve as proof of
the need for rights for women workers. Women who sought equal rights
for women, including women as workers, needed to appeal to the general
condition of humanity and use that as leverage or proof that the current
treatment of women was backward thinking instead of allowing forward
movement.

CHALLENGING THE FEMININE STYLE

The situation of working women in the early twentieth century, in its contradiction to a prevailing, domesticated gender ideology of the time, allowed for a space where a more aggressive and action-orientated speaking style from women was needed and utilized. The use of a traditional feminine speaking style as defined by Campbell and others who base the concept on descriptions of women speaking at the turn of the twentieth century would have been ineffectual in attempting to persuade an audience that nontraditional activities for women were appropriate and even necessary. Women who were already in the workforce had no incentive to use a feminine style, given their situation. Employing feminine style would have been contradictory to the position of the working woman, especially when they were arguing for improved conditions, rather than reinforcement of traditional femininity. Unlike some suffragists who suggested women would use the vote to apply the values of their domestic roles in the public sphere (usually with charities), working women were arguing for the vote to make their undomesticated and often disparaged roles acceptable.

Working women, as well as their supporters, used a more masculine than feminine speaking style in rhetorical appeals. I propose that this militancy was a strategic necessity, as these speakers were strongly advocating that their audience take immediate action to ameliorate the problems in their respective situations. There was no room for timidity, tentativeness, seduction, or pleading. A feminine communication style based on these attributes would not have been appropriate for working women, given its origins in women's domestic positioning. The women quoted here were not interested in returning to the home but rather in raising their wages or making their work situations better. In the end, working women and their advocates widen our perspective on what it means to be a woman speaking in public. Bonnie Dow warns us that difference theories like that of the feminine communication style are

> useful for understanding the shared experiences and behaviors of some women that result from their status and treatment in a patriarchal culture. Even so, they have a down side: While usefully explaining the experiences of some women, they can unwittingly elide differences among women, falsely universalizing women's experience according to a model based on the lives of white, middle-class women.[46]

The opportunity to look beyond the rhetoric of middle-class women and into the public communication of women who worked for a living thus expands understanding insignificant ways.

NOTES

1. Some communication scholars combine form and content in their assessment of feminine style. According to Blankenship and Robson the five characteristics of feminine style are: "(1) Basing political judgments on concrete, lived experience; (2) Valuing inclusivity and the relational nature of being; (3) Conceptualizing the power of public office as a capacity to 'get things done' and to empower others; (4) Approaching policy formation holistically (5) Moving women's issues to the fore-front of the public arena." Jane Blankenship and Deborah Robson, "The 'Feminine Style' in Women's Political Discourse: An Exploratory Essay." *Communication Quarterly* 43, no. 3 (Summer 1995): 359.

2. Karlyn Kohrs Campbell, "Style and Content in the Rhetoric of Early Afro-American Feminists." *Quarterly Journal of Speech* 72, no.4 (November 1986): 440.

3. Articles such as "Gender and Genre: Loci of Invention and Contradiction in the Earliest Speeches by U.S. Women" from 1995, "Style and Content in the Rhetoric of Early Afro-American Feminists" from 1986, and her book, *Man Cannot Speak for Her: A Critical Study of Early Feminist Rhetoric from 1989* all use examples from this time period to support her claim that the majority of women speaking in public used a particular kind of style she dubs the feminine communication style.

4. Bonnie Dow and Marie Boor-Tonn, "'Feminine Style' and Political Judgment in the Rhetoric of Ann Richards." *Quarterley Journal of Speech* 79, no. 3 (August 1993): 290.

5. Blankenship and Robson, "The Feminine Style in Political Discourse," 359.

6. Kathleen Hall Jamieson, *Eloquence in an Electronic Age* (New York: Oxford University Press, 1988), 88.

7. Karlyn Kohrs Campbell, "Femininity and Feminism: To Be or Not to Be a Woman." *Quarterly Journal of Speech* 31, no. 2 (Spring 1983): 104.

8. Karlyn Kohrs Campbell, "Femininity," 441.

9. Kathy Peiss, *Cheap Amusements* (Philadelphia: Temple University Press, 1986), 52.

10. Alice Kessler-Harris, *Out to Work: A History of Wage-Earning Women in the United States* (Oxford: Oxford University Press, 1982).

11. Alice Kessler-Harris, *Out to* Work, 98.

12. Quoted in Peiss, *Cheap Amusements*, 170.

13. Kessler-Harris, *Out to Work*, 128.

14. Kathy Peiss, *Cheap Amusements*.

15. One of its first activities was to open a store to help women support themselves and their families by selling crafts and foodstuffs they produced in their homes. This organization still exists today.

16. Alice Kessler-Harris, *Out to* Work, 93.

17. Susan Lehrer, *The Origins of Protective Labor Legislation for Women, 1905-1925* (New York: State University of New York Press, 1987), 227.

18. Nancy Woloch, *Women and the American Experience* (Boston: McGraw Hill, 2000), 343.

19. Kathy Porter, *A History of Suffrage in the United States* (New York: AMS Press, 1971), 249.

20. Alexander Keyssar, *The Right to Vote* (New York: Basic Books, 2000), 208.

21. Nancy Woloch, *Women and the American Experience*, 346.

22. Elizabeth Cady Stanton, "An Education Suffrage Qualification Necessary, 1897." In *Public Women, Public Words: A Documentary History of American Feminism*, ed. Dawn Keetley and John Pettegrew, Vol. 1. (Madison, Wisc.: Madison House, 1997), 264.

23. Eleanor Flexner, *Century of Struggle: The Woman's Rights Movement in the United States* (Cambridge, Mass.: The Belknap Press of the University of Harvard Press, 1959), 219.

24. Eleanor Flexner, *Century*, 247.

25. Ellen Carol Dubois, "Working Women, Class Relations, and Suffrage Militance: Harriot Stanton Blatch and the New York Woman Suffrage Movement, 1894–1909." In *One Woman, One Vote*, ed. Marjorie Spruill Wheeler (Troutdale, Ore: New Sage Press, 1995), 225.

26. Harriot Stanton Blatch, "Educated Suffrage a Fetich [sic]., 1897." *In Public Women, Public Words: A Documentary History of American Feminism*, Vol. 2, ed. Dawn Keetley and John Pettegrew (Madison, Wisc.: Madison House, 1997), 266.

27. Harriot Stanton Blatch & Florence Kelley, "Women, Work, and Citizenship, 1898." *In Public Women, Public Words*, Vol. 2, ed. Dawn Keetley and John Pettegrew, 140.

28. Ellen Carol Dubois, "Working Women," 239.

29. Ellen Carol Dubois, "Working Women," 240.

30. Eliza Turner, "Should Women Work Outside Their Homes? 1895." In *Public Women, Public Words*, Vol. 1, ed. Dawn Keetley and John Pettegrew, 359.

31. Mary Livermore, "Superfluous Women, 1883." In *Public Women, Public Words*, Vol. 1, ed. Dawn Keetley and John Pettegrew, 356–57.

32. Marguerite Mooers Marshall, "Newspaper Woman Protests Against "Maternal Legislation." *Life and Labor* 10, no. 30 (1920): 84.

33. Eva McDonald-Valesh, "Woman and Labor, 1896." In *Public Women, Public Words: A Documentary History of American Feminism*, Vol. 1, ed. Dawn Keetley and John Pettegrew, 339.

34. Anna Dickinson, "Work and wages, 1869." In *Public Women, Public Words: A Documentary History of American Feminism*, Vol. 1, ed. Dawn Keetley and John Pettegrew, 353.

35. Anna Dickinson, "Work and Wages," 353.

36. Anna Dickinson, "Work and Wages," 353.

37. Mary Livermore, "Superfluous Women," 355.

38. Lucy. A Warner, "Why Do People Look Down on Working Girls?, 1891." In *Public Women, Public Words*, Vol. 1, ed. Dawn Keetley and John Pettegrew, 343.

39. Eva McDonald-Valesh, "Woman and Labor," 339.

40. Eva McDonald-Valesh, "Woman and Labor," 339.

41. L. M. Barry, "A Report of the General Investigator on Woman's Work and Wages to the Knights of Labor, 1888." In *Public Women, Public Words: A Documentary History of American Feminism*, Vol. 1, ed. Dawn Keetley and John Pettegrew, 338.

42. Harriot Stanton Blatch, "Educated Suffrage," 342.

43. Lucy A. Warner, "Why Do People Look Down," 343.

44. Campbell, "Femininity," 104.

45. Lucy A. Warner, "Why Do People Look Down," 344.

46. Bonnie Dow, "Feminism, Difference(s), and Rhetorical Studies." *Communication Studies* 46, no. 2/3 (Spring/Summer 1995): 109.

3

CRAFTING A FEMININE PRESIDENCY

Elizabeth Dole's 1999 Presidential Campaign

Kim Reiser

Hillary Clinton's 2008 presidential campaign was historical in that no other woman has come so close to winning the nomination of a major party. However, this nation's former female presidential candidates have undoubtedly played a role in paving the way for a female president. Margaret Chase Smith, Shirley Chisholm, Patricia Schroeder, and Carol Moseley Braun are among those candidates, as is Elizabeth Dole, who, in 1999, progressed farther in her presidential campaign than any woman before her. Dole's candidacy was also notable in that, like Hillary Clinton, she was a political spouse turned presidential candidate. In reference to her 1999 campaign, Berke noted, "Never before has a politician won the Republican nomination only to see his spouse seek the same office the next time around."[1] In her campaign for the 2000 presidential election, Dole's status as a public figure was largely due to the supportive role she played during her husband's political career in the Senate (1969–1996), and as a vice presidential (in 1976) and presidential candidate (in 1980, 1988, and 1996). Throughout the 1980s, the press suggested that Elizabeth Dole should run for an office of her own,[2] a suggestion that became more pronounced after her well-received 1996 Republican National Convention speech. Identified by the public as the "better candidate of the two [Doles],"[3] Elizabeth Dole took aim at the highest office in the United States three years later.

Although she dropped out of the Republican primary race before most of her opponents, early polls placed Elizabeth Dole second to frontrunner

George W. Bush. Dole was able to garner support across party lines[4] and draw crowds of women who were both young and old, veterans of politics and new to politics.[5] Anderson argues that Dole's 1996 RNC speech "formed a rhetorical backdrop for [her] 2000 presidential bid" and she maintains that "the success of Dole's 1996 speech can be attributed, at least in part, to the fact that she highlighted her own femininity and normalized traditional gender roles."[6] Building on Anderson's insight, in this chapter I argue that Elizabeth Dole's initial success in her presidential campaign can be attributed, in part, to her use of a feminine style of speaking. However, I also argue that the same strategies that enabled Dole to feminize, and therefore make attractive, her public persona led to her downfall.

FEMININE STYLE IN POLITICAL DISCOURSE

The fact that Dole emerged from her husband's 1996 presidential campaign as a traditionally feminine political spouse and presidential hopeful shows, as Anderson and Sheeler write, that femininity and feminism are not necessarily opposing terms. They explain, "A woman can be a successful professional and a supportive spouse. She can be brilliant and attractive. She can be strong and soft."[7] In fact, throughout U.S. history, femininity has provided women a voice in the traditionally masculine political arena.

During the nineteenth century, women adopted a pattern of speaking unique to their backgrounds and experiences to face the social sanctions of their time, primarily the belief that it was unsuitable for women to speak in public. The resulting difference in women's speech has been academically identified as "feminine style." Campbell describes the style, which arose out of the process of craft learning in women's circles, as follows:

> Such discourse will be personal in tone (crafts are learned face-to-face from a mentor), rely heavily on personal experiences, anecdotes, and other examples. It will tend to be structured inductively (crafts are learned bit by bit, instance by instance, from which generalizations emerge). It will invite audience participation, including the process of testing generalizations or principles against the experiences of the audience. Audience members will be addressed as peers, with recognition of authority based on experience (more skilled craftspeople are more experienced), and efforts will be made to create identification with the experiences of the audience and those described by the speaker.[8]

Feminine style allowed women the opportunity to reshape gender norms. In other words, women could challenge injunctions against speaking in public by taking on a speaking style that was consistent with their femininity.

Although the feminine style arose out of nineteenth-century, middle-class women's experiences, it is a pattern of public speaking that has been repeated over time. Dow and Tonn explain that feminine style's recurrence may be due to the fact that although "historical conditions" for women have changed, "social roles have not."[9] They explain that women are still expected to be nurturing, emotionally supportive and empathic. In addition, they write that "current research indicates that these specific skills, as well as the way they are learned, may continue to foster development of specific communicative strategies for women." Due to these factors, women have incorporated feminine style into their political rhetoric over the past century.

Researchers have modified some of the defined characteristics of feminine style as they have seen it appear in more recent political discourse. For instance, in her 1998 analysis of Hillary Clinton, Campbell writes that feminine style avoids "such 'macho' strategies as tough language, confrontation or direct refutation, and any appearance of debating one's opponents."[10] In other words, feminine style will appear less combative than other styles of communication. Jamieson agrees with this characteristic of cooperation versus competition. She writes, "Whether in public or private communication, men are more comfortable than women in a combative 'debate' style." In addition, she purports, "Consistent with social sanctions against aggressive speech by women, they are also less likely than men to speak on controversial topics."[11]

Through their study of public discourse, Blankenship and Robson identify five characteristics of feminine style that are similar to Campbell's framework, but show modifications. They are:

1. Basing political judgments on concrete, lived experience.
2. Valuing inclusivity and the relational nature of being.
3. Conceptualizing the power of public office as a capacity to "get things done" and to empower others.
4. Approaching policy formation holistically.
5. Moving women's issues to the forefront of the public arena.[12]

I analyze Dole's use of a feminine speaking style according to the characteristics defined by Campbell, Jamieson, and Blankenship and Robson.[13]

Although Dole's use of a feminine style has gained her popularity throughout her political career, the nature of presidential campaigning created what Jamieson identifies as a "double bind."[14] Elizabeth Dole needed to enact her femininity in a role that has been traditionally marked masculine. Jamieson argues that female candidates can manage the double bind successfully and she points to the career of Maryland senator Barbara Mikulski as a model. However, I argue that the presidency magnifies the double bind challenge that women face and that Dole's specific situation made the challenge even more intense.

SURFACING STAGE

On March 10, 1999, Elizabeth Dole announced her intention to form an exploratory committee to a crowd of well-wishers in Des Moines, Iowa. Dole gave this speech during the surfacing stage of the 2000 presidential election season. Trent and Friedenberg identify surfacing as the first of four major stages of a campaign and note seven functions of surfacing: demonstrating candidates' fitness for office; initiating political rituals; providing the public opportunities to learn about the candidates; developing voter expectations about candidates' personal and administrative styles; determining main campaign issues; separating frontrunners from the rest of the candidates; and establishing candidate-media relationships.[15] Throughout my analysis of Dole's exploratory committee speech, I keep the seven functions of the surfacing stage in mind; however, recognizing that the U.S. electorate has clear expectations about the attributes they believe a person must have in order to be a viable presidential candidate, I suggest that the first of these seven functions has particular salience for female presidential candidates.

In determining a candidate's fitness for office, the electorate will consider how a candidate would act in an executive position (as mayor, governor, or president).[16] However, citing political strategist Christine Matthews, Anderson and Sheeler explain that it is always more difficult for a woman to run for an executive office than a legislative office because of voter perceptions about the chief executive role and its associations with strong masculinity.[17] According to Trent and Friedenberg, "potential presidents are not supposed to be considered wimps,"[18] referencing a weak formulation of masculinity as feminized. In addition, Trent and Friedenberg maintain that as the office becomes higher, voters become more judgmental, potentially increasing the challenge women face as they seek out the highest office in the land.

Additionally, following Benoit's conclusions that a pure generic analysis can cover up other factors affecting a text,[19] I extend my framework to look at factors such as Benoit's observations on patterns of acclaiming, attacking and defending among certain subgroups of speakers. Similar to Trent and Friedenberg, Benoit found that challengers attack more than incumbents, while incumbents acclaim more than challengers.[20] Elizabeth Dole's roles as Woman, Former First Lady Candidate, Challenger, and Republican all played a role in her presidential campaign. I consider these influences when analyzing what Elizabeth Dole's 1999 exploratory committee speech tells us about women's role in nationally elected politics.

ELIZABETH DOLE'S 1999 EXPLORATORY COMMITTEE SPEECH

The indirect manner in which Elizabeth Dole announced her campaign for the presidency set the stage for her presidential campaign. According to Trent and Friedenberg, presidential candidates formally enter the political arena through the preprimary announcement speech.[21] According to these authors this is the most clearly defined ritual not only in the surfacing stage but also in the entire campaign. Although Elizabeth Dole's 1999 speech to form an exploratory committee more closely resembles a formal preprimary announcement than any of Dole's other presidential campaign speeches, it did not directly announce her campaign.[22] However, Dole's presidential campaign had already begun. The Associated Press wrote, "Early polls have shown Texas Gov. George W. Bush and Dole far ahead of other GOP rivals. And Bush issued a statement welcoming her to the contest."[23] In addition, although this AP article was titled "Dole Moves Closer to Presidential Campaign," it discussed how Dole highlighted "her qualifications in the race for the 2000 Republican nomination."[24] The indirect communication that initiated Dole's campaign embodied feminine style. This speech, in its unique way, was the symbolic representation of Dole's start to a presidential race.

Woman versus Politician

During the surfacing stage, the central themes and issues for the campaign are also set.[25] In her exploratory committee speech, Dole introduces a central theme: woman is not synonymous with politician but is consistent with leader. She uses this theme to transform her audience's notions of the presidency. Throughout her speech she advertises herself as a uniquely female candidate who is suitable for a moral position of leadership, a candidate far removed from the immoral politics of the presidency.

The introduction to Dole's speech indicates her role as a woman is at the forefront of her campaign. Deandra, an adolescent girl of minority descent, introduces Dole to the stage. When Dole takes the stage, she calls this young lady forward and informs the audience that Deandra would like to be president of the United States someday. Dole commends this ambition, claiming: "I think that is a wonderful goal. So," Dole continues, "I wanted Deandra to stand here with me as we make an announcement that may be historic because we want everyone to know that officially I have filed my papers with the FEC to have an Elizabeth Dole Exploratory Committee for the year 2000."[26]

By associating Deandra with her potential decision to run for president, Dole appeals to those who believe that any woman of any race has the potential to be president of the United States. It is through this act that Dole defines herself as the uniquely female candidate who moves women to the forefront of politics, a goal Blankenship and Robson classify as a characteristic of feminine style.[27]

In fact, the theme "making history" was prominent throughout Dole's presidential campaign. Balz wrote, "Dole hopes to capture some of the same kind of support and enthusiasm the public showed for the women [U.S. soccer team] athletes, and as she campaigned through Iowa this week, there was evidence that the history-making aspect of her campaign was her strongest appeal."[28] "'Be a part of history,' says the sign Dole held up at campaign events this week."[29] "The message is similar to one she put on an airplane that flew over the Rose Bowl last Saturday, when the U.S. women's soccer team won the World Cup."[30]

Given that she highlighted her gender, it is perhaps not surprising that Dole was popular first and foremost with women, including those new to the political process. As one journalist noted, "The uniqueness of Elizabeth Dole's presidential candidacy is instantly obvious wherever she campaigns. The audiences are overwhelmingly female: younger women, older women, women with babies, women with husbands, women who are Republican Party veterans and women who have never participated in the political process before."[31] Andron similarly observed, "She said she was excited about the number of people who were joining her campaign even though they had never been in politics before. By way of example, Thursday's [a June 3 Greensboro, North Carolina, speech] event was organized by Bonnie McElveen-Hunter, a Greensboro businesswoman and community volunteer who said it was her first venture into politics."[32] The apolitical nature of Dole's audience furthered the message that she herself was an apolitical candidate.

Dole's persona as an apolitical female candidate conflicted with public conceptions of a presidential candidate. According to Michigan representative Lynn Rivers, the challenge this conflict creates for female candidates is particularly acute in the early stages of a woman's campaign when women's credibility is most in question.[33] Rather than allow this conflict to be a detriment to her campaign, however, Dole sought to use it to her advantage. For example, in her exploratory committee speech, Dole claims that "woman" and "politician" are oppositional terms, posing the rhetorical question: "Now what would I, as a woman, offer our country? I am not a politician, and frankly, that is a plus today."[34] The alternative image of a moral leader was a timely appeal as much of the campaigning for the 2000 presidential election took place during the aftermath of the only presidential impeachment trial since 1974. Again according to Rivers, people are more aware of corruption than ever before, making gender particularly relevant in politics because women are seen as less corrupt and more honest than men.[35]

Thus Dole sets up a framework with which her audience can view politics, a moral framework to convince her audience that a woman is a better choice than a politician for president of the United States. Dole explains:

> When I entered public service as a young woman, many years ago, it was considered a noble thing to do . . . it was a noble thing. And today, young people are turning away from public service and that is because they don't see the wonderful possibilities of public service because of the ugliness of politics . . . Politics, the politics of governing, has become so negative, so dominated by special interest, that indeed I think what is happening is that we as a people are losing faith in our institutions. The next step is we lose faith in ourselves; and then, we really have lost, haven't we?[36]

Dole's solution to this "layer, thickening layer, of cynicism and doubt"[37] is for each person to rekindle a "belief in the individual. Restoring that American sense that one person, no matter how great the challenge can make a real difference."[38] The difference, she explains, can best be made through public service.

This framework of public service allows Dole to cite her political experience in a nonpolitical way. Furthermore, the self-denying nature of a public servant is an appropriate way to feminize the presidency. It shows Dole's commitment to selfless devotion, supporting what Carol Gilligan describes as public notions of female morality.[39] In her exploratory committee speech, Elizabeth Dole illustrates a life of devotion to public service to "call America to her better nature."[40] Dole explains that her goal over her last "thirty-plus years in public service" has been to "place service over politics."[41] Dole proves this inductively, staying true to feminine style, making use of the word "serve" to list her various political experiences. For instance, Dole says that she served as the Federal Trade Commissioner and most recently has been serving as president of the American Red Cross. In addition, Dole says that she served five presidents. As Dole lists her experience, she breaks it into three categories: overseeing the management of material resources with the Department of Transportation, overseeing the management of human resources with the Department of Labor, and overseeing the management of inner resources with the Red Cross.[42] By listing her service and breaking it into these categories, Dole shows a devotion to serving others through humanitarian agendas (material resources, human resources and inner resources).

Furthermore, Dole shares details of her service with the American Red Cross, showing her humanitarian agendas attend to the daily needs of others:

> At the American Red Cross, I saw things that will haunt me the rest of my life. Praying with parents at Oklahoma City, hoping their child would still be pulled alive from that rubble. Over in Rwanda . . . I was literally stepping over dead bodies after that rush of people, million people, left the country several years ago. And this was a terrible situation where little children were held by the Red Cross there. We were trying to find some extended family. They had nothing. Their parents had been hacked to death with machetes. They had no home, no parents, no food, no clothes, no hope, no future—nothing but the humanitarian organizations to help them.[43]

Again, these examples paint an image of Elizabeth Dole as a public servant, reaching out to selflessly help others.

Dole further represents herself as a moral leader through the use of language that is spiritual in tone. Following her description of her experiences in Oklahoma City and Rwanda, Dole explains that we often take advantages in our country for granted and that we are truly blessed to be Americans. She continues: "And we have been blessed to be a blessing, haven't we—we've received that we might give. And as I saw these things that would haunt me the rest of my life, I also saw the power of the human heart."[44] She refers to people who would travel across the globe to help strangers. "This is what we yearn for. These are the values," she says, "the fact that the individual can make a difference, every individual can, and certainly honesty and integrity. This is what I think people yearn for. That is neighbor helping neighbor."[45] "We've received that we might give" is biblical. In Matthew 10:8, Jesus commands his disciples to go forth and preach. He says, "freely we have received, freely give."[46] Elizabeth Dole echoes this call as she commends the good work she has observed and urges audience members to follow this lead.

Spiritual language is also evident in Dole's use of the metaphor "mission" to illustrate her past political positions. Dole says that with the department of transportation, her "mission was to oversee the management of material resources."[47] She also says that her work with the department of labor was a "wonderful mission field, again, for me." This creates an image of a type of foreign plain through which spiritual work is carried out, despite the fact that she is talking about a branch of the U.S. government.

Another example of spiritual language is provided in Dole's discussion about drugs. She says, we must "use the bully pulpit to preach constantly that drugs are not cool; they kill,"[48] and she continues: "Let's make this a crusade and get rid of this evil on our society." Interestingly, in this last statement, Dole is making a plea for a less sinful America, which fits well with her call to bring "America to her better nature."[49] A woman, representing a gender traditionally seen as pious, would be an obvious choice for a leader to bring America to a "better" place.

Dole, through her references to morality and spirituality, appeals to piety as a source of authority. This echoes nineteenth-century women's uses of piety to enact femininity and thus access the political stage. Elizabeth Dole's use of feminine style to demonstrate her fitness for the office also provides a transition from her persona of a selfless, supportive spouse in her 1996 campaign as a potential first lady to her 1999 campaign as a first lady president. In Dole's 1999 exploratory committee speech the central themes speak loud and clear that as a potential president of the United States, Dole will represent the public as a woman and a moral leader, rather than as a "politician." In addition to transforming the office of the president, however, Dole also must demonstrate how she will enact this transformed role. Staying true to feminine style, she demonstrates that her administrative style is peerlike, a characteristic previously noted as central to feminine style.

The "Liddy Factor"

In her exploratory committee speech, Dole helped us conceive of her as a peer by using the "Liddy stroll." This presentational style involves stepping out from behind the podium and in this speech, walking down the center aisle of the audience. Dole gained popularity for this stroll in her 1996 Republican National Convention speech, which Nichols identifies as a "down-with-the audience Oprah-style performance that traded substance for Southern-charm, family lore, and nostalgia for an America that sounds a lot like Salisbury in the 1950s."[50] Even the name "Liddy stroll," a name Dole requested the press not use in stories about her,[51] creates a notion that Dole, like a familiar childhood friend, will casually guide the public rather than command them. The use of this nonverbal developed voter expectations about Dole's personal and administrative style, the fourth function of the surfacing stage.[52]

The personal style Dole creates through her exploratory committee speech is one of a family member or friend. In her introduction, she explains that due to the fact she has traveled to all one hundred counties in North Carolina, she knows the audience very well. She says, "You are almost members of my family."[53] Dole also encourages peerlike interaction. Several times during the speech, audience members respond to points she has made. In turn, Dole reacts positively to individual audience members, often addressing people by name. In addition, Dole shakes hands and greets audience members during her speech. Dole extends this interaction to the television audience by providing her Web site address and assuring her listeners that she wants to hear their interests and concerns. She says, "This is a people to people effort on my part." In other words, Dole will wait to fulfill Trent and Friedenberg's third function of surfacing, setting forth objectives, or laying out positions,[54] until she hears from people. The reason for this, she says, is to set forth policies in "a thoughtful way." Through these passages, Dole reveals a desire to work with the people, in a personal way, to improve the country.

Not only does Dole enact feminine style by addressing her audience as peers, but she also gives them credit for her successes, basing her authority on shared experience. In the introduction, Dole disassociates herself with the overflow crowds she has seen on the campaign trail. She states, "But, I don't think I'm the cause of those overflow crowds and all of that enthusiasm. I think that Americans yearn to make our country a better place. I think that's why they're turning out in great numbers."[55] Furthermore, she avoids taking individual credit for tasks completed in her positions with the department of transportation, the department of labor, and the American Red Cross. For example, she speaks of the completion of two national airports with the department of transportation. Dole introduces this experience as follows: "We also transferred two airports out of the federal government, where they were on the dole, excuse me the pun, they were in the federal dole and getting only a few million dollars so they had to be gateways to the nation's capital. Dulles and National, which should be first class facilities." She continues to explain that there had been eight attempts to get this done since 1949, but Dole and her team were able to complete the project. She explains, "Why? Because I had a team of people who were the best and the brightest and I believe that is what you need in every job that you are in; you get the best people working with you, volunteers, staff, people who really understand how to get the job done." This story reverberates the theme of working with people rather than above them.

Through her description of her governmental experiences, Dole establishes that she will maintain a peerlike administrative style. In fact, in her exploratory committee speech, Dole refrains from citing job titles.[56] She makes one reference to her title as president of the American Red Cross and references positions held under Reagan. However, Dole avoids mentioning the prominent positions she has held under four other presidents, including secretary of labor in George H. W. Bush's administration. Dole's reference to specific job titles would conflict with her theme of "public service." In addition, avoiding titles is another way Dole illustrates how she will guide versus govern as president of the United States. Dole's strategy here is consistent with the characteristic of feminine style that envisions the power of public office as empowering others, rather than gaining power for self.[57]

As I have argued, Dole's solution to the public's lost faith in its political institutions, as quoted previously, is for each person to rekindle a "belief in the individual. Restoring that American sense that one person, no matter how great the challenge, can make a real difference" through public service.[58] By encouraging each person to restore a "belief in the individual," Dole invites audience participation. Furthermore, Dole refrains from placing herself above the audience or saying outright that she is the best leader to restore hope and goodness. In contrast, she talks to her audience as peers. She encourages her audience to engage in public service. However, this leadership style potentially conflicts with public notions of the presidency as an office headed by a single entity.[59]

Dole's use of this feminine leadership style may have created questions about her credibility as a presidential candidate. Referencing her tenure at the Department of Transportation, Pope and Eddings write, "Some colleagues . . . describe [Dole] as an empty suit. 'She acted more as a caretaker than as a reformer or visionary,' says one, allowing that 'she did surround herself with good managers.'"[60] However, as Jamieson notes, women are expected to be more prosocial in their communication, stressing "relationships rather than autonomous action."[61] Therefore, Dole's popularity may have come from the same place her nonacceptance did. She has a cooperative feminine appeal, but some perceived her to be lacking in the autonomy and combativeness necessary to win a presidential election.

The Noncombative Challenger

Elizabeth Dole's use of feminine style to enact a new kind of presidency made it difficult for her to take on a challenger style in the presidential election. However, Dole was a challenger, even though there wasn't a true incumbent running in the race; Elizabeth Dole was running against eight years of Democratic administration. Trent and Friedenberg write:

> When there is no incumbent, candidates attack the record of the current administration (if they do not represent the same political party) or even an opponent's record in a previous position. Whatever becomes the focus of criticism, the object is to attack—to create doubt in voter's minds regarding the incumbent's/opponent's ability—to stimulate public awareness of any problems that exist, or to foster a sense of dissatisfaction and even unhappiness with the state of affairs generally.[62]

These expectations of a challenger conflict with public expectations of women in politics, which tend to see women as more acquiescent. As numerous scholars have noted, the forms through which one can attack while enacting a feminine style are limited.[63] Again according to Trent and Friedenberg, "Women who initiate aggressive and forceful attacks may be viewed as unfeminine, shrill, vicious, nagging, . . . and therefore dismissed as abnormal."[64] A woman's political style must not diverge too much from expectations of ideal femininity; a challenger style might seem to do that in its more critical stance. The fact that Elizabeth Dole campaigned by projecting a more traditionally feminine image magnified these constraints.

In Elizabeth Dole's exploratory committee speech, she makes only one attack. It is when she addresses the only topic in her speech that typically has more Republican appeal than feminine association—defense. Dole explains that we need increased military spending. She says, "The president recommended in his budget twelve billion dollars [for defense], but only four billion dollars of that is new money. The rest, the eight billion is just moving money around. His joint chiefs, of course, who are his top military advisors, recommended seventeen billion. I say let's go with the joint chiefs, right? We need more money."[65]

The desire to increase defense spending was repeated in other Dole campaign speeches. This was one of the few topics Dole used to challenge the current administration by "stimulat[ing] public awareness of any problems that exist." However, pressure to discuss more traditionally feminine topics was compounded by the aforementioned nature of Dole's audiences, females involving themselves in politics for the first time. For example, Dole spoke on military and foreign policy a week after a speech George W. Bush delivered on the same topics at the citadel, Charleston's military academy famous for efforts to bar women.[66] Dole's audience, also a group of college students in Charleston, South Carolina, was heavily female. She proposed a post–cold war weapons buildup to reinforce the country's nuclear arsenal, invoking President Ronald Reagan, to whom she attributed the fall of communism.[67] In addition, Schemo writes, "She [Dole] said the current Administration had been taken in by the 'empty promises' of weak treaties and by 'rogue and outlaw nations' threatening the United States with weapons of mass destruction."[68] However, in her article titled "Dole Talks Foreign Policy, but Women Want Something Else," Schemo writes that several audience members were apparently disappointed in the content of Dole's speech, due to a lack of discussion of domestic issues.[69] Therefore, the nature of Dole's audience limited the topics that she could challenge.

Dole's audiences wanted generalities and Dole, in her noncombative style, delivered these. For example, although Dole, as previously illustrated, was clearly feminine in her presentational style, she denied that she was trying to gain votes by running as a female candidate. However, as we have noted, she used the reference of "making history" in her speeches. In fact, Dole's 1999 campaign contained a number of conflicting messages. Leonard writes, "[Dole] said she was not the women's candidate. But on a host of issues—gun control, education, school safety, controlling illegal drugs—Dole hit all the hot buttons that pollsters say appeal to women. She was also cautious on what she said about abortion. She insisted she was against abortion but quick to add she would not lead a charge as president to restrict abortion rights."[70]

Dole, in her indirect style, attempted to maintain a middle ground on a host of issues. Dole defined herself as uniquely feminine, while avoiding feminist labels. She appealed, in general terms, to the concerns of women. However, Dole avoided taking direct stances on women's issues. Some pundits contend that Dole's indirect style caused her to fade into the scenery. As Givhan observed, "[Dole] was ambivalent about barreling through walls and not inclined to boast about making history. As a result, she robbed herself of a defining image."[71]

Furthermore, Elizabeth Dole's failure to challenge early in her campaign caused her to lose ground against her primary contender, George W. Bush, who led the race for the Republican nomination for president.[72] George W. Bush held views very similar to Elizabeth Dole. Balz writes, "On most issues other than gun control, where she is less conservative than Bush, Dole and the Texas governor are not in sharp disagreement. Nor does she seem eager to begin to challenge Bush directly on issues. But obliquely at least, she suggested that she has far better credentials than Bush to step into the presidency."[73] This again illustrates Dole's use of proactive, noncombative, approaches to presidential campaigning. However, this strategy worked to her disadvantage. Balz quotes Tom Gorman: "Women are drawn to her . . . and she's got more hard support than the polls give her credit for. . . . But she's going to have to get a little tougher and focused. She's still pretty chit-chatty. She'll have to start swinging some."[74]

The 2000 presidential primaries revealed that the public expects challenger candidates to enact a challenger speaking style early on in the campaign. Jamieson explains that in the 2000 presidential campaign, former senator Bill Bradley achieved success in the polls when he "began not only to respond to attack but also to launch contrastive arguments of his own in New Hampshire."[75] She continues, "Bradley's shift raises the question: Had he moved more aggressively sooner to begin contrasting his record and proposals with [Al] Gore's, would he have been able to win Iowa or New Hampshire." Although Jamieson maintains that "there is no way to know the answer to that question, . . . what intrigues us about Bradley's campaign and Senator John McCain's (R-Arizona) experience when he swore off contrast ads in South Carolina is that in each instance the candidate who held to the supposed 'high road' lost ground."[76] In her attempt to maintain a more feminine, and therefore more cooperative, speaking style Dole similarly lost ground. Dole's failure to take on a challenger role may have cost her funds. "Her policy speeches on education and defense came later and were less detailed than Bush's on the same subjects."[77] Lawrence and Drinkard write, "Arizona Sen. John McCain is only slightly ahead of Dole in fundraising, but he has had no trouble attracting media attention. Several analysts contrast his ability to stay in the news—by publicizing a new memoir, voicing controversial views on the war in Kosovo or fighting for campaign finance reform—with Dole's caution and inability to build momentum."[78] Perhaps these pundits are correct to suggest that Dole would have benefited by assuming a more aggressive, challenger style, yet there is reason to doubt whether this is true. To the contrary, I maintain that women presidential candidates are caught in a double bind whereby challenging can both hinder and help.

THE PARADOX OF FEMININITY
AND PRESIDENTIAL POLITICS

If Dole, in her 1999 presidential campaign, had enacted a challenger style, one unlike the feminine style that defined her, she may not have progressed farther than any female presidential candidate before her. As previously noted, it was Dole's personal style in her 1996 convention speech that defined her as a popular choice for a presidential hopeful. Dole's repetition of this style in her presidential campaign contributed to her success. However, her feminine persona was not perceived as credible enough to win her a spot as a Republican presidential nominee.

On October 20, 1999, Elizabeth Dole withdrew her name as a presidential candidate citing lack of funds as her primary reason. Throughout Dole's campaign, her fundraising efforts reiterated the indirectly stated theme of being first and foremost a women's candidate. Dole was challenged in obtaining financial support from sources that traditionally finance male GOP candidates. Consequently, according to a May 31, 1999, issue of *Newsweek*, the Dole campaign sought funds in nontraditional ways, such as buying subscriber lists from women's magazines.[79] Leonard writes that her fundraising was successful in that it was "unlike her rivals and unlike any female candidates before."[80] Furthermore, Leonard explains that Dole obtained a substantial amount of funds with this strategy, "almost 50 percent of her $5 million from women. But that only enhanced the perception that gender was the focus of Dole's candidacy."[81] Furthermore, the disparity between frontrunner George W. Bush's funds, secured from traditional GOP sources, and her own funds had an influence over public support. Balz explains:

> The disparity between her campaign [Dole's] and Bush's make some Republicans who otherwise like her message, admire her personally and say she has the qualifications to serve as president more inclined to support frontrunner George Bush. When Dole visited the Madison County Historical Society here this week, Jane Wiggins brought some of her summer campers to see the Republican candidate. "I thought it would be exciting for Winterset kids to see a presidential candidate," she said. But when asked whether she would be supporting Dole's candidacy, Wiggins said she doubted it—even though she was delighted with what she heard and believes Dole is as qualified as any of the other candidates to hold the presidency. "I would like to see George W. Bush as president and Elizabeth Dole as vice president," she said.[82]

Wiggins was not alone in her perception that Dole would be a more suitable vice presidential candidate than a presidential candidate; this perception was echoed in other public responses.[83] However, disparity in funds most likely wasn't the only influence on perception. Parry-Giles and Parry-Giles write that it is the use of feminine style that perpetuates stereotypes about women.[84] They contend that society is comfortable with women's use of feminine style because it depicts women in their traditional light. However, these authors also argue that this style perpetuates the idea that women are to be supportive and nurturing. For this reason, Elizabeth Dole's style, although popular, may have depicted her as more of a political spouse or a possible vice presidential nominee rather than a presidential nominee. As seen in this analysis, Dole's presidential campaign both supports Parry-Giles and Parry-Giles' theory as well as challenges it. In contrast to Parry-Giles and Parry-Giles, I would argue that the fact that Dole used a feminine style in her 1999 presidential campaign was more positive than it was negative. As previously noted, Dole's use of feminine style increased her popularity. Because Dole progressed further in her presidential campaign than any woman before her, it resulted in a visual impact via images sent to a large number of individuals. Givhan quotes Schroeder, who says, "Any time there's a woman running for president, it's history-making. It's always very important because of the visuals it [the campaign] sends out to little girls watching TV."[85] Although some would say that the visuals Dole sent to young girls perpetuated the idea that they must enact femininity to be a presidential hopeful, I would argue that these visuals showed that a woman can enact femininity and still be a viable presidential candidate. Hopefully, there will come a day when a woman will not have to "masculinize" herself to win a presidential election but will be allowed the opportunity to choose a gendered speaking style most suitable to her. Sara Ruddick writes, "It is the conjunction of feminist and maternal consciousness, of maternal sympathies and feminist solidarity, which might shift the balance with maternal practices from denial to lucid knowledge, from parochialism to awareness of other's suffering, and from compliance to stubborn, decisive capacities to act."[86]

Although Elizabeth Dole ended her presidential race in 2000, she sought a senate seat in North Carolina in 2002 and won. Among the differences between Dole's senatorial campaign and her presidential campaign was not only that she was seeking a legislative rather than an executive position, but also that Dole was able to campaign virtually as an incumbent. In a July 9, 2002, *Washington Times* article, Dinan writes, "Mrs. Dole, who once sought the Republican nomination for president, has the name recognition of an incumbent; uses events with the president, vice president and Senate Republican leader to raise an incumbent-sized treasury; and runs on the

implicit endorsement of the departing Mr. Helms."[87] Dinan also explains
that her image of an incumbent rather than a challenger was positive in that
she could enact a "typical incumbent strategy—sit quiet, don't talk about issues if you can avoid it, look sweet and wait for the other guy to stumble or
not make headway."[88] In this sense the incumbent style is conducive to feminine style, whereas as mentioned previously, the challenger style is not.

In a February 17, 2007, article in the *News and Observer*, Christensen
writes that at a GOP dinner, Dole, at the age of seventy, announced her
intent to run for reelection to the senate in 2008.[89] Furthermore, according
to Christensen, displaying "no signs of recent hip replacement surgery, she
performed her patented 'Dole stroll,' walking between the tables rather
than speaking from behind the lectern, and taking questions from the audience."[90]

These various images that political candidates bring to the campaign
process will continue to shape how we view our nation's political positions.
Jamieson writes that as women and men use feminine style at all levels of
political leadership, female candidates will be able to use this style with less
risk to their credibility.[91] Dole's use of feminine style in the political campaign process are now part of the conversation we will continue to have in
future presidential campaigns.

NOTES

1. Richard Berke, "As Political Spouse, Bob Dole Strays From Campaign
Script," *The New York Times*, 17 May 1999, A14.

2. Nichola D. Gutgold, *Paving the Way for Madam President* (Lanham, Md.:
Lexington Books, 2006).

3. David Von Drehle, "Dole's Role: Bridging the Past and the Future: Pioneer-
ing Candidate's Popularity Reflects Traditional Roots," *The Washington Post,* 13
October 1999, 7.

4. Scott Andron, "Dole Appeal Crosses Party Lines: Both Republicans and
Democrats Seem Impressed With the Popular North Carolina Native," *Greensboro
News & Record*, 4 June 1999.

5. John Nichols, "Will Any Woman Do? The Candidacy of Elizabeth Dole," *The
Progressive* 63 (July 1999): 31–33.

6. Karrin Vasby Anderson, "Hillary Rodham Clinton as 'Madonna': The Role of
Metaphor and Oxymoron in Image Restoration," *Women's Studies in Communication* 25, no. 1 (March 2002): 119–21.

7. Karrin Vasby Anderson and Kristina Horn Sheeler, *Governing Codes: Gender,
Metaphor, and Political Identity* (Lanham, Md.: Lexington Books, 2005), 167–68.

8. Karlyn Kohrs Campbell, *Man Cannot Speak For Her: A Critical Study of Early Feminist Rhetoric.* vol. 1. (New York: Praeger, 1989), 13.

9. Bonnie J. Dow and Mari Boor Tonn, "'Feminine Style' and Political Judgment in the Rhetoric of Ann Richards," *Quarterly Journal of Speech* 79, no. 3 (August 1993): 287–88.

10. Karlyn Kohrs Campbell, "The Discursive Performance of Femininity: Hating Hillary, *Rhetoric and Public Affairs* 1, no. 1 (Spring 1998): 5.

11. Kathleen Hall Jamieson, *Eloquence in an Electronic Age: The Transformation of Political Speechmaking* (New York: Oxford University Press, 1988).

12. Jane Blankenship and Deborah C. Robson, "A 'Feminine Style' in Women's Political Discourse: An Exploratory Essay," *Communication Quarterly* 43, no. 3 (Summer 1995): 359.

13. Karlyn Kohrs Campbell, *Man Cannot Speak For Her;* Campbell, "Discursive Performance;" Jamieson, *Eloquence in an Age;* and Blankenship and Robson "A 'Feminine Style.'"

14. Kathleen Hall Jamieson, *Beyond the Double Bind: Women and Leadership* (New York: Oxford University Press, 1995).

15. Judith S. Trent and Robert V. Friedenberg, *Political Campaign Communication: Principles and Practice* (Lanham, Md.: Rowan and Littlefield, 2004).

16. Trent and Friedenberg, *Political Campaign Communication.*

17. Karrin Vasby Anderson and Kristina Horn Sheeler, *Governing Codes, 173.*

18. Judith S. Trent and Robert V. Friedenberg, *Political Campaign Communication, 26.*

19. William L. Benoit, "Acclaiming, Attacking, and Defending in Presidential Nominating Acceptance Addresses, 1960–1996," *Quarterly Journal of Speech* 85, no. 3 (August 1999): 247–67.

20. Judith S. Trent and Robert V. Friedenberg, *Political Campaign Communication;* Benoit, "Acclaiming, Attacking, and Defending," 247.

21. Trent and Friedenberg, *Political Campaign Communication, 26.*

22. "Road to the White House 2000," (Washington, D.C.: C-Span, 14 March, 1999).

23. Associated Press, "Dole Moves Closer to Presidential Campaign," *Missoulian*, 11 March 1999, A5.

24. Associated Press, "Dole Moves Closer," A5.

25. Judith S. Trent and Robert V. Friedenberg, *Political Campaign Communication.*

26. "Road to the White House."

27. Jane Blankenship and Deborah A. Robson "Feminine Style.'"

28. Dan Balz, "Hoping to Be 'Part of History': Elizabeth Dole is Wowing Women Voters, But Her Bid to Overtake George W. Bush for the GOP Prize Remains an Uphill Struggle," *The Washington Post*, 15 July, 1999, 1.

29. Balz, "Hoping to Be 'Part of History,'" 1.

30. Balz, "Hoping to Be 'Part of History,'" 1.

31. Balz, "Hoping to Be 'Part of History,'" 1.

32. Scott Andron, "Dole Appeal Crosses Party Lines," 1-2.

33. "Hillary and Liddy: From Running Mates to Front Runners?" [Panel Discussion at American University] (Washington, D.C.: C-Span, 1999).

34. "Road to the White House."

35. "Hillary to Liddy."

36. "Road to the White House."

37. "Road to the White House."

38. "Road to the White House."

39. Carol Gilligan, *In a Different Voice: Psychological Theory and Women's Development* (Cambridge, Mass.: Harvard University Press, 1993).

40. "Road to the White House."

41. "Road to the White House."

42. "Road to the White House."

43. "Road to the White House."

44. "Road to the White House."

45. "Road to the White House."

46. *The Holy Bible: Old and New Testament in the King James Version* (Camden, N.J.: Thomas Nelson, 1972).

47. "Road to the White House."

48. "Road to the White House."

49. "Road to the White House."

50. Nichols, "Will Any Woman Do?" 33.

51. Karrin Vasby Anderson and Kristina Horn Sheeler, *Governing Codes.*

52. Judith S. Trent and Robert V. Friedenberg, *Political Campaign Communication.*

53. "Road to the White House."

54. Judith S. Trent and Robert V. Friedenberg, *Political Campaign Communication.*

55. "Road to the White House."

56. "Road to the White House."

57. Jane Blankenship and Deborah A. Robson, "A 'Feminine Style.'"

58. "Road to the White House."

59. Judith S. Trent and Robert V. Friedenberg, *Political Campaign Communication,* 83.

60. Victoria Pope and Jerelyn Eddings, "An Iron Fist in a Velvet Glove," *U.S. News and World Report* 121 (19 August 1996): 27.

61. Kathleen Hall Jamieson, *Eloquence in an Electronic Age,* 82.

62. Judith S. Trent and Robert V. Friedenberg, *Political Campaign Communication,* 100.

63. Karlyn Kohrs Campbell, *Man Cannot Speak*; Bonnie J. Dow and Mari Boor Tonn "Feminine Style;" Sara Hayden, "Negotiating Femininity and Power in the Early Twentieth Century West: Domestic Ideology and Feminine Style in Jeannette

Rankin's Suffrage Rhetoric." *Communication Studies* 50 (1999): 83–102; Sara Hayden, "Family Metaphors and the Nation": 196-215; Mari Boor Tonn. "Militant Motherhood: Labor's Mary Harris 'Mother' Jones." *Quarterly Journal of Speech* 82, no. 1 (February 1996). 1–21.

64. Judith S. Trent and Robert V. Friedenberg, *Political Campaign Communication: Principles and Practice* (New York: Praeger, 1983), 115.

65. "Road to the White House."

66. Diana Jean Schemo, "Dole Talks Foreign Policy, But Women Want Something Else," *The New York Times* (28 September 1999): A23.

67. Schemo, "Foreign Policy," A23.

68. Schemo, "Foreign Policy," A23.

69. Schemo, "Foreign Policy," A23

70. Mary Leonard, "Gender Issue Casts Large Shadow as Dole Quits," *Boston Globe*, 21 October 1999, A1.

71. Robin Givhan, "One Small Step for Womankind: Elizabeth Dole's Candidacy Became Merely the Symbol She Avoided," *The Washington Post*, 21 October 1999, C1.

72. Dan Balz, "Hoping to Be 'Part of History';" Richard Berke, "As Political Spouse."

73. Balz, "Hoping to Be 'Part of History,'" 3.

74. Balz, "Hoping to Be 'Part of History,'" 3.

75. Kathleen Hall Jamieson, *Everything You Think You Know About Politics: And Why You're Wrong* (New York: Basic Books, 2000), 215.

76. Jamieson, *Everything You Think*, 215.

77. Jill Lawrence and Jim Drinkard, "Out Before a Vote: 'Bottom Line is Money,'" *USA Today*, 21 October 1999, 1A.

78. Lawrence and Drinkard, "Out Before a Vote," 1A.

79. "Deep Freeze." *Newsweek* 4 (31 May 1999). Expanded Academic ASAP Database (accessed July 13 1999).

80. Mary Leonard, "Gender Issue," A1.

81. Leonard, "Gender Issue," A1.

82. Dan Balz, "Hoping to Be 'Part of History,'" 2.

83. Karrin Vasby Anderson and Kristina Horn Sheeler, "Governing Codes."

84. Shawn J. Parry-Giles and Trevor Parry-Giles, "Gendered Politics and Presidential Image Construction: A Reassessment of the 'Feminine Style,'" *Communication Monographs* 63, no. 1 (December 1996): 337–53.

85. Robin Givhan, "One Small Step," C1.

86. Sara Ruddick, "From Maternal Thinking to Peace Politics." In *Exploration in Feminist Ethics: Theory and Practice* (Bloomington, Ind.: Indiana University Press, 1992), 150.

87. Stephen Dinan, "Mrs. Dole Campaigns Like Incumbent," *Washington Times,* 9 July 2002, A01.

88. Dinan, "Mrs. Dole Campaigns," A01.

89. Rob Christensen, "Dole Says She'll Seek Re-election to Senate," *The News and Observer* (Raleigh, NC), 17 February 2007. Dole eventually lost her election bid.

90. Christensen, "Dole Says," *News and* Observer, B1.

91. Kathleen Hall Jamieson, *Eloquence in an Electronic Age*.

4

THE DIATRIBE OF ANN COULTER

Gendered Style, Conservative Ideology, and the Public Sphere

Stephen A. Klien and Margaret E. Farrar

When asked in an interview what inspires her political commentary, Ann Coulter replied, "I love America, God, and truth, and I hate liars."[1] An unapologetic cultural conservative and self-described "devout Christian,"[2] Coulter described her rhetorical persona to another interviewer in this way: "I think my TV performances, radio, books, columns, private conversations are all one. The same person, saying the same things, making the same points."[3] If this statement is to be believed, then Ann Coulter is a compelling exemplar of contradiction. While regularly accusing "liberals" of racism, sexism and an incapacity for rational argument and debate, the controversial best-selling conservative pundit has also described extremist Muslims as "ragheads,"[4] called a presidential candidate a "faggot" while the C-SPAN cameras were rolling,[5] and advocated a now infamous response to the Arab Muslim world immediately following the September 11 terrorist attacks: "We should invade their countries, kill their leaders, and convert them to Christianity."[6]

Coulter's vitriolic broadsides against "liberals" and other enemies both engage in emotionally hyperbolic, irrational rhetoric and accuse her ideological opponents of the same. She also constructs a veneer of logical, evidence-grounded argument that is fraught with illogic and manipulation, leaving her vulnerable to charges of ineffective, inappropriate public argument. Given that her five best-selling books, articles, and ubiquitous media appearances are popular with her core audience of cultural conservatives and the mainstream media sources that regularly turn to her for punditry, Coulter functions as an influential voice of contemporary conservatism. As David Carr of the *New York Times* opined, "Without the total package, Ms. Coulter would be just one more nut living in Mom's basement . . . the fact that she is one of the leading political writers of our age says something about the rest of us."[7]

The recent, rapid rise of conservative female political commentators such as Coulter, Michelle Malkin, and Laura Ingraham has received little attention by feminist scholars.[8] This is surprising, given the observation by Linda Kintz that these women in the media function hegemonically as "spectacularized . . . extreme" embodiments of gendered whiteness, reifying white supremacy in a postmodern visual culture.[9] Yet these women have carved out a unique niche in U.S. political imaginary, and they have done so with rhetoric that takes a complex and often problematic set of positions regarding the legitimacy of women as political agents. This chapter examines Coulter and her rhetoric to illuminate her rhetorical construction of discourse norms. We suggest that Ann Coulter's rhetoric involves complex yet recurrent patterns of gendered diatribe that work to the detriment of women as legitimate political agents in the public sphere.

ANN COULTER: THE RISE OF A "STILLETO-CON"

Ann Coulter's Universal Press Syndicate biography opens with these words: "Political analyst and attorney Ann Coulter has been dubbed 'the Abbie Hoffman of the Right' for her unabashed satirical commentary and her savage barbs on the Washington scene and the media world."[10] A lawyer by training, Coulter has often been described as a "constitutional law expert" and "legal analyst" during her myriad television appearances, but she is best known for her role as a deliberately controversial conservative political commentator. She describes herself on her Web site, in part, as follows:

> Coulter is the legal correspondent for Human Events and writes a popular syndicated column for Universal Press Syndicate. She is a frequent guest on many TV shows, including *Hannity and Colmes, Wolf Blitzer Reports, At Large With Geraldo Rivera, Scarborough Country,* HBO's *Real Time with Bill Maher, The O'Reilly Factor, Good Morning America* and has been profiled in numerous publications, including *TV Guide,* the *Guardian* (UK), the *New York Observer, National Journal, Harper's Bazaar,* and *Elle* magazine, among others. She was named one of the top 100 Public Intellectuals by federal judge Richard Posner in 2001.[11]

Coulter began her rise to notoriety as a legal pundit during the Monica Lewinsky scandal, making television appearances and writing columns while authoring the best-selling *High Crimes and Misdemeanors: The Case Against Bill Clinton*. Since the success of that book in 1998, Coulter has written five other best-selling works of commentary: 2002's *Slander: Liberal Lies About the American Right*, 2003's *Treason: Liberal Treachery From the Cold War to the War on Terrorism*, 2004's *How to Talk to a Liberal (If You Must): The World According to Ann Coulter*, 2006's *Godless: The Church of Liberalism*, and 2007's *If Republicans Had Any Brains, They'd Be Democrats*.

Coulter has often been identified as one of a group of what writer Mick Farren calls the "stiletto-cons"[12] and what a 1998 *Harper's Bazaar* article dubbed "Washington's Spice Girls: The New Breed of Conservative Babe,"[13] a number of female conservative media personalities who rose to media prominence in the mid-1990s and seemed to capitalize on a combination of sexual attractiveness and confrontational rhetorical style in order to gain public attention. Coulter and many of her contemporaries have been associated with the Independent Women's Forum, an influential organization of elite conservative political women formed during the Clarence Thomas confirmation hearings and supported by allied conservative foundations.[14] The "stiletto-cons" positioned themselves during the years of the Clinton-Lewinsky scandal, the Chandra Levy disappearance and the 2000 election as telegenic assets for the demands of cable television news and talk programming.[15]

Ann Coulter simultaneously advocates public rationality and decorum in political debate while blatantly violating such norms. Most intriguing to us, she is also a woman aspiring to a place of public prominence while valorizing a political ideology that places women in a subordinate subject position. In order to make sense out of Coulter's stunningly contradictory public voice, our analysis of her rhetoric is informed by three intersecting theoretical projects: the debate regarding a legitimate place for women in the Habermasian public sphere, the varied body of critical literature exploring women's responses to masculine discourse norms, and the concept of "diatribe," a discourse form often favored by cultural conservatives.

THE WOMAN QUESTION AND THE PUBLIC SPHERE

Since its publication nearly a half century ago, Jürgen Habermas's *The Structural Transformation of the Public Sphere*[16] has served as one of the most compelling accounts of the history and function of modern political communication. Habermas argued that the arena for rational political debate developed in the eighteenth century as a response to, and critique of, the monarchy in Western Europe. In coffeehouses, cafes, and in the pages of print media, Habermas contends, the ascendant bourgeois class developed the skills and dispositions necessary for participating in substantive, influential, and critical political conversation: specifically, the abilities to make and respond to reasoned argument through the utilization of objective facts, evidence, and civility rather than anecdote, emotion, and hostility. For Habermas, the public sphere (and its demise) represent not only a specific historical phenomenon but also a set of discursive norms by which to judge the robustness of democratic culture.

Although it remains enormously influential, Habermas's account of the public sphere has been critiqued by a variety of feminist theorists for what they perceive as its gender exclusivity. As these critics note, the discursive norms required for participation in the public sphere, such as reason, objectivity, and self-control, are qualities typically associated with men and masculinity, while their opposites (irrationality, subjectivity, and self-indulgence) have been ascribed to women. Women thus enter the public sphere, these critics contend, already at a disadvantage, before a single word has been uttered or an argument has been made.[17] Rather than a space of just and equitable interchange, participation in Habermas's public sphere may in fact be systematically denied to women.

Moreover, by privileging the qualities of rationality, objectivity, and restraint in debate, these critics continue, Habermas fails to recognize what might be valuable in women's political communication. This potential for excluding or devaluing women's contributions to public discourse has led some to study the historical contributions of women to traditions of rhetoric and public address. One of the fruits of this pursuit has been the discovery of the "feminine style" of discursive interaction. Campbell discusses the feminine style as a performative tradition emergent in nineteenth-century women's public address. As women struggled to gain access to and find a legitimate voice in the public sphere, they developed particular patterns of expression based largely on the articulation of lived experiences, often moving beyond abstract intellect to embrace the concrete, the emotional, the inclusive, and the personal through narrative.[18] Although the feminine style is not the exclusive domain of women,[19] it does come directly out of women's and men's different, lived experiences; that is to say, the feminine style is not "only" language, but rather it reveals a distinct epistemic stance. By acknowledging the presence of a "feminine style" in political discourse, some feminist critics hope to expand opportunities for women to be heard and understood in the public sphere.[20]

Feminist theorists have also identified a second discursive opportunity in the transformative possibilities present in radical political expression. Although Habermas's public sphere assumes that all participants are welcomed into the discursive arena, as Sparks notes, this is not a given for many individuals, and in fact deliberation "is often the goal rather than the starting point" for historically subordinated groups. These groups have required a variety of alternative means to make themselves heard, such as marches, sit-ins, boycotts, and strikes. Sparks describes these activities as acts of "dissident citizenship,"[21] or "the practices of marginalized citizens who publicly contest prevailing arrangements of power by means of oppositional democratic practices that augment or replace institutionalized channels of democratic opposition when those channels are inadequate or unavailable."[22]

Women certainly have availed themselves of these tactics as they have struggled to gain access to the public sphere. From the parades organized by first-wave suffragists to the inflammatory prose of Valerie Solanas' *SCUM Manifesto* to the creative street theater of third-wave activists such as the Radical Cheerleaders, women have utilized what might be called an "unruly dissident style" to fight for admission into the discursive arena.[23] Deem examines what she calls "minor rhetorics"[24] such as the *SCUM Manifesto* in order to reveal how an unruly, confrontational style holds liberatory potential. Such indecorous, often scatological rhetoric reveals the presence of the corporeal body in discourse, disrupting the disciplining functions of traditional civility in "rhetorics of disincorporation"[25] such as the normative ideal of Habermas's public sphere. The Radical Cheerleaders perform a contemporary example of the corporeal rhetoric of dissent that Sparks associates with dissident citizenship. Farrar and Warner contend that such confrontational, profane, postmodern advocacy expands the boundaries of the public sphere and opens additional space for the agency of public women.[26]

Yet the history of women's struggle to find a legitimate place in the public sphere underscores a powerful double bind.[27] Women have struggled historically to constitute a rhetorical voice at once authentic and "legitimate." On the one hand, in order to gain attention and effective entry into the public sphere, women have often had to rely on discursive norms stemming from their lived experiences as women. On the other hand, these rhetorical styles have also tended to mark women as "different"—sometimes essentially so—than men. This has left women vulnerable, as DiQuinzio has noted in her critique of the Million Mom March, to the charge that they are less capable (indeed, even incapable) of participation in the rational-critical discourse envisioned by Habermas's model of the ideal speech situation and the public sphere.[28] As well, women who have attempted to utilize traditionally masculine discursive forms in an attempt to gain political legitimacy have often been marked as insufficiently "feminine." Such women have then had to defend their identities as authentic, legitimate women.

As a cultural conservative ideologue, Ann Coulter is faced with yet another double bind: she is a woman seeking a legitimate place within the community of cultural conservatives, an ideology that has traditionally subordinated women. This begs an intriguing question: How does a woman gain powerful public visibility while her words simultaneously function to "keep women in their place"? Isn't her mere rhetorical existence a profound contradiction?

DIATRIBE AND MORAL CONFLICT

In order to understand the seemingly self-defeating dynamics of Coulter's rhetorical construction of ideal feminine discourse norms more fully, we turn to "diatribe," a form of public discourse generally characterized by combative, emotional and ideologically simple argument.[29] In their study of the New Christian Right and their critics of the 1980s, Pearce, Littlejohn and Alexander describe diatribe as "abusive criticism or invective . . . moral indignation as a basis for the group's response."[30] They argue that ideological moral conflicts between groups stem from utterly incommensurable ways of looking at the world. In diatribe, arguments are typically personal ad hominem attacks, and attacks by opponents are interpreted *"as evidence that [one's] own statements are valid."*[31] Moreover, while the messages produced by the diatribe are "simple and not thoughtful," and fail to "address each other's world view," each side perceives their messages as meaningful.[32] Thus, as Freeman, Littlejohn and Pearce describe,[33] arguments in diatribe are often, put bluntly, facile. Instead of reasoned argument, diatribe instead includes patterns of enemy construction that target clearly the opposing side as a powerful, evil threat, with whom reasoned engagement is unnecessary.[34]

Examining patterns of diatribe may illuminate Coulter's discourse, given its persistently and intentionally moralistic, combative tone. It may be that, by utilizing the diatribe to appropriate performative traditions of movement conservatism, Coulter tries to avoid the risks of internal self-contradiction and find a place of influence in the U.S. conservative power structure.

READING ANN COULTER'S GENDERED DIATRIBE

While her columns and television appearances utilize diatribe in virtually every instance, we have focused our attention on her first five books. These texts provide rich examples of Coulter's diatribe on a variety of different issues, have been consumed by thousands of readers, and have been the subject of heated critical commentary and media debate.[35] One of them, *How To Talk To a Liberal (If You Must)*, is a representative compilation of Coulter's columns (published and unpublished) from 1991 to 2004. What we find most intriguing are the patterned ways in which Coulter's diatribe positions her, conservatives, and other women within (and without) the normative terrain of the public sphere. By purportedly defending the notion of a rational public sphere, constructing conservatives as blameless victims of diabolical liberal enemies, and simultaneously perpetuating and complicating sexist assumptions regarding public discourse, Coulter manages to reify a gender-exclusionary public sphere by promoting masculine discourse norms and performing allegedly feminine violations of those norms at the same time.

Coulter's Defense of Rational Discourse (Sort Of)

First, Coulter frequently positions herself—and Republicans generally—as defenders of a civil, rational public sphere. In numerous instances, Coulter describes Democrats and liberals (the terms are synonymous for Coulter) as being unwilling to engage, or incapable of engaging in, reasoned deliberation. Liberals, according to Coulter, perform "drama-queen theatrics"[36] and "traffic in shouting and demagogy," working themselves into "dervish-like trance[s]" and "incanting inanities,"[37] the apparent victims of "political Tourette's syndrome."[38] Liberals "name call" rather than persuade, and attack rather than argue rationally.[39] In doing so, liberals ignore facts: "Any evidence that anyone seeks to harm America is stridently rejected as 'no evidence.'"[40] "Liberals unreservedly call all conservatives fascists, racists, and enemies of civil liberties with no facts whatsoever."[41] Indeed, they avoid, and seek to defeat them: "They invoke weird personal obsessions like a conversational deus ex machina to trump all facts."[42] In addition, liberals reject civil argument, preferring misdirection—"When arguments are premised on lies, there is no foundation for debate"[43]—and non sequitur—"If you can somehow force a liberal into a point-counter-point argument, his retorts will bear no relation to what you said."[44]

This should come as no surprise, as liberals are incapable of reason itself: "Logic is not their métier. Blind religious faith is."[45] Indeed, the quality of the argument even from the intellectual elite is horrendous: "[Liberalism] is no longer susceptible to reduction ad absurdum arguments. Before you can come up with a comical take on their worldview, some college professor has written an article advancing the idea."[46] The causes for this illogic are often located in some form of mental illness: they make "paranoid accusations based on their own neurotic impulses,"[47] and suffer from a "psychological block" preventing their minds from working.[48]

By contrast, Coulter constructs her commentary as a model of rational argument. The best example of this construction may be her first book, *High Crimes and Misdemeanors,* in which she builds a case for impeaching President Bill Clinton based not only on "evidence," but on a systematic application of legal definitions and principles grounded in the testimony of authorities from English common law and the U.S. constitutional framers. Coulter moves from deductive to inductive argument structure in books like *Slander, Treason,* and *Godless,* in which she uses collected anecdotal examples and narrative recountings of events to make broader claims regarding the liberal mindset and agenda. And all of the books except *How To Talk To a Liberal* (which is primarily a collection of columns) are concluded with pages of footnotes, citing documented evidence to ground her claims.[49]

While describing herself and Republican politicians as rational, reasonable, and sane (while painting her opponents as irrational, fanatical, and crazy), Coulter uses diatribe to mask her argumentative shortcomings. Rather than the measured, case-making rhetoric espoused by Habermas, after *High Crimes and Misdemeanors* Coulter usually relies on the vilification of her opponents as a primary persuasive tactic. By Coulter's logic, because liberals are incapable of engaging in rational discussion, one doesn't *need* to engage them—although Coulter magnanimously avers that conservatives *do* engage them, unavoidably, making them "the most tolerant (and long-suffering) people in the world."[50] Instead, Coulter merely has to draw attention to the faults of her enemies. That is to say, by accusing her opponents of rhetorical misbehavior, Coulter herself can engage in this same misbehavior while simultaneously absolving herself of responsibility for it. The illogic of her contradiction is utterly irrelevant. Her propensity for diatribe is especially evident when Coulter shifts quickly from discussion about discursive competence to descriptions of moral depravity. The closing moments of *Godless* illustrates this point: "We [conservative Christians] can't discover penumbras that will suddenly allow us to endorse genocide, sex with animals, gay marriage, strip clubs, premarital sex, or whatever the latest liberal fad is. The truth is the truth whether we like it or not."[51] Here, diatribe lets Coulter gets away with blatant straw person and hasty generalization fallacies, as well as placing widely divergent behaviors on the same moral plane, while proclaiming to champion the "truth" as divinely decreed.

At the same time, Coulter argues that the point of political discourse is to outrage and offend one's opponent: "[You] must outrage the enemy. If the liberal you're arguing with doesn't become speechless with sputtering, impotent rage, you're not doing it right."[52] Note, of course, that just eight pages earlier Coulter denounces the use of "stratagems to prevent conservatives from talking."[53] This inconsistency is excusable because of the clarity of Coulter's moral universe: "Nothing too extreme can be said about liberals, because it's all true."[54] In the diatribe, such completely unprovable claims are used as foundational premises for subsequent argument. Hence a key requirement for rational-critical discourse in a Habermasian public sphere—the need for argument grounded in truth—is both lauded and utterly violated by Coulter regularly.

Coulter's Rhetoric of Victimage

Coulter also situates conservatives as the *victims* of the left rather than as *perpetrators* of rhetorical and political wrongs. Such a strategy has been a staple of the cultural conservative diatribe since the emergence of a "rhetoric of personal victimage" by conservative Christians in the late 1970s directed at "secular humanists," a small but powerful group of antagonists.[55] Coulter's diatribe continues this pattern, deploying elaborate conspiracy theory that ascribes all social ills in a simple binary moral universe to "liberals," the single source of all evil, who seek to obliterate important cultural traditions. This enemy is paradoxically as powerful, clever and deadly as they are irrational and incapable.

Liberals, according to Coulter, are mean, and just don't fight fair. She warns: "Prepare for your deepest, darkest secrets to become liberal talking points. . . . [P]repare to have your every foible unveiled as if you were caught raping kittens. Even if you've led a blameless life, liberals will invent absurd stories about you."[56] This pattern is established from the start in

High Crimes and Misdemeanors, in which liberal attacks on Linda Tripp's appearance are identified as responses to her courage in protecting herself and telling the truth. In *Slander*, Coulter rightly condemns Democrats' "attacks on women for being ugly." Such an attack is, in her words, "a hideous thing, always inherently vicious."[57] This is an interesting claim, though, given how Coulter does not seem to think that her descriptions of the "fat Jewish girl" Monica Lewinsky,[58] the misguided crusades of "ugly feminists,"[59] or her description of a "physically repulsive" sex educator[60] —all in the space of nine pages—are "inherently vicious."

According to Coulter's formulation, these insults are somehow consistent with the rational, reasonable, and civil discourse routinely practiced by conservatives, often to their detriment: "On any television political roundtable you will see Republican politicians droning on about what a fine human being some heinous Democrat is . . . only to have the heinous Democrat turn around and accuse the Republican of near complicity in genocide."[61] Coulter claims that "arguments by demonization, rather than truth and light, can be presumed to be fraudulent. . . . But ad hominem attack is the liberal's idea of political debate."[62] Of course, sixteen pages later, Coulter compares Democrats to the Ku Klux Klan.[63]

Coulter also regularly identifies and criticizes the sources of power allegedly used by liberals in their assaults on America. These include "total hegemonic control of all major means of news dissemination in America,"[64] resulting in pervasive liberal bias and constant misinformation of the public for political ends. For Coulter, this discrimination by the fanatical liberal media against reasonable conservatives is quite personal; she routinely reminds readers how long she remained ignored, unpublished, unrecognized, and unrewarded for her contributions to political debate.[65] But the liberals don't just control the media. They control history: "The battle for truth is purely propagandistic. Liberals can't persuade, they can only harrumph. But they write the history books."[66] This is important, as liberal history is anti-American: "Whether they are rooting for the atheistic regimes of Stalin or Mao, satanic suicide bombers and terrorists, or the Central Park rapists, liberals always take the side of savages against civilization."[67] Liberal support of "savagery" extends to siding with anti-American Muslims against Christian Americans when designing school curricula after 9/11,[68] and deeming abortion the "holiest sacrament," concluding that "1.3 million aborted babies in America every year is something to celebrate."[69]

The evil of liberalism can be summed up in a simple binary for Coulter, paraphrased from ex-Communist Whittaker Chambers: "Liberals chose Man. Conservatives chose God."[70] For Coulter, then, "liberals" constitute an evil minority that exercises sufficient power to threaten America and its mainstream-conservative value system. They are a pervasive threat, and Coulter is fighting back for the victims. Such moral conflict is constructed as a holy war, which eliminates the public sphere as a viable mechanism for public reconciliation.[71]

Coulter's Ambivalent Gender Position

Finally, Coulter further entrenches assumptions about gender and public discourse while at the same time occupying a position that unsettles these same assumptions. In many places in her texts, Coulter, not surprisingly, frequently endorses an essentialist understanding of gender roles. "There are differences between boys and girls," she reminds us solemnly.[72] For an example of these differences: "We pretty much emerge from the womb with an instinctive understanding that all research and development costs fall to the male," she argues about women's inability to respect men who split a restaurant check.[73] And like many conservative pundits, Coulter decries feminists' role in eliminating "the very institutions that protect women: monogamy, marriage, chastity, and chivalry."[74] As she claims,

> It was much better when everyone pretended that all [men's] little projects—philosophy, math, science, world government, and so on—were more important than carrying on the human race. Back in the prelapsarian fifties, women worked if they happened to fall into the .01 percent of the population who are able to have interesting jobs or they retired in their twenties to raise children . . . As far as I'm concerned this was a division of labor nothing short of perfect.[75]

Yet Coulter's reinscription of gender binarism goes beyond the conservative *content* of her opinions. Coulter's language also reinforces the gendered dichotomy of "reasonable" and "unreasonable" rhetoric that has troubled feminist scholars such as Landes. For example, she frequently identifies liberals and Democrats as feminine or effeminate, criticizing their "womanly crying about guns,"[76] their "female taunting about weapons of mass destruction,"[77] and their "girly guilt-mongering" on public education.[78] It is important to note that Coulter frequently equates "female" with "irrational," particularly in *Treason*:

- What do liberals want? Freud would have gone crazy with these people. Figuring out what women want is easy compared to liberals[79];

- [Liberals'] minds are fine, but the woman wells up in them[80];
- Only the movie industry could produce that level of womanly hysteria.[81]

Moreover, Coulter argues that Democrats intentionally *use* irrational women as part of their political strategy. In a chapter of *Godless* titled "Liberals' Doctrine of Infallibility: Sobbing, Hysterical Women," Coulter argues that when liberals were finally forced to engage in a dialogue with the right due to conservative successes in talk radio and television, they resorted to a strategy that would protect their monopoly on truth: overly emotional discourse resulting from personal trauma. She writes,

> Finally, the Democrats hit on an ingenious strategy: They would choose only messengers whom we're not allowed to reply to. That's why all Democratic spokesmen these days are sobbing, hysterical women. . . . Democrats with a dead husband, a dead child, a wife who works for the CIA, a war record, a terminal illness . . . They've become the "Lifetime" TV network of political parties.[82]

The Democrats, Coulter continues, used the "gaggle of weeping [9/11] widows" and antiwar activist Cindy Sheehan—"with that weird disconnect between the viciousness of her comments and her itsy-bitsy, squeaking voice"[83]—in addition to emasculated men such as "a paralyzed, dying Christopher Reeve" and "a disabled Vietnam veteran" to advance their political message.[84] Coulter argues that these women (and feminized men) were used as political stooges, not as political agents acting on their own accord.

Of course, both her gender essentialism and critique of unreasonable, emotional rhetors puts Coulter in an unusual and (by her own standards) troubling position. Coulter obviously defies many gender stereotypes. Far from accepting that some domains should remain exclusively male (their "pet projects"), Coulter has established herself as a lawyer and as a political pundit—two of the most traditionally masculine pursuits. She is a working woman who has not (despite her claims that such a situation would be "nothing short of perfect") retired in her twenties to become a happy homemaker with children in tow. Moreover, in some places in her texts she recognizes that the very essentialism she claims to endorse has worked against her ambitions; when describing the few magazines that would publish her early work, she names "Ronald Reagan's favorite publication, *Human Events*—even though it had to break a half-century 'no girls' rule to hire me."[85] Coulter's hero is anti-ERA activist Phyllis Schlafly, an avowed antifeminist who was able to achieve success in a male-dominated political scene while also being a successful mother. Coulter contrasts Schlafly against feminist ERA activist and "spectacular flop" Gloria Steinem[86] in a telling manner:

> While Schlafly was writing about military policy, getting presidential candidates nominated, drafting Republican platforms, and raising six children, Steinem was writing a book about self-esteem. . . . Steinem never had children and now goes around prattling about how unhappy her life has been.[87]

Coulter's celebration of Schlafly not only constructs an ideal political woman—strong woman but antifeminist, professional, and maternal—but also ironically reveals an element of essential womanhood (i.e., marriage and motherhood) that Coulter lacks. By her own logic, Coulter is an incomplete woman.

Coulter's own rhetoric also leaves her open to charges of emotional irrationality—the same charges she levels against liberals and the same charges that have been used throughout history to silence women's attempts at political speech. Despite the thin veneer of rational argument that she provides, her writings consist mainly of hyperbole, insult, and unsubstantiated opinion. Her frequent use of sarcasm and the personal slights she chronicles at every opportunity distance her further from rationalism. In brief, she promotes the value of reasoned discourse but violates it in a number of ways. When she argues utilizing traditionally masculine "rationality" norms, her factual and logical inaccuracies reveal her inadequacies. When she goes on the extreme attack, she resembles the "harpies" she refers to in her rants against female advocates.

STANDING IN HER OWN WAY?

Ann Coulter provides an illuminating case study of the potential for, and limitations on, the use of diatribe as a rhetorical strategy to assert a legitimate place in the public sphere. Diatribe in and of itself degrades the rational, collaborative negotiation of public moral conflict.[88] It might be possible to reconceptualize diatribe as a "minor rhetoric" or "unruly dissident style" to gain attention and confront dominant power structures. However, in the hands of a cultural conservative who is also a woman, the diatribe is truly a double-edged sword.

Spindel points out that media demand for the "stiletto-cons" ebbed after the terrorist attacks of September 11, 2001, as mainstream news turned its attention to terrorism and war.

> Apparently the opinions of Ingraham, Fitzpatrick and Coulter were welcomed during a prosperous age when the most pressing news headlines— sex scandals and contested elections—were a bit surreal and, ultimately, not as weighty as the issues we face today. Now, in shaky economic times and with a protracted war on the horizon, the message of the networks seems to be that the entertaining girls have been dismissed and the expert men brought in.[89]

Spindel goes on, however, to point out that Coulter's visibility continued to escalate even after September 11, as evidenced by her notorious anti-Islamic columns and best-selling books.[90] Somehow, Coulter was able to largely escape the fate of her fellow conservative pundettes by shifting her political targets and amplifying her rhetorical attacks. Her success, however, may have been shortlived.

Coulter's brand of hyperbolic political rhetoric cannot fairly be described as representative of contemporary conservative commentary in general. David Hogberg, for instance, opines that Coulter's discourse "has a side that is vile and ugly,"[91] and characterized her February 10, 2006, CPAC speech and Q&A session, in which she referred to Muslims as "ragheads," as "stupid," "racist," "snippy," "immature," and an exercise in "idiocy."[92] Fellow conservative women have weighed in against Coulter as well. *National Review* columnist Florence King has critiqued Coulter's rhetoric, particularly her characterization of then-*Today* anchor Katie Couric as "the affable Eva Braun of morning TV,"[93] as lacking wit and sophistication—"she would not hesitate to choose a sledgehammer over a stiletto."[94] King also offered a succinct explanation for Coulter's style: "At her best, Coulter writes well, but the chief source of her success is that she is a perfect match for the American ideal: smart as a whip but dumb as a post, educated but not learned, sexy but not sensuous, all at the same time."[95]

Some critics, such as *National Review Online* writer Kathryn Jean Lopez, responded to her homophobic slurring of John Edwards as a "faggot" at the end of her 2007 CPAC speech by focusing on how her style hurts conservatism: "The rhetorical firebombs distract from what the less provocative, and sometimes much more reasonable, have to say."[96] This sentiment was echoed by Amy Ridenour of the National Center for Public Policy Research, who declared,

I'm sorry to see that Ann Coulter once again made certain news coverage of CPAC would be focused upon her instead of upon the conservative movement's goals and principles. . . . It would be better, in my opinion, to not have a CPAC at all than to have one that presents conservatism as a hostile, people-hating ideology.[97]

When Coulter has raised the ire of fellow conservatives, it has been her rhetorical style rather than her content that has prompted criticism.

Indeed, when the *National Review* dropped Coulter "in the wake of her [post 9/11] invade-and-Christianize-them column,"[98] *National Review Online* editor Jonah Goldberg cited her sloppiness as a writer and her self-serving willingness to publicly dissemble as the reasons why the magazine stopped running her column. Coulter apparently wrote a follow-up column responding to her critics that *National Review* refused to run on the basis of its demonstration of "Ann at her worst—emoting rather than thinking, and badly needing editing and some self-censorship, or what is commonly referred to as 'judgment.'"[99] Moreover, *National Review* had less of a problem with Coulter's positions than with her packaging. Explaining why relatively incendiary points of view on Islam from writers like William F. Buckley Jr. have been published while Coulter's no longer are, Goldberg argues:

> The only difference between what we've run and what Ann considers so bravely iconoclastic on her part, is that we've run articles that accord persuasion higher value than shock value. It's true: Ann is fearless, in person and in her writing. But fearlessness isn't an excuse for crappy writing or crappier behavior.[100]

Goldberg variously describes Coulter's self-perceptions as "the thin blonde line between freedom and tyranny" and "'Joan of Arc battling the forces of political correctness.'"[101] What makes this particular episode intriguing for us is the way that Coulter has been positioned (partly by self-design, partly not) as a gendered voice running counter to established norms of rational discourse. Coulter's discourse thus ultimately abandons a traditionally masculinist model of rational discourse to a flagrantly "irrational" violation of that model, performing traditionally stereotypical feminine patterns of emotional excess and embodied sexuality.

WHITHER COULTER, WHITHER WOMEN?

These criticisms of Coulter from fellow conservatives share a kinship with more vitriolic criticism from her ideological opponents. Taken together, the public criticisms of Coulter's discourse evidence some intriguing patterns. First, while she is often criticized for her imprecise, manipulative use of researched evidence sources, Coulter's primary fault is her use of ill-considered hyperbole in her rhetorical style, particularly when attacking those she deems enemies. Second, such style is typically described as inconsistent with norms for rational, civil discourse and subsequently often does more harm than good for her ideological allies. Third, Coulter's use of nasty hyperbole is frequently explained as a way for Coulter to gain and maintain public attention for herself. Finally, Coulter's use of this style is often paired with a corporeal gendering of Coulter herself—her blond hair, her thin physical frame, her choice of short skirts and heels, and her penchant for leveraging her sex appeal to gain attention.[102] Taken together, it seems that Coulter embodies and performs a number of vexing constraints faced by conservative women seeking legitimate entry into the public sphere; the diatribe form, often successful for her core constituency of cultural conservatives, is a risky rhetorical form that not only limits her accessibility to the broader public, but also appears to backfire even within her base of support.

At the time of this writing, Coulter's recent media controversies have resulted in a number of newspapers across the country dropping her column. *Media Matters for America* reported that, while thirty-nine papers nationally still carry her column, eleven have dropped it, and nine papers have pledged to drop it as of September 2007.[103] At the same time, Crown Forum Publishers released her latest book in October 2007 and it spent five weeks on the *New York Times* best-seller list. Whether Coulter remains a force for conservative media or drowns in the wake of her own controversy, her discourse highlights the importance of examining the intersection of political ideology, gender, and legitimate public agency.

NOTES

1. Chris Stamper, "10 Questions With a Top 10: Ann Coulter," *World Magazine,* Oct. 5, 2002. Lexis-Nexis Academic Universe, http://www.lexis-nexis.com/ (accessed 9 July 2007).

2. Stamper, "10 Questions With a Top 10: Ann Coulter."

3. Mick Farren, "Princess of the Stiletto-Cons," *Los Angeles City Beat,* Sept. 4, 2003, http://69.94.104.186/article.php?IssueNum=13&id=207 (accessed June 3, 2007).

4. Max Blumenthal, "Conservative Ann Coulter describes Muslims as Ragheads; Senate Leader Ducks Comment," *The Raw Story,* Feb. 10, 2006, http://rawstory.

com/news/2005/Ann_Coulter_describes_Muslims_as_ragheads_ 0210.html (accessed June 8, 2007).

5. Adam Nagourney, "G.O.P. Candidates Criticize Slur by Conservative Author," *New York Times.com,* Mar. 4 2007, http://query.nytimes.com/gst/fullpage.html?res=9500E0D81731F937A35750C0A9619C8B63 (accessed June 6, 2007).

6. Ann Coulter, "This is War," *Ann Coulter.com,* Sept. 12, 2001, http://www.anncoulter.org/columns/2001/ 091301.htm (accessed July 6, 2007).

7. David Carr, "Deadly Intent: Ann Coulter, Word Warrior," *New York Times .com,* June 12, 2006, http://select.nytimes.com/search/restricted/article?res=FB0D 14FC38550C718DDDAF0894DE404482 (accessed Feb. 24, 2007).

8. The work of Barbara Spindel on the conservative Independent Women's Forum provides the most focused scholarly treatment of Coulter, but she is not the primary focus of her analysis. We discuss Spindel's argument below. Barbara Spindel, "Conservatism as the 'Sensible Middle': The Independent Women's Forum, Politics, and the Media," *Social Text* 77 (2003): 99-125; Barbara Ruth Spindel, *"Human Beings First, Women Second": Antifeminism and the Independent Women's Forum* (Ann Arbor Michigan: UMI, 2004). Linda Kintz names Coulter as one of "The Blondes" (female conservative pundits), along with Laura Ingraham, Kellyanne Fitzpatrick Conway, and Barbara Olson. Linda Kintz, "Performing Virtual Whiteness: George Gilder's Techno-Theocracy," *Cultural Studies* 16 (2002): 735-773. Christine Rosen of the American Enterprise Institute makes a brief mention of Coulter in a commentary piece for *Society* as an example of conservative women who are seen by critics as "the benighted, self-loathing, misogynistic pawns of powerful men" (32), and whose "extreme" tone "contribute[s] more to the polarizing vacuity of contemporary political debate than to conservative intellectual culture" (32), ultimately harming the cause of conservative women. Christine Rosen, "The Future of Women and Conservatism," *Society* 42 (2005): 32–35. Angela Dillard name drops Coulter in another *Society* commentary, contrasting her antifeminism against conservative feminist Katherine Kersten. Dillard recounts once hearing Coulter "bemoan the passage of the nineteenth Amendment on the grounds that women have made a "real mess" of the right to vote." Angela D. Dillard, "Adventures in Conservative Feminism," *Society* 42 (2005): 25–27. None of these treatments engage in any analysis of Coulter's discourse itself. Published critique of Coulter has mainly come from authors seeking to debunk Coulter's arguments and attack her politics. These works fall into two categories. First are works on the conservative media in which treatment of Coulter is only a portion of the whole. See Eric Alterman, *What Liberal Media? The Truth About Bias and the News* (New York: Basic Books, 2004); Al Franken, *Lies and the Lying Liars Who Tell Them: A Fair and Balanced Look at the Right* (New York: Dutton, 2003); S. T. Joshi, *The Angry Right: Why Conservatives Keep Getting It Wrong* (New York: Prometheus Books, 2006). Second are book-length satires and lampoons blending humor with critique. See Katherine Black, *Idiocy! Taking Conservative Behind the Woodshed: A Parody of Ann Coulter's Books and Right-Wing Ideology* (Bloomington, Ind.: 1st

Books Library, 2004); Susan Estrich, *Soulless: Ann Coulter and the Right-Wing Church of Hate* (New York: Regan Books, 2006); Joe Maguire, *Brainless: The Lies and Lunacies of Ann Coulter* (New York: William Morrow, 2006); Unanimous, *I Hate Ann Coulter!* (New York: Simon Spotlight Entertainment, 2006). In these works, critique is often serious and substantive, but is intended for a mass audience and is not pursued from a scholarly standpoint. Besides similar brief treatments by Spindel and Kintz, there appears to be no published scholarship on the other female conservative pundits of this period at the time of this writing.

9. Linda Kintz, "Performing Virtual Whiteness," 759.

10. Universal Press Syndicate, Inc., "Creator Bio—Ann Coulter," *Universal Press Syndicate,* 2005, http://www.amuniversal.com/ups/ features/ann_coulter/bio. htm (accessed July 9, 2007).

11. "Ann Coulter" [web bio], *Ann Coulter.com,* http://www.anncoulter.com/cgi-local/content.cgi?name=bio (accessed June 6, 2007).

12. Mick Farren, "Princess of the Stiletto-Cons," *Los Angeles City Beat,* Sept. 4, 2003, http://69.94.104.186/ article.php? IssueNum=13&id=207 (accessed June 3, 2007). Use of the diminutive term "pundette" to describe these women has also been widely used.

13. Barbara Ruth Spindel, "Conservatism," 182.

14. Spindel, *"Human Beings First"*; "Conservatism."

15. Spindel, *"Human Beings First,"* 171.

16. Jürgen Habermas, *The Structural Transformation of the Public Sphere: An Inquiry Into a Category of Bourgeois Society,* trans. Thomas Berger with Frederick Lawrence (Cambridge, Mass.: MIT Press, 1991).

17. See especially Joan B. Landes, "The Public and Private Sphere." In *Feminists Read Habermas: Gendering the Subject of Discourse,* ed. Johanna Meehan (New York: Routledge, 1995), 91–116; Landes, *Feminism, the Public, and the Private* (New York: Oxford University Press, 1998); Lynn Sanders, "Against Deliberation," *Political Theory* 25, no. 2 (June 1997): 347–76.

18. Karlyn Kohrs Campbell, *Man Cannot Speak For Her, Vol. 1: A Critical Study of Early Feminist Rhetoric* (New York: Greenwood Press, 1989). Jamieson also discusses the historical emergence of the "effeminate" style—as a style marginalized in favor of a "manly" style throughout rhetorical history, but one that enabled participation of women in the public sphere, and is currently important due to its particular effectiveness in televisual political rhetoric. Kathleen Hall Jamieson, *Eloquence in an Electronic Age* (New York: Oxford University Press, 1988): 75–76. Campbell's earlier work on the "feminine style" is cited by Jamieson in her discussion, and is most usually cited by subsequent scholars as foundational to this line of study. We have therefore focused on Campbell's discussion here. See also Jane Blankenship and Deborah C. Robson, "A 'Feminine Style' in Women's Political Discourse: An Exploratory Essay," *Communication Quarterly* 43, no. 3 (Summer 1995): 353–66. According to Blankenship and Robson, the feminine style is

manifested when rhetors focus on concrete experience, inclusivity, empowerment, holistic policy analysis, and women's concerns.

19. Indeed, Parry-Giles and Parry-Giles have persuasively argued that the "feminine style" has often been successfully co-opted by male presidential candidates and campaigns; it is thus often used in ways that stand at cross-purposes to the normative ideal expressed by Blankenship and Robson and others. Shawn J. Parry-Giles and Trevor Parry-Giles, "Gendered Politics and Presidential Image Construction: A Reassessment of the 'Feminine Style,'" *Communication Monographs* 63, no. 1 (December 1996): 337–53.

20. See, for instance, Bonnie J. Dow and Mari Boor Tonn, "'Feminine Style' and Political Judgment in the Rhetoric of Ann Richards," *Quarterly Journal of Speech* 79, no. 3 (August 1993): 286–302.They argue that the use of feminine style has the potential to "offer alternative modes of political reasoning" and contribute to the formation of a "feminist counter-public sphere" when used in the pursuit of a feminist political philosophy. Dow and Tonn, "'Feminine Style,'" 288, 299.

21. Holloway Sparks, "Dissident Citizenship: Democratic Theory, Political Courage and Activist Women," *Hypatia* 12, no. 4 (Fall 1997), 74–110.

22. Sparks, "Dissident Citizenship," 75.

23. Jennifer L. Borda, "The Woman Suffrage Parades of 1910–1913: Possibilities and Limitations of an Early Feminist Rhetorical Strategy," *Western Journal of Communication* 66, no. 1 (Winter 2002): 25–52; Melissa Deem, "From Bobbitt to SCUM: Re-memberment, Scatological Rhetorics, and Feminist Strategies in the Contemporary United States," *Public Culture* 8, no. 3 (Spring 1996): 511–37; Margaret E. Farrar and Jamie L. Warner, "Rah-Rah-Radical: The Radical Cheerleaders' Challenge to the Public Sphere," *Politics & Gender* 2, no. 3 (September 2006): 281–302.

24. Melissa Deem, "Stranger Sociability, Public Hope, and the Limits of Political Transformation," *Quarterly Journal of Speech* 88, no. 4 (November 2002), 444–54. Deem discusses the politically transformative potential of "minor rhetorics" for "minoritarian peoples in a majoritarian landscape": "I am concerned with what I term 'minor rhetorics,' following Deleuze and Guattari's work on 'minor literature.' Minor rhetorics use the language of the majority in such a way as to make that language stutter; they slow down, interrupt, or halt the movement of language. This conception of rhetoric short circuits appeals to transcendence and pushes language to its extreme" (Deem, "Stranger Sociability," 447).

25. Deem, "Stranger Sociability," 449.

26. Farrar and Warner, "Rah-Rah-Radical."

27. The concept of "double binds" on public women has been examined in Kathleen Hall Jamieson's influential work *Beyond the Double Bind: Women and Leadership* (New York: Oxford UP, 1995). Jamieson identifies five contradictory positions that constrain the leadership efficacy of women: "Womb/Brain" (a woman may either be a mother or a thinking agent, and is less than ideal for not being

both), "Silence/Shame" (a woman may either be a shameful immodest speaker or ignored utterly), "Sameness/Difference" (a woman may be like a man or different, and problematic either way), "Femininity/Competence" (a woman may either have a legitimate female identity or be judged an able actor, and is less than ideal for not being both), and "Aging/Invisibility" (women who age are deemed ugly and incompetent rather than wise and accomplished). Clearly, the rhetorical double binds we describe here involve pervasive elements of several of these traditional categories.

28. Patrice DiQuinzio, "Love and Reason in the Public Sphere: Maternalist Civic Engagement and the Dilemma of Difference," *Women and Children First: Feminism, Rhetoric, and Public Policy,* eds. Sharon M. Meagher and Patrice DiQuinzio (Albany, N.Y.: SUNY Press, 2005), 227-246.

29. W. Barnett Pearce, Stephen W. Littlejohn, and Alison Alexander, "The New Christian Right and the Humanist Response: Reciprocated Diatribe," *Communication Quarterly* 35 (1987): 171-192.

30. Pearce, Littlejohn, and Alexander, "The New Christian Right," 177.

31. Pearce, Littlejohn, and Alexander, "The New Christian Right," 177 (emphasis in original).

32. Pearce, Littlejohn, and Alexander, "The New Christian Right," 177.

33. Sally A. Freeman, Stephen W. Littlejohn, and W. Barnett Pearce, "Communication and Moral Conflict," *Western Journal of Communication* 56, no. 4 (Fall 1992): 311–29.

34. Freeman, Littlejohn, and Pearce, "Communication and Moral Conflict," 318–19.

35. At the time this analysis was conducted, Coulter's sixth book, *If Democrats Had Any Brains, They'd Be Republicans,* was preparing for release in October 2007. We have not included this volume in our study, as it is comprised almost exclusively of compiled quotations from previous writings, but we have observed that Coulter exhibits similar patterns in the new book. The publisher, Crown Forum, describes the book on its jacket as "the definitive collection of Coulterisms"—quotations from previous writings and appearances—as well as "brand-new commentaries and hundreds of never-before-published quotations." We can hardly wait.

36. Ann Coulter, *Treason,* 10.

37. Ann Coulter, *How To Talk To a Liberal,* 1.

38. Ann Coulter, *Slander,* 7.

39. Ann Coulter, *Godless,* 10.

40. Ann Coulter, *Treason,* 2.

41. Coulter, *Treason,* 5.

42. Ann Coulter, *How To Talk To a Liberal,* 1.

43. Ann Coulter, *Slander,* 3.

44. Ann Coulter, *How To Talk To a Liberal,* 3.

45. Ann Coulter, *Slander,* 2.

46. Ann Coulter, *Godless,* 280.

47. Ann Coulter, *Slander,* 17.

48. Ann Coulter, *Treason*, 29.

49. Critics have alleged Coulter's apparent tendency to make use of endnote citation that ranges from sloppy inaccuracy to manipulative distortion of facts, including the popular press authors cited in note 1. We will generally leave the fact-checking to others; our primary interest is in the rhetorical function of copious endnotes as "evidence" of rational, well-grounded argument in Coulter's books.

50. Ann Coulter, *Slander*, 204.

51. Ann Coulter, *Godless*, 281.

52. Ann Coulter, *How To Talk To a Liberal*, 10.

53. Coulter, *How To Talk To a Liberal*, 2.

54. Coulter, *How To Talk To a Liberal*, 10.

55. W. Barnett Pearce et al., "The New Christian Right," 174.

56. Ann Coulter, *How To Talk To a Liberal*, 18.

57. Ann Coulter, *High Crimes and Misdemeanors*, 17.

58. Ann Coulter, *Godless*, 4.

59. Coulter, *Godless*, 9.

60. Coulter, *Godless*, 13.

61. Ann Coulter, *How To Talk To a Liberal*, 13.

62. Ann Coulter, *Slander*, 10.

63. Coulter, *Slander*, 26.

64. Coulter, *Slander*, 14.

65. See, for example, the chapter in *How To Talk to a Liberal* titled "What You Could Have Read If You Lived in a Free Country" (320-344).

66. Ann Coulter, *Treason*, 95.

67. Coulter, *Treason*, 285.

68. Ann Coulter, *How To Talk To a Liberal*, 36-39; *Godless*, 2.

69. Ann Coulter, *Godless*, 78.

70. Ann Coulter, *Treason*, 9.

71. Ironically, Coulter accuses liberals of precisely this tactic with regard to demonization of the "religious right": "Having created a mythical enemy and trained the public to reflexively hate it, the myth can later be deployed to discredit anyone." Coulter, *Slander*, 190. Of course, in diatribe, this kind of inconsistency is unremarkable.

72. Ann Coulter, *How To Talk To a Liberal*, 172.

73. Coulter, *How To Talk To a Liberal*, 393.

74. Coulter, *How To Talk To a Liberal*, 392.

75. Coulter, *How To Talk To a Liberal*, 396.

76. Coulter, *How To Talk To a Liberal*, 8.

77. Coulter, *How To Talk To a Liberal*, 64.

78. Ann Coulter, *Godless*, 152.

79. Coulter, *Treason*, 15.

80. Coulter, *Treason*, 29.

81. Coulter, *Treason*, 78.

82. Ann Coulter, *Godless*, 101.

83. Coulter, *Godless*, 103.

84. Coulter, *Godless*, 102.

85. Ann Coulter, *How To Talk To a Liberal*, 388.

86. Ann Coulter, *Slander*, 38.

87. Coulter, *Slander*, 38.

88. Sally A. Freeman et al., "Communication and Moral Conflict."

89. Barbara Ruth Spindel, *"Human Beings First,"* 173.

90. Spindel, *"Human Beings First,"* 175.

91. David Hogberg, "Not Funny," *American Spectator Online*, Feb. 13, 2006, in the Lexis-Nexis Academic Universe, http://www.lexisnexis.com/us/lnacademic/ (accessed July 9, 2007).

92. Coulter's use of the "raghead" epithet in the 2006 CPAC speech was too much even for fellow conservative female lightning rod Michelle Malkin, who also decried the speech as racist on her weblog of February 12, 2006. Malkin also criticized Coulter's use of the word "faggot" to insult John Edwards at the 2007 CPAC meeting, arguing on a March 5 episode of FOX News's *The O'Reilly Factor* that such a statement would overshadow the political importance of the meeting for fellow conservatives. Malkin called Coulter's remark a "rhetorical fragging . . . a bomb that was apparently meant to hurt the left, but ended up hurting Ann's own fellow ideological soldiers."

93. Florence King, "Watch Ann Go Whoosh!—Analyzing La Coulter," *National Review*, Aug. 7, 2006, in the Lexis-Nexis Academic Universe, http://www.lexisnexis.com/us/lnacademic/ (accessed 9 July 9, 2007).

94. King, "Watch Ann Go Whoosh!"

95. King, "Watch Ann Go Whoosh!"

96. Kathryn Jean Lopez, "Ann Alternatives," *National Review*, Mar. 21, 2007, in the Lexis-Nexis Academic Universe, http://www.lexisnexis.com/us/lnacademic/ (accessed July 9, 2007).

97. Amy Ridenour, "Ann Coulter at CPAC," *Amy Ridenour's National Center Blog*, Mar. 4, 2007, http://www.nationalcenter.org/Z030507=ann-coulter-at-cpac.html (accessed July 8, 2007).

98. Jonah Goldberg, "L'Affaire Coulter," *National Review Online*, Oct. 3, 2001, in the Lexis-Nexis Academic Universe, http://www.lexisnexis.com/us/lnacademic/ (accessed July 19, 2007).

99. Goldberg, "L'Affaire Coulter." He further contends that *NRO*'s original run of the infamous anti-Islamic column was an error; he assumed the column was coming to him pre-edited when it in fact was not.

100. Goldberg, "L'Affaire Coulter."

101. Goldberg, "L'Affaire Coulter."

102. With the exception of *High Crimes and Misdemeanors*, all of Coulter's books—including her latest 2007 volume—feature a photo of herself on the cover. Her long blond hair is featured prominently, and her four latest books feature

figure-clinging black outfits (sleeved leotard and slacks, sleeveless leather vest, low-cut tank dress, spaghetti-strap dress) that reveal increasing amounts of skin with each publication. In addition, the conservative Young America's Foundation sells two posters featuring Coulter ("The Conservative Movement Starts Here—Posters"). In one she stands with a group of other conservative media figures; she stands near the center, hands on hips, wearing a black leather jacket, miniskirt and pumps. In another, titled "The Beauty of Conservatism," she is a solitary figure in a black spaghetti strap dress, viewed in a head-and-chest shot from the side but turning to face the camera out of the corners of her eyes in classic "male gaze" pose. This poster sells for $4.87. Coulter is literally a pin-up girl for young conservatives.

103. "Ann Coulter Action Center," *Media Matters for America*, http://mediamatters.org/action_center/ann_coulter/ (accessed Sept. 28, 2007).

5

MADAM SECRETARY

Is the Female Voice a Difference That Makes a
Difference in National Security Discourse?

Heather Aldridge Bart and Heidi Hamilton

Madeleine Albright and Condoleezza Rice, as the nation's first female
secretaries, provide precedents for women's leadership in matters of state
dealing with both war and peace. While their service brings hope to those
wishing to see a female U.S. president, their rhetoric is grounded in traditional, masculine discourse that provides little challenge to the gendered
construction of national security discourse.

We use textual analysis of Albright's and Rice's public comments on the
foreign policy crises of Kosovo and Iraq respectively to discover ways their
discourse is different from the traditional or masculine international relations (hereafter, IR) discourse. While any number of rhetorical moments
could be studied, these two case studies offer an ongoing situation with
which each was identified and through which their rhetoric developed.
While it would be an overgeneralization to claim that either case epitomizes
their IR rhetoric on other issues, both cases significantly represent how
the secretaries demonstrated their approach to IR.[1] Examination of the
rhetorical enactment of the role of secretary of state by each reveals much
congruous with masculine enactment of national security discourse; thus
illustrating that one's sex does not necessarily equate with gendered styles
of discourse, especially when the context demands particular discursive arguments. However, while the transformation is far from complete, nuggets
of difference by Albright and Rice create lines of argument about national

security that stress feminine values and challenge the masculine framework of foreign policy.

FEMINIST INTERNATIONAL RELATIONS THEORY

Some rhetorical scholars have suggested a "feminine style" of communicating increases opportunities for women candidates.[2] Others argue, however, that the feminine style masks the substance of the messages, and the substance further entrenches the patriarchy.[3] This chapter looks not at style but at substantive elements to discover how masculinity is entrenched or challenged.

Feminist IR theory identifies substantive elements that constitute the traditional (to be read masculine) bases upon which purveyors of foreign policy situate their discourse. Claiming the language used to justify policy is based on the language of the theories governing "national security," feminist IR theory provides a framework for examining the gendered nature of discourse itself. Because traditional national security discourse is masculine, women must operate within that discourse to be seen as effective. We examine the discourse of Albright and Rice for their adherence to traditional or masculine lines of argument and for signs of departure. In doing so, we illustrate how rhetorical scholars might move beyond style to substance in studying gendered political communication. Specifically, feminist IR redefines security, security-seeking behaviors, and power, expanding them beyond the traditional-masculine to suggest alternative (feminine) discourse for conducting foreign policy. These three concepts are the organizing principle for our textual analysis.

Security

Feminist IR theorists argue that traditional-masculine definitions of security are centered on the state. Jill Steans notes that realist and neorealist perspectives hold that the "state provides for the security of the individual by virtue of her or his membership of the national community."[4] Jacqui True notes security is "examined only in the context of the presence and absence of war, because the threat of war is considered endemic to the sovereign state-system where security is zero-sum and by definition national."[5] The state acts to maintain conditions that keep its people free from externally imposed violence; this conception of security, however, "ignore[s] other forms of insecurity and their gendered dimensions."[6]

Feminist IR scholars offer examples of what a redefinition of security might encompass; in doing so, they indicate its rhetorical dimensions. Ann Tickner advocates examining national security in terms of development, basic material needs, and environmental sustainability, noting that "thinking about military, economic and environmental security in interdependent terms suggests the need for new methods of conflict resolution which seek to achieve mutually beneficial, rather than zero-sum, outcomes."[7] Feminist critics also point to the division between domestic (family) violence and international violence, suggesting that "violence, whether it be in the international, national or family realm, is interconnected."[8] Steans explains: "[Human security] has been articulated in narrow terms as the need to provide an adequate level of food, health care and other social and economic resources to meet basic needs. A more expansive conception of human security goes beyond a basic needs approach, to include all that is needed to live a dignified life as a human being."[9]

Security-Seeking Behavior

Security-seeking behaviors create and maintain the aforementioned state of security. The basic argument posits that cooperation is necessary to prevent conflict. The tools to secure cooperation are diplomacy (also called persuasion) and economic resources to assist with diplomacy. Realists emphasize alliances and the preservation of a balance of power rather than "security through disarmament, development and respect for human rights."[10] In her challenge to traditional conceptions, Christine Sylvester argues for cooperation to "include but also take us beyond our fixations on either-or constructs of conflict versus cooperation, war versus peace, strategy versus death."[11] Thus, security-seeking activities would go beyond adversarial uses of power to force compliance or military might to deter violence, instead accounting for the possibility of mutual security. The traditional tools of foreign policy (e.g., treaties and diplomacy) need not be abandoned but repurposed by an underlying philosophical change.

Rhetoric grounded in this redefinition also would reflect a need in humans to come together instead of falling into anarchy. The rhetoric of traditional-masculine security-seeking behaviors involves language of alliances and strategic partnerships to ensure peace. If feminist IR reconceptualizes human nature as both conflictual and cooperative, then rhetoric needs to incorporate imagery and language that envisions a world where chaos and anarchy are not the necessary outcome of a decrease in power.

Power

The concept of power is inextricably linked to the concepts of security and security-seeking behavior. Power assists in gaining the cooperation of others and ensures compliance if necessary. True summarizes the connections between security and power: "State security apparatuses create their own security dilemmas by purporting androcentric control and 'power-over' to be the name of the game; a game we are persuaded to stay in, in order to achieve the absolute and relative gains of state security."[12] Feminist IR theorists argue that coercive power definitions blind us to other possible understandings. Tickner notes that while "power as domination is a pervasive reality in international relations, there are also elements of co-operation in interstate relations which tend to be obscured."[13]

From a rhetorical perspective, a feminist national security discourse would move away from coercive constructions of power. Policymakers would recognize that the United States does not have power over others as an autonomous entity who wields power independent of an "other"; and instead acknowledge the "power" that others bring to the table. This reconstituted notion of power also would argue for cooperation as an ends, not simply a means to an end (e.g., peace, stability, the avoidance of conflict).

MADELEINE ALBRIGHT

At the onset of Albright's term as secretary of state (January 23, 1997), the United States was amid the crisis between Serbia and Bosnia-Herzegovina. In Serbia, the Kosovo region had declared its independence in 1992, and suffered a massive crackdown by Serbian President Milosevic. In the period between 1992 and 1997, the Kosovar Albanians maintained a provisional government not recognized by Serbia, and the Kosovar Liberation Army (KLA) conducted violent attacks aimed at driving back Serbs in Kosovo. These clashes escalated to the point of gaining international attention.

Security

Albright's term is marked by her orchestration of actions taken to force Milosevic's concession to international demands, ending ethnic cleansing in Kosovo. As the crisis develops, Albright points to U.S. interest in Kosovo based on the region's history, noting, "Kosovo is a small part of a region with large historic importance and a vital role to play in Europe's future. The region is a crossroads where the Western and Orthodox branches of Christianity and the Islamic world meet. It is where World War I began, major battles of World War II were fought, and the worst fighting in Europe since Hitler's surrender occurred in this decade."[14] Albright further argues that humanitarian crises become military crises, explaining that the "refugees being created by Serbian policies" constituted a security threat because "the influx of refugees tends to destabilize countries in terms of how they are able to deal with them."[15] Lastly, Albright defines security vis-à-vis U.S. interests in Kosovo by noting the risk of conflict spreading into southern Europe. She argues, "Regional conflict would undermine NATO's credibility as the guarantor of peace and stability in Europe. This would pose a threat that America could not ignore."[16]

A change from these traditional security definitions emerges as Albright calls attention to the plight of women and children. By focusing on women and children, Albright draws upon fundamental elements of humanity rather than masculinist concerns that would justify war. Albright describes stopping the rape and murder of women and children as the "right thing to do" three times on March 26, 1999,[17] and again on March 28,[18] and April 5.[19] Speaking to Jim Lehrer, Albright emphasizes the atrocities saying "that seeing this kind of ethnic cleansing and the huge numbers of people that have been expelled from Kosovo and the horrible massacres and rapes and burning of houses, that that [sic] could not be allowed to go on."[20]

Albright refutes her opponents by making an additional argument that war crimes violate universal rights and must be opposed prima fasciae.

> Others suggest that until we can help all the victims of ethnic violence, we should be consistent and not help any. Still others believe that by trying to bring stability to the Balkans, we're taking on a job that is simply too hard. Finally, there are some—overseas and even here at home—who see NATO's actions as part of a master plan to impose our values on the world. Such criticisms are not original. They echo voices heard half a century ago when America led in rebuilding war-torn societies across two oceans, helped to reconcile historic enemies, elevated the world's conception of human rights, and attempted and achieved the impossible by supplying more than two million people in Berlin entirely by air for more than nine months. From that time to this, the United States has defended its own interests, while promoting values of tolerance and free expression that are not "Made in America" or confined to the West, but rather *universal and fundamental* to world progress and peace.[21]

Her passionate defense anchors the actions of the United States to the most transcendent of justifications—universal human rights. Albright makes the human rights violations more personal:

> Perhaps we should substitute for Banja and Batlava more familiar names, such as Lincoln or Plainville, Arlington or Bedford—America's home towns—and imagine them sacked and plundered; our neighbors and family members murdered, raped or expelled. Perhaps we should imagine that the hand we out-stretch asking for help is our own.[22]

Clearly, her argument changes security from the masculine (peace in the international realm) to security grounded in the feminine (peace within the home and society). Albright argues that we cannot stand by when others are so fundamentally threatened.

Security Seeking

As with security, Albright's arguments about security seeking are traditional-masculine in nature: allies are sought, diplomacy is attempted, sanctions are enacted, and noncompliance results in escalating threats. Her arguments regarding Kosovo reflect a reliance on alliances, treaty obligations, and a code of conduct for civilized nations. Toward the conflict's beginning, referencing the Contact Group consisting of countries interested in the Balkans, including all NATO members with additional nations like Albania, Bosnia, and Macedonia, Albright indicates that "we agreed to impose punitive measures against those responsible for the violence."[23] By October 1998, Albright argues that it is "time for the Alliance to move to the next phase of its decision-making—that is, to take the difficult but necessary decision to authorize military force if Milosevic fails to comply."[24] Throughout the course of the bombing, Albright is quick to point to the unity of the alliance and to place the blame for the bombing squarely on Milosevic. In April, Albright reiterated: "NATO is playing its rightful role as a defender of freedom and security within the Euro-Atlantic region. Because our cause is just, we are united. And because we are united, we are confident that in this confrontation between barbaric killing and necessary force . . . we will prevail."[25] Albright references the unity of the alliance numerous times in press conferences with various foreign ministers until the bombing campaign ended.

Albright offers one curious departure from the traditional in an op-ed piece published in the *Wall Street Journal*:

> The crisis in Kosovo should cause a re-examination of the paradigms of the past. As the world has changed, so have the roles of key institutions such as the EU, NATO and the United Nations. And so have American interests. In today's world of deadly and mobile dangers, gross violations of human rights are everyone's business. As for the use of force, Kosovo tells us only what we should have already known. Yes, in confronting evil and otherwise protecting our interests, force is sometimes required. Now, as before Kosovo, it is not wise to formulate assumptions based on any single experience about exactly when and how force should be applied. In coping with future crisis, the accumulated wisdom of the past will have to be weighed against factors unique to that place and time. This is why foreign policy is more art than science.[26]

While not departing from masculine modes of security-seeking, Albright makes a point of arguing for change in our thinking about security threats and means of response. She suggests that "evil" must be opposed. While defending the idea that force is a last resort (a traditional concept), she also contends that we must reorient our thinking to consider acting without assuming force will eventually result. Her argument challenges masculine-traditional assumptions regarding involvement in "humanitarian" crises.

Additionally, the solution implemented—making Kosovo an autonomous part of Bosnia—reflects the paradigm change of which Albright speaks. Security seeking required cooperation by both Bosnians and Kosovars to keep the peace. A masculine-traditional resolution to the crisis would have been total surrender and imposition of conditions on the "loser." In this case, Milosevic is "forced" to surrender but the imposition of conditions does not include independence for Kosovo. This compromise forced Kosovars to be interdependent and act responsibly with their autonomy from Bosnian rule.

Power

Albright's rhetoric regarding power is, again, very traditionally grounded. Logically, the security-seeking activities described above require both credible threat and use of force to gain compliance. Albright argues "we learned in Bosnia, and we have seen in Kosovo, that President Milosevic understands only the language of force. Nothing less than strong engagement from NATO will focus the attention of both sides; and nothing less than firm American leadership will ensure decisive action."[27] "Power over" language permeates her arguments. When discussing bombings' end, Albright employs the ultimate "power over" language, saying, "You never exactly know when the moment of cracking comes, but we're very glad that it has, and the Serbs have *surrendered*."[28]

A second way Albright addresses power is to define how it should be used by civilized nations, arguing, essentially, it not be used indiscriminately against sovereign nations. Albright first points out that Milosevic, as an elected leader of a sovereign nation," has responsibilities not only to his own people but to the international community for trying to pursue civilized behavior."[29] Further, Albright indicates Milosevic abrogated his nation's sovereignty as "he has started four wars against his neighbors and what he was doing with his own people."[30] Finally, Albright argues for using force only as a last resort, "It is not our desire to use force for the sake of using force but in order to get compliance with the Security Council resolution."[31] Thus, Albright's primary arguments regarding power acknowledge the need for military power, but they also caution against overreliance on force. None of her arguments address other sources of power a nation might have— like economic or moral credibility. Likewise, these arguments favor the traditional-masculine formulation as power over rather than a mutual concept, which might reflect a more feminist IR approach.

Nuggets of difference appear in Albright's arguments regarding Kosovo as she offers a reconceptualization of sovereignty as nonabsolute. Albright discusses sovereignty and the necessity to limit one's own sovereign claims for the greater good. Albright argues:

> Great nations who understand the importance of sovereignty at various times cede certain portions of it in order to achieve some better good for their country. Arms control agreements for instance, are ways of making agreements that in some way, say to a highly sovereign country, I'm not going to have all the weapons that I really could produce because I think that there is value to my people if I limit my weapons so that the other side limits theirs. The way we are all operating as a global community means that we are looking at how the nation-state functions in a totally different way than people did at the beginning of this century and will be doing at the beginning of the next.[32]

Albright's arguments are in the context of the proposal for Kosovo as self-ruling without being an independent state from Serbia. The very proposal challenges traditional notions of power because it is based on the idea of mutual power, achieving peace by ending the paradigm of "power over" and total victory (for either Serbia or Kosovo).

In addition to the sovereignty comments, Albright makes several points that indicate a preference for mutual power based on economic growth and interdependence. Albright states:

There is nothing foreign about foreign policy anymore. When we make innovative investments in peace, prosperity and democracy overseas, as we now
propose, we help to secure those blessings for our own citizens here at home.
And when we fail to make the needed investments, we place our own future
in jeopardy.[33]

Albright notes that mutual economic development would "enable countries throughout the region to participate fully in the major economic and
political institutions of the Trans-Atlantic community" which "would greatly
serve America's interest in expanding the area within Europe where wars
simply do not happen."[34]

Summary

Overall, Albright's rhetoric during the Kosovo crisis favors traditional-
masculine conceptions of security, security seeking, and power. Her arguments reflect the fact that the United States pulled together a coalition of
allies and negotiated a settlement with Milosevic and the Kosovar Albanians. Albright also indicates that the NATO-initiated bombing campaign
was a last resort to solve the humanitarian crisis created by Milosevic's
ethnic-cleansing campaign. Each of these rhetorical moves appears rooted
in a masculine, realist approach to IR discourse.

Albright's arguments, at times, diverge from traditional-masculine notions,
for example, injecting the plight of women in Kosovo as a justification for action and personalizing the suffering of Kosovar Albanians. Despite continuing
her discussion of traditional forms of security seeking, Albright calls for more
action on humanitarian crises asking for a reorientation of our thinking about
those crises. Finally, regarding power, Albright draws the concept of power
toward integration and cooperation and away from the hard-line focus on sovereignty. These departures seem minor in the overall arguments, but they are
important in opening space for change without drawing too sharp a contrast to
the dominant, masculine discourse of war and security. Traditional-masculine
arguments allow for her to maintain credibility as the chief foreign policy officer and afford her the freedom also to draw the feminine into the discussion
in a way that does not seem threatening.

CONDOLEEZZA RICE

As the second female secretary of state, the war on terrorism and the Iraq
war largely mark Rice's tenure. The latter started on March 19, 2003, when

Rice was still national security advisor. On January 26, 2005, starting President Bush's second term in office, Rice became secretary of state, after Colin Powell's resignation. Given both the Bush administration's preoccupation with, and particularly the public prominence of, the issue, this section looks primarily at Rice's rhetoric concerning the Iraq war.

Security

In Rice's public statements, Iraqi security becomes defined in terms of violence and its effects on the Iraqi people, including the Iraqi state's ability to protect its citizens. For example, when discussing U.S. worries, she mentions "sectarian murders, death squads going into a neighborhood, lining up the men, shooting the men, and sending the women into exile."[35] Concerns include securing borders in order to stop violence; following the Iraqi Neighbors' Conference, she states:

> There was quite a lot of talk by the neighbors of the importance of securing the borders and that means stopping the flow of foreign fighters, it means stopping the flow of arms and sophisticated technology to those—to not just to foreign fighters, also to militias and those who are killing innocent Iraqis as well as endangering multinational forces.[36]

These comments largely assume traditional-masculine notions of state security, where the state and its people are free from violence.

Rice also discusses Iraq's impact on United States and global security, again within the traditional realist framework. For instance, she remarks that "this mission, bringing a stable and secure Iraq, is also essential for the security of the United States of America."[37] In other comments, she states, "What happens in Iraq has profound consequences, which will affect each and every one of us: the nation of Iraq, its regional neighbors, and indeed, the entire international community."[38] While she may not specifically discuss violence or killing, the assumption of collective security in a global context remains.

As a movement away from this masculine approach to foreign policy, Rice does consider expanded security issues, although this tends to occur during broader speeches about world security, of which Iraq is only part of the picture. Rice mentions that administration foreign policy realizes

> security is only achieved when people, especially those on the margins of society, gain freedom and justice and opportunity within their countries and when democracy is on the march. . . . the non-negotiable demands of human dignity

. . . free speech and tolerance of difference, freedom of worship, equal justice and property rights and finally, but not last, respect for women.[39]

She reiterates these same themes when discussing the Middle East at the Southern Baptist Convention: "Human beings share certain basic aspirations. They want to choose those who are going to govern them. They want a good job, an education, protection from injustice, the freedom to worship as they please, the future that will be better for their children."[40] While these remarks do not account for all the factors of internal violence, and specifically violence against women, they do indicate a more feminist approach in understanding the deeper roots of security as stemming from more than just the lack of fighting.

Security Seeking

When discussing security seeking, Rice's rhetoric maintains a traditional-masculine stance, dovetailing with security definitions. She discusses security-seeking behaviors in two contexts: U.S. relationship with Iraq and relationships with other countries. In terms of Iraq, Rice contends that the U.S. presence there is to cooperate with the Iraqi government in order to achieve security and stability. Before a Senate committee, she testifies, "the most urgent task before us now is to help the Iraqi Government—and I want to emphasize help the Iraqi Government—establish confidence among the Iraqi population that it will and can protect all of its citizens."[41] On various occasions, she discusses the different means that the United States uses to achieve these goals. At the Iraq Neighbors Conference, she asserts:

> The United States has spent about 20.6 billion of American taxpayer dollars to try and help with reconstruction in Iraq and we're going to continue to do it because we fundamentally believe that a stable, secure, democratic Iraq will be at the heart of a Middle East that can be stable, secure and democratic and therefore a strong pillar for international peace and security.[42]

Beyond the economic tools, of course, are military forces. U.S. forces "are also there to help to train Iraqi security forces that can then help Iraq secure itself."[43] In each of these instances, Rice ties the means of U.S. cooperation back to that traditional notion of security, and each of the means suggests U.S. attempts to influence how Iraq achieves this security.

Rice also summarizes the U.S. role within multinational forces and the larger Middle East community. Rice explains the formation of an

International Compact, involving the United Nations, the World Bank, and neighboring countries designed to provide debt relief and financial and technical assistance, stating, "[The goals] extend much further—providing powerful incentives for the Iraqi government to function more effectively."[44]

She reiterates that U.S. forces do not fight alone. In a press briefing, she comments, "The multinational force is there under a UN Security Council resolution so this is not an American force; this is a multinational force that's there under a UN mandate."[45] In another press conference, she remarks on the international community's role by reminding "the multinational forces in Iraq of which the United States is a part are there, of course, by UN Security Council resolution and at the request of the Iraqi Government."[46] This placement of U.S. forces within the multinational force should not be viewed as a lack of U.S. power, however; given the Bush administration's emphasis on building a "coalition of the willing" in Iraq, Rice's statements occur within the very traditional-masculine framework of building alliances in order to secure the peace, and in this case, an alliance willing to use force.

Power

Given the aforementioned rhetoric regarding security and security-seeking activities, Rice focuses power on very traditional definitions, emphasizing both diplomatic efforts but particularly military efforts. In explaining how the U.S. plans to achieve its goals, she talks about diplomatic initiatives. To the Senate Foreign Relations Committee, she states, "We do have a regional approach. It is to work with those governments that share our view of where the Middle East should be going. It is also to work with those governments in a way that can bring support to the new Iraqi democracy."[47] Furthermore, Rice emphasizes the combined use of diplomacy with the military use of force in Iraq. In remarks to a Senate committee, she talks about "our political-military strategy" in which the United States is striving to

> clear the toughest places—no sanctuaries to the enemy—and to disrupt foreign support for the insurgents. We are working to hold and steadily enlarge the secure areas, integrating political and economic outreach with our military operations. We are working to build truly national institutions by working with more capable provincial and local authorities.[48]

Even when discussing the troop surge starting in early 2007, she comments, "I want also to emphasize that we see this not just as a military effort, but also as one that must have very strong political and economic elements."[49]

Through discussing U.S. uses of power in the recent past, Rice reiterates traditional notions of power as the ability to influence and exert power through military action. She asserts that "it was the right strategic decision that Saddam Hussein had been a threat to the international community long enough that it was time to deal with that threat."[50] In other remarks, she words U.S. actions more strongly: "I am confident that the decision to overthrow Saddam Hussein and give the Iraqi people an opportunity for peace and democracy is the right decision."[51] In 2007, she describes it as "the liberation of Iraq from Saddam Hussein."[52] Obviously, the ultimate use of power is the actual overthrow of a government through military force.

She further justifies these actions within the larger context of the war on terrorism. In one statement, she comments, "We have taken the fight to the enemy, and we are making America safer."[53] In remarks to U.S. personnel in Iraq, she states, "We were going to have to go on the offense . . . we couldn't play defense because the terrorists only have to be right once and we have to be right 100 percent of the time. And that's an unfair fight, and therefore we decided we had to go on the offense. And that meant coming to the source of the problem here in the Middle East."[54] Rice thus pushes traditional notions of military force as "a last resort," saying in effect that it is the only recourse.

In her rhetoric, nuggets of difference emerge in terms of using power. She speaks in several places in the language of partnership, which might imply a mutual interdependence, more indicative of the feminist emphasis on cooperation. For example, "The United States wants to be a supportive partner in that work, that we are prepared to do whatever we can to help the Iraqi Government."[55] When speaking to the British, she uses similar rhetoric:

> We have partners in the world and I don't think of it in terms of junior partners and subordinate partners. . . . You then, of course, have goals in common and you can sometimes then have disagreements about tactics. There's no doubt about that. And the only way to overcome those differences is through constant dialogue and constant discussion.[56]

In these instances, an attempt appears to move beyond the masculine exertion of power over, at least with U.S. partners; although the context in which these remarks are made could cause a more cynical viewing. The true feminist IR concept would recognize mutual interdependence and the need for stability with a variety of world players, not just strategic partners, which still implies a traditional emphasis on alliances.

She also suggests that once free, power over may be limited. In remarks to the Southern Baptist Convention, she states, "We are leading the cause of freedom not because we believe that free peoples will always agree with us. They will not. That is their right and America will defend that right."[57] Here she presents an acknowledgement of the limits of traditional notions of power.

Summary

Overall, Rice's rhetoric follows traditional-masculine foreign policy arguments. Security is defined as the absence of state violence and killing, and comments about the use of security-seeking means and power reinforce this security definition. Particularly present, given the Iraqi situation, is the emphasis on military means to achieve goals, whether those means are tied to diplomacy or separate, as an effort to stop violence or go on the offensive to prevent it. This military emphasis further entrenches a masculinist mindset to viewing the world, limiting options for perceiving and responding to global security issues. Diverging from the traditional, her rhetoric mentions larger goals beyond freedom from violence that citizens should expect, and she acknowledges that the United States cannot always exert power over other states. Sometimes, the United States needs to treat states as partners, and at other times, free states will, and should be allowed to, disagree with U.S. policy. At these moments, her rhetoric may allow for change, taking into account more feminist values toward IR, although overall her discourse, more so than Albright, largely remains rooted in a masculine, traditional framework.

EXPANDING THE DISCOURSE

The similarities between Rice and Albright's rhetoric may be explained in that both operated in the context of military action. Given this context, one would expect similar tropes that tap into accepted principles for military use. Additionally a paradigm shift from these two chief foreign-policy officers would be unexpected. Any such pronouncements would certainly upset the order and shake the confidence of allies and enemies alike. Furthermore, a man might be able to speak outside of the traditional discourse by virtue of being a man in a masculine framework. As the first two female secretaries of state, these women have already broken new ground. Radical departures from traditional-masculine discourse would be seen as inappropriate and could negatively impact domestic and international perceptions of them. Thus, little surprise exists in finding a large portion of their rhetoric reflects traditional, realist principles. The interesting elements from their rhetoric are found in the nuggets of difference from the traditional-masculine.

Both Albright and Rice discuss security in ways that expand the concept. While neither redefines the concept as far as feminist IR scholars would like, their rhetoric opens some space for dialogue on the nature of security and for action based upon that dialogue. For example, by placing the rape and torture of Kosovar women and girls into the realm of requiring action, Albright opens up the scope of security to domestic insecurities. Rice's rhetoric also suggests valuing human dignity, religious freedom, and respect for women. Thus, violating or threatening these constitutes a threat to security within a state. Both women broaden the concept of security by defining what creates insecurity within the state.

With regard to security seeking, Rice does not provide any substantive difference from traditional, realist concerns. While Albright's rhetoric presents no new tactics for security seeking, she challenges traditional thinking about "humanitarian" crises and reticence to seek solutions. Albright encourages greater depth of understanding about the roles various institutions could play in solving these kinds of security issues—rather than assuming force.

Finally, with regard to power, Rice's and Albright's rhetoric similarly looks more at cooperation and interdependence, which feminist IR theory suggests are normally obscured by more traditional-masculine discourse. Rice uses the language of partnerships, while Albright invokes language of integration and interdependence. Such language is more in keeping with the kind of gendered revisioning feminist IR calls for. Albright's rhetoric opens the door to reconsidering sovereignty as absolute, and Rice offers a nod to the limits of power to force agreement on all issues.

Closer examination of Albright's and Rice's rhetoric leads back to the fact that one's sex does not necessarily equate with gendered styles of discourse. Both Rice and Albright demonstrate their ability to "speak like a man." Ultimately, this skill may be key to their being viewed as credible practitioners of foreign policy in times of crisis. The work of two women at the highest levels of foreign policymaking demonstrates women can be seen as credible leaders of national security. However, Albright's and Rice's success in the field of foreign policy during military action also demonstrates that success comes at the price of maintaining masculine discourse of power and security that obscures women's roles and feminine values in the larger world community.

The fact that points in their rhetoric diverge from the typical, realist underpinnings offers some hope that one's gender might introduce opportunities for opening up dialogue and considering alternative ways of thinking, speaking, and acting in foreign policy. Even though the nuggets of difference are not on a grand scale, their presence allows for the possibility that a woman in the presidency would have a basis upon which to situate discourse that moves beyond the traditional-masculine tropes of security, security seeking, and power. By successfully situating their discourse in the traditional, they open doors for women seeking to participate at the highest levels in foreign policy making while, simultaneously, reifying the masculine nature of that discourse. By including discourse that differs from the traditional-masculine, Albright and Rice open up space for masculine discourse to be challenged and changed by women and men alike.

NOTES

1. For Rice, we examine the period from her beginning as secretary of state through summer 2007. While this is not the end of this conflict, it denotes a period when the surge of military forces increased in response to insurgent attacks and arguably, her diplomatic role decreased.

2. Bonnie J. Dow and Mari Boor Tonn, "'Feminine Style' and Political Judgment in the Rhetoric of Ann Richards." *Quarterly Journal of Speech*, 79, no. 3 (August 1993): 286–302 ; Karlyn Kohrs Campbell and Claire E. Jerry. "Woman and Speaker: A Conflict in Roles." In *Seeing Female: Social Roles and Personal Lives*, ed. Sharon Brehm (Westport, Conn.: Greenwood Press, 1988), 123–33 ; Jane Blankenship and Deborah C. Robson "A 'Feminine Style' in Women's Political Discourse: An Exploratory Essay." *Communication Quarterly* 43, no. 3 (Summer 1995: 353–66).

3. Shawn J. Parry-Giles and Trevor Parry-Giles, "Gendered Politics and Presidential Image Construction: A Reassessment of the 'Feminine Style.'" *Communication Monographs* 63, no. 1 December 1996): 337.

4. Jill Steans, *Gender and International Relations: An Introduction* (New Brunswick, N.J.: Rutgers University Press, 1998), 107.

5. Jacqui True, "Feminism." In *Theories of International Relations*, ed. Scott Burchill and Andrew Linklater (New York: St. Martin's Press, 1996), 234.

6. Brooke A. Ackerly and Jacqui True, "Studying the struggles and wishes of the age: feminist theoretical methodology and feminist theoretical methods." In *Feminist Methodologies for International Relations*, ed. Brooke. A Ackerly, Maria Stern, Jacqi True (Cambridge: Cambridge University Press, 2006), 252.

7. Ann J. Tickner, "Hans Morgenthou's Principles of Political Realism: A Feminist Reformulation (1988)." In *International Theory: Critical Investigations*, ed. James der Derian (New York: New York University Press, 1995), 63.

8. Ann J. Tickner, *Gender In International Relations: Feminist Perspectives on Achieving Global Security* (New York: Columbia University Press, 1992), 63.

9. Jill Steans, *Gender and International Relations: Issues, Debates and Future Directions* (Cambridge: Polity Press, 2006), 73-74.

10. Steans, *Gender and International Relations: Issues, Debates*, 65.

11. Christine Sylvester, *Feminist Theory and International Relations in a Postmodern Era.* (Cambridge: Althenaeum Press Ltd, Gateshead, Tyne & Wear, 1994), 207.

12. Jacqui True, Jacqui. "Feminism," 235.

13. Ann J. Tickner, "Hans Morgenthou's Principles of Political Realism," 62.

14. Madeleine Albright, "Statement before the House International Relations Committee, Washinton, D.C.." Para. 11–14. *U.S. Department of State.* April 21, 1999.

15. Madeleine Albright, "Interview with Middle East Broadcasting Corporation, Washington, D.C." Para. 21. *U.S. Department of State.* March 25, 1999. http://secretary.state.gov/www/statements/1999/000325.html.

16. Madeleine Albright, "Interview on PBS Newshour with Jim Lehrer]" Para. 15–17. *U.S. Department of State.* May 7, 1999. http://secretary.state.gov/www/statements/1999/990507b.html.

17. Madeleine Albright, "Interview on ABC-TV's Good Morning America with Diane Sawyer, Washington, D.C.." *U.S. Department of State.* March 26, 1999. http://secretary.state.gov/www/statements/1999/990326.html; "Interview on Kosovo on CNN's Early Edition, Washington, D.C." *U.S. Department of State.* March 26, 1999. http://secretary.state.gov/www/statements/1999/990326a.html; "Interview on Kosovo on Fox News' Fox and Friends with Julie Kirtz, Washington, D.C." *U.S. Department of State.* March 26, 1999. http://secretary.state.gov/www/statements/1999/990326b.html.

18. Madeleine Albright, "Interview on CBS's "Face the Nation," Washington D.C." *U.S. Deparment of State.* March 28, 1999. http://secretary.state.gov/www/statements/1999/990328.html.

19. Madeleine Albright, "Interview on NBC's "Meet the Press" with Tim Russert and Andrea Mitchell, Washington, DC." *U.S. Department of State.* April 5, 1999. http://secretary.state.gov/www/statements/1999/990404.html.

20. Madeleine Albright, "Interview on PBS Newshour with Jim Lehrer." Para. 32. *U.S. Department of State.* May 7, 1999. http://secretary.state.gov/www/statements/1999/990507b.html.

21. Madeleine Albright, "Remarks and Q&A Session with the Council on Foreign Relations, New York New York." Para36-38/ *U.S. Deparment of State.* June 29, 1999. http://secretary.state.gov/www/statements/1999/990628.html. Emphasis ours.

22. Madeleine Albright, "Press Remarks on the Ethnic Cleansing in Kosovo Report, Washington, D.C.." Para. 7. *U.S. Department of State.* May 10, 1999. http://secretary.state.gov/www/statements/1999/990510.html.

23. Madeleine Albright, "Statement at the Contact Group Meeting on Kosovo, Bonn, Germany." Para. 6. *U.S. Department of State.* March 25, 1998. http://secretary.state.gov/www/statements/1998/980325.html.

24. Madeleine Albright, "Press Conference on Kosovo, Brusels, Belgium." Para. 6. *U.S. Department of State.* October 8, 1998. http://secretary.state.gov/www/statements/1998/981008.html.

25. Madeleine Albright, "Statement before the House International Relations Committee, Washinton,D.C.." Para. 57. *U.S. Department of State.* April 21, 1999. http://secretary.state.gov/www/statements/1999/990421.html.

26. Madeleine Albright, "To win the peace...The Wall Street Journal." Para. 15. *U.S. Department of State.* June 14, 1999. http://secretary.state.gov/www/statements/1999/990614a.html.

27. Madeleine Albright, "Remarks and Q&A Session at the U.S. Institute of Peace, Washington, D.C.." Para. 21. *U.S. Department of State.* February 4, 1999. http://secretary.state.gov/www/statements/1999/990204.

28. Madeleine Albright, "Interview on PBS Newshour with Jim Lehrer." Para. 14. *U.S. Department of State.* May 7, 1999. http://secretary.state.gov/www/statements/1999/990507b.html. Emphasis ours.

29. Madeleine Albright, "Press Conference, October 8, 1998, London, United Kingdom." Para. 22. *U.S. Department of State.* October 8, 1998. http://secretary.state.gov/www/statements/1998/981008a.html.

30. Madeleine Albright, "Interview on PBS Newshour with Jim Lehrer." Para. 20. *U.S. Department of State.* May 7, 1999. http://secretary.state.gov/www/statements/1999/990507b.html.

31. Madeleine Albright, "Press Conference, October 8, 1998, London, United Kingdom." Para. 15. *U.S. Department of State.* October 8, 1998. http://secretary.state.gov/www/statements/1998/981008a.html.

32. Madeleine Albright, "Press briefing following meeting with Conact Group on Kosovo, Kleber Centre, Paris, France." Para. 30. *U.S. Department of State.* February 14, 1999. http://secretary.state.gov/www/statements/1999/990214a.html.

33. Madeleine Albright, "Remarks to the U.S. Chamber of Commerce, Washinton, D.C.." Para. 22. *U.S. Department of State.* April 14, 1999. http://secretary.state.gov/www/statements/1999/990414.html.

34. Madeleine Albright, "Remarks and Q&A Session with the Council on Foreign Relations, New York New York." Para. 25 *U.S. Deparment of State.* June 29, 1999. http://secretary.state.gov/www/statements/1999/990628.html.

35. Condoleezza Rice, "Interview with the New York Daily News editorial board, New York, New York." Para. 59. *U.S. Department of State.* June 8, 2007. http://state.gov/www/secretary/rm/2007/06/86255.htm.

36. Condoleezza Rice, "Press availability following the Iraq neighbor's Conference, Sharm el-Sheikh, Egypt." Para. 10. *U.S. Department of State.* May 4, 2007. http://state.gov/www/secretary/rm/2007/may/84293.htm.

37. Condoleezza Rice, "Remarks to U.S. mission personnel in Iraq, Baghdad, Iraq." Para. 5. *U.S. Department of State.* February 17, 2007. http://state.gov/www/secretary/rm/2007/feb/80645.htm.

38. Condoleezza Rice, "Remarks at the International Compact with Iraq Ministerial, Sharm El-Sheikh, Egypt." Para. 4. *U.S. Department of State.* May 3, 2007. http://state.gov/www/secretary/rm/2007/may/84210.htm.

39. Condoleezza Rice, "Remarks at the Independent Women's Forum upon receiving Woman of Valor Award, Washington, D.C." Para. 7 & 9. *U.S. Department of State.* May 10, 2006. http://state.gov/www/secretary/rm/2006/66139.htm.

40. Condoleezza Rice, "Remarks at the Southern Baptist Convention annual meeting, Greensboro, North Carolina." Para. 23. *U.S. Department of State.* June 14, 2006. http://state.gov/www/secretary/rm/2006/67896.htm.

41. Condoleezza Rice, "Iraq: A new way forward, testimony before the Senate Foreign Relations Committee, Washington, D.C." Para. 17. *U.S. Department of State.* January 11, 2007. http://state.gov/www/secretary/rm/2007/78605.htm.

42. Condoleezza Rice, "Remarks from the intervention at the Iraq Neighbors Conference, Sharm el-Sheikh, Egypt." Para. 18. *U.S. Department of State.* May 4, 2007. http://state.gov/www/secretary/rm/2007/may/84292.htm.

43. Condoleezza Rice, "Press availability following the Iraq neighbor's Conference, Sharm el-Sheikh, Egypt." Para. 8. *U.S. Department of State.* May 4, 2007. http://state.gov/www/secretary/rm/2007/may/84293.htm.

44. Condoleezza Rice, "Remarks at the International Compact with Iraq Ministerial, Sharm El-Sheikh, Egypt." Para. 8. *U.S. Department of State.* May 3, 2007. http://state.gov/www/secretary/rm/2007/may/84210.htm.

45. Condoleezza Rice, "On-the-record briefing on Iraqi political developments, Washington, D.C.." Para. 34. *U.S. Department of State.* April 22, 2006. http://state.gov/www/secretary/rm/2006/64972.htm.

46. Condoleezza Rice, "Press availability following the Iraq neighbor's Conference, Sharm el-Sheikh, Egypt." Para. 8. *U.S. Department of State.* May 4, 2007. http://state.gov/www/secretary/rm/2007/may/84293.htm.

47. Condoleezza Rice, Iraq: A new way forward, testimony before the Senate Foreign Relations Committee, Washington, D.C." Para. 14. *U.S. Department of State.* January 11, 2007. http://state.gov/www/secretary/rm/2007/78605.htm.

48. Condoleezza Rice, "Iraq and U.S. policy, Opening remarks before the Senate Foreign Relations Committee, Washington, D.C." Para. 22. *U.S. Department of State.* October 19, 2005. http://state.gov/www/secretary/rm/2005/55303.htm.

49. Condoleezza Rice, "Iraq: A new way forward, testimony before the Senate Foreign Relations Committee, Washington, D.C." Para. 3. *U.S. Department of State.* January 11, 2007. http://state.gov/www/secretary/rm/2007/78605.htm.

50. Condoleezza Rice, "Remarks at BBC Today-Chatham House lecture, Blackburn, United Kingdom." Para. 32. *U.S. Department of State*. March 31, 2006. http://state.gov/www/secretary/rm/2006/63969.htm.

51. Condoleezza Rice, "Remarks with British Foreign Secretary Jack Straw and Blackburn Town Hall, Backburn, England." Para. 20 *U.S. Department of State*. April 1, 2006. http://state.gov/www/secretary/rm/2006/63980.htm.

52. Condoleezza Rice, "Remarks from the intervention at the Iraq Neighbors Conference, Sharm el-Sheikh, Egypt." Para. 11. *U.S. Department of State*. May 4, 2007. http://state.gov/www/secretary/rm/2007/may/84292.htm.

53. Condoleezza Rice, "Remarks at the 88th Annual American Legion Convention, Salt Lake City, Utah." Para. 11. *U.S. Department of State*. August 29, 2006. http://state.gov/www/secretary/rm/2006/71636.htm.

54. Condoleezza Rice, "Remarks to U.S. mission personnel in Iraq, Baghdad, Iraq." Para. 5-6. *U.S. Department of State*. February 17, 2007. http://state.gov/www/secretary/rm/2007/feb/80645.htm.

55. Condoleezza Rice, "Remarks at stakeout with Secretary of Defense Donald Rumsfeld, Baghdad, Iraq." Para. 2. *U.S. Department of State*. April 27, 2006. http://state.gov/www/secretary/rm/2006/65347.htm.

56. Condoleezza Rice, "Remarks at BBC Today-Chatham House lecture, Blackburn, United Kingdom." Para. 30. *U.S. Department of State*. March 31, 2006. http://state.gov/www/secretary/rm/2006/63969.htm.

57. Condoleezza Rice, "Remarks at the Southern Baptist Convention annual meeting, Greensboro, North Carolina." Para. 22. *U.S. Department of State*. June 14, 2006. http://state.gov/www/secretary/rm/2006/67896.htm.

6

RACING JESSE JACKSON

Leadership, Masculinity, and the Black Presidency

Paul Achter

Postmodern discourses are often exclusionary even when, having been accused of lacking concrete relevance, they call attention to and appropriate the experience of "difference" and "otherness" in order to provide themselves with oppositional political meaning, legitimacy, and immediacy.

—bell hooks[1]

In June of 1983, the *New York Times* published a survey revealing that nearly one in five white voters would not vote for a black candidate for president, even if that candidate was qualified and was the party nominee.[2] For some readers, such a revelation might have induced shock or even outrage; for others the poll would merely reflect an obvious and ugly reality. The survey was prompted by the Rev. Jesse Jackson's attempt to become the first black, Democratic nominee for president.

A news story exploring the prevalence of white racism in the United States was not uncommon when Jesse Jackson campaigned for the presidency in 1984 and 1988. The mainstream press framed Jackson's candidacies as an index for measuring racial progress, and in some cases, as an outright referendum on race in the United States. Jackson's own critiques of white establishment politics helped assure that his race—his blackness— would seem to foreground all representations of him. Discussions of Jackson during this time were particularly complex since the continuation of civil rights battles finds itself in "multicultural" and "multiracial environments" complicated by "social, political, and legal constructions of race, ethnicity, gender, class, and religion, among others."[3] The symbolic generation and exchange of identity markers therefore has a particular rhetorical significance for contemporary "race" studies that Jackson's presidential campaigns are uniquely suited to bring to our attention.

This chapter is an analysis of news coverage of Jesse Jackson's presidential campaigns as they attempted to traverse the terrain of a candidacy that prompted, at once, both widespread celebration and widespread suspicion in the mainstream press. News discourse about political campaigns has traditionally focused more on personalities than campaign "issues." Sanford Schram[4] argues that in the "postmodern presidency," news discourse directed toward tearing down "appearances" to find the "real" candidate, results in campaign discourse that reflects the personal characteristics of candidates more than ever. This intense focus on the body means that a candidate's "personal qualities" can encompass not only extramarital affairs, past drug use, or professional comportment, but qualities seen as *essential* to a candidate's identity—namely race and gender.[5] Intense focus on Jackson's so-called essential gender and race reinforced normative gender-race categories and contained him by defining him in negation to the norms of white masculinity.

This essay maintains that coverage of Jesse Jackson as a potential president in dominant print news media reveals a series of longstanding, often assumed but understated expectations for the presidency that function to contain him. Deriving from colonial discourses, and reinforced in cold war imagery, "The metaphor of containment has since been transformed into cultural demonization of female and racialized Others."[6] In campaign discourse, I argue, the conflation of manhood and leadership in campaign news discourse requires a candidate's successful exhibition of masculinity but simultaneously functions to promote understandings of candidates within confining racial roles that obstruct such an exhibition. In examining the discourses surrounding the presidential candidacies of Jesse Jackson in 1984 and 1988, I argue that news media interpretations of the qualities of potential presidential candidates can contain those who do not meet the implicit requirements of whiteness and masculinity taken as common sense aspects of the presidency. Defining so-called difference candidates against the standards of white masculinity not only reinforces gender and race as literal, immutable categories, it also severely limits our thinking about race, gender, and the wide range of expressions of leadership in U.S. political culture.

I begin by tracing the intersections of masculinity, leadership, and the presidency in political culture. Second, I illustrate some current incongruities between black and white masculinities. In the third section of the chapter, I argue that Jesse Jackson has few contemporaries that might otherwise guide understandings of his candidacy into more constructive channels. Moreover, media coverage of Jackson's strength as a speaker functioned to align him with the problematic, feminine qualities associated with rhetoric, which made rhetoric a pejorative term and destabilized Jackson's gender. I conclude reflecting on what this means for Barack Obama, and by illustrating the complexities of a cultural discourse that must acknowledge the existence of racism and simultaneously assure readers that it is not prevalent.

MASCULINITY, LEADERSHIP, AND THE PRESIDENCY

When we speak of masculinity, we speak of a mutable and layered concept. There is not one "masculinity" but rather, dominant "masculinities" that emerge in concert with cultural events, prevailing norms, trends, and values. What qualities are thought to be constitutive of the "approved way of being an adult male in any given society" shifts and adjusts culturally as it is embodied and articulated.[7] Masculinity is important to the political candidate, because, as David Marshall puts it, "masculinity continues to connote power, control, and mastery," all qualities inherently associated with leadership.[8] Particular signs of masculinity shift with historical and cultural contexts and prevailing structures of feeling. Gender scholars accordingly refer to hegemonic masculinity to denote a prevailing set of standards commonly regarded as signifiers of adult maleness in a culture at any given time. Trujillo has argued that hegemonic masculinity in U.S. culture is exhibited through physical force and control, occupational achievement, familial patriarchy, frontiersmanship, and heterosexuality.[9] Trujillo applies the standards of hegemonic masculinity in a study of baseball superstar Nolan Ryan, whose exhibition of masculinity is a uniquely white one.[10]

Michael Kimmel's evaluation of several presidents' displays of masculinity is instructive in understanding this relationship between leadership and masculinity.[11] President Kennedy, Kimmel shows, embodied a competitiveness his biographer labeled "almost compulsive" but balanced it with "a fresh-scrubbed handsome, energetic charisma—qualities that LBJ lacked in equal abundance."[12] Kimmel argues that after Jimmy Carter, Presidents Reagan and Bush regained the manhood of the office with "the compulsive masculinity of the schoolyard bully, defeating weaker foes such as Grenada and Panama, a defensive and restive manhood, [a manhood] of men who needed to demonstrate their masculinity at every opportunity."[13] The ability of a candidate to display a "proper" masculinity can become a determining factor in the rhetoric of the campaign; projecting a winning image is nearly synonymous with projecting leadership and masculinity. In the 1988 race, news media depictions of George Herbert Walker Bush as a "wimp" prompted his campaign to spend nearly his entire advertising budget attempting to overcome the perception.[14] Where Bush would eventually overcome this constraint by exploiting the masculine machinery of office, the same actions risk binding women between damaging stereotypes. As Karrin Vasby Anderson notes, "Women who try to adapt similarly assertive leadership personae simply feed the stereotypes associated with "bitch." If, however, a woman responds by softening her image she risks being criticized for lacking leadership capabilities."[15] Perhaps women candidates come under scrutiny because they are a more obvious trace of gendered imagery at work in presidential campaigns. For example, the campaign film, featured in most conventions as a prelude to the anointing of the selected candidate, demonstrates the heavy reliance by candidates on masculine imagery. Parry-Giles and Parry-Giles argue that campaign films construct images for the candidates according to male-oriented myths, ideals, and values such as aggressiveness, competitiveness, and confidence.[16] The authors also observe that such values are often anchored to the institutions of athletics, family, and military—institutions that "work in concert with the meaning of masculinity in contemporary political discourse."[17]

Explorations of a candidate's family life in campaign rhetoric provide an easy crossover to paternalistic roles presidents are expected to play while in office and are thus a key resource for masculine display. Parry-Giles and Parry-Giles's[18] conclusions about campaign films underscore a now well-attested observation that campaign discourse portrays candidates as paternal characters.[19] In 1988, for example, George H. W. Bush's large family was featured repeatedly in the campaign film and in commercials used during the election race, connecting the paternalistic qualities Bush exercised with his family and those he might exhibit as president. Bush's campaign film, Parry-Giles and Parry-Giles argue, "forms a metaphoric link between the extended Bush family and the United States, suggesting that Bush function as the patriarch of both."[20] We know, then, that the performance of normative manhood is important in campaign rhetoric and is one standard voting audiences use in evaluating candidates.[21] What is less explicit is an understanding of how gender roles have taken on whiteness in historical representations of male leaders. What qualities of whiteness pervade the presidency would rarely surface for inspection. According to Nakayama and Krizek,

> "White" is a relatively uncharted territory that has remained invisible as it continues to influence the identity of those both within and without its domain. It affects the everyday fabric of our lives but resists, sometimes violently, any extensive characterization that would allow for the mapping of its contours.[22]

As Stuart Hall points out, however, all difference is ambivalent, capable of evoking excitement, energy, threat, and discomfort simultaneously.[23] Although whiteness is an unacknowledged aspect of presidential masculinity, news discourse about candidates coming from outside traditional race and gender domains brings both whiteness and masculinity into sharper focus. That is, Jesse Jackson's race and gender difference, which could make him seem problematic as a president, could be also used to underscore the historical importance of his presence in the campaign.

Tracing the Problems of Black Masculinity

A discussion of black masculinities must acknowledge how the historical residues of slavery leave behind lingering cultural representations about black men that set black masculinities and white masculinities in competition.[24] African American society is often perceived "in terms of a perennial 'crisis' of black masculinity whose imagined solution is a proper affirmation of black male authority,"[25] and a number of scholars acknowledge the centrality of black masculinity to the perception of racial issues in the United States.[26]

Representations of black candidates originate in the conceptions of black male citizenship during slavery.[27] The success of slavery derived in part from the ability of slaveholders to construct living patterns for black males that controlled their access to leadership roles in the family. Through these weapons, slaveholders dominated the everyday lives of their slaves and solidified a visual and verbal vocabulary about the masculine qualities of black males. Although slavery attempted to reduce *all* its subjects to animal or chattel status regardless of gender, white slaveholders perceived black men as a particular threat to the plantation's social order and thus tightly controlled their activity as a perceived way to protect their position as slave master. As Angela Davis explains, slavery, therefore, did not encourage men as family leaders:

> Because husbands and wives, fathers and daughters were equally subjected to slavemasters' absolute authority, the promotion of male supremacy among the slaves might have prompted a dangerous rupture in the chain of command . . . Black men could not be candidates for the figure of "family head" and certainly not for "family provider." After all, women and children alike were all providers for the slaveholding class.[28]

Protection of the role of slave master was accomplished through a number of means not limited only to material control of the movements of slave men. Slaveholders granted themselves free sexual access to slave women that constituted a means of psychological power over slave men and women.

Though it was stripping male slaves' access to women and defiling existing relationships, slave culture paradoxically built and operated under the myth of black male hypersexuality. As Harper observes, "The black man historically has been perceived as the bearer of a bestial sexuality, as the savage 'walking phallus' that poses a constant threat to an idealized white womanhood and thus to the whole U.S. social order."[29] The practice of lynching, for example, which was usually carried out subsequent to a white woman's accusation of rape by a black man, attests to the strength of this observation.

In circulating the perception of black men as sexual threats and stripping them of the basic father role, slavery thus subjected male slaves to a unique and lingering form of control that subsequently "provoked contradictions and dilemmas for black men in society."[30] Those contradictions derive from the paradox of being made powerless within slave culture, yet expected to exhibit masculinity as defined by a predominantly white group. Resolving the contradiction has, in fact, occupied a central research program in the social sciences. Most notably, the Moynihan Report argued that the "failure" of the black family was conterminous with the "failure" of black men and that slavery and Jim Crow had forced submissiveness on black males that could be traced to the underdevelopment of paternal figures in black communities.

The "problem" of black masculinity thus owes its legacy to historical discourses that emasculated black malehood while simultaneously using white standards of masculinity to ascertain the progress of race relations in the United States. This problem continues to find its expression in new forms. Ideological constructions of the black male, particularly in professional sports, emphasize his physical and sexual qualities. Concurrently, the legacy of the Moynihan Report is echoed in many discussions about criminality, genetics, and intelligence.[31]

Circulation and Representation

Walter Goodman once said of local news in New York City, "If a rule went out excluding entertainers, athletes, and criminals from a night's report, the only black faces you could be sure of seeing would be those of the anchors."[32] The circulation of black images in the news media has often come at the expense of the people represented. Goodman's observation about news media has its roots in the work of Sterling A. Brown, whose groundbreaking study *The Negro in American Fiction* revealed the striking differences between white and black authors' portrayals of black characters.[33] Eventually broadening his study to poetry and stage productions, Brown identified a series of recurring caricatures, including the "tragic mulatto," the "brute Negro," the "wretched freedman," the "contented slave," and the "comic negro."[34] Such severely restricted roles are still familiar in mainstream mass media but are asserted with more subtlety.[35] Stuart Hall calls this inferential racism: the "apparently naturalized representations of events and situation relating to race, whether 'factual' or 'fictional,' which have racist premises and propositions inscribed in them as a set of unquestioned assumptions."[36] Orbe found, for example, that primary characterizations of the black males on MTV's popular reality drama *The Real World* drew upon stereotypes of black males as angry, threatening, hypersexual.[37] Lulle similarly argues that coverage of Mike Tyson's rape trial drew on just two primary racist predicates.[38]

The absence of covertly racist and reductionist representations of black men in mainstream media is an opportunity to examine the broader logics that contain and control black images. As Hall remarks, inferential racism "enable[s] racist statements to be formulated without ever bringing into awareness the racist predicates on which the statements are grounded."[39] With this type of reasoning at work, a black man, Willie Horton, becomes a pawn in the 1988 presidential campaign commercial for George H. W. Bush, who successfully linked Horton's image to Michael Dukakis's perceived "soft" stance on crime. The assumptive link between blackness and criminality has similarly motivated white criminals to blame their crimes on black men, a practice that has prompted massive and expensive manhunts.[40] Although representations of black masculinity as threat are still implicated in racist logics, black masculinity has also been strongly shaped by a rhetoric of whiteness that requires black men to display white signs of leadership.[41]

If a successful candidacy required minimizing race in order to embody a presidential type of manhood predicated upon normative displays of reason, discipline, and other qualities of a hegemonic masculinity, Jesse Jackson was ill suited to the task. Where prominent black men before or after him chose to "bleach" their exhibition of masculinity in the face of this obstacle, this was impossible because Jackson and journalists covering him continually made race and racism part of the campaigns.[42] The circulation of "blackness" as Jackson's key signifier and his own failure to display a white masculinity functioned to simplify the portrayal of a complex, unconventional presidential candidate leave unchallenged normative gender roles.

ENTERING THE POLITICAL SCENE:
JESSE JACKSON IN 1984 AND 1988

In comparing depictions of Jackson during his presidential runs, we see precisely how Jackson is contained in a culture that celebrates both the dignity of every identity and how difference condenses and confines discussions of his candidacy. While Jackson's run for the presidency is ascribed a variety of diverging meanings, an ascription of Jackson's blackness serves as the primary filter through which his candidacy is explained by print media. But this is not a monolithic process or an easily simplified one. The tone of dominant print coverage of Jackson, for example, indicates a position of compassion and hope even as it tends to operate under the presumption that political campaigns are meritocracies and black and white candidates operate on equal footing.[43] The black press, by contrast, writes from the premise that the white establishment has ignored, often willfully, Jackson's and the black community's distinctness. It argued that Jackson's candidacy was not necessarily synonymous with progress on race issues while the establishment press points to Jackson's presence in the campaign as evidence to the contrary.

Virtually all coverage of Jackson celebrated Jackson's candidacy as a significant achievement for race relations in the United States and with many good reasons. Yet the press also constructed foundational characterizations of Jackson incompatible with the conventional expectations for the office of the presidency. Coverage of Jesse Jackson's 1984 and 1988 candidacies focused intently on Jackson's "blackness," and this "blackness" serves as the foundation for a series of characterizations of Jackson that help frame and direct the meaning of his display of masculinity. Barack Obama's 2008 campaign, by contrast, avoided overidentifying the candidate with any one group, including blacks, fighting against what Obama had called "the temptation to view my candidacy through a purely racial lens" and sounding a theme of unity that preempted some of the controversy Jackson's candidacy experienced.[44] Still, the mainstream press asked—as it did about Jackson—if America was "really" ready for a black candidate, critics argued that he was underqualified, and prominent public figures attributed his popularity to affirmative action.[45] Obama's campaign, like Jackson's, had frequently centered on race topics, which included criticism from blacks that he was not black enough and calls from biracial Americans who wanted Obama to claim himself as one of them.[46] These efforts all briefly drove race to the forefront of the campaign, even as Obama's continued efforts to transcend race meant that he rebuffed efforts to get him to show his racial bona fides.

The Obama campaign resisted narrow race identification because they realized that emphasis on their blackness "naturalizes" black presidential candidates and constitutes them in narrow terms of differences and essences that are problematic for black men. In the 1984 and 1988, race was the critical hook for stories about Jesse Jackson and the press delighted in discussing the questions his candidacy raised. Popular press coverage of his campaign commented on the novelty of Jackson's run by labeling him "the first major black candidate," by making mention of the candidacies of other "minor" black candidates[47] or by regarding the campaign as a sign of the continuation of civil rights. For a time, popular black periodicals such as *Essence*, *Jet*, and *Ebony* covered Jackson with great enthusiasm, but they accepted that Jackson was a candidate for blacks and they scolded the white mainstream press for caricature and misrepresentation in their coverage of him.[48] In an *Essence* column in 1984, Louis Farrakhan refuted widespread criticisms of Jackson as egotistical and inexperienced. Farrakhan argued that when Jackson was criticized as having too little experience, it meant that he was not as qualified as any of the white candidates running.[49]

Jackson's "blackness" in the dominant press was created and shaped by surrounding Jackson with stereotypical markers of his race. A *U.S. News and World Report* article emphasized the significance of race in the meaning of the campaign for its readers, continually referencing Jackson's attendance at "all black" high schools and colleges. Of his departure from the University of Illinois after one semester, Thornton and Mashek note that Jackson left "because white students humiliated him and he was not given a chance to try out for the quarterback position."[50] The article identifies Jackson's heroes as African American leaders Martin Luther King Jr., Malcolm X, and Adam Clayton Powell. Descriptions of Jackson emphasize the importance of blackness to understanding the presidential candidate:

> The candidate describes his health as excellent although he has sickle-cell-anemia trait—a chronic blood disease that affects many blacks. To stay in shape, he often takes a basketball with him on the campaign trail and plays pickup games with aides. Normally careful about his diet, he admits a weakness for fried fish and will go out of his way to find restaurants specializing in Southern cooking.[51]

Representations of Jackson in news discourse illuminate Hall's notion of an "inferential racism" wherein racist predicates are offered and audiences are nudged toward racist conclusions.[52] It is significant, then, that in three sentences Jackson's distinctly "black" disease, his weakness for Southern soul food, and his love for the game of basketball are all highlighted. Equivalent markers for the white candidates in this context are more difficult to imagine. Whiteness, as Nakayama and Krizek observe, needs no such markers to announce itself—it is most often an assumed and discursively invisible perspective.[53] With Jackson in the nomination race, however, *U.S. News* was compelled to draw attention to "Jackson's seven white rivals," underscoring the importance of race in determining the meaning of Jackson's candidacy.[54] Such a characterization of Jackson's blackness serves as the foundation for positioning him within a series of narratives and stock role images unique to black experience. Moreover, Jackson's presence in the Democratic nomination race is formulated as a sign of growth in the ongoing narrative regarding race relations in the United States.

Anchored by emphasis on his "race" as a perceptual starting point, Jesse Jackson's display of masculinity was contained in the 1984 and 1988 campaigns by three primary characterizations. In what follows, I detail these three strategies. First, the tone of the discourses surrounding the campaign subordinated Jackson to his opponents and to the wider American audience, complicating Jackson's efforts to exhibit leadership in its hegemonic, paternalistic form. Second, by way of praising him for his speaking abilities, discourses of the campaign produced an image of Jackson as performer. Such an image draws upon the traditional stock image of the "comic Negro" and thus fails to distinguish Jackson from other prominent black Americans—namely athletes and entertainers. Third, Jackson's status as a black performer on the stage of presidential politics ascribes to him an ambivalent standing in public life that resonates with the status of rhetoric in society. Jackson's primary claim to superiority as a political candidate (as articulated in coverage of him) is his oratorical prowess, but this strength can be viewed simultaneously as his greatest weakness and as the grounds for his dismissal as a suitably masculine contender for the presidency.

A Symbolic Candidacy

Most observers of the both the 1984 and 1988 campaigns speculated that Jackson had little chance of winning the Democratic nomination, much less the presidency.[55] Despite dismal odds that he would win, Jackson's candidacy continued to attract widespread attention largely because, as the *New York Times* put it, "His candidacy [showed] enough strength to influence politics beyond this year's campaign."[56] In the absence of the usual horse-race coverage, the meaning of Jackson's presence in the race took less traditional forms. In each case, these forms accentuated Jackson's blackness and diminished the threat his candidacy might pose to the political system. For example, Jackson's candidacy was frequently interpreted as a symbolic continuation of the civil rights movement. The *New York Times* quoted Alvin Poussaint, a Harvard psychiatrist, who said, "At a time when the civil rights movement seemed long past and blacks felt they had lost ground under the Reagan Administration, Mr. Jackson showed them they could fight back."[57] The article further argued that Jackson seemed "to be paving a road for other black candidates to walk upon."[58] *U.S. News* asserted that "for blacks, many count on Jackson's candidacy . . . to force all candidates to pay attention to the needs of minorities and to blaze the way for a generation of black candidates at all levels of government."[59] Elevating one exceptional black person as a symbol of racial progress can be problematic, however. The use of superstar athletes and entertainers as symbols of diminished racism is all too common. In 1986, for example, William F. Buckley observed, "It is simply not correct . . . that race prejudice is increasing in America. How does one know this? Simple, by the ratings of Bill Cosby's television show and the sales of his books. A nation simply does not idolize members of a race which that nation despises."[60] Television and other mass media provide constant opportunities for talking about and making sense of race, but news norms and institutional pressures allow few opportunities to look beyond personality for an understanding of race or racial progress. In this and other campaign coverage, Jackson is figured as an unfinished product while the white establishment pats itself on the back and celebrates him as an index of improving race relations. As a representative of a gradual movement toward the presumed, inevitable development of black candidacies in American politics, Jackson is a boy among men.

It is important to note that Jackson's own discourse can facilitate this perception of his incompatibility for paternalistic masculinity expected of presidents.[61] Jackson's efforts to give voice and representation to the Rainbow Coalition, for example, subordinates him to his audience and leads eventually to his occupation of the role of servant rather than leader or father figure. Whereas white candidates typically place themselves within paternal, masculine narratives that position them as leaders of their own family and, by proxy, the American family, Jackson seeks to critique the family setup. Moreover, Jackson was a respected orator, which led to distrust. Those covering Jackson admit that there is a "dispute over whether Jackson is more style than substance," and even those who might be regarded as Jackson's allies questioned his public comportment.[62] In an article before the 1984 nominating conventions, the *New York Times* noted that "civil-rights leaders and black politicians have called him an opportunist who cares less about the substance of his change and the hard work it requires than about the spotlight he can grab with fiery speeches and press conferences."[63] Other critics complained that "he seizes the spotlight but fails with tedious follow-up work" and that despite his "extraordinary gift for language . . . in terms of what kind of president he would make, I think there are some pretty disturbing answers."[64] The very qualities that drew audiences to Jackson led to value judgments that echoed contemporary connotations of rhetoric itself. In coverage of his campaigns, Jackson would be represented as the embodiment of rhetoric and performance writ large on the campaign scene.

The Great Communicator?

During his 1984 campaign, the *Washington Post* wrote of Jesse Jackson's appeal: younger voters "identify with the snappy dresser, the 'get down' street-smart side of Jackson that is just below the surface. They have Michael Jackson and Mr. T. and Dr. J. and now they have Jesse."[65] By emphasizing Jackson's performances, and particularly his speeches and audience reactions to them, the writer draws from the entertaining, comic Negro stock character that serves as a component of the images of so many prominent black Americans.[66] Lacking true peers in the instrumental realm of political culture, Jackson was often approached as a popular hero. The *Washington Post* article was published in the style section.

As a performer or entertainer, Jackson is set apart from other candidates through an emphasis on his oratorical ability, an emphasis focused particularly on the emotional effect he often inspires in audiences. A common sentiment among those covering each campaign is captured by a *Newsweek* article that referred to Jackson as "the best-known black and the most gifted orator in American politics."[67] *Newsweek* declared him "the party's prime performer and perhaps its most serious threat."[68] Although he would not win in 1984, another *Newsweek* article noted the other candidates were so boring that "the winner needs to have Jesse Jackson standing next to him in San Francisco . . . and it wouldn't help if a little of Jackson's charisma rubs off in the process."[69]

Portrayals of Jackson like these, however, created a political scene in which Jackson came to be an almost ornamental presence. Through an emphasis on his rhetoric and the emotions it engendered in audiences and in journalists Jackson was discounted as an aesthetic figure—talented at rousing emotions but suspect in regard to political practice. Jackson was and is still frequently regarded as a grandstander, an opportunist whose aggressive seeking of public relations and inspiring rhetoric ultimately ignores "the substance" and "hard work" required of politicians.[70] Political analysts noted that Jackson had an exceptional "feel for language," a "gift for oratory," and "a homing instinct for the camera."[71] Those on his campaign trail likened his speeches to revivals and some critics accused Jackson of running a campaign of jingles.[72] The grounds for praising Jackson—his exceptional performance in debates, moving speeches, his charisma—are therefore simultaneously the grounds for containing him within the hegemonic standards for masculinity and the presidency.

Jackson's rhetorical prowess, his key strength, hurts his candidacy in two ways. First, it allows media to frame him as a performer rather than as a politician, a move that relegates Jackson to the *Washington Post*'s style section as a figure who is meant to be enjoyed and admired but not invested with significant political power. Second, in the characterizations of Jackson as a performer lacking in "substance" we can detect the reemergence of challenges to rhetoric that have been with us since the earliest Western histories of the art were written, conceptions that elevate other forms of discourse by associating rhetoric with negative terms. In each case, characterizations of Jackson's strengths hinder his ability to establish himself as a leader. To exhibit masculinity or leadership requires logical thinking and emotional control, traits not commonly associated with one another in mainstream discussions of rhetoric. When, twenty years later, Hillary Clinton and John McCain repeatedly demeaned the rhetorical skills of their black opponent, Barack Obama, they hoped to benefit from these same negative connotations. Framing the campaign as a choice between "substance and action" and Obama's "merely" beautiful speechmaking, McCain and Clinton invoked a lingering white suspicion of black men with great rhetorical power.

Tying successful black men to the inferior status of rhetoric risks undermining their ability to perform within the hegemonic gender parameters of the presidency. In political contexts, the constitution of boundaries between the feminine-masculine and the seductive-reasonable has important consequences because rhetoric has been understood as "the feminine alternative to male violence."[73] If military service connotes masculinity and rhetorical skill seems to connote feminine qualities derived from notions of rhetoric as flattery and seduction, then we have progressed little from Plato's characterization of the art as "a certain habitude" that produces "a kind of gratification and pleasure."[74] In *Theories of the Symbol* Todorov writes, "right up to Kant, pleasing, the rhetorical function par excellence . . . is women's business (the function of moving . . . belongs to men)."[75] Given these cultural biases, the raising up of Jackson and Obama as rhetorical geniuses functions as a dismissive gesture insofar as it feminizes their difference and makes their oratorical skill into a problem.

As he ran for president, the image of Jesse Jackson was imbued with the markings of marginalization on two levels. Within larger society, the prominence of Jackson's race—the creation of "blackness"—in features about him push him to the margins of political culture and reinscribe the dominance of whiteness (even while this process remains elusive). Insofar as Jackson's image is drawn from stock images of black males circulated in mass media, the frame narrows, particularly in a presidential race, which intensifies the search for masculine, paternal qualities, qualities that are circumscribed in white male experience and thought to be urgently lacking in black American male experience.

Casting Jackson's image backward as an extension of the civil rights movement positions him in a growth narrative from which it becomes difficult to enact normative masculine presidential leadership. Rather than appearing as a carefully developed presidential "product," Jackson's character becomes that of an unfulfilled, incomplete outsider. The prophetic role Jackson assumes in his campaign speeches further complicates his efforts to embody the will of the people, whose criteria for "finished products" in presidential candidates conflicts with Jackson's insistence on personal and national growth. Second, characterizations of Jackson as gifted rhetorical performer marginalize his candidacy, for political culture is saturated not only by the norms and practices of white male officeholders but also by the expectation set by the norms of journalism and by candidates for clear, reasoned discourse. Supposed "neutral" and "objective" discourse not only obscures the construction of race, but it also implicitly relegates to rhetoric, and to Jesse Jackson, an inferior status. Praising Jackson's performative abilities positions him outside those norms and therefore simultaneously reinforces and elevates the white, hegemonic masculinity shaping the norms of the American presidency.

THE INCLUSIVE PRESIDENCY

> The peremptory demand for favorable judgments of worth is paradoxically—perhaps one should say tragically—homogenizing. For it implies that we already have the standards to make such judgments. The standards we have, however, are those of North Atlantic civilization. And so the judgments implicitly and unconsciously cram the others into our categories.
>
> —Charles Taylor[76]

The presidential campaigns of Jesse Jackson open up for scholars of political communication far too many questions for full exploration here, including questions about what this means in terms of Barack Obama. Given Obama's rise, Jackson's campaigns have gained renewed importance for their ability to historicize and illuminate how stereotype and public arguments about race work in political campaigns.[77] Charles Taylor's "politics of difference" is a compelling contextual explanation for the complexities involved in talking about race today. Media rhetoric about black candidates, while ostensibly in support of a progressive race agenda, can function rather to contain candidates within a relatively narrow set of characterizations and narratives. This occurs in part because efforts at equality are predicated on the marking of difference that requires a constant awareness of divisions based on race, class, gender, and sexuality. Thus in differentiating among "personal" qualities of political candidates, media discourse continually creates, modifies, and critiques candidates at the level of their bodies. Our consciousness about difference is always accompanied by evaluation of the meaning of that difference. Within a culture where the distinctiveness of individuals or "minority" groups are celebrated, markers of race that predominate coverage of Jesse Jackson's presidential runs continue to frame our understanding of his candidacy in problematic ways. Moreover, popular understandings of Jackson as an entertaining orator undermine his ability to perform presidentiality when the unstated premise is that the ability to speak well implies an inability to govern. Barack Obama's candidacy is of course a more recent test of the expectations for the presidency and a snapshot of the how the politics of difference works today. Perhaps press coverage has been kinder to Obama. For his part, Obama's tendency toward inclusiveness is evident in the conciliatory attitude that marks his public performances and his measured rhetoric. Obama has preempted public controversies about race by telling and retelling stories about his white mother and his Kenyan father, a move that enables him to refuse identification with any one racial group and claim common ground with blacks, whites, and multiracial people. Jackson, on the other hand, was from the south, and his blackness was often at the forefront of coverage of his campaign. This is not to suggest that Obama has not been stereotyped in problematic ways. On the contrary, his opponents throughout the campaigns race-baited audiences by suggesting Obama had "terrorists" for friends and by using his middle name in attempts to slur him.[78] The point is that when he has talked about race and white racism in substantial ways, the purpose, in part, is to calm fears and defuse the issue of his race. When the conservative media insisted that he dissociate himself from inflammatory clips of statements made by his pastor, Jeremiah Wright, Obama's response was the "More Perfect Union" speech, which was a vitally important moment in his primary campaign. "More Perfect Union" was a calm and thorough treatment of race and racism in the United States that skillfully managed many racial misgivings, one that chided white people and black people for their mistakes but—importantly—was careful not to alienate anyone. Obama's life story, his rhetoric of racial conciliation, and his attempt at sweeping transcendence of race and political party allow him to reach out to a broad range of white people that may not have felt a part of Jackson's more class- and race-based "Rainbow Coalition."

For critics, part of the project of understanding the presidency is in making visible the normative whiteness of the office that accompanies so much campaign discourse, for a large part of the American experience is the ongoing dialogue about race. The presidency is deeply endowed with the myths and symbols that have always provided meaning and purpose to the American experience. As this study indicates, a research program on the presidency must include attention to the processes by which prevailing forms of white, Euro-American masculinity become tools of evaluation of presidential candidates. Presidential candidates, as Fisher[79] has noted, allow Americans to understand themselves and what they symbolize as nation. Critical work that focuses on symbolic expectations for the presidency may help us better determine how that symbolism disadvantages black candidates.

NOTES

1. bell hooks, "Postmodern blackness," *Postmodern Culture* 1, no.1 (1990).

2. F. S. Joyce, "Fiery Jesse Jackson Attracting Politicians' Praise and Criticism." *New York Times* (June 27, 1983): A1.

3. Steve R. Goldzwig, "Civil Rights in the Postmodern Era: An Introduction," *Rhetoric and Public Affairs* 2, no. 2 (Summer 1999): 171–76.

4. Sanford Schram, "The Post-Modern Presidency and the Grammar of Electronic Engineering," *Critical Studies in Mass Communication* 8, no. 2 (June 1991): 210–16.

5. Although it is difficult to imagine class becoming a realistic issue in presidential politics—only very well financed and/or well-connected candidates seriously contend for the nominations—a similar case could be made for class as a key prism through which candidates would be seen in contemporary politics.

6. Karrin Vasby Anderson, "'Rhymes With Rich': 'Bitch' as a Tool of Containment in Contemporary American Politics," *Rhetoric and Public Affairs* 2, no. 4 (Winter 1999): 601.

7. David D. Gilmore, *Manhood in the Making: Cultural Concepts of Masculinity* (New Haven and London: Yale University Press, 1990): 1.

8. David Marshall, *Celebrity and Power: Fame in Contemporary Culture* (Minneapolis: University of Minnesota press, 1997): 217.

9. Nick Trujillo, "Hegemonic Masculinity on the Mound: Media Representations of Nolan Ryan and American Sports Culture," *Critical Studies in Mass Communication* 8, no. 3 (September 1991): 291.

10. In *Manhood* Gilmore makes a similar case, listing logical thinking, leadership, ability to plan ahead, resourcefulness, emotional control, assertiveness, toughness (physical and psychological), dominance, decisiveness, independence, ambitiousness, self-reliance, forcefulness, reliability, analytical ability, competitiveness as primary qualities associated with masculinity. The list appears to speak for men without regard to ethnicity (Gilmore, 1990, p. 32).

11. Michael Kimmel, *Manhood in America: A Cultural History* (New York: The Free Press, 1996).

12. Kimmel, *Manhood in America*, 269.

13. Kimmel, *Manhood in America*, 292.

14. Trevor Parry-Giles and Shawn Parry-Giles, "Political Scopophilia, Presidential Campaigning, and the Intimacy of American Politics," *Communication Studies* 47, no. 3 (Fall 1996): 191–205.

15. Karrin Vasby Anderson, "'Bitch' as Containment," 616.

16. Shawn J. Parry-Giles and Trevor Parry-Giles, "Gendered Politics and Presidential Image Construction: A Reassessment of the 'Feminine Style,'" *Communication Monographs* 63, no. 1 (December 1996): 337–53.

17. David Marshall, *Celebrity and Power*, 217.

18. Shawn J. Parry-Giles and Trevor Parry-Giles, "Gendered Politics and Presidential Image Construction."

19. Many critics advance this claim. See, for example, Sanford Schramm, "Post-Modern Presidency"; Walter Fisher, "Romantic Democracy"; David Marshall, *Celebrity and Power*.

20. Trevor Parry-Giles and Shawn J. Parry-Giles, "Political Scopophilia," 198.

21. See, for example, David E. Procter, Roger C. Aden, and Phyllis Japp, "Gender/Issue Interaction in Political Identity Making: Nebraska's Woman vs. Woman Gubernatorial Campaign," *Central States Speech Journal* 39, no. 3:4 (Fall/Winter 1988): 190-203; Denise M. Bostdorff, "Vice-Presidential Comedy and the Traditional Female Role: An Examination of the Rhetorical Characteristics of the Vice Presidency," *Western Journal of Speech Communication* 55, no. 1 (Winter 1991): 1–27; Bonnie J. Dow and Mari Boor Tonn, "'Feminine Style' and Political Judgment in the Rhetoric of Ann Richards," *Quarterly Journal of Speech* 79, no. 3 (August 1993): 286–302.

22. Thomas K. Nakayama, and Robert L. Krizek, "Whiteness: A Strategic Rhetoric," *Quarterly Journal of Speech* 81, no. 3 (August 1995): 291.

23. Stuart Hall, "The Spectacle of the 'Other.'" From *Representation: Cultural Representations and Signifying Practices*, ed. Stuart Hall (Sage Publications, 1997), 238

24. Richard Majors and Janet Mancini Billson, *Cool Pose: The Dilemmas of Black Manhood in America* (Lanham, Md.: Lexington Books, 1990); Kenneth Clatterbaugh, *Contemporary Perspectives on Masculinity: Men, Women, and Politics in Modern Society* (Boulder, Colo: Westview Press, 1997), 163–65.

25. Philip Brian Harper, *Are We Not Men?: Masculine Anxiety and the Problem of African-American Identity* (New York: Oxford University Press, 1996), x.

26. Philip Brian Harper, *Are We Not Men?*; two books by Michael Eric Dyson, *Reflecting Black: African-American Cultural Criticism* (University of Minnesota Press: Minneapolis, 1993) and *Race Rules: Navigating the Color Line* (Reading, Mass.: Addison Wesley Publishing Company, 1996).

27. For perceptive studies of persisting negative stereotyping of black males in the news media, see Robert Entman, "Modern Racism and the Images of Blacks in Local Television News," *Critical Studies in Mass Communication* 7, no. 4 (December 1990): 332–45; Mark Orbe, "Constructions of Reality on MTV's 'The Real World': An Analysis of the Restrictive Coding of Black Masculinity," *Southern Journal of Communication* 64, no. 1 (Fall 1998): 32–47.

28. Angela Y. Davis, *Women, Race, and Class* (New York: Random House, 1981), 7–8.

29. Philip Brian Harper, *Are We Not Men?* 9.

30. Robert Staples, *Black masculinity: The Black Male's Role in American Society.* (San Francisco: The Black Scholar Press, 1982), 2.

31. E. Michele Ramsey, Paul Achter, and Celeste Condit, "Genetics, Race, and Crime: An Audience Study Exploring the Effects of *The Bell Curve* and Book

Reviews," *Critical Studies in Media Communication* 18, no. 4 (December 2001): 1–22.

32. John Hoberman, *Darwin's Athletes: How Sport Has Damaged Black America and Preserved the Myth of Race* (Boston: Houghton Mifflin, 1997), xxxiii.

33. Sterling A. Brown, *Negro in American Fiction* (Washington, D.C.: The Associates in Negro Education, 1937).

34. Janette Lake Dates and William Barlow, *Split Image: African Americans in the Mass Media* (Washington, D.C.: Howard University Press, 1993), 2.

35. Stuart Hall, "The Whites of Their Eyes: Racist Ideologies and the Media," in *Gender, Race, and Class in Media: A Text Reader*, ed. Gail Dines and Jean M. Humez (Thousand Oaks, Calif.: SAGE, 1991), 18–22. See also Entman, "Modern Racism."

36. Hall, "The Whites of Their Eyes," 20.

37. Mark Orbe, *Constructions of Reality on MTV's "The Real World."*

38. Jack Lule, "The Rape of Mike Tyson: Race, the Press and Symbolic Types," *Critical Studies in Mass Communication* 12, no. 2 (June 1995): 176–95.

39. Stuart Hall, "The Whites of Their Eyes," 20.

40. Philip Brian Harper, *Are We Not Men*, 143–44.

41. Michael Eric Dyson, *Race Rules*; John Hoberman, *Darwin's Athletes.*

42. In other contexts, a "problem" of black masculinity refers to the efforts being made by millions of families to involve black men in leadership roles in their families and communities. See, for example, Geoffrey Canada, *Reaching Up for Manhood: Transforming the Lives of Boys in America* (Boston: Beacon Press, 1998); D. Belton, *Speak My Name* (Boston: Beacon Press, 1995); Joseph L. White and James H. Cones III, *Black Man Emerging.* (New York: Routledge, 1999). The Million Man March was one notable effort in which black male solidarity was formulated as a symbolic answer. For an excellent discussion of how other black figures navigate the contradictory expectations in their performance of race, see Dyson (1996). Dyson points out that Colin Powell, for example, does attempt to *transcend* his race, but that Louis Farrakhan attempts rather to "*translate* race into the idiom of black self-determination" (p. 164).

43. Jackson received 18 percent of the popular vote at the 1984 Democratic National Convention. He ran his campaign at a considerable disadvantage, however, collecting just under $6 million in campaign funds. His opponents, by comparison, collected $21 million (Gary Hart) and $31 million (eventual nominee Walter Mondale). Jackson did not run paid television advertisements. *Essence* (November 1984): 20.

44. Barack Obama, "A More Perfect Union." March 18, 2008, http://my.barack obama.com/page/content/hisownwords.

45. James Hannaham, "Multiracial Man," Salon.com, February 2, 2008, http://www .salon.com/opinion/feature/2008/02/02/biracial_obama/print.html; Katharine Q. Seelye and Julie Bosman, "Ferraro's Obama Remarks Become Talk of Campaign,"

New York Times, March 12, 2008, http://www.nytimes.com/2008/03/12/us/politics/12campaign.html.

46. James Hannaham. "Multiracial Man." See also Debra J. Dickerson, "Colorblind," Salon.com, January 22, 2007, http://www.salon.com/opinion/feature/2007/01/22/obama/; Ta-Nehisi Paul Coates, "Is Obama Black Enough?" *Time*, Feb. 1, 2007, http://www.time.com/time/printout/0,8816,1584736,00.html; Rick Klein and Joseph Williams, "Obama's Silence on Imus Alarms Some Blacks; Candidate Faces First Test on Handling Issues of Race," *Boston Globe*, April 11, 2007; Benjamin Wallace-Wells, "Is America too Racist for Barack? Too Sexist for Hillary?" *Washington Post*, November 12, 2006; B01.

47. Before Jackson just seven black Americans had declared their candidacy for an American presidential nomination in a major party: Frederick Douglass in 1856, George Edwin Taylor in 1904, Rev. Clennon King in 1960, Charlene Mitchell, Dick Gregory and Eldridge Cleaver in 1968, and Shirley Chisholm in 1972. In Jannette Lake Dates and Oscar H. Gandy Jr., "How ideological constraints affected coverage of the Jesse Jackson campaign," *Journalism Quarterly* 62 (1985): 595-600.

48. Audrey Edwards, "Winning With Jesse," *Essence* 15 (July, 1984): 72-74.

49. Louis Farrakhan, "Farrakhan on Jesse Jackson," 92.

50. J. Thornton and J.W. Mashek, "Jesse Jackson Shakes Up Race for White House," *U.S. News and World Report* (1983, December 19): 43.

51. Thornton and Mashek, "Jesse Jackson Shakes Up Race," 43.

52. Stuart Hall, "The Whites of Their Eyes."

53. Tomas K. Nakayama and Robert L. Krizek, "Whiteness: A Strategic Rhetoric."

54. J. Thornton and J. W. Mashek, "Jackson Shakes Up Race," 43.

55. Thornton and Mashek, "Jackson Shakes Up Race," 43; D. E. Rosenbaum, "Jackson Makes Formal Bid For Presidency in 1988," *The New York Times* (October 11, 1987): 36; W. Shapiro, Howard Fineman, M. G. Warner, "Eight is Enough," *Newsweek* (November 14, 1983): 52.

56. Faye S. Joyce, "Jackson Candidacy is Giving New Shape to Politics in U.S." *The New York Times* (April 13, 1984): A1.

57. Joyce, "Jackson Candidacy," A1.

58. Joyce, "Jackson Candidacy," A1.

59. J. Thornton and J. W. Mashek, "Jackson Shakes Up Race," 43.

60. Herman Gray, "Television, Black Americans and the American Dream," *Critical Studies in Mass Communication* 6 (1989): 294.

61. In campaign speeches, for example, Jackson frequently adopts and develops a prophetic persona in accordance with his desire to solidify the blocs of voters comprising his "Rainbow Coalition." While biblical in origin, the prophetic ethos is frequently adopted in American oratory. Zulick argues that it allows speakers to assume the role of "visionary social critics." Margaret Zulick, "The Agon of Jeremiah: On the Dialogic Invention of Prophetic Ethos," *Quarterly Journal of Speech* 78, no. 2 (May 1992): 2. In his celebrated 1984 address to the Democratic National Convention as well as his 1988 address, Jackson spoke of himself as a supplicant

not only to his constituency, but also to God, the party, and the nation. He asked that voters understand his mistakes in the campaign and "charge it to my head and not to my heart . . . I am not a perfect servant. I am a public servant. I'm doing my best against the odds. As I develop and serve, be patient. God is not finished with me yet" (para. 22; *Congressional Quarterly Almanac*: 100th Congress, 2nd session. Washington, D.C.: Congressional Quarterly, Inc, 1988). Jackson's leadership, as he saw it, was incumbent upon the understanding, grace, and forgiveness of those who would support him; it is a sort of biblical populism.

62. J. Thornton and J. W. Mashek, "Jackson Shakes Up Race," 43.

63. Ronald Smothers, "The Impact of Jesse Jackson," *The New York Times* (March 4, 1984): 41.

64. Faye S. Joyce, "Jackson Candidacy," A10, A13.

65. M. MacPherson, "Pain and Passion: The Mystique of Jesse Jackson; Seizing the Moment, Reaching the Crowds," *The Washington Post* (May 21, 1984): D1.

66. D. M. Alpern, R. Manning, M. Warner, "Democrats: Stormy Weather," *Newsweek* (December 19, 1983): 48.

67. "What Makes Jesse Jackson Run?" *Newsweek* (November 14, 1983): 3.

68. D. M. Alpern, R. Manning, M. Warner, "Democrats: Stormy Weather," 43.

69. W. Shapiro, Howard Fineman, and M. Warner, "Eight is Enough," 52.

70. Ronald Smothers, "The Impact of Jesse Jackson," 41.

71. Ronald Smothers, "The Impact of Jesse Jackson," 41; Joyce, "Jackson Candidacy," A1.

72. MacPherson, "Pain and Passion," D1; Marshall Frady, *Jesse: The Life and Pilgrimage of Jesse Jackson* (New York: Random House, 1996), 63.

73. Celeste M. Condit, "Opposites in an Oppositional Practice: Rhetorical Criticism and Feminism," in *Transforming visions: Feminist Critiques in Communication Studies*, ed. Sheryl Perlmutter Bowen and Nancy Watt (Cresskill, N.J.: Hampton Press, 1993), 205.

74. Plato, *Gorgias*, in Patricia Bizzell and Bruce Herzberg, *The Rhetorical Tradition* (Boston: Bedford Books, 1990): 70.

75. Tzvetan Todorov, *Theories of the Symbol*. Translated by Catherine Porter. Théories du Symbole (Ithaca, N.Y.: Cornell University Press, 1982), 74.

76. Charles Taylor, "The Politics of Recognition," in *Multiculturalism*, ed. A. Gutman (Princeton, N.J.: Princeton University Press, 1994), 25–44; 61–73.

77. Patricia A. Sullivan, "Signification and African-American Rhetoric: A Case Study of Jesse Jackson's 'Common Ground and Common Sense' Speech," *Communication Quarterly* 41, no. 1 (Winter, 1993): 1–15.

78. Georgie Anne Geyer, "Ayers a pointless campaign ploy," *Chicago Tribune*, October 10, 2008, http://www.chicagotribune.com/news/nationworld/chi-oped1010 geyeroct10,0,7804826.story; "Another McCain-Palin Introducer Declares 'Barack Hussein Obama,' Huffington Post, October 8, 2008, http://www.huffingtonpost.com/2008/10/08/another-mccain-palin-intr_n_132996.html

79. Walter Fisher, "Romantic Democracy."

7

GOVERNOR MOM

Jane Swift and the Body Politic

Wendy Atkins-Sayre

In January 2001, George W. Bush chose Massachusetts governor Paul Cellucci to be the Canadian ambassador. This innocuous choice became controversial when Lieutenant Governor Jane Swift, pregnant with twins, stepped in to replace Cellucci. Swift's pregnancy stirred debate over motherhood, the rights and duties of mothers, and the position of pregnant women in society. As *Salon* writer Amy Benfer noted, "Given that she is a public figure, we all feel free to speculate about her private life with impunity, to use her as a blank slate on which we can project all of our cultural anxieties about motherhood, gender, and power."[1] And speculate we did—mostly about her body. Opponents described and ridiculed her maternal form, questioned the effect of the pregnancy on her politics, and asserted that her "maternal instincts" should keep her at home. What became clear as the controversy unfolded was that the combination of pregnancy and power disturbed many people. The issue of mothers in politics has surfaced more recently, with the addition of Alaska governor Sarah Palin as the Republican vice presidential candidate. Although Palin's example was less controversial before reaching the national stage, the governor has experienced similar controversy over her ability to juggle politics and motherhood.[2] In fact, their stories are so parallel that Jane Swift was recruited to head up a "truth squad" focused on defending Palin as a vice presidential pick.[3]

Surprisingly little has been written about the way that mothers struggle to maintain their images while holding positions of power. Instead, past research has looked at the ways in which the maternal persona has been strategically used by women to gain a morally superior position. Some early women leaders, for example, chose to embrace the "womanhood" image and argued that women were in a unique position to care for society because of their feminine virtues, including the ability to mother.[4] More contemporary examples show women employing the maternal persona for similar reasons.[5] This strategy, however, has been criticized as "reductive and essentialist" and, in the end, a move backward for women.[6] Although past research has examined the strategic use of the maternal image, what has not been explored is how the fact of motherhood and pregnancy, in particular, affects the image of women in power.

This chapter examines how pregnancy and power are articulated through the discourse that emerged in response to Swift. Specifically, a rhetorical analysis of the discourse surrounding Jane Swift's pregnancy and assumption of office shows a reduction of Swift to her body, symbolically placing her in the private realm, making a public, political life problematic.[7] In order to better understand the discourse, the chapter will explore the context of the discourse, analyze the discourse in response to Swift's pregnancy, and draw conclusions about this case and maternity and power more broadly.

JANE SWIFT AND MATERNITY IN U.S. POLITICS

Although the controversy surrounding Jane Swift's second pregnancy quickly attracted national attention, Swift was already a controversial figure before she became governor. She won her first state senate election as the youngest state senator (age twenty-five) in Massachusetts history.[8] Swift later ran for U.S. Congress but lost the election after a troubled campaign. Nevertheless, Swift made a strong showing in the election and Republicans were impressed with her potential. She was appointed to two state positions by the next two governors and, in 1998, Swift accepted Governor Paul Cellucci's call to run for lieutenant governor on his ticket.

Shortly after announcing her intention to run, Swift declared that she was pregnant with her first child and that the baby was due two weeks before the November election.[9] The first woman to run for statewide office while pregnant, Swift's pregnancy stirred discussions over whether women should hold office while dealing with pregnancy, birth, and motherhood. Voters questioned Swift's decision to run while pregnant, her youth, and her supposed use of the pregnancy for political gain. As one analyst questioned, "Do you really want to be the candidate who beats up on an eight-month-pregnant woman?"[10]

Cellucci and Swift won the election and, two years after winning the lieutenant governorship, Swift was poised to become the acting governor of Massachusetts. With twins due imminently, Swift stepped into the acting governorship as Cellucci became ambassador. The director of the Center for the Study of Women in Politics analyzed the explosive response to Swift:

> I think people have a hard time wrapping around the idea of a woman governor to begin with, but to have one who's pregnant with twins, that's almost beyond the pale . . . Throw in the question of whether or where the governor will pump milk for breast-feeding after the babies are born . . . and you have a total and complete cognitive dissonance.[11]

Despite facing criticism from numerous fronts, Swift announced in 2001 that she would run for the governorship the following year. Shortly thereafter she withdrew from the race, however, stating that her decision to leave the office was based on her belief that Mitt Romney (then best known as organizer of the Salt Lake City Olympics) had a better chance to maintain Republican control of the governor's office. Swift also stated that she was unwilling to decrease the amount of time that she spent with her family, claiming "something has to give."[12]

There were a number of reasons that Swift's assumption of office could have been controversial. She was a Republican leading a primarily Democratic state; she had a history of past controversies; she was the youngest U.S. governor in more than a century; she was a woman who had eschewed any feminist positions; and she was a woman in a state with a dismal record of electing women to public office.[13] Swift faced the same constraints that many women face when entering the political arena: having a low number of role models[14] and managing a complex image.[15] Despite the number of potential issues that constrained her, for Swift the focus of controversy was on her pregnancy. As Orleck argues, motherhood is

> always a politicized role, especially in its most romantic and idealized portrayals. Notions of "good motherhood"—underscored by popular images of maternal devotion and self-sacrifice—serve to regulate not only who becomes a mother but what it means to be a mother in a particular milieu.[16]

In the case of Jane Swift, her pregnant body was used as a focal point for discussion over the construction of motherhood and its significance for women with political aspirations.

RHETORICALLY ANALYZING
THE ATTACK ON JANE SWIFT

The discourse surrounding Swift's pregnancy presented a wide range of political leanings, philosophies, and opinions on pregnancy and work. A close reading of this discourse shows that the combination of politics and pregnancy presented a complicated response from a host of parties; supporters and attackers transcended divides in voicing their opinions on Swift. In the end, the attacks on Swift reduced her to her body, making a political image of Swift more troubling.

Before analyzing the attacks, however, it is necessary to note the complexity of the discourse surrounding Swift's case. Some of the reports merely discussed her pregnant state and the controversy surrounding the pregnancy without making evaluative statements. Many of the international articles about Swift's pregnancy, although primarily noting the novelty of the situation, commented on the controversy that erupted over Swift's right to work.[17] Although the controversy over Swift's pregnancy and ascension to office might be read as a simple division between conservative and liberal, feminist and antifeminist, the controversy was much more complicated. Swift, a Republican, was attacked by Democrats and Republicans alike; feminists both supported Swift as an example of a strong woman and attacked her as setting a bad example for women's need for family leave. Articles that generally supported Swift often commented on the irony of the politics involved in Swift's situation, with Democrats, traditionally supportive of women, attacking the pregnant Republican Swift.[18] Republicans, meanwhile, argued that Democrats were using her case for political gain.

In addition to conflicts over political beliefs, columnists often commented on their ambivalences over supporting Swift in light of their feminist beliefs.[19] They argued that despite their ideological commitment to women's equality, they struggled with the idea that Swift could manage both a state and a newly expanded family at the same time. As feminist writer Elayne Clift wrote in the *Christian Science Monitor*, "I have every confidence that the great state of Massachusetts will weather its governor's having newborn twins just fine. What I am less certain about is this: When deadlines loom, who's going to do what by when? It's never been simple."[20] Far from being a liberal versus conservative or feminist versus antifeminist issue, Swift's case created complex controversies in many circles.

Aside from comments on the political nuances of the situation, supporters of Swift argued that she faced a situation not unlike thousands of working women in America. Outraged at the attacks on Swift, many of her supporters claimed a double standard was at work. Male politicians had dealt with the birth of children, severe illnesses, and side jobs without any discussion of their abilities to handle it all.[21] As syndicated columnist Leonard Pitts wrote, "There's something creepy and paternalistic about the response to Swift's pregnancy, something that suggests we somehow stumbled into a time warp and ended up in 1954."[22]

Interestingly, then, the attacks on Jane Swift and the decisions that she made came from a host of different people—feminists, conservatives, liberals, men, and women. The more striking and, perhaps disturbing, discourse was the impassioned attack on Swift's pregnant body. It served to punish Swift, placing her back in the private realm by hyperembodying her and reducing her to her body. This synecdoche becomes apparent through the emergence of three themes in this discourse: Swift was reduced to her body, her body was then held responsible for her political actions (erasing her mind out of the equation), and, in turn, she was encouraged to remain in the private, domestic realm. Once she was reduced to her body, there was no place for her in politics.

THEORIZING THE BODY

Ideas about women's role in society, including opinions on control over their bodies, are directly connected to the way that women's subjectivity is constructed. As Rose Weitz argues, "Throughout history, ideas about women's bodies have played a dramatic role in either challenging or reinforcing power relationships between men and women. We can therefore regard these ideas as political tools in an ongoing political struggle."[23] The construction of the gendered body has been used to empower and to disempower individuals. Susan Bordo, for example, argues that a mind-body dualism is central to Western thought.[24] The mind is always privileged over the body because it is seen as the entity that leads the thoughtless mass of the body. Women are generally associated with the body—the part that is led by the (masculine) mind.[25] As Bordo writes, "That which is not-body is the highest, the best, the noblest, the closest to God; that which is body is the albatross, the heavy drag on self-realization."[26]

Pregnancy only intensifies the mind-body split, emphasizing woman's "otherness" as the changing body serves as a strong visual reminder of difference. As Robyn Longhurst observes, "Pregnancy, both culturally and biologically, poignantly marks the sexual difference. The enlarging of the breasts ready for the infant, the swelling of the stomach, the threat of the body leaking fluids and splitting itself into two, all this marks women's sexual Otherness."[27] With a pregnancy, women seem to lose the autonomy that they once had. Suddenly, the woman is constantly reminded that she is now sharing her body with another being, altering the personhood of the mother. Kristin Luker argues, "The act of conception therefore creates a pregnant woman rather than a woman who is pregnant; it creates a woman whose life, in cases where roles or values clash, is defined by the fact that she is—or may become—pregnant."[28] If women are able to overcome differences, pregnancy makes that accomplishment much more difficult because of the material reminders of our differences.

There is something particularly disturbing about pregnancy that makes it tempting to solidify difference. Pregnancy, in many ways, is seen as a very private experience.[29] The marked sexuality of the occurrence causes some of the reaction.[30] Pregnancy is primarily seen as something that should be connected to the home, the private realm. It is separated from the masculine public realm[31] and should be hidden and contained in the private. Pregnancy and motherhood (and the way that we talk about them) emphasize the reception of the public-private divide between genders, where men are seen as maintaining a public, active role while women are symbolically placed in the private, static sphere.[32] In the nineteenth century, that split was best described through the idea of the cult of true womanhood, in which true women were to be pure, pious, submissive, and domestic.[33] Motherhood and domesticity tied women to the home, where they were expected to make the home a "cheerful place"[34] and provide moral guidance for the family. Political activity certainly had no place in the true woman's life; thus women were shunned for speaking publicly and expressing interest in politics.[35]

The Body Politic

Although times have changed, contemporary women are still faced with similar constraints. Female politicians are forced to maintain a carefully constructed image that balances the feminine and the masculine.[36] Moreover, women are expected to adapt their speaking styles to their traditional roles, adopting a more "feminine style."[37] As Campbell writes, there is a "continuing demand that women who play public roles or function in the public sphere discursively enact their femininity."[38] In other words, although more women are playing public roles, they are forced to balance that activity with acts that emphasize their feminine side, their connection to the image of the private sphere. Adding to this difficult balancing act is the pressure of intensive mothering,[39] or the "new momism,"[40] that has emerged in recent years. That is, the idea that "to be a remotely decent mother, a woman has to devote her entire physical, psychological, emotional, and intellectual being, 24/7, to her children."[41] Clearly this image of motherhood is inconsistent with a public, political image. Thus, Swift faced a larger social issue as she attempted to move beyond biases against mothers.

Her Buttons Were Straining: A Focus on the Body

The mind-body split was apparent in the discussions concerning Swift. Whether attacking or supporting, the discourse embodied her through realistic and "humorous" depictions of her bodily state. This rhetoric was a critical part of creating a focus on her body as symbolic of her whole. The question of Swift's weight, a topic that provided some of the most degrading examples of attack, was frequently a subject of humor in local papers both before and after her pregnancy. Even articles that were fairly neutral in reporting Swift's condition noted her appearance: "It's hard to picture anything but birth when looking at her standing in the sunshine, the fabric of her maternity shirt straining against the bottom buttons."[42] Reporters noted that she was "not sure how much weight she has gained," that she craved oranges, and that she "doesn't like it when strangers touch her belly."[43] These articles (and others like it) made Swift's body—not her mind—the focus of the discussion.

Visual imagery was an important part of Swift's media coverage. Many of the articles included pictures of Swift's swelling body, but they more frequently described the changes Swift was experiencing in detail. The images presented of motherhood in media discourse about Swift were often idyllic. Kathleen Parker, a conservative syndicated columnist, noted, "Babies need their soft, overplump, familiar-smelling, hairlessly lactating, soft-speaking mothers to coddle, coo and soothe them into toddlerhood."[44] Thus, mothers must look, smell, and talk a particular way, adopting a "motherly" persona, in order to provide for their babies. The focus on the pregnant body occurs not only because of the spectacle of the swelling body, but also because of the emphasis on the manifestation of the maternal body.

The comments on Swift's weight and her swelling body served as the gaze that pregnant women frequently face, making it difficult to separate the image of the pregnant Swift from Swift the politician. As *Boston Globe*'s Joan Vennochi wrote of Swift's pregnancy:

> Any woman who is or has been pregnant knows how this wonderful but all-consuming physical condition comes to define you, at home and in the workplace. People look at you and think almost exclusively about what is happening in your belly, not in your brain. No matter how happy a woman is about impending motherhood, it is disconcerting to know much of the world sees a breeding machine, not a thinking machine.[45]

The constant focus on Swift's body served to usurp her mind such that her political abilities were in doubt. In Swift's case, the mind-body split was so pronounced in the discourse that she was reduced to her pregnant body, making her ability to lead the state more challenging. This distraction from the political issues becomes even more apparent when examining the discourse that argued that Swift's pregnant body would have dominance over her mind.

Dreaming of Baby: A Focus on Motherhood Affecting Politics

Critics often questioned the effect that Swift's pregnancy and motherhood had on her political career, arguing that the pregnancy had granted her political gains, had affected her mind, and would contort her political agenda. The state of Swift's body and the confused subjectivity that the pregnancy created, critics argued, controlled her politics. One *Boston Globe* staffer wrote, "And the glow the national media bestowed on Swift was only intensified by the birth of her twins. Her approval ratings, dismal for months, shot up."[46] The pregnancy, they argued, stifled political attacks on Swift because, as a former Swift political opponent noted, "It's hard to slap around a new mom."[47] Some critics even facetiously suggested that Swift should use her new motherhood role to her advantage, as in this statement from conservative Boston radio personality and *Boston Herald* columnist Howie Carr: "Here's my advice for acting Gov. Jane Swift. Get pregnant again. It's what women do now in corporate America when they think they're about to get fired. You can't fire a pregnant woman."[48]

The condition of Swift's mind was also called into question as writers argued that her pregnancy and mothering responsibilities would (and should, in some cases) interfere with her abilities to perform as governor. As Bill Maher, host of television's satiric *Politically Incorrect*, stated, "As I've said a hundred times on this show, everybody can't do everything. And if you're pregnant, especially with twins, you can't be the governor of a state. It's a huge job. I think it's the height of arrogance."[49] While Maher argued that Swift would fail at managing both the governorship and her role as mother, *Atlantic Monthly* senior correspondent Wendy Kaminer explained more explicitly why Swift's pregnancy would affect the state:

> Of course, Swift's husband can care for their infant children (and he is reportedly planning to do so). But he can't bear them; he can't recuperate from childbirth for her (if recuperation is necessary); he can't experience whatever hormone swings lay in store for her, catch up on her sleep for her, or keep her from being happily distracted by the mere thought of her two new babies.[50]

Thus, women are described as virtually incapacitated by their pregnancies because they are at the mercy of their bodies.

Moreover, journalists and pundits often questioned the impact that motherhood would have on her decision-making abilities. At times, authors described a harried mother juggling work and family, creating images of Swift conducting this balancing act. As one *Boston Herald* writer commented:

> I make this peace offering to soon-to-be-acting Gov. Swift: I will refrain from calling you Gov. "Not Too Swift" if you will refrain from burping the babies during the State of the State speech. No TV cameras in the delivery room. No spitting up on executive orders. No diaper changes in the corner office. Go someplace else more appropriate for that.[51]

These examples, and others like them, used humor to get the audience to imagine what Swift would do with the arrival of her twins.

Even her supporters suggested that her pregnancy would and should affect her thoughts. They urged Swift to use her unique position as a mother to push through legislation that would help mothers. Ann Crittenden, *American Prospect* writer, argued:

> A female governor with young children may be ideally equipped to grasp what other mothers go through and what they need to make their job of nurturing more successful. She might use her empathy and experience to push for parent education, or paid parental leaves, or health coverage, or a quality preschool education for all children in her state.[52]

Others asked her to "be the leader" in fighting for family supportive legislation.[53] It is noteworthy that even feminist-friendly journalists (like Crittenden and Ellen Goodman) fell into the message of the pregnant body guiding her political mind. In the end, Swift's pregnancy became the impetus for change in her popularity, her ability to handle the duties of the office, and even in her policies, according to the media discourse. Swift became little more than a pregnant woman who happened to be acting governor.

Barefoot and Pregnant: A Focus on Mothering "Duties"

Given the focus on how Swift's pregnancy would affect her abilities to govern, much of the discourse surrounding Swift's assumption of office generalized and argued that because women are biologically destined to have children, all women should be prepared to leave the job during and after a pregnancy. As Kathleen Hall Jamieson notes, this argument represents the classic womb-brain double bind. She explains:

> One could have either career or marriage and motherhood, but not both . . . When that bind fell, a second replaced it. One could have both career and family, but not at the same time. Now women are confronted with the corollary assumption: They can have both at the same time, but only at the cost of cheating one or the other.[54]

Like most responses to pregnancy, there was a plea to make Swift's pregnancy private—to ask her to step down from office and enter the static, private world where she could properly mother. Swift's case became the sounding board for anti–working mother rhetoric. As conservative syndicated columnist Kathleen Parker argued, Swift should "announce her temporary retirement from public office so that her girls can have a mother."[55] *New York Times* columnist Gail Collins was more explicit in explaining why Swift needed to shift her priorities: "A pregnant woman can certainly be governor, but I think I speak for us all in suggesting that a semi-homeless [Massachusetts provides no housing for the governor] extremely pregnant woman is not in the perfect position to suddenly take over the job."[56] The pressure of intensive mothering seems to lurk behind many of the comments targeted at Swift. Her body—her mothering capacities—defined who she was in the public eye and, therefore, what actions she must take. Given that synecdoche, Swift's public lifestyle was inconsistent with societal expectations.

The public seemed to feel a need, perhaps even perceived a right, to advise Swift on how to perform motherhood. The message extended beyond Swift, however, as many of the authors made sweeping statements about mothers in the workplace. Specifically, they claimed that women were bio-logically destined to stay at home and be with the children that they created and that Jane Swift (and other working mothers) hurt all women by fighting against that "natural role." *Ottowa Citizen* columnist Adamson suggested:

> The phrase "working mother" should be obliterated from the planet—as though women who do the right thing by looking after their own child are not working. Children need a parent at home. It seems odd that we have got to the point where this opinion needs to be defended. I say "a parent" because sure, in exceptional cases, dads need to stay home. But still, I would say that women ought to be the ones who do so. It is natural. We carry the children for nine months.[57]

The idea of the father staying home (and in Swift's case, this did happen) was routinely excluded from a list of possible solutions. Columnist Kathleen Parker made a similar claim about the biological need for women to stay home with the children, claiming, "to insist that a dad is just as good as a mom for newborns is to ignore biology. What happens to mother and child during those nine months transcends mere physicality. Call it hormonal, chemical, psychological, but ignore it at a great risk to humanity."[58] There was a clear elevation of the issue with this argument; Swift and women like her were said to be harmful to all of society.

The biological argument served to divide men and women—to "otherize" women. If women are uniquely responsible for giving birth to and caring for children, then they are bound to that role. There was also an emphasis on the private aspects of pregnancy and motherhood: "Swift should *stay home* with her kids"; "Children need a parent *at home*."[59] Not only are women uniquely built to care for children ("It is natural"[60]), but they should be compelled to do so in the privacy of the home. In particular, the pressure of "intensive mothering" demands a more domesticated woman who forgoes career for motherhood.[61] That action certainly cannot happen while women are in political office.

THE CONTINUING STRUGGLE

The discourse surrounding Swift's simultaneous pregnancy and ascension to governor shows a public struggling with the place of pregnant women (and perhaps all women) in politics and a general tension between preg-nancy and power. At the very least it shows that many people were willing to take advantage of Swift's situation in order to grandstand about women's need to focus on mothering. Although there were certainly defenders of Swift, most of the rhetoric attacked her decision or right to hold office while pregnant and then mothering twins. The focus on her pregnant body brought unlikely groups together in their attack. Her selection as acting governor could have been debated on a number of different levels: her political party, her inexperience, or her past controversies. Despite those options, however, her assumption of office was deemed most controversial because of the state of her body.

The discourse that emerged suggests that there remains a tendency to shift the focus to a woman's body with a pregnancy. Pregnancy makes the differences between men and women apparent; it "otherizes" the woman and can serve a subjugating role in putting woman back in her place. What Swift faced was a rhetoric that served to place her in the position that many felt she should accept. She was hyperembodied and "otherized." With the focus on Swift's body (the descriptions of her growing body and the questions about the effect of her pregnancy on her politics), her image and role as governor was diminished and, consequently, questioned. The danger of the mind-body split that Bordo and Jamieson describe is that the inevitable focus on woman's pregnant body means that intellectual activities (education, career, leadership, etc.) are downplayed.[62] Thus, pregnancy subtly divides women away from others and has a limiting effect on what women are capable of doing.

Moreover, pregnancy makes it apparent that the public-private split has been breached and Swift experienced negative reaction because of this violation. Pregnancy and childrearing is still seen as a very private, domestic occurrence,[63] despite an embracing of "intensive mothering" or mothering made central to a woman's life.[64] When women graphically expose their pregnant bodies, for example, they are met with consternation. Actress Demi Moore's 1991 nude *Vanity Fair* cover was "shocking" (and, some noted, "disgusting") enough to warrant an added plastic wrapper that hid all of the "offensive" parts of the photograph.[65] Publicly breastfeeding mothers face a similar response. The pregnant body, even if it is Demi Moore, is not considered appropriate for the public realm.

Nowhere is this rejection of the public pregnant body more apparent than in politics. The political world is seen as fast paced, powerful, public, and rational—the antithesis of the private, emotion-driven world of the mother. As Annelise Orleck writes:

> Perhaps the most deeply rooted of these [feelings and opinions] is the notion that mothers are by definition apolitical, isolated with the children in a world

of pure emotion, far removed from the welter of politics and social struggle. Underlying this static image of the mutually absorbed madonna and child is the unstated belief that bearing and raising children alters a woman's consciousness in an essentially conservative way, quieting and grounding even the most rebellious of women.[66]

Not only do we assume that women want to be absorbed in the maternal, we almost insist that they retreat into that world. Swift experienced a similar response in the demand that she (and other working mothers) retreat back into the private realm to ensure that her children were properly reared. Consequently, Swift's political career was called into question because it was inconsistent with a socially sanctioned, private, intensive mothering lifestyle.

The question becomes whether this hyperembodied, otherized, and privatized state is only an issue when women are pregnant. Generally there is a "risk" of pregnancy with many women. Does this "risk" remain in the minds of voters or employers? Trite pharmaceutical disclaimers come to mind: "Warning: women who are pregnant or at risk of becoming pregnant should avoid politics." At the very least, the discourse suggests that Americans are troubled by pregnant women and new mothers holding positions of power; many people still believe that women should be in the private sphere, at least when young children are involved. This has profound effects on women's ability to rise to positions of power. If women are still expected to take the "critical early years" off to be with their children, their career paths are severely affected.

Swift's case is an apt illustration of Kathleen Hall Jamieson's concept of the double bind, a stricture that women face in many endeavors. In what Jamieson calls, the "no-choice choice," she analyzes the womb-brain double bind, writing:

> Women could use their brains only at the expense of their uteruses; if they did, they risked their essential womanhood. Exercise of the uterus was associated with the private sphere, exercise of the brain with the public. Here was a question of woman's proper place: Those who chose to exercise their intellects in public life upended the natural order, endangered the family, and called into questions whether they were really women.[67]

In fact, Jamieson's description of the double bind that women face continues to speak to Swift's situation in 2001. More recent examples have complicated our understanding of the double bind. The current Spanish defense minister, seven months pregnant, is shown in newspaper photographs inspecting her troops "in a chic maternity outfit," for example.[68] Alaska governor and vice presidential candidate Sarah Palin gave birth to her fifth child (a child with Down Syndrome) while in office and was back at work three days later.[69] In both cases, there was discussion of the oddity of the situation, but no general outcry as with Swift. In Palin's case, however, that changed once she was launched onto the national political scene, with similar hand-wringing over the challenges that she might face as mother and vice president. A pessimistic reading would suggest that although Palin escaped scrutiny originally (perhaps because of a less public pregnancy), future women will continue to experience resistance to combining public lives and maternity, especially when there is more at stake with their positions. That resistance will not only be based in the public-private split that still lingers when pregnancy is involved, but it will also call into question the mind-womb split that suggests that women cannot and should not act in the same way when they are pregnant.

This brings to the forefront additional research questions that should be explored. The literature has begun to explore the strategic use of the maternal image, however there is a need to further understand how images of mothers are shaped by discourse.[70] Although the maternal image can be used to create a feminine persona and, therefore, create some political clout, there is a difference between embracing an image or employing maternal rhetoric and dealing with the political fallout from a pregnancy. Although there may be an advantage to appearing maternal, there are limits to how maternal one can look as she juggles a position of power. There is a need for more research into the perception of pregnancy and power. A second area for future research is exploring more about the body and how its construction affects discourse (and vice versa). Is pregnancy a unique case of this perceived mind-body split? Are there other situations that lead people to conclude that the body leads the mind? There is clearly more to be explored in this area.

Although Swift faced more scrutiny than most women, she confronted a limitation that women across the nation continue to face daily: biases against working mothers. As syndicated columnist Leonard Pitts wrote of Swift's critics:

> It's galling that this bunch of goobers would try to use Swift's babies as an excuse to, in effect, take her job. But frankly, there's something else that troubles me even more. I mean, if this is the garbage they try with a woman who has a high-profile position, a full time staff and a six figure salary, my goodness . . . Just imagine what they do with a woman who does not.[71]

The response to Swift's pregnancy is quite telling and may reflect feelings that many women encounter. Pitts's comments make it clear why it is important to understand the discourse surrounding Jane Swift. The related news and commentary surrounding her pregnancy and motherhood presented opinions that, at least ostensibly, represent those of other individuals who may not *voice* their opinions, but who act on them nonetheless. The discussion shows that there is still work to be done in defeating these arguments. Efforts to do so need to focus not just on celebrating examples of women who have successfully managed the balancing act but also on defeating notions of the mind-body split, images of changed subjectivity during pregnancy, and the public-private divide.

In a 2001 interview, Swift said, "Look, I'm not going to pretend or refuse to address any way that my being a mother affects how I do my job as governor . . . On the other hand, when the time is over, I do not want the only thing people remember to be Mother Jane."[72] Unfortunately, Swift's wishes have not been met. Despite her modest political accomplishments, Jane Swift is primarily remembered as yet another female politician who tested the water for women. Her example shows the degree to which pregnancy and power are still seen as incongruous, bringing to light the remnants of outdated beliefs about women and their roles in society.

NOTES

1. Amy Benfer, "A Pregnant Pariah," *Salon.com*, 25 January 2002, http://www.salon.com (accessed 25 January, 2002).

2. Jennifer Harper, "Palin Triggers Feminism Reversal: 'Mommy War' Evolves in Race," *Washington Times*, 17 September 2008, Lexis-Nexis (accessed 16 October 2008); Jodi Kantor and Rachel Swarns, "A New Twist in the Debate Over Mothers," *New York Times*, 2 September 2008, http://www.nytimes.com (accessed 16 October 2008); Jodi Kantor, Kate Zernike, and Catrin Einhorn, "Fusing Politics and Motherhood in New Way," *New York Times*, 8 September 2008, http://www.nytimes.com (accessed 16 October 2008).

3. Stephanie Ebbert, "Swift Signs on to Lead the Defense of Palin's Record," *Boston Globe*, 11 September 2008, Lexis-Nexis (accessed 16 October 2008).

4. Karlyn Kohrs Campbell, "Femininity and Feminism: To Be or Not To Be a Woman," *Communication Quarterly* 31, no. 2 (Spring 1983): 101-8; Bonnie Dow, "'Womanhood' Rationale in the Woman Suffrage Rhetoric of Frances E. Willard," *Southern Communication Journal* 56, no. 4 (Summer 2001): 298–307; Mari Boor Tonn, "Militant Motherhood: Labor's Mary Harris 'Mother' Jones," *Quarterly Journal of Speech* 82, no. 1 (February 1996): 1–21.

5. Sara Hayden, "Family Metaphors and the Nation," *Quarterly Journal of Speech* 89, no. 4 (Fall 2003): 196–215; Valeria Fabj, "Motherhood as Political Voice," *Communication Studies* 44, no. 1 (Winter 1993): 1-18. See also Alexis Jetter, Annelise Orleck, and Diana Taylor, *Politics of Motherhood* (Hanover, N.H.: University Press of New England, 1997) for more contemporary examples.

6. Annelise Orleck, "Tradition Unbound: Radical Mothers in International Perspective," in *The Politics of Motherhood: Activist Voices from the Left to Right*, ed. Annelise Jetter, Alexis Orleck, and Diana Taylor (Hanover, N.H.: University Press of New England, 1997), 5.

7. For the analysis, I collected texts from Lexis-Nexis and other general databases (ProQuest and EBSCOHost), from internet magazines and newspapers, and from various web sites. Originally examining over one hundred articles that discuss Swift's pregnancy and the response to that pregnancy, I searched for emerging themes in the discourse. I then narrowed down the number of articles being more closely examined in this chapter.

8. Seth Gitell, "See Jane Govern," *Worcester Phoenix*, 21-28 January 2000, http://www.worcesterphoenix.com (accessed 25 January 2002).

9. Carey Goldberg, "A Pregnant Candidate Discovers She's an Issue," *New York Times*, 15 May 1998, Lexis-Nexis (accessed 15 February 2002).

10. Goldberg, "A Pregnant Candidate."

11. Quoted in Elizabeth Mehren, "Pregnancy, Politics Collide in Boston," *Los Angeles Times*, 11 May 2001, Lexis-Nexis (accessed 8 March 2002).

12. Joanna Weiss, "They Understood the Dilemma," *Boston Globe*, 20 March 2002, http://www.boston.com/dailyglobe (accessed 20 March 2002).

13. Mark Sappenfield, "Swift Rise, Steep Fall, and a Shot at History," *Christian Science Monitor*, 16 February 2001, http://www.csmonitor.com (accessed 26 January 2005); Betty Taymor, *Running Against the Wind* (Boston: Northeastern University Press, 2000).

14. Center for American Women and Politics, "Women in Elective Office 2008," http://www.rci.rutgers.edu/~cawp/Facts/Officeholders/cawpfs.html (accessed 1 May 2008).

15. Barbara Lee Family Foundation, *Keys to the Governor's Office: Unlock the Door: The Guide for Women Running For Office* [Brochure], Brookline, Ma.: Barbara Lee; Karrin Vasby Anderson and Kristina Horn Sheeler, *Governing Codes: Gender, Metaphor, and Political Identity* (Lanham: Lexington Books, 2005).

16. Annelise Orleck, "Tradition Unbound," 5.

17. See, for example, Louise Branson, "All Eyes on Governor as She Juggles New Babies and Career," *Straits Times* (Singapore), 22 May 2001, Lexis-Nexis (accessed 8 February 2002); Laura Peek, "Rights of Pregnant Governor Disputed," *Times* (London), 12 May 2001, Lexis-Nexis (accessed 15 February 2002); Robert Tait, "Opponents Say Pregnancy Makes Governor Unfit," *Scotsman*, 12 May 2001, Lexis-Nexis (accessed 8 February 2002).

18. See, for example, Leonard Pitts, "Motherhood or Career: Governor Faces a Challenge," *Milwaukee Journal Sentinel*, 19 May 2001 (accessed 8 February 2002).

19. Nicole Brodeur, "Baby Steps, Big Choices in Office," *Seattle Times*, 15 May 2001, Lexis-Nexis (accessed 9 February 2002); Elayne Clift, "Jane Swift, and the Feminists' Dilemma," *Christian Science Monitor*, 23 May 2001, Lexis-Nexis (accessed 28 January 2002).

20. Elayne Clift, "Jane Swift."

21. Nicole Brodeur, "Baby Steps;" Elayne Clift; "Jane Swift"; Ellen Goodman, "Governor Mommy's Challenge," *Boston Globe*, 22 February 2001, Lexis-Nexis (accessed 8 February 2002); Pitts.

22. Leonard Pitts, "Motherhood or Career."

23. Rose Weitz, "A History of Women's Bodies," in *The Politics of Women's Bodies: Sexuality Appearance, and Behavior* (2nd ed.), ed. Rose Weitz (New York: Oxford University Press), 3.

24. Susan Bordo, *Unbearable Weight: Feminism, Western Culture, and the Body* (Berkeley: University of California Press, 1993).

25. Kathleen Hall Jamieson, *Beyond the Double Bind: Women and Leadership* (New York: Oxford University Press, 1995).

26. Susan Bordo, *Unbearable Weight*, 5.

27. Robyn Longhurst, *Bodies: Exploring Fluid Boundaries* (London: Routledge, 2001), 44.

28. Kristin Luker, *Abortion and the Politics of Motherhood* (Berkeley, Calif.: University of California Press, 1984), 200.

29. Paradoxically, some women argue that it is also very public. The pregnant woman becomes the target of wandering hands wanting to rub the swelling stomach, the gaze that lands on the stomach, and the advice for what she can do with her body (and the growing fetus) (Longhurst). There is an odd public-private dichotomy to pregnancy.

30. Sandra Matthews and Laura Wexler, *Pregnant Pictures* (New York: Routledge, 2000).

31. Robyn Longhurst, *Bodies*.

32. Jeanne Boydston, *Home and Work: Housework, Wages, and the Ideology of Labor in the Early Republic* (New York: Oxford University Press, 1990); Karlyn Kohrs Campbell, *Man Cannot Speak For Her: A Critical Study of Early Feminist Rhetoric* (New York: Praeger, 1989); Linda K. Kerber, "Separate Spheres, Female Worlds, Women's Place," *Journal of American History* 75, no. 1 (June 1988): 9–39; Aileen S. Kraditor, *Up From the Pedestal: Selected Writings in the History of American Feminism* (New York: New York Times Book Company, 1975); Barbara Welter, "The Cult of True Womanhood: 1820–1860," *American Quarterly* 18, no. 2 (Summer 1966): 151–74.

33. Barbara Welter, "Cult."

34. Barbara Welter, "Cult,"163.

35. Karlyn Kohrs Campbell, "The Discursive Performance of Femininity: Hating Hillary," *Rhetoric and Public Affairs* 1, no. 1 (Spring 1998), 1–19; Phillis M. Japp, "Esther or Isaiah? The Abolitionist-Feminist Rhetoric of Angelina Grimke," *Quarterly Journal of Speech* 71, no. 3 (August 1985), 335–48; Susan Zaeske, "'Promiscuous Audience' Controversy and the Emergence of the Early Woman's Rights Movement," *Quarterly Journal of Speech* 81, no. 2 (May 1995), 191–207.

36. Barbara Lee Family Foundation; Dan Kennedy, "Jane's Defense, Weakly," *Phoenix.com*, 28 January 2002, http://www.bostonphoenix.com (accessed 28 January 2002).

37. Bonnie J. Dow and Mari Boor Tonn, "'Feminine Style' and Political Judgment in the Rhetoric of Ann Richards," *Quarterly Journal of Speech* 79, no. 3 (August 1993), 286–302.

38. Karlyn Kohrs Campbell, "The Discursive Performance of Femininity," 15.

39. Sharon Hays, *Cultural Contradictions of Motherhood* (New Haven: Yale University Press, 1996).

40. Susan J. Douglas and Meredith W. Michaels, *Mommy Myth: The Idealization of Motherhood and How it Has Undermined All Women* (New York: Free Press, 2004).

41. Susan J. Douglas and Meredith W. Michaels, *Mommy Myth*, 4.

42. Beth Whitehouse, "She's a Working Mother Who is Pregnant With Twins. Can Jane Swift Govern Both Massachusetts and her Growing Family?" *Newsday*, 30 April 2001, Lexis-Nexis (accessed 8 February 2002).

43. Whitehouse, "She's a Working Mother."

44. Kathleen Parker, "Stay Home, Governor, While Your Girls are Babies," *USA Today*, 24 May 2001, Lexis-Nexis (accessed 8 February 2002).

45. Joan Vennochi, "At Senate Hearings, Sexism Swiftly Appears," *Boston Globe*, 16 March 2001, Lexis-Nexis (accessed 1 February 2002).

46. Yvonne Abraham, "A Growing Confidence Despite Embarrassments, Criticism," *Boston Globe*, 18 October 2001, Lexis-Nexis (accessed 8 February 2002).

47. Daniel McGinn, "A Mom for Massachusetts: A Young Governor Faces a Tough Job—and New Twins," *Newsweek*, 26 February 2001, Academic Search Premier (accessed 15 February 2002).

48. Howie Carr, "Swift Glowing a Little More with Kennedy Out of the Picture," *Boston Herald*, 14 March 2001, Lexis-Nexis (accessed 8 February 2002).

49. Quoted in Gayle Fee and Laura Raposa, "Inside Track: Maher: Jane is Incorrect Politically," *Boston Herald*, 14 February 2001, Lexis-Nexis (accessed 8 February 2002).

50. Wendy Kaminer, "Mama's Delicate Condition," *American Prospect*, 23 April 2001, ProQuest (accessed 28 January 2002).

51. Joe Sciacca, "Shakeup in Corner Office Gives Swift a Second Chance," *Boston Herald*, 12 February 2001, Lexis-Nexis (accessed 1 February 2002).

52. Ann Crittenden, "A Pregnant Governor: An Exchange," *American Prospect*, 7 May 2001, Lexis-Nexis (accessed 28 January 2002).

53. Ellen Goodman, "Governor Mommy's Challenge," *Boston Globe*, 22 February 2001, Lexis Nexis (accessed 8 February 2002).

54. Kathleen Jamieson, *Double Bind*, 54.

55. Kathleen Parker, "Stay Home."

56. Gail Collins, "All at Once, Swift Struggles to Balance Career, Family," *Milwaukee Journal Sentinel*, 12 May 2001, Lexis-Nexis (accessed 8 February 2002).

57. Rondi Adamson, "See Jane Stay at Home Instead of Playing Governor Mom," *Ottawa Citizen*, 25 April 2001, Lexis-Nexis (accessed 8 February 2002).

58. Kathleen Parker, "Stay Home."

59. Rondi Adamson, "See Jane," emphasis added.

60. Adamson, "See Jane."

61. Susan J. Douglas and Meredith W. Michaels, *Mommy Myth*; Hays, *Cultural Contradictions*.

62. Susan Bordo *Unbearable Weight*; Jamieson.

63. Robyn Longhurst; *Bodies*; Matthews and Wexler, *Pregnant Pictures*.

64. Susan J. Douglas and Meredith W. Michaels, *Mommy Myth*; Hays, *Cultural Contradictions*.

65. Robyn Longhurst; *Bodies*; Matthews and Wexler, *Pregnant Pictures*.

66. Annelise Orleck, "Tradition Unbound," 3.

67. Kathleen Jamieson, *Double Bind*, 17.

68. Jocelyn Noveck, "When Motherhood Comes at an Inconvenient Career Moment," *Boston Globe*, 18 April 2008, http://www.boston.com (accessed 2 May 2008).

69. Lisa Demer, "Palin Confirms Baby Has Down Syndrome," *Anchorage Daily News*, 2 May 2008, http://www.adn.com/news/alaska/v-printer/story/382560.html (accessed 2 May 2008).

70. See, for example, Hayden, "Family Metaphors;" Fabj, "Motherhood;" Jetter, Orleck, and Taylor, *The Politics of Motherhood*..

71. Leonard Pitts, "Motherhood or Career."

72. Quoted in Sally Jacobs, "Swift's Unusual Ride to the Governor's Office," *Boston Globe*, 8 April 2001, http://www.boston.com (accessed 2 May 2008).

8

BEYOND LESBIAN IDENTITY

Exploring the Use of Narrative in Kathy Webb's
Successful Campaign for the Arkansas State Legislature

Christina Standerfer

Until 1965, no woman had been elected in her own right to the Arkansas State House of Representatives. Today twenty-one of the one hundred Arkansas state representatives are women.[1] In general, women have made considerable progress in the last forty years in storming the traditionally male-dominated bastion of American politics.[2] No state exists that has not elected a woman to some office. Even voters in southern states, which have been studied extensively in regard to their unique political culture that traditionally excludes women and other politically underrepresented groups, have embraced women candidates for certain offices.[3] Given these changes over the last half century, it seems a fair assumption that women running for most political offices are not immediately viewed as novelties.

The same cannot be said for openly lesbian, gay, bisexual, or transgendered (LGBT) candidates. According to the Gay and Lesbian Victory Fund,[4] as of October 2006 there were about 350 openly gay elected officials nationwide; and of the 7,382 seats in state legislators, 57 were occupied by openly gay individuals. Seven states still had no openly LGBT elected officials at any level of government and thirteen states still had no openly LGBT state legislators. Considering conservative estimates that at least 10 percent of the U.S. population is LGBT, openly gay and lesbian citizens are woefully underrepresented in political offices. Before the May 2006

Arkansas Democratic primary, Arkansas was counted among the states that had no openly gay elected official at any level of government. That changed with the election of Kathy Webb.

In 2006, Kathy Webb became the first openly gay individual elected to the Arkansas State House of Representatives. In fact, according to an August 9, 2006, press release from the Gay and Lesbian Victory Fund, Webb was the first openly gay elected official in Arkansas history. Webb, whose only previous campaign experience as a candidate had been a successful run for an executive position with the National Organization of Women more than two decades earlier, handily beat three male opponents in the Democratic primary. She received nearly 57 percent of the vote and faced no Republican opposition in the November general election. Webb has described her victory as the result of a "perfect storm"—conditions and opportunities came together in just the right way to achieve victory. Make no mistake, though, about the nature of the perfect storm Webb describes: it did not happen serendipitously. This perfect storm was orchestrated in part by Webb and her campaign staff paying careful attention to how Webb was presented to potential voters.

While a growing body of academic research concerning perceptions of women candidates and the challenges they face exists, few studies have addressed the perceptions and challenges of openly gay and lesbian candidates.[5] None has addressed rhetorical dimensions of an openly gay or lesbian candidate's campaign. In this essay I explore the rhetorical strategies used by the Webb campaign to both acknowledge Webb's sexual orientation and to steer discourse about the election to pertinent local issues such as water quality, education, and health care. Using Walter Fisher's narrative theory and Gerard Hauser's rhetorical norms of the public sphere,[6] I argue that the success of Webb's campaign hinged on defining the candidate through the intersection of three narratives told about and lived by Webb: "The Tale of the Exemplary Lesbian," "The Account of the Competent Woman," and the story of "Us Acting Together." Moreover, analysis of the narratives constructed in this campaign offers valuable lessons for any candidate regardless of sex, sexual orientation, or political affiliation, as this case exemplifies how intersecting narratives may be used to create possibilities for crossing boundaries and inviting voters to become active participants rather than spectators in the democratic process. Explicating these claims requires first reviewing the theories of Fisher and Hauser.

STORIES TOLD, STORIES LIVED:
THE NARRATIVE NATURE OF PUBLIC DISCOURSE

While the idea that humans are essentially storytellers is founded in so-phistic ideas of *mythos* and *nomos*, Walter Fisher must be credited with resurrecting the rhetorical functions of narratives. Fisher lamented the de-terioration of "everyday argument" and the ever-narrowing venues in which traditional rational debate occurred. Fisher argued that humans are essen-tially storytelling animals, and he proposed the "narrative paradigm" as an alternative to the traditional rational model of argument. He described this paradigm as "a dialectical synthesis of two traditional strands in the history of rhetoric: the argumentative, persuasive theme and the literary, aesthetic theme."[7]

People's willingness to believe or participate in any story is grounded in "their inherent awareness of *narrative probability*, what constitutes a co-herent story, and their constant habit of testing *narrative fidelity*, whether the stories they experience ring true with the stories they know to be true in their lives."[8] In essence, people accept, live, and live by stories that have internally consistent plots and comport with stories they previously have heard and participated in. As Fisher further noted, "Some stories are better than others, more coherent, more 'true' to the way people and the world are—in fact and value."[9] These more coherent, more "true" stories are the ones people deem to have the most narrative rationality; and they guide people's public judgments and action.

In regard to public discourse, then, the judgments and actions of citizens are not necessarily guided by evaluation of the strengths of arguments based on rules of advocacy but rather by identification with stories told and lived. Fisher suggests that given this turn away from traditional ways of as-sessing and making arguments, the narrative paradigm "provides a radical democratic ground for social-political critique" in that narrative rationality "is inimical to elitist politics, whether fascist, communist, or even demo-cratic."[10] Fisher asserts that "voters are not fools" who are "straitjacketed by social determinants or moved by subconscious urges triggered by devilishly skillful propagandists." Rather they are moved by their perceptions and appraisals of "central and relevant questions of public policy, of govern-ment performance, and of executive personality." Fisher concludes: "These perceptions and appraisals of political discourse and action become stories, narratives that must stand the tests of probability and fidelity";[11] however,

Fisher offers no specifics concerning how social actors determine the probability and fidelity of stories told or lived beyond stating that narrative rationality is "ruled by matters of history, biography, culture, and character."[12] Fisher's notion of narrative rationality, then, does not explicitly take into account how stories lived and told by diverse people may be negotiated. Hauser's notion of the rhetorical criteria of the public sphere offers one way to bring Fisher's idea of narrative rationality into sharper focus.

STORIES SHARED: THE VERNACULAR OF THE PUBLIC SPHERE

The function of the public sphere as delineated by Jürgen Habermas is to influence and authorize state activities through critical rational debate.[13] Gerard Hauser questioned the desirability of the public sphere as envisioned by Habermas and proposed a vernacular rhetoric model of publics and public spheres.[14] According to Hauser, publics invent themselves and then make sense of and act upon that invention based on cultural narratives more so than the force of others' arguments. These narratives are told and retold among social actors as the means by which these social actors come to share a common reference world. Narratives fuse the past and the future and allow social actors to make meaning of their present. As such it is the symbolic action, the rhetoric, of these social actors that brings a public into being, gives that public meaning, and defines that public's possibilities for actions. No public exists in isolation from other publics, but rather it influences and is influenced by other publics based on perceived levels of interdependence. As such, cultural narratives among members of a public require coordination or negotiation to serve the best interests of the public involved.

To aid in this coordination or negotiation, Hauser advocates adopting a rhetorical model of a network of multiple public spheres evident in actual social practices. In doing so, Hauser rejects norms for gauging the quality of public discourse and public argument based solely on any universal rationalistic template. Instead, Hauser offers five rhetorical norms or criteria by which public discourse tied to particular issues or particular publics may be gauged and criticized: *permeable boundaries, activity* (the ability of social actors to engage issues), use of *contextualized language* not colonized by technocrats or epistemic elites, *believable appearance* (means for social actors to appear believable before strangers), and *tolerance* for divergent perspectives. While Hauser's rhetorical norms of public discourse make intuitive sense, finding actual case studies that exemplify these norms is difficult. Hauser's own use of these norms to explicate the discourse related to the Meese commission's report on pornography revealed that in that particular case *none* of the norms was met. In fact, it seems far easier to find cases in which the norms are not met than cases in which they are, given the proliferation of public discourse that is identity-based or high-jacked by the language of technocrats or experts.[15] The practical import of these norms to generate productive and prudent public discourse requires investigation of cases in which they are met.

In sum, while Fisher's notion of narrative rationality does not explicitly take into account how stories lived and told by diverse people may be negotiated, Hauser's notion of rhetorical norms of the public discourse offers insights concerning both conditions necessary for such negotiations and ways social actors may facilitate these negotiations to bring about prudent civic judgment and actions. I now turn to the stories lived and told by Kathy Webb's campaign to consider how these narratives contributed to the success of the campaign and offer evidence of the practical import of Hauser's rhetorical norms of public discourse in relation to Fisher's notions of narrative rationality.

KATHY WEBB'S CAMPAIGN: FROM IDEA TO ACTION

During the election cycle of 2006, the race for District 37 of the Arkansas State Legislature would have no incumbent as the current legislator had served three terms, the maximum according to Arkansas's term limit laws for state offices. District 37, situated in Pulaski County in central Arkansas, the most densely populated area of the state, includes portions of one of the most affluent neighborhoods (Hillcrest) in Little Rock, the state capital, as well as portions of the downtown area and a mainly working-class neighborhood (Capitol View) that runs along one side of the interstate loop that divides the city. The district, which is racially and economically diverse, has a history of electing some of the more liberal members of the state legislature.

In 2005, Webb started thinking about the possibility of running for state legislative representative from District 37.[16] As she described it, she saw the possibility of running and winning as a "maybe"—she had grown up in the district, most of her family still lived in the district, she attended a large church in the district, and she had received positive publicity from a restaurant she owns that specializes in Asian cuisine using organic and

locally grown ingredients. She also considered the fact that an openly gay
person had never run in Arkansas and that the time and the district might
be right for her candidacy. On a trip to Atlanta in spring 2005, she noticed
an ad in a gay-oriented newspaper for a Victory Fund mini training for gays
and lesbians interested in running for political office. She signed up for the
training.

Later that summer, she and Alice Lightle, a prominent local lawyer (now
judge) and political lobbyist who would become her campaign manager,
attended a more extensive training for potential candidates sponsored by
the Gay and Lesbian Leadership Institute. The four-day training was held
in Colorado Springs, Colorado. According to the Gay and Lesbian Leadership Institute Web site, their trainings focus on three areas of campaigns:
fundraising, message, and planning and strategy.[17] By the end of the training Webb had decided to run for office and Lightle agreed to manage the
campaign. Upon returning to Little Rock, Webb and Lightle set about putting together a campaign team that included Debbie Willhite, a nationally
known political strategist and political consultant, who had orchestrated
Webb's successful 1982 campaign for an executive board position with
NOW.

Webb would face three opponents, all men, in the primary. Two of her
opponents, Jesse Gibson and Jerry Larkowski, were attorneys; Larkowski
had resigned as chair of the Pulaski County Election Commission to run for
office. The other opponent, Jordan Johnson, a public relations consultant,
was associated with one of the largest advertising agencies in the area and
had secured backing from some of the most prominent power brokers in
the state; his mother was already serving in the Arkansas legislature having
run two successful campaigns. As stated earlier, despite this formidable
opposition, Webb won the primary handily with nearly 57 percent of the
vote.

According to Webb's campaign manager, the success of the campaign
hinged on the execution of three interdependent elements: (1) raising a lot
of money and raising it early; (2) having an organized campaign strategy;
and (3) presenting Kathy as Kathy. In regard to raising money, all in all,
Webb's campaign raised a little less than $130,000; no other candidate in
the race raised even half that amount. Adhering to the lessons learned at
the Gay and Lesbian Leadership Institute, Webb and her staffers ran a
disciplined campaign. The strategies for getting Webb's name and message out to voters included using yard signs, mobilizing volunteers, direct
mail, and door-to-door campaigning ("walking the district"). But, as Webb's
campaign manager also noted, the ability to raise money and run an orga-

nized campaign were the direct result of "Kathy being Kathy." Unpacking the tautological concepts of "Kathy being Kathy" and "presenting Kathy as Kathy" requires consideration of the stories lived by and told about Kathy Webb during the campaign.

PRESENTING KATHY AS KATHY: STORIES LIVED AND TOLD IN THE WEBB CAMPAIGN

The phrase "Kathy being Kathy" by all accounts translates to Webb being an honest and a civic-minded person; however, the success of this understanding of Webb resonating with potential voters required their belief and participation in three intersecting narratives: (1) "The Tale of the Exemplary Lesbian"; (2) "The Account of the Competent Woman"; (3) the story of "Us Acting Together." In explicating the importance of these narratives to the success of Webb's campaign, I have drawn rather arbitrary lines among them. In practice, the narratives blended together seamlessly, and it was this integration of the stories that was crucial to moving potential voters to regard and to accept Kathy Webb's story as more than simply that of an exemplary lesbian. For no matter how compelling the narrative of an exemplary lesbian might be, in the end one can never be sure how ready the world is "for lesbians in general."[18] In short, the story of the Exemplary Lesbian alone cannot account for victory at the polls; however, it is where the overarching narrative of "Kathy being Kathy" begins.

Being "More Than": The Tale of the Exemplary Lesbian

Jacqueline Taylor, who characterizes herself as an "exemplary lesbian," notes that lesbians in general are invisible; however, when they are rendered visible, "it is often as emblems of corruptions and depravity or as avenging furies."[19] Exemplary lesbians are supposed to counteract those negative stereotypes by being "so charming, articulate, well-groomed, and well, *normal*, that all those prejudices melt away and the assembled audience suddenly sees the veil lift from their eyes."[20] Of course, being an "exemplary" lesbian first requires being an "out" lesbian: being known publicly as a lesbian.

Coming out was something Webb had done years before. She has been out since the 1970s, and during the campaign she made no attempts to hide her sexual orientation. Her perception was that people probably already knew she was a lesbian, but they were interested in how she would handle her public identity. Both Webb and Lightle told the story of Webb meeting with a representative of an organization from which she was seeking endorsement. In the course of outlining her experience, education, her platform, she mentioned also that she was a lesbian. After she had finished her pitch, the man paused for a moment, smiled, and said, "This is interesting. I wondered if you would bring that up [meaning her sexual orientation]." He then offered his support citing Webb's "openness, honesty, and courage" as well as her qualifications as the reasons for his decision.

When I asked Webb if her sexual orientation was ever raised as an issue in the campaign, she indicated that one opponent had try to imply that she would not be effective in the legislature because the Arkansas legislature was still the bastion of "good old boy politics" where women in general, much less a lesbian, could not easily gain voice. When I asked her how she handled it, she indicated that during a debate sponsored by the Pulaski County Democratic Women, she preempted this opponent's attack by opening with, "You may have heard that I am a lesbian. Well, you know, that's true. But I'm also a small-business owner who has met with all sorts of people and dealt with all sorts of issues." She went on to catalog how, as a restaurant owner, she had direct experience dealing with issues of education, health care, environmental concerns, and hunger. As Webb told an interviewer for *Advocate* magazine: "A few people were pretty hostile about my involvement with NOW, and there was some questioning about whether I could be effective in the legislature given my sexual orientation . . . But voters decided, based on my record, that I would be effective, so that got nipped in the bud."[21]

Webb also made it clear that she did not want to run as a "gay candidate." As she stated, "From day one, I wanted to make it clear that I wanted to work for everyone in the district." Her past experiences point to the sincerity of this statement. Webb has a history as an activist, but an activist who focuses on a wide range of issues, not just gay issues. She served on NOW's national executive board for six years, she has been a board member for Planned Parenthood, and she has been active in organizations that address issues of hunger, literacy, and the environment. She is a Stonewall Democrat and has been a Rotarian. She serves on the administrative board of her church and has served on ACLU's task force on gay and lesbian issues. She also has earned a wide variety of awards. She was the first woman to receive a National Manager of the Year Award from Domino's Pizza; she was named Humanitarian of the Year by the Arkansas Hospitality Association; in 2004, *Little Rock Monthly* named Webb one of "Ten Women We Love." As Willhite noted, being a lesbian is part of Kathy's identity but is not her whole identity. Lightle expressed Webb's attitude of self as a proficiency in not "over-defining herself."

Not overdefining Webb is a bit more complicated than it first appears and is the key to an audience's acceptance of the Tale of the Exemplary Lesbian narrative. Fulfilling the role of exemplary lesbian, as Taylor suggested, requires being perceived as "normal." By incorporating other social roles (successful businesswoman, lauded community volunteer, award winner) into the account of her life, Webb offered a narrative that not only rendered her "normal" but positioned her as what Herbert Simons has termed a "super-representative" of the people she wished to serve: someone who seemed enough like potential voters that they could identify with her but also just different enough based on past accomplishments to be seen as having the expertise and experience to represent potential constituents well.[22] Not overdefining is accomplished through the juxtaposition of the potentially negative "lesbian" label with the potentially positive "successful businesswoman" and "award-winning, community-minded volunteer" labels, thereby rendering Webb "exemplary," and it is from this juxtaposition that the narrative of the Account of the Competent Woman could emerge.

Getting Things Done: The Account of the Competent Woman

As indicated earlier, Webb was the only woman running in this four-person race. She used this fact and her age to her advantage. Webb not only ran "as a woman," she ran as an *older* woman stressing her *experience* in a race in which her opponents were three considerably younger men (Webb was fifty-six; Larkowski, thirty-nine; Gibson, thirty-one; and Johnson, twenty-eight the year of the campaign). As she stated in an article for the *Arkansas Times*, a weekly free press publication that offered profiles of the candidates in the race: "I think with my public policy experience, my community involvement, and my practical experience, that I can make a difference in the legislature on the issues that are important to the people of this district."[23] The issues she emphasized in her speeches and public appearances included education, economic development, and health care. Previous studies suggest that focusing on these types of social welfare issues gives female candidates significant advantage over male candidates in that voters associate domestic social issues favorably with female candidates and often perceive women generally as more proficient than men in dealing with these kinds of issues.[24]

The Account of the Competent Woman narrative evident in Webb's public appearances and statements to the press was echoed in the direct mail campaign. The direct mail pieces included seven large (8" x 11") full color pieces on glossy card stock and two smaller mail-outs. The tag line on each piece was some variation on "Kathy Webb gets it done." Of the seven large glossy pieces, three focused on specific issues: education, economic development, and a local environmental issue concerning development on Lake Maumelle, a primary water source for Pulaski County residents. In each of these, the tag line was preceded by a phrase relevant to the subject of the piece—"When it comes to economic development, Kathy Webb gets it done"; "Protecting our water supply, Kathy Webb gets it done"; "When it come to education, Kathy Webb gets it done."

The other four large pieces focused generally on Webb's qualifications based on awards won (Entrepreneur of the Year, Humanitarian of the Year) and her experience as a small-business owner. The smaller pieces focused on Webb's endorsements. One of these featured a quote from the endorsement she received from the *Arkansas Democrat Gazette*, the daily newspaper with the largest circulation in Arkansas. The other piece featured endorsements from citizens from different walks of life, including a retired Methodist bishop.

As stated earlier, one of the lessons learned at the Victory Fund training Webb and Lightle attended was "communicate a consistent message." Most research that has focused on consistency of message in political campaigns suggests voters perceive candidates as more favorable if their messages are consistent over time and among different forms of communication activities and interactions.[25] Webb's direct-mail campaign showed consistency of message from one piece to another as well as with statements she made to the press and during public appearances. Woven together these messages present a convincing narrative of a competent woman. Perhaps more significant, the message evident in each mail-out piece is internally consistent.

All the direct-mail pieces featured pictures of Webb interacting with people—at picnics, on people's porches, in her restaurant's kitchen, in her work clothes talking with employees. These *action* shots reinforced the theme that "Kathy Webb gets it done." Rather than the usual staid head shot of a candidate in his or her business suit or the conventional family portrait shots that are featured on most direct-mail pieces produced for localized races, these materials offered voters images of Webb that gave them reasons to believe she really *is* someone who can get things done. The message, then, is not merely consistent from one piece to another, it is *internally consistent* in its visual and verbal presentation of Webb as a woman of action. In fact, the inconsistency between the visual and written message in campaign materials that feature "action" words and "static" images may serve to undermine the written message, particularly when considering many people's tendency to at least glance at pictures featured on unsolicited mail they receive even if they do not take the time to read the words.

As stated earlier, women candidates tend to fare better in local races if they "run as women" stressing their concern for traditionally "feminine" issues (education, health care, children's welfare) as voters tend to perceive women in general as more competent than men in addressing these types of issues. The competent woman narrative evident in Webb's campaign clearly positioned her as a *traditional* woman running on *traditional* "feminine" issues. This reinforced not only her competency as a candidate but, perhaps more important, her competency *as a traditional woman*. The strategy also complicates the Exemplary Lesbian narrative. "Kathy being Kathy" involves living and telling both the Tale of the Exemplary Lesbian *and* the Account of the Competent Woman. These narratives, while powerful, are not necessarily complementary nor can they alone account for Webb's overwhelming success at the polls. In fact, they may be viewed as competing narratives given ingrained stereotypes of lesbians as anything but competent *traditional* women. However, the final narrative evident in Webb's campaign, the Story of Us Acting Together, not only bridges the Exemplary Lesbian and Competent Woman narratives, but it also invites voters to do more than contemplate Webb's individual story—it encourages them to participate in that story.

Putting the Voters in the Frame: The Story of Us Acting Together

As indicated earlier, in the visual images of Webb's direct-mail pieces she was not pictured alone—she is shown talking with a variety of people: women and men, young and older, people of color, and people of faith. As such, the pictures convey a message that traditional headshots or family portraits cannot: *they position the voter as active participant in Webb's world*. Traditional pictures of candidates smiling into the camera do not do that—in fact they place the voter outside the frame positioning the voter as spectators rather than participant. The pictures featured in Webb's direct-mail campaign invite the voter into the frame by offering images that correspond to ones present in nearly every family album.[26] This is a powerful rhetorical move that invites the voter to cross the boundary between her/himself and the candidate and to see similarities between the story lived by Webb and the story lived by the voter. This creates the possibility not only for Webb's story to ring true with the voter—it also creates an intersection or even a merger of those stories. In short, it renders Webb and the voter visible and active within the same frame—no longer separated by real or perceived differences.

Moreover, this narrative of Us Acting Together was reinforced when Webb actually met people at the doors to their homes when she walked through the district to ask people directly for their votes. Webb's family had lived in the district for more than forty years, so often when she walked the neighborhoods, she would encounter people who knew her family. She would hear comments like, "Oh! Yes we know you, your father [Webb's father is a retired Methodist minister] married us over forty years ago!" or "Your brother [who is retired from teaching history at a local university] convinced me to major in history," or "You're the 'Rice Depot' [the Arkansas Rice Depot is a local nonprofit for which Webb volunteers] lady, right?" People would then launch into stories about their connection with her family or organizations with which Webb was associated.

Webb also made connections with people by paying attention to her surroundings. She told a story of walking up to a young man's home and noticing an "Astros" bumper sticker on his car. She did her usual introduction of "Hi. I'm Kathy Webb and I'm running for state representative." She then followed with, "I'd appreciate your vote even if you are an Astros fan." This provided entrée for the man to ask her about her favorite team (the Cardinals) and to chat about baseball. In this way, Webb made a personal connection with a potential voter.

In fact, during the course of the campaign, Webb was able to make personal connections with many voters. Webb started walking the district February 1, 2006, and walked at least four hours a day every day, rain or shine, right up to the day of the primary, May 23, 2006. She managed to go through targeted areas twice, and she was the only candidate who went door-to-door to residences in downtown Little Rock. The campaign team devised a system to identify supporters, undecided voters, and those definitely voting for one of the other candidates. Webb would note on cards she carried as she walked whether people she talked to at a particular residence were "1s" (definitely supporting), "3s" (undecided), or "5s" (supporting another candidate) after she left. Residences identified as definitely supporting or undecided were marked for second visits.

As the election neared, the campaign team hired a firm to conduct a telephone poll of the people who had been identified as undecided from Webb's door-to-door contact and canvassing. This poll indicated that 70 percent of the people polled said they had decided to vote for Webb. Lightle recounted that at first she did not believe the poll could be accurate, but she realized if it were and those polled actually voted, Webb would win the primary without a run-off, which she eventually did. This seems a clear indication that the narrative of Us Working Together not only invited voters to share their own stories and to participate in Webb's story, it spurred them to act on that invitation. It also suggests the rhetorical power of the intersecting narratives that comprise the overarching theme of "Kathy being Kathy."

THE RHETORICAL POWER OF
WEBB'S INTERSECTING NARRATIVES

By openly acknowledging her sexual orientation while simultaneously focusing on traditionally "feminine" issues and inviting others to participate in the democratic process, Webb participated in the overarching "Kathy being Kathy" narrative that opened up the possibility of voters accepting the narrative rationality of a story that might not necessarily comport with their negative stereotypes of lesbians. As Fisher might state, the "Kathy being Kathy" narrative may be a new story that voters choose "to adopt to better account for their lives or the mystery of life itself."[27] It is a story that also adheres to the rhetorical norms of believable appearance and tolerance, in that the story suggests the sincerity of Webb's public actions based on public persona derived from public roles rather than private identity; moreover, by focusing on issues common among voters Webb is creating opportunities for coalitions to be formed among people with divergent perspectives.

In regard to public appearances, press meetings, and the direct-mail campaign, the combination of the acknowledgement of sexual orientation, the focus on competency both as a candidate and as a woman, and the positioning of the voter as an active participant provides an excellent example of how rhetorical norms of permeable boundaries, contextualized language, and activity may be met. The stories lived and told through Webb's door-to-door campaigning offer more evidence of how the narratives of Webb's life and the narratives of voters' lives intersected. The stories in these instances provided narrative rationality and good reasons to vote for Webb based on an ever-widening the circle of shared narratives bound by "matters of history, biography, culture, and character."[28] And it is in these quotidian exchanges between Webb and the people she met that the rhetorical norms of public discourse are most clearly met. In her walks through the various neighborhoods of the district, Webb crossed many boundaries, spoke in a language familiar to her interlocutors, invited others to be active, and appeared believable. In doing so, she invited others to practice tolerance, to listen to diverse voices, and to seek common ground on which to make prudent civic judgments.

Theorists who decry the state of American politics often link its decline to the pejorative impact of identity politics on public dialogue. In *Democracy on Trial*, Jean Bethke Elshtain claimed our public language has become overwhelmed by declarations predicated on narrow self-interests. These self-interests are largely derived from our allegiances to some group identity based on race, ethnicity, gender, sexual orientation, (dis)abilities, or other categories. She further evinced that this retribalization of the American public into "fixed identity groups" results in a politics of displacement "that dislodges the concerns of the citizen and public life in favor of politicizing all features of who and what we are."[29] Dialogue that might lead to transcendence of differences for a common good is silenced as a result. Attacking others' opinions is equated with attacking their identities; ideology usurps democracy and everybody loses.

By claiming her sexual orientation as part of her identity but not all of her identity, by centering her discourse on issues important to people in her district, and inviting voters to participate in her story, Kathy Webb participated in a discourse that was issue-based rather than identity-based. In doing so, she created a space for active democratic participation by a variety of people. Webb herself indicated that her favorite story from the campaign was a conversation she overheard between two elementary school girls. One girl said to the other, "Who are you for in the District 37 race?" The other girl replied, "Why Kathy Webb!" The first girl then answered, "Me, too!" Webb indicated she was surprised such young children would even know about the District 37 race much less know who might be running. But she was heartened that her entry into the race raised awareness and might engender civic participation and civil dialogue for years to come. As Jacqueline Taylor so eloquently noted:

> As exemplary lesbian I occupy a rare discursive space. . . . I take pleasure in speaking my truth, in telling a story often omitted, in putting my lesbian life on the record. In the telling, I learn more about who and what I am. In telling, I participate in a dream that if we all tell our stories to one another, if we can learn to listen to those stories with our hearts, we will learn to live with one another in a community of mutual respect. In the telling, I become part of something larger than myself.[30]

By telling her story through a series of intersecting narratives, Webb invited others to participate in that story and in doing so made history as the first openly gay person elected to office in Arkansas.

NOTES

1. While this represents significant strides for Arkansas women interested in public service through political office, it does not represent proportional parity as the most recent statistics available from the U.S. Census Bureau indicate 51 percent of Arkansas's 2.8 million residents are female.

2. Paul S. Herrnson, J. Celeste Lay, and Atiya Kai Stokes, "Women Running 'as Women': Candidate Gender, Campaign Issues, and Voter-Targeting Strategies," *The Journal of Politics* 65, no. 1 (February 2003): "In 1951, only 10 women held seats in the U.S. House of Representatives, one served on the U.S. Senate, 242 were in state legislatures, and there were no female governors. By 2001, these numbers increased to 59 in the House, 13 in the Senate, 1656 in state legislatures, and five governors. Albeit small proportionally, the number of women elected officials has grown as a result of several factors, including the strides women have made in education, in the workplace, and in other societal institutions" (244).

3. David Lublin and Sarah E. Brewer report that when women routinely run for and win election to "process-oriented" county level positions (e.g., county assessors and clerks). (Lublin and Brewer, "The Continuing Dominance of Traditional Gender Roles in Southern Elections," *Social Science Quarterly*, 84 (June 2003): 379–96.

4. Victory Fund is a non-profit organization that "provides strategic, technical, and financial support to openly LGBT candidates and their campaigns" (http://www.victoryfund.org/about_us).

5. Of these studies, many have relied on experimental designs rather than actual case studies (see Ewa A. Golebiowska, "Group Stereotypes and Political Evaluation," *American Political Research* 29, no. 6 (November 2001): 535–65; Rebekah Herrick and Sue Thomas, "Gays and Lesbians in Local Races: A Study of Electoral Viability," *The Journal of Homosexuality* 42, no. 1 (March 2002): 103–26).

6. Walter R. Fisher, "Narration as a Human Communication Paradigm: The Case of Public Moral Argument," *Communication Monographs* 51, no. 1 (March 1984):1–22; Gerard A. Hauser, *Vernacular Voices: The Rhetoric of Publics and Public Spheres* (Columbia: University of South Carolina Press, 1999).

7. Fisher, "Narration," 2.

8. Fisher, "Narration," 8.

9. Fisher, "Narration," 10.

10. Fisher, "Narration," 9.

11. Fisher, "Narration," 10.

12. Fisher, "Narration," 8.

13. Jürgen Habermas, *The Structural Transformation of the Public Sphere: An Inquiry into a Category of Bourgeois Society* (Cambridge, Mass.: Polity, 1989); Jürgen Habermas, "The Public Sphere: An Encyclopedia Article (1964), *New German Critique*, 3, (1974): 49–55.

14. Gerard A. Hauser, *Vernacular Voices*.

15. See, for example, Jean B. Elshtain, *Democracy on Trial.* (New York: Basic Books, 1995); Amy E. Grim, "Citizens Deliberate the 'Good Death': The Vernacular Rhetoric of Euthanasia" (Ph.D. dissertation, University of Colorado, 2005).

16. The account of the campaign that follows is based primarily on interviews with Webb; her campaign manager, Alice Lightle; and her primary political consultant, Debbie Willhite.

17. "Candidate & Campaign Training" (Gay & Lesbian Leadership Institute) http://www.glli.org/training/candidate_campaign (January 31, 2008).

18. Jacqueline Taylor, "On Being an Exemplary Lesbian: My Life as a Role Model," *Text and Performance Quarterly* 17, no. 1 (January 2000): 58–73.

19. Taylor, "On Being," 60.

20. Taylor, "On Being," 61 (emphasis in original).

21. Fred Kuhr, "First in Their Houses," *Advocate*, November 7, 2006, 37.

22. Herbert Simons, *Persuasion in Society* (Thousand Oaks, Calif.: Sage, 2001), 80.

23. "Full House Race in Little Rock," *Arkansas Times* [Little Rock], April 13, 2006, 2.

24. Herrnson, Lay, and Stokes, "Women Running 'as Women,'" 244. The reverse holds for male candidates who are generally perceived to be better at handling issues of law enforcement and crime.

25. Kathleen Hall Jamieson, *Everything You Think You Know about Politics . . . and Why You Are Wrong* (New York: Basic Books, 2000).

26. In fact, on one piece, the pictures are even rendered as "snapshots" that look as if they were lifted from a family album.

27. Fisher, "Narration."

28. Peter J. Frost, Larry F. Moore, Meryl Reis Louis, Craig C. Lundberg, and Joanne, Martin, *Reframing Organizational Culture* (Thousand Oaks, Calif.: Sage, 1991), 221.

29. Elshtain, *Democracy*, 36.

30. Lynn C. Miller, Jacqueline Taylor, and M. Heather Carver, *Voices Made Flesh* (Madison: University of Wisconsin Press, 2003), 210.

9

TRAVERSING THE WIFE-CANDIDATE DOUBLE BIND

Feminine Display in the Senate Campaign Films
of Hillary Clinton and Elizabeth Dole

Janis L. Edwards

The contemporary tensions over women's place in the political sphere are effectively illustrated by the dichotomies presented in cultural expectations for political leaders and political wives. Perceptions of ideal leadership are still significantly derived from perceived masculine traits such as dominance, strength, and hierarchical control.[1] These expectations are further manifested in our national political history,[2] and continue to influence public affairs, most particularly the institution of the presidency.[3] Conversely, the political wife best embodies her role as the inverse of masculinized qualities, displaying compliance, deference, softness, and cooperation. The ubiquitous newspaper images of Cindy McCain standing silently near her husband on the 2008 campaign trail[4] visually resembled the simultaneous presentation of news images of stoic political wives standing by as their errant husbands delivered apologias for corrupt or illicit activities. Supportive silence and embodied femininity is the preferred image of the political wife, initially the primary role women assumed in American politics.

Gender ideologies such as Republican motherhood, developed as strategies of political efficacy and social control, further shaped and defined the appropriate spheres of activity for the ultimate political spouse, the first lady.[5] The "zero-sum game" of political marriage[6] revolves around this gendered dichotomy, compromising agency for the wife of a political leader, who "risks making her husband appear weak should she appear to compromise his authority or decision making by acting too strongly publicly."[7]

The demands of political wifery bear heavily on women who, in addition to their established marital connections to campaign politics, seek public office themselves. In 2000 and 2002, two high-profile women successfully made the transition from political wife to political officeholder. Both Hillary Clinton and Elizabeth Dole presented campaign films as part of their initial, formal campaign messages in their successful bids for seats in the U.S. Senate, which, I contend, facilitated the transition by presenting a reassuring, gendered image component to their specific challenges. My argument begins with a summary of the constraints facing these women as political wives making a transition to elected leadership roles. I then consider the genre of the presidential campaign film and how its characteristics translate to the specific uses of biographical documentaries by Clinton and Dole. I argue that the uncommon use of campaign films by these women provided a multimodal (but largely visual) means by which to straddle the double binds that constrain the dichotomous perceptions of wifery and leadership through display of a feminized "social" political style. The films served to reassure voters of these political wives' traditional femininity and facilitate a rhetorical transition into new roles as elected political leaders, a transition that could not be effectively addressed in verbal form.

THE CHALLENGE OF A SYMBOLIC OFFICE

The position of first lady of the nation has no Constitutional grounding, no formal job definition, and no salary, but it has been inscribed in the national imaginary for centuries as adjunct to the image of the president and "the single most visible symbol of American womanhood."[8] The role is fraught with contradictions, however, that stem from political and cultural ambiguities about gender roles. Americans revere their first ladies, honoring them in history,[9] regarding them gently in national memory, electing them to the annual (since 1940) list of most-admired women, and consuming their photographs, stories, and recipes in periodicals. Although first ladies attain their position by being anchored to their husbands, public affection for first ladies regularly exceeds public esteem for the president, and the celebrity status of first ladies endures even when their husbands suffer death or disfavor. But Americans can also revile their first ladies when they seem to deviate from the ceremonial and familial expectations of the office, particularly if they are too outspoken.[10] A first lady who seems to act as a copresident invites swift criticism. While she may deflect criticism of her husband's administration through her charm and favor,[11] a first lady, in her public visibility and association with the president and the political center of the country, is also vulnerable to political critiques.

The first lady's position within her marriage exemplifies the "two-person career" that requires cooperative effort for the success of the husband's position.[12] In political campaigns, wives serve as adjuncts to the candidates, their images often displayed on political buttons and signs as though they were the candidates running for office. A wife also serves as a surrogate on the campaign trail and has been highlighted in recent nominating conventions as an important partner to the nominee and a significant component to the campaign. But once in office a wife is expected to avoid an appearance of meaningful, public political influence or activism. Research indicates that a number of first ladies have been active and influential in political affairs, not always behind closed doors.[13] As Robert P. Watson notes, "spousehood" was one of the earliest avenues of political influence available to women.[14] But tradition has prevailed in that a first lady is judged by her faithful performance of the ceremonial aspects of symbolic presidential performance, a performance linked more to personal display than to oratory. She can speak as a supporter of uncontroversial "feel-good" causes and act as an international good will ambassador[15] but, to avoid censure, her ceremonial visibility must be countered by instrumental silence.

The political ambiguities that militate against a vocal, activist first lady involvement in political and governmental affairs are mirrored by cultural ambiguities that accompany presentation of the first lady as an archetype of idealized womanhood and a representative of "cherished U.S. values."[16] These values resist change. As historian and author Kristie Miller has noted, "People expect the first ladies to be more traditional than they expect the women in their own lives to be."[17] Perhaps this apparent longing for tradition explains why, as recently as 1996 a *Washington Post* writer referred to the "three C's of first ladyhood as Chemistry, Caring, and Charm,"[18] aspects of personality that implicitly exclude public sphere competence. While segments of the American public celebrate "liberated" iterations of first lady performance, the tradition-bound conservatism of the first lady image, steeped in early American versions of middle-class propriety, contrasts with cultural tensions over women's evolving roles in contemporary society. As such, "first ladies become 'sites' for the symbolic notion of female identity."[19]

First ladies, in reality, are not as passive as traditional perceptions of the role might suggest. Anderson suggests that political wives possess agency through the enactment of *social style*, a proposed iteration of Hariman's concept of political style as a "coherent repertoire of rhetorical conventions depending on aesthetic reactions for political effect,"[20] and enacted "through rules for speech, interaction, and performance."[21]

Anderson proposes the following as constitutive of social style. (1) it is gendered feminine, and through the ceremonial presence, challenges the dominance of political masculinities. (2) It focuses on "decorum, minimization of speech, and attention to the body." (3) It "enacts political power while disguising its nature as political" in reaction to the double bind for first ladies that demands sublimation to sanctioned power sources. (4) It is "defined by the constraint of conforming to norms of femininity while, at the same time, developing a tacit ability to employ femininity in order to achieve political agency."[22] A spouse who exhibits social style is thus able to act or speak as she simultaneously exhibits conformance to the norms of the first lady role.[23]

Hillary and Elizabeth as Political Spouses

Enter Hillary Rodham Clinton in 1992. While not the first presidential spouse to have a university education and an independent career, Mrs. Clinton was the most professionally accomplished presidential spouse to enter the White House. Her husband touted her intelligence and capabilities as an added attraction to his administration's potential. Hillary Clinton was, and remains, a polarizing figure. While many voters embraced her, a significant number also saw her as "aggressive," "strident," and "power hungry," and gave her a high disapproval score as first lady. Hillary's professional qualifications and intelligence, and her initial active involvement in White House governmental affairs, mirrored mainstream cultural tensions about women's roles in society. Hillary recognized her image as a reflection of the social milieu. After she left the White House, she acknowledged, "We were living in an era in which some people still felt deep ambivalence about women in positions of public leadership and power. In this era of changing gender roles, I was America's Exhibit A."[24] As a symbol of the "new" American woman and her place in evolving gendered politics, Hillary commanded the attention of the media and scholars situated in a larger project reevaluating the position of the presidential first lady, a situation that remained energized by her subsequent political ambitions.

When Robert Dole challenged Bill Clinton for the presidency in 1996, the emergent interest in an evolving version of first ladies was heightened by the addition of Elizabeth Hanford Dole[25] to the campaign scene. Like Hillary, EHD was also a very accomplished political wife. Although best known by Americans in her spousal role, EHD had been a prominent professional in Washington politics for decades, serving as a cabinet officer in two presidential administrations and as head of the Red Cross. In her examination of the first lady role on the 1996 campaign trail Denise M. Bostorff[26] outlined the numerous media constructions of that campaign as a contest between the wives. Notably, the July 1, 1996, issue of *Time* featured a cover story that asked, "Who would be the better first lady?" highlighting the similarities and differences between the two women and repeating the widespread notion that they should hold a debate. While the media may have been entranced with the stories of the two women as individuals, their placement within political marriage was never eclipsed. One *Washington Post* writer summarized the candidate couples as two coordinated units.

> There is Bill Clinton, whose skin is pink and whose persona is soft. And there is Bob Dole, whose eyebrows and wit are as dark a thunderclouds. If Hillary hardens Bill, Elizabeth brightens Bob. There is a symmetry between the couples; in each pair, one plays the honeyed Southerner, while the other shows Midwestern reserve.[27]

In fact, the media cited numerous similarities between HRC and EHD, concentrated on the professional lives of the two women, and the implications of change for the first lady role. In their capacity as wives, EHD was generally assessed as more in keeping with the "supportive wife" image, perhaps because of her effectiveness at campaigning and a notable Republican convention performance.[28] However, like Hillary, Mrs. Dole eventually kept a low profile in the campaign so as not to exacerbate concerns that she would "outshine her husband."[29] The coverage of the first lady "candidates" reflected many of the accumulated findings about media bias directed toward women candidates, particularly the dominance of concern with appearance and personaliuty over policy issues. Media coverage of HRD and EHD in 1996 also differed in the level of neutrality accorded each woman, with Dole's coverage significantly more positive than Clinton's.[30] First lady was the only position HRC and EHD would simultaneously seek, although both women made subsequent unsuccessful bids for president (in 2008 and 2000, respectively) and successful bids for seats in the U.S. Senate. Their images as wives would combine with other exigencies to affect their Senate campaigns, Clinton's in 2000 and Dole's in 2002. The choice each candidate made to frame and project her image in a campaign film feature combines with the content of those films to suggest a recognition of the strategic need for a rhetorical transition from a subordinate "wife" image to that of a leader.

GENDER AND DISPLAY IN CAMPAIGN FILMS

As technologies developed in the nineteenth and early twentieth centuries that conveyed visual images, they were quickly adopted for political effect, beginning with the 1896 one-minute short *William McKinley at Home*. "Film was thus absorbed into the presidential spectacle, framed in an aesthetic of factuality"[31] prompted by the example of the photograph. The candidate biographical film became a "predictable and stable form of political documentary"[32] by the mid-twentieth century, specifically for presidential candidates.[33] As the presidential campaign film has evolved into a genre that replaces the rhetorical functions of the speech introducing the party's nominee at the convention[34] it has come to be seen as "a force in the campaign and a sign of its health."[35]

The obvious advantage to film as a medium for the construction of a candidate's image is its accommodation of multiple channels of rhetorical display. Display is a concept that reaches back to the classical roots of rhetorical theory and the manifestations of epideictic rhetoric, although it also functions as an ordinary term. Ludmilla Jordanova defines display as involving "commonplace associations about (1) how things look or appear, (2) exhibition or demonstration, and (3) showiness or ostentation.[36] As Lawrence J. Prelli observes, the idea of display may be invoked by verbal images, but it also has special resonance for texts that are visual or incorporate visual aspects in an attempt to constitute meaning. "Displays," notes Prelli, "are manifested rhetorically in the 'demonstration' of a scientific finding, of a political grievance, of a preferred identity."[37] Drawing from Perelman, Prelli argues that the situated audience is also important in the functions of rhetorical display, as singling out aspects of a presentation "draws the attention of the audience to them and thereby gives them a presence that prevents them from being neglected."[38] Campaign films, in their functions of display, incorporate critical processes in their making that serve to highlight desirable factors of a candidate's image and conceal others, a process Prelli labels "rhetorical selectivity."[39] This selectivity results in a message constructed verbally, visually, and aurally in campaign films through a combination of candidate representations and self-presentations, testimonials, narratives, symbols, music, and scenes of action or reflection, designed to evoke particular audience responses. As with all rhetorical expression, audiences bring their own valuing perspectives, which may or may not resonate with the constructions of image presented to them.[40]

Although the biographical campaign film is closely associated with presidential nominees, Edwards[41] notes that the use of film is increasing as a component of political convention stagecraft. Campaign films and their convention off-shoots relate to the observations of Parry-Giles and Parry-Giles on the general, pervasive "visuality of postmodern presidentialities," which seeks to satisfy "voters accustomed to a televisual diet of intimacy and personal display."[42] The use of the Internet as a generative tool for campaign messages offers candidates one way to reach out to voters visually, especially since 2004. But, when Hillary Clinton (in 2000) and Elizabeth Dole (in 2001) formally launched their Senate campaigns, their uses of the long-form biographical film to assist the moment were noteworthy for being atypical.

The Clinton and Dole Senate films were similar enough to presidential campaign films in form, function, and situational exigency that the parameters established by scholarship on presidential campaign films as a genre[43] constitute a fruitful starting point for analysis. As scholars have indicated,[44] the presidential campaign film is gendered in terms of the inscription of masculinity on the candidate's image. That biographical films are generally not a significant feature in the rhetorical armory of women's campaigns for office is noteworthy, since visual representations play a significant role in the social constructions of femininity and, by extension, the image of women in politics. The human urge to seek visual pleasure, or scopophila, is itself a gendered phenomenon, contributing as it has to the development of cinematic theories of gender relationships of power. Scopophilia is also sexualized in its objectification of women in particular. Visual presentations of female candidates are potentially more volatile than visual presentations of men, partly due to the prohibitions against sexualization of the body in politics that Manning and Short-Thompson discuss in their contribution to this volume[45] and to the defining capacity for stereotypes that are inherent in visual representation.

In another respect, the campaign film (or any other televisual format) transcends specific gender concerns in contemporary politics in its contribution to an epistomophiliac impulse, or "pleasure of knowing." As Parry-Giles and Parry-Giles explain,

> Because politics is so heavily mediated by technologies dependent upon visual cues and images for their impact, voters come to know and experience politics in profoundly visual ways. They expect to see their candidates in increasingly intimate contexts, and the visual evidence . . . validates their political knowledge and understanding.[46]

A candidate-centered film, produced by and for a campaign, provides an opportunity for a candidate to control his or her image, in contrast to representations provided by other media-originated images circulated in print and on television and the Internet, representations which may play on stereotypes or be unflattering to the candidate. The visibility of campaign films in early stage, televised campaign rituals is especially important in this respect.

In addition to the presidential campaign film's presentation of pseudo-personal knowledge within the parameters of scopohilia's impulse, specific characteristics emerge that typify the genre, regardless of varied exigencies that may bear on campaign messages. Morreale[47] has identified eight generic formal features of presidential campaign films: (1) They are structured around short vignettes which advance the candidate's character through such means as testimonials, archival film and photographs, and direct address—all signifiers for documentary objectivity and veracity; (2) they employ narration, with an anonymous yet omniscient off-camera narrator; (3) they offer testimonials from others about the candidate's character or experience, following a tradition of using surrogates on the campaign trail; (4) they use rhetorical depiction—"simple, mythic pictures, verbal or nonverbal, that embody common values and goals"[48]—as an inventional strategy to provide a familiar and symbolic connection between audiences and the candidate that creates a communal bonding; (5) stock (previously existing) images are used to provide connections between the candidate and historical events. Stock footage not only is cost-effective, it may also be seen as imbued with documentary authenticity; (6) original film or video footage shot for the campaign film purposes (or for other candidate televisual messages) allows for selected depictions of the candidate, testimonials, or other scenes that advance the desired displays; (7) they typically have some portions with background music that helps set the tone of the depictions and provide extra emotional displays; and (8) there is typically a lack of overt special effects such as animation, graphics, and superimpositions. Morreale notes that special effects are undesirable because they detract from the documentary aura of campaign films, an important criteria for presentation of the rhetorical content as factual and authentic.

In the course of constructing generic elements, presidential campaign films present mythic images,[49] images which may be archetypal, images of the candidate's persona as it relates to the party, or national images of the country and its people. Gender, as one of the most evident aspects of subjectivity, grounded in cultural ideals, may be included as a mythologizing element in campaign films,[50] visually manifested in ways subtle or obvious. Presidential campaign films commonly project gender markers such as clothing, activities (such as chopping wood or engaging in athletics), and implied relationships between the candidate and others (especially family members).

Presidential campaign films serve as a vital framework for analysis of the HRC and EHD campaign films because, according to Parry-Giles and Parry-Giles, gender is particularly relevant as a construct in these ritualized campaign rhetorical forms. The presidential campaign films they cite in their argument simultaneously employ a feminine style while "perpetuating masculinist conceptions of political leadership,"[51] suggesting the film stands as one site of negotiation of gender constraints and contradictions in campaigns. The dichotomies of gender, the simultaneity of feminine style and masculinist implications Parry-Giles and Parry-Giles describe as elements of presidential campaign films, are enabled by the multimodal form of the film medium, and the intervention of the camera, stylistic devices, and narrators. Direct address by the candidate cannot "show *and* tell" contradictions and contrast as effectively as mediated display that provides a collage of images, narrations, and testimonials.

A consideration of these aspects of presidential campaign films—their personalizing functions, their generic characteristics, and their mythologizing and gendering aspects—against the campaign films of HRC and EHD suggests that their films strategically highlight and affirm each woman's traditional femininity and embodiment of the "social" political style, stemming from her identity as a political wife, preparing the way (through a discrete, predominantly visual form) for advancement of a new (orally demonstrated) image as a political leader.

Hillary: The Film

Hillary Clinton's status as a sitting first lady complicated her Senate campaign and required a renovation to her wifely image aimed at voters who were inclined to see her as a fire-breathing dragon who had been overly ambitious in her political reach in the White House and her aspirations beyond.[52] She faced additional exigencies in her campaign, particularly the concern that she was a carpetbagger, whose residential ties to New York were calculated and tenuous. HRC combated this criticism with a series of "listening tours" throughout New York State in which she met with voters and formed her platform. Although her intentions were already obvious, HRC made her official announcement as the Democratic candidate for junior senator from New York on July 6, 2000, at a large public hall gathering on the campus of State University of New York in Purchase, New York. The announcement was preceded by speeches of endorsement and support from various New York State Democratic dignitaries, and directly preceded by the twenty-minute campaign film titled, simply, *Hillary*. The title signaled the personal tone of the film and had the added value of symbolically distancing HRC from association with the recently impeached president and the stigmas of the Clinton administration.

The opening scene of *Hillary* departs significantly from the standards of narration and testimonial exhibited in presidential campaign films. Rather than opening with an "authoritative male voice" and "esteemed leaders"[53] *Hillary* opens with a child's voice singing a simple ditty about hope over a picture of a lakeside setting. The child is identified as Kelly MacDonald, whose family met HRC on her listening tour, and who exhibits a clear fondness for the candidate-first lady. From there, the film segues easily into HRC's childhood, via photographs of Hillary as a tot, as Dorothy Rodham recounts stories about her daughter's early years. Of particular note is a story about Hillary's concern for the welfare of migrant workers and their families in a labor camp where the family extended charity. The anecdote evolves into Hillary's own reverie about her corresponding moment of awareness about class and income differences in America, fueled by her mother's difficult childhood experiences, as well. As HRC's life story continues into her accomplishments at Wellesley and as a young attorney working on the Watergate hearings, these accounts are continually woven into a theme of HRC's personal and professional interest in children's issues. As people such as famed pediatrician Berry Brazelton, New York State official Carl McCall, and Eileen Weiss and Nan Rich (with their connections to women's commissions and organizations) offer testimony about HRC's work on behalf of family and child policy and health concerns, emotive images of hospitalized children, and HRC's interaction with them, appear on the screen. Cora McHenry and Dr. Betty A. Lowe, important officials in Arkansas hospital and education programs, respectively, speak to HRC's centrality in programs designed to benefit children, such as the Home Interaction Program for Pre-School Youngsters. Although the theme is one that bestows competence on HRC—she gets results—her success is facilitated by her direct, personal involvement in the recipients' lives.

From Arkansas, the scene shifts to New York State, bypassing mention of HRC's years and position in the White House. Some citizens of Rome, New York, gather to speak of their impressions of HR, especially her likeability, her character, and her personable nature, although they also note that she "works hard" on issues. The personality of HRC is then put on display as HRC talks about her skills at making salads and omelettes, and friends laughingly share anecdotes about Hillary's familiar shortcoming (her poor eyesight, her embarrassingly loud laughter, and her inability to carry a tune) as well as her personal assets—a sense of humor and loyalty as a friend.

Another section follows in which HRC is shown in professional attire, meeting with people, as New York State officials and others speak admiringly of her ability to "electrify a room" and be an effective leader. Dorothy Rodham repeats a statement made early in the film, that Hillary could "play with the boys." A brief voice clip accompanies the image of her address at the 1995 UN World Conference on Women in Beijing. A more extensive section follows, returning to personal images of HRC, apparent home movies that include her daughter Chelsea as a young child. These images move to still photos taken in more recent White House years. Separately, and off-camera, HRC and her mother, Dorothy, speak glowingly of Chelsea and of each other, and the bonds between mother, child, and grandchild, as pictures of Chelsea or of Hillary and Chelsea play on the screen. The pictures include footage from an unofficial diplomatic trip to India as first lady. While this section is extensive, the film actually concludes with a transition from HRC delivering her commencement address at Wellesley in 1969 to her subsequent visit to Wellesley as first lady in 1994. Her black attire provides a visual transition to the live version of HRC, standing on stage in a black pantsuit, ready to deliver a hard-hitting speech outlining her platform for her U.S. Senate campaign.

Hillary: The Image

HRC's campaign film contrasted with her speech in substance and tone, and also with her rhetorical style. Although Bostdorff notes that Hillary "emphasized female traits almost entirely" as first lady on the 1996 campaign trail[54] and she had softened her image following the failure of the health care initiative,[55] the HRC pre-2008 speaking style was not famous for its feminized characteristics, nor was the woman herself.[56] As Campbell has observed, HRC's speaking style "typically omits all of the discursive markers by which women publicly enact their femininity. Her tone is usually impersonal . . . her ideas unfold deductively . . . all kinds of evidence is used." [57] The contrast between the Hillary presented in the film and the self-presentation of Hillary in her announcement speech is notable and suggests the duality of first lady and leadership expectations.

The film, as might be expected, follows some of the conventions of presidential campaign films (it is a biographical candidate message connected to a campaign, after all). The film employs short vignettes, narration, testimonials, and lacks special effects. It acts to personalize the candidate, both in its overall structure, which centers on explaining and defining HRC, and in many of its content features which focus on Hillary the *person* who laughs at little too loudly and "makes a mean tossed salad." In fact, the film promotes a special sense of intimacy between viewer and candidate at those moments when Hillary addresses the camera to further the film's purpose (as opposed to news footage of her activities) or testimonials address her human qualities (as opposed to her policy stances and political competence). In other words, the film invites us to share the candidate's domestic life, in terms familiar to her closest friends, her mother, and her experiences with her daughter.[58] The use of stock images that refer to American politics and history is virtually absent in *Hillary*. Instead, the bank of images the filmmakers incorporate seem to derive almost exclusively from personal family archives: here is Hillary on a tricycle, here she is with her young siblings, here she is at her college commencement, clowning with fellow Watergate hearing junior staff, interacting with her tiny daughter, here is her daughter at a dance recital.

The "mythology" forefronted in these and other images is not one that speaks of the Great Leader or national mythologies, but of gender. While the film does offer some glimpses of Hillary's interest and effectiveness where policy issues are concerned, they are woven into a narrative about Hillary the woman, friend, mother—not so much the wife—who embodies the virtues of an American first lady as exemplar of femininity. She is portrayed as warm, gracious, loving, and mothering, humanized by the recollection of her political passions as rooted in childhood experiences and her adult relationships with women, rather than through her political associations with her husband.

As such, HRC's image in her campaign film adheres more to Anderson's proposal of "social style" than to the assertive "fighter" image of HRC's announcement speech.

The candidate is repeatedly gendered feminine in the film, with photographic and verbal references to her relationships (especially with other women), a concentration on her role as a mother, and an almost ubiquitous association with the color pink. The only serious references to her activities as first lady include her speech on women's rights in Beijing and an international trip shared with her daughter. Both of these are consistent with the legitimized ceremonial performances of the first lady role. Perhaps most notably, in terms of the display social style, the film "enacts political power while disguising its nature as political." The film rarely, and even tentatively, moves to political subjects. It repeatedly returns to a more personal and domestic version of Hillary Clinton, even as it all but bypasses her years in the White House. The film is clearly produced for a political purpose, but the political agency and intent of the Clinton candidacy is outlined by the speech that follows the film, not the film itself.

The film asks viewers to *like* Hillary and to understand what motivates her to serve. But the service, and the motivations, are vague in terms of her ambitions to represent New York in the U.S. Senate, whereas her speech lays out a specific agenda. HRC's statewide listening tour of New York is evident in the film as a reaction to the candidate's personality and personableness, marked, most significantly, by a young child's affection and admiration.

Elizabeth Dole: The Film

Elizabeth Dole had scheduled her formal announcement for the Senate for September 11, 2001, but the more momentous events of the day intervened. Perhaps as a result, the Dole film was not shown nationally. It is also different than the Clinton film in other respects. It is shorter, at seven minutes, and clearly addresses one of the significant exigencies of the Dole campaign, her ties to North Carolina. While Hillary Clinton's ties to New York were ephemeral, the carpetbagging issue was not evident in her film. EHD, on the other hand, had been born and raised in North Carolina but had not lived there for more than forty years and had to move her official address from Washington, D.C., to her mother's home in Salisbury in order to qualify as a candidate. While the issue was moot, as suggested by EHD's dismissals of any comparison with Hillary's situation during interviews, one of the campaign film's chief functions was to tie EHD definitively to Salisbury, North Carolina. In spite of this focus, the film also presents EHD in a highly gendered manner, perhaps to counter any perceived public resistance to electing a woman to succeed Jesse Helms in the Senate.

The film opens with a male narrator who recites descriptive terms associated with Elizabeth Dole: trailblazing success, work ethic, warm and loving marriage, work for five presidents, "literally" saving thousands of lives, wanting to tuck everyone she meets under her wind. As the announcer extols these virtues, the words "trailblazing, driven, caring, smart, loving, gentility" rendered in script and reproduced in various sized fonts float across the screen below soft-focus, sepia-toned, close-up images of a smiling yet contemplative Dole. The effect might be likened to a Hallmark greeting card. The narrator goes on to locate EHD's achievements and sensibilities in her home town of Salisbury.

Others take up the task of describing Elizabeth Hanford for the camera, including Salisbury citizens, a former mayor, and Dole's centenarian mother. The scene of Dole's mother in her (presumably) living room, with its golden wash of soft-focus light, abundant flowers, and framed family photographs sets a visual theme for the film. Salisbury and EHD are blended together nostalgically as viewers embark on a journey of town locations significant to Elizabeth. Not all of the locations are historically valid; staged, hazy footage of a young woman running and skipping toward a gothic-style building, schoolbooks in hand, represents Elizabeth's high school years, although the more recently built local school is first shown on camera. The scene of the very modern Salisbury Red Cross office is also an anachronism, but EHD's portrait hangs there, as if to equate professional accomplishment with community rootedness.

From there the film breezes quickly through EHD's college and early professional years, illustrated briefly through the narrative continuity device of the framed photographs, and including the "work for five presidents" cited in the introduction, until we arrive at her marriage to Bob Dole. Separately, Bob and Elizabeth Dole give an on-camera account of their meeting and courtship. The Dole marriage is described as "the ultimate partnership" and "one of the world's warmest, most mutually caring marriages."

Specially filmed scenes of the Doles show them bathed in warm, hazy light, evidently sitting and walking on the streets of Salisbury, interspersed with scenes where Bob speaks of his wife's qualities and a few of her accomplishments, as the visual scenes reinforce EHD's own statement, "This is my home." Another testimonial from a community official notes Dole's work on seat belt laws as Transportation Secretary, while brief, vague citizen testimonials follow, most of them reinforcing the message of EHD's roots in North Carolina. Again, scenes from the town are played across the screen as the narrator remarks, "She was born in Salisbury to try and help make the world a better place." The closing scene appears, a picture of the North Carolina flag, washed (as much of the film was) in hazy filters, and the narrator's final laudatory remarks on the candidate, backed by an angelic female chorus.

Elizabeth Dole: The Image

Elizabeth Dole's senate campaign film is clearly designed to contradict any view of Dole as an opportunistic interloper or crafty political protege. Despite her chronological and geographical distance from North Carolina, EHD is represented as part and parcel to Salisbury itself, intertwined with the community's past and present, even functioning as a leader among her peers in her school years. EHD's long identification with her southern roots, including retention of an accent, assist in development of the image connecting the candidate with North Carolina.[59] The visual references to the town are frequently deployed during verbal references to Elizabeth; her marriage, with its actual ties to Kansas and Washington, D.C., is visually rooted in Salisbury. While a few pictorial choices emphasize EHD's political policy work, the camera only dwells on her Red Cross leadership. The combination of photos with Princess Diana and with the children of other countries and the verbal explanation of Dole's work emphasize the Red Cross as an example of a caring profession. The camera techniques of focus, lighting, and superscript create a feminized, genteel image associated more with first ladies (although Dole never was one) than senatorial leaders. Just as Margaret Chase Smith employed a large rose as her Senate emblem, the implication is that Mrs. Dole would not be a "pretend man" in the Senate, following from Dole's cultivated feminine image in 1996.[60] The possible inference of contrast between Mrs. Dole and Senator Clinton may be drawn here, as extensions of their relative public personae and their described "obsession" with each other during the 1996 presidential campaign.[61]

Like the Hillary Clinton campaign film, Dole's routinely adopts some of the conventions of the presidential campaign film, with its inclusion of short vignettes, brief testimonials, and narration. Dole's film, like Clinton's, is absent the nationally drawn, mythical depictions common to presidential campaign films. Instead, Salisbury is represented as a mythic place, in its scenic presence and awash in soft focus presentation. This mythic presentation of Salisbury is keyed by the film's evident theme and purpose—to associate Elizabeth Dole with North Carolina. But because EHD is equated with Salisbury, the content features present EHD as a mythologized figure. The implied influence of EHD on her home town is one element that drives this mythic view, but, as in the Clinton film, gender is also a key mythic construct. Unusually "feminized" portraits of EHD introduce the film, backed by music that enhances the experience of reflection and recollection that pervades the film. EHD's leadership is mentioned but often downplayed in favor of a more homespun version of prominence, portrayed within her childhood and adolescent associations and, most significantly, within her marriage. This aspects is accentuated by the hyperbolic description of her marriage as unique in its warmth, caring, and partnership. While the film does not address EHD's relationship with her stepdaughter, the presence and testimony of her mother echoes similar accentuations in HRC's fim. The warm and hazy camera focus not only underscores the nostalgic motif but also feminizes through its suggested warmth and softness.

The film also is consistent with the "social" style adopted by first ladies,[62] in that there is a minimization of speech, the candidate is "embodied" in the physical presence and memory of Salisbury, and the narrative is feminized by its use of domestic picture frames almost exclusively to project EHD's professional experience, bathing them in the same nostalgic references to her childhood and marriage. Even the testimonies offered about her work in the Red Cross and on the seat belt issue are offered by women. Again, despite the film's development as a political message, EHD's political power and experience is subsumed within the film by the personal narrative of her roots and her marriage.

TRANSITIONING THE DOUBLE BIND

In making a transition in public perception between the role of wife and the role of (successful) candidate, Hillary Clinton and Elizabeth Dole faced limited options. To ignore the dynamics that necessitate an image transition would be to disregard the potent contrasts between meeting expectations as a wife and as a candidate. Both women were clearly aware of these issues, HRC by seeking to soften her strident image in the media during the first Clinton administration, EHD through the celebratory response to her appearances in 1996 on behalf of her husband. Indeed, EHD's failure to alter her highly feminized campaign style for her first bid as a (presidential) candidate in 2000 has been criticized as a contributing factor to her failure to gain visibility in that race. On the other hand, if EHD were to emerge as a candidate who exhibited the required "toughness" to succeed could be jarring compared to her existing wifely *public* persona, resulting in cognitive dissonance, even for voters who were unaccustomed to seeing a woman as a representative of their state. Hillary's situation was somewhat different, in that her *public* toughness sometimes operated as a detriment among voters who saw in her an inadequate embodiment of the first lady role she already held.

It is revealing that both women should choose to present televisual messages in presenting their campaigns, although HRC's was more widely disseminated than Dole's. Other senatorial candidates are not known for using the film medium as an important instrument of rhetorical selectivity. Even more noteworthy is the relative absence of policy stands in these films, and the concentration on a feminized persona for each candidate. The threads of national myth and institutional authority woven throughout presidential campaign films are absent here. Although Dole's film mythologizes place, the selected place is her "home town" of Salisbury. Rather each film my-thologizes gender, positioning each subject as an appropriate (in traditional terms) embodiment of womanly being, in terms of motives—service to children's needs for HRC, service to hearth, home, and community for EHD—and in terms of relationships—motherhood and friendship for HRC, marriage for EHD. While both films offer some testimony and his-tory that speak to the capabilities of the candidates, the films present dis-plays that heighten their performance of traditional, wifely gender expecta-tions, in contrast to their subsequent performances of leadership.

Although the Dole film is clearly invested in addressing a critical exi-gency of her campaign, the nature of her connections to North Carolina, Clinton's film disregards similiar exigencies in her campaign. What these films do share is an attempt at feminine display, employing aspects of the "social style" of leadership, proposed by Anderson as an element of first lady agency, to provide a reassuring portrait of two political wives *as* wives, in preparation of a transition over the double bind between a domestically inscribed role and a public-sphere role in politics. Whereas Parry-Giles and Parry-Giles have argued that presidential campaign films expose the under-pinnings of hegemonic masculinity in presidential politics, in the cases of HRC and EHD, campaign films functioned to liberate these women from the constraints of their wifely personas and launch them into leadership roles, still arguably masculinized but not male defined. Although these two films, and these two campaigns, may be unique in their required transi-tions from wife to candidate, these observations suggest the importance of visuality in a first lady or women candidate's attempts to control her image. Women's visual display as objects of the male gaze has been a point of criti-cism about media representations of political women. The efficacy of these films in HRC's and EHD's successful bids for high office suggests visual display may also be an effective tool for image management for women in negotiating the double binds of their gendered status.

NOTES

1. Marcia Lynn Whitaker and Hedy Leonie Isaacs, "Gendering the Political Executive's Space: The Changing Landscape?" in *Women in Politics: Outsiders or Insiders?* 4th ed. Lois Duke Whitaker, ed. (Upper Saddle River, N.J.: Pearson/ Prentice Hall), 201–9.

2. Mark E. Kann, *The Gendering of American Politics: Founding Mothers, Founding Fathers, and Political Patriarchy* (Westport, Conn.: Praeger, 1999).

3. Karin Wahl-Jorgensen, "Constructed Masculinities in U.S. Presidential Campaigns: The Case of 1992," in *Gender, Politics, and Communication*, Annabelle Sreberny and Liesbet van Zoonen, eds. (Cresskill, N.J.: Hampton Press Inc, 1996), 57.

4. Although Cindy McCain did some speaking on the campaign trail she did not campaign independently, as Michelle Obama did.

5. Shawn Parry-Giles and Diane M. Blair. "The Rise of the Rhetorical First Lady: Politics, Gender Ideology, and Women's Voice, 1789–2002," *Rhetoric and Public Affairs* 5 (2002), 565–600.

6. See Muir and Taylor's chapter in this volume for a further explication of the zero-sum idea in gendered politics outlined by Kathleen Hall Jamieson in *Beyond the Double Bind: Women and Leadership* (New York: Oxford University Press, 1995).

7. Ashley Quesinberry Stokes, "First Ladies in Waiting: The Fight for Rhetorical Legitimacy on the 2004 Campaign Trail," in *The 2004 Presidential Campaign: A Communication Perspective*, ed. Robert E. Denton Jr. (Lanham, Md.: Roman & Littlefield, 2005), 173.

8. Maureen H. Beasley, *First Ladies and the Press* (Evanston, Ill.: Northwestern University Press, 2005), xix.

9. First lady portraits and inaugural ball gowns are museum staples. Honorary and uncritical historical biographies are plentiful.

10. Janis L. Edwards and Huey Rong Chen, "The First Lady/First Wife in Editorial Cartoons: Rhetorical Visions Through Gendered Lenses," *Women's Studies in Communication* 23, no. 4 (Fall 2000) 367-391 for a discussion of public "disciplining" of outspoken first ladies.

11. Karlyn Kohrs Campbell, "The Rhetorical Presidency: A Two-Person Career," in *Beyond the Rhetorical Presidency*, ed. Martin J. Medhurst. (College Station, Texas A & M University Press, 1996), 181.

12. Campbell, "The Rhetorical Presidency," 180.

13. For a summary work on first ladies and their varied roles, see Robert P. Watson, *The Presidents' Wives: Reassessing the Office of First Lady* (Boulder, Colo.: Lynne Reinner Publishers, 2000). For additional discussions of first ladies and the policy realm, see Robert P. Watson and Anthony J. Eksterowicz, eds, *The Presidential Companion: Readings in First Ladies* (Columbia: University of South Carolina Press, 2003).

14. "First Ladies and Their Influence on Politics, Policy, and the Presidency," in *Women in Politics: Outsiders or Insiders?* 4th ed, ed. Lois Duke Whitaker (Upper Saddle River, N.J.: Pearson/Prentice Hall, 2006), 210–25.

15. Charles Tien, Regan Checchio, and Arthur H. Miller, "The Impact of First Wives on Presidential Campaigns and Elections," in *Women in Politics: Outsiders or Insiders?* 3rd, ed. Lois Duke Whitaker (Upper Saddle River, N.J.: Prentice Hall, 1999) 149–68.

16. Karlyn Kohrs Campbell, "The Rhetorical Presidency." 188.

17. Quoted in Darlene Summerville, "First Lady Takes Time Defining Her Role," *Tuscaloosa News*, February 2, 2009, 8A.

18. Laura Blumenfeld, "And One of Them Shall Be First," *Washington Post Weekly Edition*, April 8–14, 1996: 6.

19. Karrin Vasby Anderson, "The First Lady: A Site of 'American Womanhood,'" in *Inventing a Voice: The Rhetoric of American First Ladies of the Twentieth Century*, ed. Molly Meijer Wertheimer (Lanham, Md.: Rowman & Littlefield, 2004) 17–30.

20. Robert Hariman, *Political Style: The Artistry of Power* (Chicago: University of Chicago Press, 1995).

21. Karrin Vasby Anderson, "The First Lady: A Site of 'American Womanhood,'" 23.

22. Anderson, "The First Lady" A Site of 'American Womanhood,'" 25.

23. These are among the reported descriptors catalogued in Lisa M. Burns, *First Ladies and the Fourth Estate: Press Framing of Presidential Wives* (DeKalb, Ill.: Northern Illinois University Press, 2008), 140–41.

24. *Living History* (New York: Simon & Schuster, 2003), 124.

25. For the sake of clarity and simplicity I will refer to Elizabeth Dole as EHD and Hillary Clinton as HRC in the remainder of this essay.

26. "Hillary Rodham Clinton and Elizabeth Doles as Running 'Mates' in the 1996 Campaign: Parallels in the Rhetorical Constraints of First Ladies and Vice Presidents," in *The 1996 Presidential Campaign: A Communication Perspective*. ed. Robert E. Denton Jr. (Westport, Conn.: Praeger, 1998), 199–227.

27. Laura Blumenfeld. "And One of Them Shall be First," 7.

28. Karrin Vasby Anderson offers an analysis of the highly gendered aspects of Dole's convention speech in "From Spouses to Candidates: Hillary Rodham Clinton, Elizabeth Dole, and the Gendered Office of U.S. President" *Rhetoric and Public Affairs* 5, no. 1 (Spring 2002), 105–32.

29. Denise M. Bostdorff, "Running Mates," 210.

30. Dianne G. Bystrom, Laurie M. McKinnon, and C. K. Chaney, "The First Lady and the First Estate:Media Coverage of Hillary Clinton and Elizabeth Dole in the 1996 Presidential Campaign," in *The Electronic Election: Perspectives on the 1996 Campaign Communication*, eds. Lynda Lee Kaid and Dianne G. Bystrom (Mahwah, N.J.: Lawrence Erlbaum, 1999), 81–95.

31. Thomas W. Benson and Brian J. Snee, "New Political Documentary: Rhetoric, Propaganda, and the Civic Prospect," in *The Rhetoric of the New Political Documentary*, eds. Thomas W. Benson and Brian J. Snee (Carbondale, Ill.: Southern Illinois University Press, 2008), 3

32. Benson and Snee, "New Political Documentary," 8.

33. In an earlier effort, this author found examples of long format campaign films other than those produced on behalf of presidential nominees practically nonexistent, particularly for women candidates.

34. J. Cherie Strachan and Kathleen E. Kendall, "Political Candidates' Convention Films: Finding the Perfect Image—An Overview of Political Image Making," in *Defining Visual Rhetorics*, eds. Charles A. Hill and Marguerite Helmers (Mahwah, N.J.: Lawrence Erlbaum Associates, 2004.)

35. Thomas W. Benson and Brian J. Snee, "New Political Documentary," 9.

36. "Medicine and Genres of Display," in *Visual Display: Culture Beyond Appearances*, eds. Lynne Cooke and Peter Wollen (NY: Free Press, 1995), 216.

37. Lawrence J. Prelli, "Rhetorics of Display: An Introduction," in *Rhetorics of Display*, ed. Lawrence J. Prelli (Columbia: University of South Carolina Press, 2006), 1.

38. Chaim Perelman, "Choice, Presence, and Presentation," in *The Realm of Rhetoric* (Notre Dame, Ind.: University of Notre Dame Press, 1982), 35; q. in Prelli, "Rhetorics of Display," 7.

39. Lawrence J. Prelli, "Rhetorics of Display," 12.

40. Although campaign films may be treated as examples of candidate rhetoric, I do not mean to suggest their construction is not the collective result of interventions by the films' creative team and the candidate's political advisors.

41. "Presidential Campaign Films in a Televisual Convention Environment: The Example of 2004," *The 2004 Presidential Campaign: A Communication Perspective*, ed. Robert E. Denton, Jr. (Lanham, Md.: Rowman & Littlefield, 2005), 75–92.

42. Shawn J. Parry-Giles and Trevor Parry-Giles, *Constructing Clinton: Hyperreality & Presidential Image-Making in Postmodern Politics* (New York: Peter Lang, 2002), 28.

43. Joanne Morreale argues for a generic view of presidential campaign films in *The Presidential Campaign Film: A Critical History* (Westport, Conn.: Praeger, 1996), an assumption that infuses subsequent research.

44. See, for example, Shawn J. Parry-Giles and Trevor Parry-Giles, "Gendered Politics and Presidential Image Construction: A Reassessment of the 'Feminine Style,'" *Communication Monographs* 63, no. 1 (December 1996), 337–53; and Janis L. Edwards and Stacey Smith, "Mythic Images in Campaign 2000 Presidential Bio-Films," in *The Millenium Election*, eds. Lynda Lee Kaid, John C. Tedesco, Dianne Bystrom, and Mitchell S. McKinney (Lanham, Md.: Rowman & Littlefield, 2003).

45. Jimmie Manning and Cady Short-Thompson, "Gendered Bodies: Considering the Sexual in Political Communication," in *Gender and Political Communication in America: Rhetoric, Representation, and Display*, ed. Janis L. Edwards (Lanham, Md.: Lexington, 2009).

46. Shawn J. Parry-Giles and Trevor Parry-Giles, *Constructing Clinton*, 28.

47. Joanne Morreale, *The Presidential Campaign Film*.

48. Morreale, *The Presidential Campaign Film*, 17

49. Morreale, *The Presidential Campaign Film*, 14–21.

50. Edwards and Smith, for example, in "Mythic Images" argue that depictions of masculinity in campaign films signal transitions in the prevailing archetypes of the mythic leader or common man.

51. Shawn J. Parry-Giles and Trevor Parry-Giles, "Gendered Politics."

52. The judgment that Hillary's ambitions were excessive and inappropriate was a regular formulation in political discourse. Editorial cartoons were especially vivid in this regard, according to Edwards and Chen, "The First Lady/First Wife in Editorial Cartoons." Political cartoonists regularly reviled Hillary for trying to assert her dominion over Bill, inserting herself into the swearing-in ceremony and, once in the White House, displacing her husband the *real* president. The image construction contradicted Bill Clinton's espoused pride in his wife's potential partnership in the administration.

53. Joanne Morreale, 16–17.

54. Denise Bostdorff, "Hillary Rodham Clinton and Elizabeth Dole as Running 'Mates,'" 214.

55. HRC's "softened" image makeovers in the White House years were regularly acknowledged in the media. See, for example, Lloyd Grove, "The Woman with a Ticket to Ride. Hillary Clinton's New Image: Fresh From the Oven," *Washington Post*, July 16, 1992: C1; and Marian Burros, "Hillary Clinton Asks Help in Finding a Softer Image," *New York Times*, January 10, 1995: A1.

56. Among a number of statements about HRC's professional manner, a former secretary is alleged to have stated, "there wasn't one stereotypically womanly or feminine thing about her." In Karlyn Kohrs Campbell, "The Discursive Performance of Femininity: Hating Hillary," *Rhetoric & Public Affairs* 1, no. 1 (Spring 1998): 12.

57. Karlyn Kohrs Campbell, "The Discursive Performance of Femininity," 6.

58. Admittedly, family relationships are a part of any number of presidential campaign films, although Parry-Giles and Parry-Giles, in "Gendered Politics," position these accounts as evidence of a patriarchal component of hegemonic masculinity.

59. The evocation of "southerness" in Dole's rhetoric is described by Nichola Gutgold in "Just Like 'Azaleas in the Spring': Elizabeth Dole as Daughter of the South," in *Telling Political Lives*, eds. Brenda DeVore Marshall and Molly A. Mayhead (Lanham, Md.: Lexington Books, 2008), 95–107.

60. Karrin Vasby Anderson, "From Spouses to Candidates," 121.

61. Nancy Gibbs and Michael Duffy, "Just Heartbeats Away," *TIME*, July 1, 1996, 25.

According to Gibbs and Duffy in their *TIME* article, the public perceptions of Hillary Clinton and Elizabeth Dole are a reversal of the insider assessment. Where Hillary is seen publicly by many as cold, even as a "dragon lady," she is described by associates as "the velvet fist in an iron glove . . . wonderful to work for, and devoted to her aides," while the southern charm of Elizabeth is described as the iron fist in the velvet glove, more stern with aides, and "working on her third press secretary in six months" (28).

62. Karrin Vasby Anderson, "The First Lady, A Site of 'American Womanhood.'"

10

POLITICAL SYMBOLISM IN *CHISHOLM '72:* UNBOUGHT & UNBOSSED

Teresa Bergman

Shirley Chisholm's 1972 presidential bid is rarely referenced in the U.S. mainstream media. Chisholm was the first black woman to run for the U.S. presidency, and the first woman to mount a meaningful presidential campaign in the twentieth century,[1] but her groundbreaking campaign is mostly lost in the U.S. collective memory. The 2004 documentary *Chisholm '72: Unbought & Unbossed* attempts to recuperate the significance of her campaign and remind U.S. audiences of her historic position in U.S. presidential contests. This film is particularly instructive in terms of highlighting how Chisholm's race and gender became the two main fractures in her campaign. Unlike the 2008 Democratic presidential primary where these fissures were highlighted separately via the candidacies of Barack Obama and Hillary Clinton, Chisholm's 1972 campaign embodied both. The debates surrounding Chisholm's national bid for the presidency illuminate an early foray into the ways in which gender and race function as political symbols in a national electoral campaign.

The study of political symbols concerning women and African Americans provides an hermeneutic for understanding their persuasive power and repeated use. These identities are set in contrast to the prevailing white male political tradition, inviting observation of the symbolic uses of identities. Political communication scholar Virginia Sapiro observes that women "are interpreted through a narrow set of culturally embedded symbols."[2] Political science professor Joel Olson observes that "races are political categories.

They are produced by power; they do not exist prior to it."[3] The challenges for scholars and the public alike are to translate the power behind racial political categories and the narrowness of female symbols in the political realm in order to recognize their regressive role in political communication. The documentary film *Chisholm '72: Unbought & Unbossed* employs symbols of race and gender to recuperate Chisholm's legacy, yet one result of their usage is that these symbols also rhetorically limit and diminish a contemporary audience's understanding of Shirley Chisholm. Her legacy as a community activist, a member of Congress and a vocal advocate of progressive causes is lost and is replaced by race and gender symbols. Although the film ultimately limits its depiction of Chisholm's candidacy to her race and gender, the documentary is instructive in the ways in which mediated representations of race and gender continue to rely on dated symbolic stereotypes even for "serious" candidates.

Communication scholars interested in collective memory and photography point to the pivotal role visual images play in not only contributing to the production of collective memory but also to infusing memories with an ideological point of view.[4] Roland Barthes, a prominent critic on the ideological functions of photography and film, defines photographic images as "constituted either by a universal symbolic order or by a period rhetoric, in short by a stock of stereotypes."[5] Rhetorician Michael Calvin McGee cogently observes how "ideology in practice is a political language, preserved in rhetorical documents, with the capacity to dictate decision and control public belief and behavior."[6] In order to understand how the visual political symbols used in this film invoke stereotypes of women and African Americans, I begin with an analysis of how this documentary formulates its rhetorical position. This is followed by an analysis of the film's symbolic political imagery focusing primarily on its representations of the women's movement, the black power movement, and the 1972 Democratic Convention. I conclude with a discussion of the implications of using of these sounds and images in the contemporary political climate as more women and people of color enter U.S. electoral politics.

CHISHOLM '72: UNBOUGHT & UNBOSSED

The 2004 documentary film *Chisholm '72: Unbought & Unbossed* is seventy-seven minutes long and the director is Shola Lynch.[7] This independent documentary production screened at the 2004 Sundance Film Festival and was broadcast nationally as part of the public television series P.O.V.

The film is structured as a conventional narrative documentary film using an expository format to develop its points. An expository format in a documentary film functions primarily to advance a rhetorical position where the film "assembles fragments of the historical world into a more rhetorical or argumentative frame than an aesthetic or poetic one."[8] Although this film does not use a narrator, which is one of the characteristics of an expository documentary, the film does use "voices that propose a perspective, advance an argument or recount history."[9]

One of the first voices heard in the film is that of Shirley Chisholm stating, "I am not a candidate of Black America, although I am black and proud. I am not a candidate of the Women's Movement although I am a woman and equally proud of that. I am a candidate of the people of America."[10] Structurally reinforcing the position is the last scene of the film, in which an older Shirley Chisholm (she died on January 1, 2005) looks into the camera and declares how she would like to be remembered: "I don't want to be remembered as the first Black woman who went to Congress and I don't want to be remembered as the first woman who happened to be black to make a bid for the presidency. I want to be remembered as a woman who fought for change in the twentieth century. That's what I want." Despite her clearly stated desire, this documentary offers little information concerning the nature of change for which she stood, except to define her candidacy as the first black woman to run for the U.S. presidency; this is exactly how she did not want to be remembered. The film's director, Shola Lynch, focuses on Chisholm's "viable political strategy"[11] instead of the issues that gave rise to Chisholm's candidacy, which results in an extremely limited depiction of Shirley Chisholm and her presidential bid.

The Sensory Synecdoche

There are several reasons why Chisholm's race and gender overshadow her legislative achievements and political stances. One reason is the film's liberal use of visual and audio symbols as shorthand for her political views. The documentary film tradition has long relied on metaphors in order to communicate larger themes[12]; however, this documentary relies so heavily on short visual and audio clips to define historical movements that they function as a sensory synecdoche. In rhetoric, a synecdoche is the use of a single example or small part to stand in for the whole. I am using the term "sensory synecdoche" in this context in order to examine this film's use of distinctive images and sounds to represent or serve as a substitute for complicated historical events. A sensory synecdoche functions similarly to a sound bite where a sentence or even phrase from a political candidate or public personality's longer speech is used over and over as a defining moment. William Safire defines a sound bite as a piece "that catches the rhetorical highlight of a speech, a quotation that is bright, snappy and memorable."[13] A sensory synecdoche expands the definition of a sound bite to include the images and soundtracks that often accompany visual clips, and these audio and visual representations are intended to capture iconic actions that are bright, snappy and memorable. The combination of images, location sound, voice-over narration and musical soundtrack performs several functions on the audience that are significantly different from a sound bite. They can evoke memory, can create a contemporary interpretation of the particular referenced event(s), or perform some combination of the two, depending on the audience's experience and knowledge of the depicted events. The documentary sensory synecdoche relies on sight and sound and thus flattens memory to these two senses. Audiences cannot feel the air of the depicted protests or smell the environment or taste anything in this represented sensorium; however, as opposed to a sound bite, visuals and soundtracks provide other access points and references that can invoke various metonymies.[14]

In documentary film, sensory synecdoches are evocative, based in historical actuality, and deeply ideological. Similar to sound bites, sensory synecdoches eschew an in-depth analysis of the contextual information surrounding the bite in favor of gleaning complete meaning from the clip itself. Even though the documentary "truth" of photographic images and sound recording has come under justified scrutiny, and the increasingly sophisticated advancements in digital technology have served to highlight that point, the sensory impact of video and audio recordings of historic actuality is still profound. Documentary film theorist Michael Renov calls into question this reliance on representing the truth in documentary film: "Documentary practitioners have frequently assumed their right to didacticism based on assumptions of truth . . . or at least standards of objectivity."[15] Renov, along with many contemporary media scholars, observes how easy it is to manipulate all visual and auditory recordings and that their truth claims are tenuous at best and largely interpretive.[16] Given the exegetical nature of documentaries, it is important to examine how sensory synecdoches evoke a range of meanings that may not necessarily represent the "truth" of historical events but are meaningful nonetheless.

The documentary sensory synecdoches in *Chisholm '72: Unbought & Unbossed* are particularly potent in the sections describing the black power movement and the women's movement, and they each appear twice in the film. At forty-six seconds into the film, there is an introductory montage describing the black power movement and the women's movement that provides a historical context for the viewer. The accompanying soundtracks to this montage include Chisholm's initial declaration (as quoted above) and a music score intended to replicate the music of the 1970s. The opening includes five images depicting African Americans: a still image of a Black Panthers' handbill held in a black hand announcing 2,000 Free Full Bags of Groceries; moving images of African Americans with fists waving at the National Black Political Convention; the famous black-and-white photo of Black Panther party members dressed in black leather jackets, black berets, long Afro hairstyles, with their arms interlocked; African American women in fashionable fur coats; and a close-up of an African American woman at the Black Power convention. Although this sequence is only seven seconds long, it packs a powerful metonymic punch.

These symbolic images function metonymically to invoke the memory of the militant edge of the black power movement of the 1960s and 1970s. The raised fists of the Black Panthers quickly bring to mind their radical tactics. Although the sequence is clearly intended to remind audiences of the historical moment in 1972, the contemporary use of these images as shorthand for the black power movement raises significant concerns. Robert Hariman and John Lucaites note how "one can reassess the role of visual practices in the public media and discern specific problems, anxieties and attitudes that define public culture in particular historical moments."[17] The use of these particular images function symbolically to remind viewers of the historic use of violence associated with African American political activism. Although these are images from the late 1960s and early 1970s, it is their use in a 2004 context that gives an indication of some contemporary problems and anxieties concerning African Americans and political power. These extremely evocative images function as a sensory synecdoche to narrowly define African American political power as angry and violent.

Immediately following this sequence in the opening montage are images delineating the women's movement with the same 1970s music in the background. This sequence is also seven seconds long and contains the following images: two scenes of women's rights marches in split-screen with the top image in black and white of an urban street with two women holding signs that read "Love Me Less. Respect Me More." Another sign reads, "Backlash to Tokenism Uncle Toms," and there is a woman playing drums, and another is dressed in a Victorian dress holding an unreadable sign. The bottom image is of another women's rights march with women holding a long banner with red lettering that reads, "Abortion. Women's Right to Choose."

Women's National Abortion Action." After the split screen images of the marches, the next image is a black-and-white shot of an older black woman with thick glasses, which is followed by a younger white woman in a vest and tailored shirt holding her glasses preparing to speak publicly. This sequence ends with a vintage black-and-white fashion clip of a 1960s female model turning to show off her jacket, boots, and mod clothing. Inserted onto this clip is a color graphic that reads, "I'm Female. I'm Proud." This model ends the clip by looking down into the camera as she strikes a pose by jutting out her hip. The intention of this sequence is again to remind audiences of the historical moment, but the use of these visual symbols in 2004 as shorthand for the women's movement illuminates both historical and current anxieties. Images of women marching in the streets and demanding abortion rights invokes a narrow element of the women's movement, and these images work metonymically to remind audiences that women in this public sphere were so angry that they took to street protest marches, but their concerns and identities were formed and defined by fashion.

The use of these documentary sensory synecdoches sets up the symbolism that defines Shirley Chisholm's candidacy throughout the film. Her explicit political messages are briefly referenced only three times and they are not in the form of a synecdoche. There is a short clip from a speech near the beginning of the film where she declares that if elected she would withdraw U.S. troops from Vietnam, and at fifty-eight minutes into the film a media critic states that there is "very little difference on the policy level between her and McGovern" (although McGovern's positions are not explained in the film either). At fifty-nine minutes, a former campaign volunteer explains the goal of Chisholm's campaign was to go to the smoke-filled rooms of McGovern and Humphrey and agree to release her delegates if she could get a promise to fund Head-Start and to end the war in Vietnam. These sparse references connote very progressive positions for 1972; however, they are extremely understated and fleeting. Instead, the film relies on its descriptions of the black power movement and the women's movement as shorthand for defining Chisholm's politics and candidacy. This strategic move ultimately limits our understanding of Shirley Chisholm as a presidential candidate. Her ethos is constitutively defined by her gender and race even though the candidate herself balked at that definition.

Black Power Movement

The section of the film that explains the role of African American support for Chisholm's presidential bid illustrates a deeply reductive rendition of the black power movement.[18] This sequence begins at twenty-six minutes and lasts for approximately six minutes before segueing into the section on the women's movement. This section opens with interviews of Congressman Ron Dellums, Reverend Walter Fauntroy and poet-activist Amiri Baraka, with each recalling Chisholm's difficulties in gaining African American support for her presidential run. Baraka specifically describes her role at the 1972 Black National Political Convention held in Gary, Indiana. The film then provides a sequence of images from this convention that function as the second documentary sensory synecdoche of the black power movement. The depicted newscast and this film's representation of the Black National Political Convention are indicative of how narrowly African Americans were reproduced in the political realm in the United States.

There are ten sets of images in this two-minute section, and the overall impression is one of angry, dissatisfied and somewhat chaotic African Americans. The sequence begins with black-and-white footage of an ABC newscaster announcing the convention and then cuts to location footage. The same 1970s style music that was used earlier in the film ramps up as the reporter in Gary, Indiana, reports on the convention. The first images are of crowds of African Americans entering the convention center followed by two images inside the convention hall of the crowd with fists raised high. Next is historical footage of Baraka intercut with contemporary interview footage explaining why Chisholm did not get the convention's endorsement. Following is a black-and-white still image of an unsmiling black male attendee staring straight into the camera followed by another still of many black male attendees all with their fists raised with similar serious expressions. The segment ends with historical footage of Baraka as chair of the convention conducting a voice vote on whether to endorse a candidate for president. He is visibly frustrated with the lack of a clear direction in the vote, and this scene is intercut with shots of the crowd that clearly number in the thousands. The voiceover narration during these last two images is that of the ABC newsman intoning, "The National Black Political Convention spent most of their two days bogged down in procedural problems. The closest vote of the night came on whether to endorse a political candidate. Backers of Shirley Chisholm worked hard for her endorsement." By the end of this sequence, the reproduction of race is clear. The news media and this documentary's coverage of the convention was presented as disorganized and populated with fist-raising African Americans who did not look happy.

This sequence of the black power movement works to narrowly define black men in the political sphere as angry and offers no explanation or justification for their anger: "The branding of any individual African American man (and by extension, all black men), as angry has worked to absolve the rest of America of any responsibility to struggle with, respond to, or even consider any claim he—or they—might make."[19] The film uses this sensory synecdoche to define the 1970s black power movement, and it works metonymically to define Shirley Chisholm in the political sphere. After seeing all of these images of black Americans engaged in the political sphere as angry, and Shirley Chisholm is a black candidate running for president, the viewer is led to conclude that she, too, must be angry. This negative portrayal of African Americans "underscores the importance of the play of threats and reassurances in the emotional aspects of symbolic politics."[20] This symbolic depiction of angry black Americans certainly can be read as threatening and not reassuring due to the previous use of Black Panther film footage to represent the black power movement. In this filmic context, the audience is given one metonymic option in how to interpret Chisholm's sharp confrontational verbal style, and it is one that connotes violence. The film's depiction of the 1970s women's movement offers a similarly restricted symbolic definition of Chisholm as a female in the political sphere.

Women's Movement

The section on the women's movement intends to evince the state of women and the women's movement at the time. This sequence begins at thirty-four minutes and lasts four minutes, and the images include a 1960s television advertisement of a mother concerned that her son's working wife cannot take care of him the way a wife should and several fashionably dressed women walking in urban settings. The voiceover narrator is Susan Brownmiller, who explains that women were perceived as really nice and that women could not get store credit cards in their own name, that insurance on a car for an unmarried woman was much higher, and that all these things were considered natural until the explosion of the women's movement. The next set of images include black-and-white footage of women's street protests with banners which read, "Abolish All Abortion Laws" and "Equal Jobs & Equal Opportunities." Helen Reddy's anthem "I Am Woman" plays in the background to the following images: a mass bra burning; women practicing self-defense moves in a street march; a series of women's marches with women shaking their fists. This sequence and the Reddy song end with a clip of Shirley Chisholm with her arm upraised giving an impassioned speech about how the political establishment is working to keep her out of power because she is a woman.

The final three interviews of the women's movement sensory synecdoche are of Betty Friedan (who supported Chisholm), Bella Abzug (who did not support Chisholm), and Gloria Steinem (who partially supported Chisholm).[21] In many ways, this section works well to counter Virginia Sapiro's observation that women are "stereotypically seen as mothers, housewives, or sex objects, [and] that none of these roles are seen as compatible with political leadership."[22] I would argue that the intent of this section is to be read in just this manner. However, these particular images, when coupled with the Reddy song, function as a sensory synecdoche that narrowly defines the 1970s women's movement and, hence, Shirley Chisholm. Missing from the film are any references to the actual legislative and community work that Chisholm achieved for women's issues. She had an impressive record in the New York Assembly of proposing legislation directly aimed at benefiting women, which included, "opening day care centers for working women, and those on public assistance, unemployment insurance for domestic workers, and seniority protection for public school teachers who took maternity leave." Chisholm was also able to see some of her proposals enacted. "Her proposed program for low-income students to attend college, SEEK, became law" as did the unemployment insurance bill and legislation ensuring seniority for schoolteachers who took maternity leave.[23] Chisholm was hardly known for bra burning or self-defense maneuvers, as these sensory synecdoches would imply. For contemporary audiences, the use of the bra-burning image and the street marches of women with their fists raised works metonymically to identify the 1970s women's movement as one of anger and excess. Moreover, because Chisholm is a woman in the political sphere and identified with the women's movement, she too must be angry and excessive. This section ends with a clip from a Chisholm speech that depicts her right arm upraised as she speaks angrily and loudly reinforces this symbolic meaning.

The film correctly identifies the double bind that Chisholm found herself in as the first female black presidential candidate. However, the film creates its own double bind for understanding her symbolism. As a black candidate, she must be angry, and as a female candidate she must be angry, all of which are threatening political symbols. Interestingly, this reductive portrayal appears to be countered by her representation at the 1972 Democratic presidential convention and her desire to be a "serious" candidate.

Ending at the 1972 Democratic Presidential Convention

The 1972 Democratic convention comprises the final section of the film, and the entire event is framed within the context of backroom deal making between Shirley Chisholm, the Black Caucus, and presidential candidate George McGovern. Political scientists McClain, Carter and Brady observe that "the biggest problem" for Chisholm's presidential campaign, "seemed to be people taking her seriously."[24] Within this sixteen-minute section, the audience learns how delegate selection worked for the Democratic presidential convention and that Chisholm's knowledge of this process is meant to define her "seriousness." This segment of the film offers fascinating insider footage of the political brokering and maneuvering not usually available for public consumption. This portion of the film is detailed and does not show any fists waving or bras burning, but instead it depicts the complex convention negotiations of the time. As a political symbol, this section portrays Chisholm as a deeply committed participant in the Democratic convention process, and there are no sensory synecdoches used to represent her role. The section ends with Chisholm's "unity speech" in which she withdraws from the race and commits to working to unseat President Richard Nixon. There is a still photo of Chisholm on the podium, arm in arm with George McGovern, Thomas Eagleton, Edmund Muskie, and Hubert Humphrey.

IMPLICATIONS

For contemporary audiences there are several instructional insights to be gleaned from this film. African American and female candidates are still represented with similar threatening political symbols that have to do with anger and excess.[25] Even well-intentioned documentary filmmakers who set out to reclaim the memory of Shirley Chisholm can activate a metonymy that has little to do with understanding the actual candidate. One of the questions that remain unanswered is whether these documentary sensory synecdoches depicting angry African Americans and women ever cease to be viewed as threatening. The candidacies of Barack Obama and Hillary Clinton clearly indicate that there has been progress, yet synecdochic attempts are still made to depict women and African Americans in the political sphere as angry and excessive. I am hopeful that as women and African Americans occupy more positions of power in the political sphere, the historic images of each as angry and excessive will lose their persuasive force in defining women and African Americans as *only* angry and excessive. Perhaps these images will eventually be recognized for what they are— images of historic actuality that capture one part of a much larger rights movement—nothing more and nothing less. Until that time, scholars and the public can "take a more explicit theoretical and empirical account of the fact that the specific individual and context matters."[26] Not all women who participated in the 1970s women's movement are the same, nor are all African Americans who participated in the 1970s black power movement the same. Shirley Chisholm chose a course uniquely responsive to the time, and it is the particulars of her life and work that enables audiences to fully understand her contribution as more than the first black woman to run for the U.S. presidency.

NOTES

1. Margaret Chase Smith's name was entered in nomination for the Republican ticket in 1964, but the event is widely viewed as symbolic, and Chase Smith did not vigorously campaign.

2. Virginia Sapiro, "The Political Uses of Symbolic Women: An Essay in Honor of Murray Edelman," *Political Communication* 10, no. 2 (April–June1993), 141–54.

3. Joel Olson, "Abolition of White Democracy," (Minneapolis: University of Minnesota Press, 2004), http://site.elibrary.com.ezproxy.pacific.edu:8992 (accessed March 24, 2008).

4. Robert Hariman and John Louis Lucaites, "Performing Civic Identity: The Iconic Photograph of the Flag Raising on Iwo Jima," *Quarterly Journal of Speech* 88, no. 4 (2002); Barbie Zelizer, *Remembering to Forget: Holocaust Memory through the Camera's Eye* (Chicago and London: University of Chicago Press, 1998).

5. Roland Barthes, *Image—Music—Text*, trans. Stephen Heath (New York: Hill and Wang, 1977), 18.

6. Michael Calvin McGee, "The 'Ideograph': A Link between Rhetoric and Ideology," *Quarterly Journal of Speech* 66, no. 1 (February 1980): 5.

7. *Chisholm '72—Unbought & Unbossed* was released by P.O.V., American Documentary Inc., the Independent Television Service, National Black Programming Consortium and the Corporation for Public Broadcasting

8. Bill Nichols, *Introduction to Documentary* (Bloomington: Indiana University Press, 2001), 105.

9. Bill Nichols describes the additional forms of documentary as: "poetic documentary which reassemble[s] fragments of the world poetically, . . . observational documentary which eschew[s] commentary and reenactment [and] observe[s] things as they happen, . . . [t]he filmmaker in a participatory documentary interview[s] or interact[s] with subjects [and] uses archival footage to retrieve history, . . . reflexive documentary which question[s] the documentary form [and] defamiliarize[s] the other modes, . . . performative documentary which stress[es] [the] subjective aspects of a classically objective discourse." *Introduction to Documentary*, 102-38.

10. All future unmarked quotations are taken from the film *Chisholm '72—Unbought & Unbossed.*

11. Shola Lynch, *Shirley Chisholm Fought the Good Fight* (Volume 112, Issue 1) (Crisis Publications, 2005 [cited May 6 2008]); available from http://search.ebscohost.com.ezproxy.pacific.edu:8992/login.aspx?direct=true&db=a9h&AN=16024942&site=ehost-live.

12. Bill Nichols describes the prevalent use of metaphors in the documentary film tradition as ways to describe larger themes: "The selection and arrangement of sounds and images are sensuous and real; they provide an immediate form of audible and visual experience, but they also become, through their organization into a larger whole, a metaphorical representation of what something in the historical world is like." Nichols, *Introduction to Documentary*, 74.

13. William Safire, "On Language; Sound Bite, Define Yourself!" *New York Times*, November 13, 1988.

14. Metonymy is the use of one relationship to stand in for or represent a larger set of relationships.

15. Michael Renov, *The Subject of Documentary* (Minneapolis: University of Minnesota Press, 2004), 147.

16. Bill Nichols, *Representing Reality* (Bloomington: Indiana University Press, 1991); Brian Winston, *Claiming the Real: The Documentary Film Revisited* (London: British Film Institute, 1995); Marita Sturken, Lisa Cartwright, *Practices of Looking: An Introduction to Visual Culture* (Oxford: Oxford University Press, 2001); Michael Renov, ed., *Theorizing Documentary* (New York: Routledge, 1993); Trinh T. Min-ha, "The Totalizing Quest of Meaning," in *Theorizing Documentary*, ed. Michael Renov (New York: Routledge, 1993).

17. Robert Hariman and John Louis Lucaites, *No Caption Needed; Iconic Photographs, Public Culture, and Liberal Democracy* (Chicago: University of Chicago Press, 2007), 44.

18. For a more complex analysis of the Black Panthers, see Curtis J. Austin, *Up against the Wall: Violence in the Making and Unmaking of the Black Panther Party* (Fayetteville: University of Arkansas Press, 2008); David Hilliard, ed., *The Black Panther Party: Service to the People Programs* (Albuquerque: University of New Mexico, 2008); Judson R. Jeffries, ed., *Black Power in the Belly of the Beast* (Champaign: University of Illinois Press, 2006); Andrew Witt, *The Black Panthers in the Midwest: The Community Programs and Services of the Black Panther Party in Milwaukee, 1966–1977* (London: Routledge, 2007).

19. Vorris Nunley Adam Banks, Howard Rambsy, Keith Gilyard, et. al., "Just Another Angry Black Man?" *Black Issues in Higher Education*, April 11, 2002, 1.

20. Virginia Sapiro, "The Political Uses of Symbolic Women," 147.

21. Gloria Steinem endorsed Shirley Chisholm only in states where she was running (a total of twelve) and endorsed George McGovern in the other thirty-eight states. Gloria Steinem, "Shirley Chisholm: Front-Runner," *New York Magazine*, January 10, 2005.

22. Virginia Sapiro, "The Political Uses of Symbolic Women," 142.

23. Julie Gallagher, "Waging 'The Good Fight': The Political Career of Shirley Chisholm, 1953–1982," *Journal of African American History* 92, no. 1 (2007): 399.

24. Niambi M. Carter Paula D. McClain, Michael C. Brady, "Gender and Black Presidential Politics: From Chisholm to Moseley Braun," *Journal of Women, Politics and Policy* 27, no. 1/2 (2005): 58.

25. The footage of Rev. Jeremiah Wright angrily speaking has been used, and I anticipate will continue to be used, to prove that Barack Obama is also an angry black man.

26. Virginia Sapiro, "The Political Uses of Symbolic Women," 143.

PRESS FRAMING OF FIRST LADIES' POLITICAL ACTIVISM

Lisa M. Burns

The press and the American people have been fascinated with the first lady since the beginning of this nation's history. Lewis L. Gould argues, "These women offer a significant perspective on how their fellow citizens regard marriage, child rearing, women in society, and gender relations within the United States."[1] The press has historically presented first ladies as important social figures and models of American womanhood. Yet the political influence of first ladies has always been scrutinized, calling into question women's place in U.S. political culture.

In this chapter I examine press coverage of first ladies' political activities in the twentieth century, highlighting how gender framed journalists' discussions of the political efficacy of presidents' wives.[2] The analysis focuses on a few key examples of how these women's political activities were portrayed by the press. What links the cases together is the critique of first ladies' political influence that appears in press coverage. These cases show how journalists rhetorically constructed boundaries that sought to question and limit first ladies' political power.

GENDER FRAMING AND THE FIRST LADY POSITION

The first lady may be a symbolic role, but its inclusion in discussions of gender and political communication is warranted by the uniqueness of the position. The first lady office is full of contradictions. The position is not outlined in the Constitution, yet it has been a part of the American presidency since its inception. The first lady role is inherently gendered because its holders assume office through marriage, not election. The institution has no set rules or guidelines, yet the first lady assumes important duties and faces high expectations, including the notion that she somehow represents the "ideal" American woman.[3] Gould asserts, "The public expects the first lady to fulfill a multitude of roles flawlessly, and there is criticism at any departure from perceived standards. At the same time the criteria for success as a first lady constantly change as the public's view of women evolves and develops."[4] The position is unique in that it forces its holders to straddle the public and private spheres, placing these women at the center of U.S. political culture yet questioning the extent of their influence.

Over the years, first ladies have been asked to perform a variety of public and private roles, from that of hostess, escort, and volunteer to advisor and policymaker.[5] Because the first lady is a gendered role, there are social norms and expectations associated with the "performance" of the position. The public nature of the position gives first ladies some latitude of performance in the public sphere, yet they must also conform to gender standards that often equate women's roles with the private sphere of home and family. Therefore, while the position has been shaped by the discourse and actions of each first lady, those in the role have never had complete control over the construction of the position because of historical, social, and political constraints that attend to women's position in American culture. Discourse about the first lady is as significant as each woman's performance of the position, as both "function culturally to shape notions of femininity and so both foster and constrain women's agency."[6]

One of the most prominent sites of public discussion about first ladies is press coverage. Since very few people ever have direct contact with the first lady, the majority of the public's information about the position comes from the press. The evolution of the position has undergone press scrutiny since the days of Martha Washington. However, popular interest in presidents and first ladies increased significantly after 1900 thanks to mass-circulation magazines and the emergence of human-interest journalism.[7] Throughout the years, stories about first ladies have covered a broad range of topics, from the first lady's fashion sense to her political activities.

Media framing helps to explain how gender ideologies have pervaded first lady press coverage. Jamieson and Waldman offer the following definition of media framing: "The metaphor of a frame—a fixed border that includes some things and excludes others—describes the way information is arranged and packaged in news stories."[8] Frames work by drawing upon the prior knowledge of individuals in order to explain and classify new information.[9] Feminist media critics contend that gender is a primary framing device used by journalists. When women are the subject of news narratives, gender is often the primary, if not the only, frame. By employing social standards to frame news narratives, either consciously or unconsciously, journalists often reinforce so-called traditional gender roles that view home and family as women's primary sphere of influence and politics as a chiefly male domain.[10] Thus, gendered framing shapes how journalists construct narratives about women, especially first ladies. Such framing is especially evident in press coverage of first ladies' political activities. The examples in this chapter illustrate how first ladies' political involvement has been both praised by the press for expanding women's political influence and critiqued for going beyond "traditional" gender frames and trespassing too far into the male political sphere.

FIRST LADY AS GOVERNMENT OFFICIAL

Eleanor Roosevelt and the Office of Civilian Defense

The early twentieth century was a period of great social change, particularly for American women. Glenna Matthews argues that women achieved "a new kind of public power" during this era: "They began to win electoral office, they saw the enactment of major public policy for which they had struggled, and they enjoyed an increasing public presence." However, she notes that "women's power and women's access to public influence still fell far short of that exercised by men."[11]

News of women's increased political activity filled the newspapers and women's magazines of this era, which boasted millions of female readers.[12] Likewise, the political activities of first ladies received increased attention. But no previous first lady generated more press coverage than Eleanor Roosevelt, and only a handful of her successors matched the amount of column space devoted to her. By the eve of World War II, Roosevelt was already widely regarded in the press as the most active first lady in history. She was the first president's wife to testify in front of a congressional committee (on two occasions), the first to address a political nominating conference, and the first to hold a formal position with a government organization.[13] For reporters, Roosevelt represented the expansion of women's, and the first lady's, political roles. Her brief tenure as the associate director of the

Office of Civilian Defense, which generated some of the most negative press coverage during Roosevelt's twelve years as first lady, serves as an example of both the opportunities and constraints faced by first ladies who assume political leadership roles.

When Roosevelt assumed her duties as the associate director of the Office of Civilian Defense (OCD) on September 29, 1941, the *New York Times* noted it was "the first government job ever held by the wife of the President of the United States." Roosevelt told reporters "she was planning to be 'on the job' every morning and remain as long as possible, although other commitments would occupy part of her time." She said her overall objective was "'giving every person, man, woman and child, wishing to volunteer their services in the interests of civilian defense, an opportunity to train for the work they wish to do.'"[14] Once on the job, newspaper articles about the OCD identified Roosevelt by her associate director title rather than referring to her as the "first lady" or "president's wife," a journalism convention that conveys status and authority to public officials. In doing so, reporters recognized the OCD position as an official post and not simply an extension of Roosevelt's first lady duties.

Roosevelt got to work right away, developing plans for various volunteer efforts. She spent much of her time touring defense preparedness programs around the country and speaking to various groups, urging them to support civilian defense efforts. After the United States officially entered the war, Congress questioned the civilian leadership of the OCD and considered putting the OCD under military control. Roosevelt argued that the office "should remain under civilian direction because its function is 'one that cannot be fulfilled by the Army.'" When a House committee questioned whether either Roosevelt or OCD director Mayor Fiorello LaGuardia had "sufficient time at their disposal to devote to their respective duties," Roosevelt responded that she routinely devoted "'about twelve hours a day'" to the OCD.[15] On January 14, 1942, both Roosevelt and LaGuardia testified before the congressional committee considering the matter. Their testimony helped to convince the group to drop the proposal to transfer control of the OCD to the War Department.[16]

But in early February, Roosevelt came under fire when a dancer was named head of children's activities in the OCD's physical fitness division at a salary of $4,600 a year. Mayris Chaney was consistently identified in the press as Roosevelt's "dancer protégé." The appointment of actor Melvyn Douglas to direct OCD theatrical activities was also called into question. A group of Republican congressmen demanded an inquiry into OCD expenditures, and on February 7, 1942, the House voted 88 to 80 to "forbid the use of civilian defense funds for "instructions in physical fitness by dancers, fan dancing, street shows, theatrical performances or other public entertainment." During the House debate, one representative "suggested that a 'Bundles for Eleanor' movement be started in tribute to Mrs. Roosevelt's ability to get jobs for her friends."[17] Soon after, politicians started calling on Roosevelt to resign her post. A Nebraska senator urged both LaGuardia and Roosevelt to "'remove themselves immediately from the OCD so that the real work can go forward.'" The senator stated, "'The time is past for boondoggling. If communities wish to organize dancing and calisthenics, I am sure they can do it themselves without direction from the throne.'"[18] The indirect reference to Roosevelt as a monarch was a clear critique of her influence. A New York assemblyman suggested that Roosevelt be replaced with "a person who can and will devote full time to the duties of that important position," which ignored the many hours that Roosevelt had devoted to her OCD position.[19]

Roosevelt responded to her critics, telling reporters that she "would welcome the chance to tell Congress 'the truth' about OCD appointments" and had "no intention of resigning her own post as associate director." She defended herself, noting that she had suggested but had not appointed Chaney and had nothing to do with the selection of Douglas. At a press conference, she stated, "'I assume they will do me the courtesy of allowing me to give them the facts. They have offices, and I have feet. As the person criticized, I imagine I shall be given the opportunity of meeting with them and telling them the truth about the questions they have raised.'"[20] But that invitation was never extended, and Roosevelt announced that she would "relinquish her associate directorship" just four days after defending herself in the press. The news made front page headlines. In her comments, Roosevelt noted that she had always planned on stepping down once the OCD was organized, but admitted to leaving sooner because of political pressure. She told reporters, "'I realize how unwise it was for a vulnerable person like myself to try a government job. . . . It is a little bit unusual for the wife of the president to go into an official job even if she doesn't get any pay and pays her own travel expenses.'"[21] Under the headline "Mrs. Roosevelt Quits OCD to Free Agency of Attack," the *New York Times* printed the full text of her resignation letter, in which she stated that if she remained in her post, "'I would only make it possible for those who wish to attack me, because of my beliefs, to attack an agency which I consider can prove its usefulness so completely to the people that it should be free of attack.'"[22] A few days later, on her weekly NBC radio program, Roosevelt took on her critics, describing them as "'a small and very vocal group of unenlightened men'" who "had seen fit to make me of greater importance than I have ever before thought I could be.'"[23] Even though she attempted to downplay the importance of what transpired, it is clear from Roosevelt's comments that she resented being forced from her post for personal and political reasons.

The controversy over Roosevelt's political influence as OCD associate director is an example of how the press and public reacts when a first lady expands her role "too far" beyond the traditional boundaries of the position. Even Roosevelt pointed to the unusualness of the first lady in an official government role as one of the reasons why she came under attack, and ultimately resigned. Her personal influence, related to political appointments, was harshly critiqued by Congress. But the press offered another perspective. A *New York Times* editorial argued that "since she is the president's wife, no one could ever be sure whether she was acting for herself alone or for Mr. Roosevelt. Of necessity she exercised an influence out of proportion to the defined powers of her office." According to this editorial, Roosevelt clearly violated the boundaries of the first lady position by assuming an official political post and by showing a personal interest in politics. In doing so, her influence was judged as going beyond the "defined powers of her office," even though there are no definitive guidelines for the first lady position. Such framing gives the press the power to construct the boundaries of a first lady's influence and then judge whether a first lady has violated those boundaries. The editorial further noted, "Her failure was inevitable. In no way does it reflect on her ability, her good-will and her unselfish devotion to the general welfare," suggesting that Roosevelt would "serve the country all the better now that she has no official tag."[24] According to this reasoning, she failed because she assumed duties that were beyond the boundaries of first lady influence, and she would be able to be more effective once her political efficacy was contained to an "unofficial" position. Several of Roosevelt's successors would find themselves constrained by similar press framing of their political activity.

First Lady as Political Activist:
Betty Ford, Rosalynn Carter, and the ERA

The social and political unrest of the 1960s and 1970s provided a fertile environment for the so-called rebirth of feminism.[25] The revival of an organized social movement in the 1960s has been referred to as the "second wave" of feminism. According to Barbara Ryan, the "ideological and material contradictions developing in women's lives—as well as the actual constraints of the homemaker role" during the cold war era played an important part in the resurgence of a feminist movement in the 1960s.[26] But the "new" feminism did not resonate with all Americans. The movement faced ridicule from many men, women, and media outlets as well as vigorous attacks from well-organized opponents who embraced women's traditional domestic roles. Despite these challenges, the call for women's liberation was successful in generating widespread discussions of gender roles during this period.

The women's liberation movement influenced the way journalists framed the first lady's duties. For journalists, the activities of these first ladies were compared to women's increased activism and evolving roles in the workplace and public life. Reporters accentuated first ladies' political activities like presidential advisor, surrogate, and political advocate. Such framing infused the first lady institution with a sense of empowerment and gave rise to the first lady as an influential political activist. First ladies Rosalynn Carter and Betty Ford were viewed as playing an important role in the "co-career" they shared with their husbands. They were also viewed as women with their own political interests.

While press framing during this era celebrated first ladies as political activists, news coverage also critiqued their growing influence; the resulting coverage represented the ideological contestation over women's changing roles. As a 1975 story in *McCall's* proclaimed, "While there is a loss of privacy and anonymity as First Lady, there is also direction, a well-defined role, an exalted status and a chance to influence public opinion that is unparalleled for any other woman in this country."[27] The activist first ladies of this era used their status as political celebrities to influence public opinion on a variety of subjects. In doing so, they also witnessed the limits of their political efficacy, at least in the estimation of journalists, who at times challenged this growing public and political influence of first ladies. Such coverage continued to mark the boundaries of "proper" first lady performance. Articles about Rosalynn Carter's tour of several Latin American countries promoting her husband's foreign policy agenda and press coverage of Betty Ford and Rosalynn Carter's lobbying on behalf of the Equal Rights Amendment illustrate reporters' reactions to first ladies' growing political advocacy.

First Lady as Presidential Surrogate: Rosalynn Carter's Latin American Trip

Rosalynn Carter was framed by the press as one of her husband's closest advisors. The *New York Times* pointed out that "Mr. Carter has described his wife as his 'best friend and chief advisor.'"[28] Carter said, "'Jimmy respects my judgment on things, that's all. I think I have some influence on him.'"[29] Carter became famous for sitting in on Cabinet meetings and for advising her husband on political appointments, which were viewed as very political acts. She also chaired two committees, the President's Commission on Mental Health and the White House Conference on Aging, both of which resulted in legislation.

Carter's most prominent role was when she acted as a surrogate for her husband, discussing foreign policy during a twelve-day tour of the Caribbean and Latin America, which made daily headlines in both the United States and abroad. She told reporters that her visit was "'on behalf of the President to express his friendship and good will and to conduct substantive talks with the leaders of these nations on issues of bilateral, regional, and global importance.'"[30] As the first president's wife to undertake such an important political assignment abroad, she often found herself having to defend her trip. Her response was, "'I think that I am the person closest to the President of the United States, and if I can help him understand the countries of the world, that's what I want to do.'"[31] To prepare, Carter took Spanish lessons and was "briefed by 40 experts on Latin America in 13 sessions lasting two to five hours each."[32] David Vidal of the *New York Times* noted that, before the trip, "there was widespread skepticism that it could produce any results," particularly since Carter was visiting a region "dominated by a male culture" and "would be unable to gain the ear of male leaders, often military men, on issues as varied and complex as nuclear proliferation, commodity prices, arms sales, trade and third-world development problems and, of course, human rights." However, Vidal concluded, "Mrs. Carter has achieved a personal and diplomatic success that goes far beyond the modest expectations of both her foreign policy tutors at the State Department and her hosts."[33] Adding the role of diplomat to the first lady's duties increased the political influence of the first lady position.

However, with this added influence came increased press scrutiny. Kandy Stroud characterized Carter as "a tough, shrewd power-behind-the-throne, ambitious both for herself and her husband."[34] Similar comments were made by Meg Greenfield, who claimed there were many "downsides" of a politically active wife: "She is variously regarded as the seductress, the bewitcher, the mysterious power behind the throne, the possessor of unfair advantage and the wielder of undue influence."[35] These quotes sexualized public womanhood, harkening back to the days when women who dared to enter the public sphere were called "Jezebels," comparing them to the biblical wife who exercised "undue influence" on her husband.[36]

Carter's Latin American trip sparked editorials about the appropriateness of the first lady assuming a diplomatic role. The *New York Times* questioned "whether it was somehow insulting to send the First Lady if the President and Vice President were too busy with other countries," implying that both her gender and unofficial position were an issue. However, the editorial concluded that "it is the quality of her ambassadorship that should concern us, not the range of subjects on which the President might wish to exploit her prestige and proximity."[37] Greenfield, in a *Washington Post* op-ed, disagreed, claiming that "the question raised by her Latin American trip is not whether Rosalynn Carter is capable of serving as an agent of her husband's government, but rather whether she should." Greenfield asserted, "If Mrs. Carter is going to conduct diplomatic discussions abroad and enter into policy matters in a systematic way at home, her efforts and her influence are going to have to be judged as those of an ordinary professional." She concluded that "before it's over, Mrs. Carter—a remarkable woman—will have demonstrated whether or not a political wife who comes out of the kitchen can stand the heat."[38] For Greenfield, the issue was accountability. However, her final comment regarding political wives coming "out of the kitchen" unnecessarily gendered the question of Carter's political activism. The critiques of Carter's diplomatic role are strikingly similar to the criticism Roosevelt faced for her OCD leadership. Journalists seem more interested questioning the appropriateness of a first lady assuming such a political role rather than these women's actual performance of their roles. This press preoccupation with a first lady's "proper" role evidences the constraints these women face when they attempt to exercise their political influence, even if they are doing so as their husband's surrogate.

First Lady as Political Activist:
Betty Ford, Rosalynn Carter, and the ERA

Carter also faced critical press coverage for her support of the Equal Rights Amendment, as did her predecessor, Betty Ford. The women's liberation movement benefited from the first lady media spotlight thanks to Ford's and Carter's lobbying on behalf of the ERA. The *Ladies' Home Journal* asserted that Ford's "championing of the women's rights movement—and specifically the Equal Rights Amendment—has meant much to its supporters."[39] According to a February 1975 *New York Times* article, Ford was "making telephone calls and writing to legislators in several states where the amendment has recently come up for action, including Illinois, Missouri, North Dakota, Arizona, and Nevada."[40] Ford described her lobbying as a "'very soft sell'" and explained to *McCall's* that she "'merely asked that the amendment be allowed to get to the floor and to let the people vote their conscience.'"[41] Carter followed Ford's example, making phone calls to legislators urging their support of the ERA. A headline on the front page of the *Washington Post* on January 19, 1977, proclaimed, "Indiana Ratifies the ERA—With Rosalynn Carter's Aid." According to the article, Carter "called Democratic state Sen. Wayne Townsend, known to be wavering in the caucus, and persuaded him to switch his vote," making Indiana the "thirty-fifth state to ratify the Equal Rights Amendment."[42] Later that month, after Virginia failed to ratify the amendment by one vote, Carter was reportedly "working to change votes" by "calling several state legislators."[43] The press considered such activism by first ladies on behalf of the feminist movement unprecedented, even though their actions were extensions of previous first ladies' social reform efforts. By publicly using the power of the first lady position to lobby for feminist legislation, Ford and Carter provoked a mix of praise and criticism that often played out in the press.

Both first ladies were frequent targets of anti-ERA groups. In February 1975, the *Washington Post* reported that Ford's response was to "keep lobbying for the Equal Rights Amendment in spite of heavy criticism from opponents of the measure who picketed the White House" with placards reading "Stop E.R.A." and "Happiness is Stopping E.R.A." Ford directly challenged anti-ERA arguments in the press: "'You get all this silly business about co-ed facilities as an argument against the amendment. Think about it: how many campuses have sexually integrated dorms and are perfectly accepted?'" She also took on Stop ERA leader Phyllis Schlafly, saying, "Phyllis Schlafly has her great motherhood thing. I've been through motherhood. I think it's marvelous. But I'm not so sure mothers shouldn't have *rights*."[44] Ford's vocal support of the ERA generated criticism. At first, White House mail was "running three to one against her outspoken support of passage of the Equal Rights Amendment." One of the letters asserted, "'What right do you have as a representative of all women to contact the legislators and put pressure on them to pass the hated E.R.A.?'"[45] Ford responded in the *McCall's* article, saying, "'I see no reason why as first lady I cannot go right ahead like any other woman.'"[46] A 1975 profile in *Ladies' Home Journal* claimed, "She has stood by her support of the Equal Rights Amendment, provoking some criticism, but making many proud that a first lady would campaign so forcefully for women's rights."[47]

The anti-ERA movement also criticized Carter's lobbying efforts on behalf of the ERA. Schlafly organized a White House protest against Rosalynn

Carter following her calls to Indiana and Virginia legislators regarding the ERA. She told the *Washington Post* that "'state legislators around the country resent this improper White House pressure.'" The 150 demonstrators carried signs that read, "Rosalynn Carter—if my daughter is ever drafted it will be your fault!" and "Mrs. Carter, you have no right to lobby ERA!" Carter declined comment, but her press secretary said that she would "'continue to work in support of ERA.'"[48] Following the protest and a "surge of critical calls," Carter "stopped announcing all of her activities on behalf of the E.R.A.," although she continued to lobby on its behalf.[49] Unlike Ford, who publicly challenged her detractors, despite criticism, Carter responded to the pressures of her critics by silencing the publicity surrounding her activism. But in both cases, supporting the ERA pitted Ford and Carter against other women, which undermined the feminist notion of "sisterhood" and characterized the debate over women's rights as little more than a "political catfight."[50]

The framing of the ERA battle foreshadowed the backlash against feminism that would be evident in the coming decades. The first ladies of this era, through their political activism, prompted journalists to "reconsider the relationship between presidential spouses in order to infer the extent and character of a form of influence exerted largely outside public scrutiny."[51] Thus, journalists took it as their job to capture the extent of these women's influence. This reaction to the political activism of the period evidenced the limits of first ladies' influence, representing another type of backlash, this one aimed at containing the increased political power of presidents' wives. This backlash would reach its peak at the end of the twentieth century.

First Lady as Policymaker:
Hillary Clinton and Health Care Reform

On the verge of a new millennium, Americans were still debating women's "proper" place in society. The 1980s and 1990s were characterized by the conflict between the ideals of second-wave feminism and the feminist backlash, resulting in what some scholars and journalists have called the "postfeminist" era.[52] The rise of the New Right and the election of Ronald Reagan in 1980 brought the feminist backlash to the political foreground. Susan Faludi contends, "Just as Reaganism shifted political discourse far to the right and demonized liberalism, so the backlash convinced the public that women's 'liberation' was the true contemporary American scourge— the source of an endless laundry list of personal, social, and economic problems."[53] Feminism had become a symbolic lightening rod for the problems of modern family life at the end of the century. Like many politicians, the media depicted feminism as an extreme ideology, despite the fact that many of the advances sought by the women's movement, especially women's rights to pursue education and employment, had been embraced by U.S. culture.[54]

The last two decades of the twentieth century were in many ways a culmination of one hundred years of debate over women's proper place in American society. At the end of the twentieth century, first lady press coverage continued to serve as a site of ideological contestation over women's roles, with the debate over gender performance arguably more heated than ever. During this era, journalists became preoccupied with assessing the influence of presidents' wives and questioning the first lady's "proper place" in American politics and culture. The scrutiny of these women's influence became so intense that any perceived exercise of power, whether in private or public, resulted in extremely negative press coverage, as was the case with coverage of Hillary Rodham Clinton's leadership role in health care reform.

Clinton received front-page press scrutiny when she was appointed to "the most powerful official post ever assigned to a First Lady," chairing a committee "to prepare legislation for overhauling the nation's health-care system."[55] Reporters highlighted the novelty of a first lady venturing so far into traditionally masculine political territory. The New York Times reported, "Breaking decades of tradition, Hillary Rodham Clinton will set up shop in the West Wing of the White House, alongside the President's senior staff members, where she will help formulate policy on health care and other domestic issues."[56] She made front-page news when she traveled to Capitol Hill for a "closed-door policy discussion with leaders from both parties." Calling the visit a "vivid display of her clout," the New York Times claimed that the trip was the latest manifestation of Clinton's political influence, underscoring her importance "within the power structure of Washington."[57]

When Clinton testified before Congress, one editorial noted, "She is a strong, separate source of power inside the administration with a mandate of authority from the president and an operational base from which to carry it out."[58] Gwen Ifill of the New York Times stated that, by "influencing public policy," Clinton's role had "been expanded far beyond that of previous presidents' wives." Yet the article noted, "Questions about the scope of the power she wields from her West Wing office located a staircase away from the Oval Office have not subsided." She concluded that Clinton's health care role solidified "her position as the power beside, rather than behind the throne," echoing earlier concerns about the extent of her influence.[59] The language in these articles underscored the boundary-violating aspects of Clinton's role. By tying her visits to her "influence" and "power" rather than framing them as a routine part of her position as a task force chair, journalists implied that her actions were atypical for a first lady. The articles also talked very little about the substance of her visits, instead focusing on how these visits were tied to the performance of the first lady position.

After the failure of health care reform, Clinton "retreated" from taking the lead in shaping policy, playing a "less public" role according to press reports.[60] Even though the proposal came from the administration, journalists regularly referred to it as Clinton's plan. Articles talked about "the failure of *her* efforts to overhaul the nation's health care system."[61] Such framing made her the sole person held accountable for the plan, and its failure. Clinton herself told reporters she was willing to take "some of the blame" for the administration's plan being "misunderstood," although she also pointed to the organized attack against the plan by political opponents.[62] She told a group of reporters, "'I think I was naïve and dumb, because my view was 'results speak for themselves.' I regret very much that the efforts on health care were badly misunderstood, taken out of context and used politically against the administration.'"[63] A 1997 article claimed that her "failed attempt" at reforming health care "taught" Clinton the limitations of the first lady position.[64] Journalists routinely equated the failure of health care reform to Clinton's violation of the boundaries of the first lady role rather than to the numerous political and business interests that would have worked against any plan to overhaul the existing system at the time. The impression readers were left with was that health care reform failed because of Clinton's leadership (or lack thereof), which undermined the political efficacy of both Clinton and the first lady position. Such coverage also served as a way to rhetorically contain the power of the first lady position by using the failure of health care reform as an example of what can happen when a first lady oversteps her boundaries, assuming a policymaking role reserved for elected officials. The irony is that the "boundaries" journalists are so eager to police were largely constructed by media coverage, since after more than two hundred years, there is still no official description of the first lady's role.

FRAMING THE BOUNDARIES OF FIRST LADIES' POLITICAL INFLUENCE

Throughout its history, the first lady institution has served as a site of contestation regarding women's "proper" place. Through their press framing as role models for American women, first ladies became powerful symbols of women's expanding social and political roles. By treating first ladies as public figures functioning in the political sphere, news coverage helped to normalize women's public participation and political efficacy. Yet the boundaries of gender and role performance constructed and reified by media framing have simultaneously empowered and contained the women who have held the first lady position. By defining what was deemed a proper or improper political role for a first lady, journalists helped at times to expand women's political influence, while also creating many of the invisible boundaries that first ladies were subsequently accused of trespassing.

For journalists, the tipping point seems to be when a first lady is perceived to be wielding power that is deemed the province of elected officials, or worse, to be seeking political power for herself. Such was the case with Roosevelt's role as OCD associate director, Carter's Latin American trip, and Clinton's leadership of her husband's health care task force. The idea of a first lady assuming an official political position or speaking on behalf of the president was deemed by the press as violating the boundaries of first lady performance by extending these women's influence into the political sphere historically dominated by men. Ford and Carter also faced criticism for lobbying elected officials and forcing their personal political views on the public, which reporters and anti-ERA supporters framed as an improper use of their influence.

In sum, the gendered press framing of first ladies' political activities furthers the assumption that women remain less central to U.S. political culture by critiquing the legitimacy of women's participation as political leaders, advocates, and policymakers. As Witt, Paget, and Matthews argue, "The press coverage of women in politics is an artifact of this country's age-old but unresolved debate over women citizen's proper roles versus 'proper women's' place."[65] By the end of the century, the performance of gender roles and the subsequent gendered performance of the first lady position were the subject of a heated debate. Journalists, through their gendered framing of first ladies' political activities, helped create boundaries that marked the "proper" performance of the first lady position. When a first lady was suspected of exerting too much political influence, press critiques sought to contain her power. The rhetoric employed in such cases reflected the cultural fears over women's power and place within U.S. political culture. Thus, at the end of the century, journalists were still pondering the "proper" place of women and the "proper" role of the first lady, trying to figure out how this uniquely gendered position fits into U.S. political culture.

NOTES

1. Lewis L. Gould, *American First Ladies: Their Lives and Legacies* (New York: Garland Publishing, 1996), xix.

2. This study examines articles from two major U.S. newspapers, the *New York Times* and *Washington Post*, and from three leading women's magazines, *Ladies' Home Journal, McCall's,* and *Good Housekeeping.*

3. Betty Boyd Caroli, *First Ladies* (New York: Oxford University Press, 1995), xvii.

4. Gould, *American First Ladies*, xv.

5. Robert P. Watson, *The President's Wives: Reassessing the Office of First Lady* (Boulder, Colo.: Lynne Rienner Publishers, 2000), 72.

6. Karrin Vasby Anderson, "The First Lady: A Site of 'American Womanhood,'" in *Inventing a Voice: The Rhetoric of American First Ladies of the Twentieth Century,* ed. Molly Meijer Wertheimer (Lanham, Md.: Rowman & Littlefield, 2004), 18.

7. Lewis L. Gould, "First Ladies," *American Scholar* 55 (1986): 529.

8. Kathleen Hall Jamieson and Paul Waldman, *The Press Effect: Politicians, Journalists, and the Stories That Shape the Political World* (New York: Oxford University Press, 2003), xiii.

9. Shanto Iyengar and Donald R. Kinder, *News That Matters: Television and American Opinion* (Chicago: University of Chicago Press, 1993), 64.

10. Pippa Norris, *Women, Media, and Politics* (New York: Oxford University Press, 1997), 6.

11. Glenna Matthews, *The Rise of Public Woman: Woman's Power and Place in the United States, 1630–1970* (New York: Oxford University Press, 1992), 172.

12. Carolyn Kitch, *The Girl on the Magazine Cover: The Origins of Visual Stereotypes in American Mass Media* (Chapel Hill: The University of North Carolina Press, 2001), 4.

13. Maurine H. Beasley, *First Ladies and the Press: The Unfinished Partnership of the Media Age* (Evanston, Ill.: Northwestern University Press, 2005), 3–4; Lisa M. Burns, "First Ladies as Political Women: Press Framing of Presidential Wives, 1900–2001" (Ph.D. diss., University of Maryland, College Park, 2004), 145.

14. "OCD Job Assumed by Mrs. Roosevelt," *New York Times*, Sept. 30, 1941.

15. "First Lady Backs Civilians for OCD," *New York Times*, Jan. 13, 1942.

16. "Conferees Return OCD to LaGuardia," *New York Times*, Jan. 15 1942.

17. "House Forbids OCD Funds for 'Dancers,' Donald Duck," *New York Times*, Feb. 7, 1942.

18. "Mrs. Roosevelt Criticized," *New York Times*, Feb. 11, 1942.

19. "First Lady Ouster Urged," *New York Times*, Feb. 10, 1942.

20. "Hearing is Asked by Mrs. Roosevelt," *New York Times*, Feb. 10, 1942.

21. "First Lady Says She Will Quit OCD," *New York Times*, Feb. 13, 1942.

22. "Mrs. Roosevelt Quits OCD to Free Agency of Attack," *New York Times*, Feb. 21, 1942.

23. "Mrs. Roosevelt Berates Critics," *New York Times*, Feb. 23, 1942.

24. "Mrs. Roosevelt Resigns," *New York Times*, Feb. 21, 1942.

25. Matthews, *Rise of Public Woman*, 223.

26. Barbara Ryan, *Feminism and the Women's Movement* (New York: Routledge, 1992), 36.

27. Myra MacPherson, "The Blooming of Betty Ford." *McCall's*, Sep. 1975, 122.

28. Wayne King, "Rosalynn Carter, a Tough, Tireless Campaigner," *New York Times*, Oct. 18, 1976.

29. Judy Klemesrud, "For Mrs. Carter, a Rest at Last," *New York Times*, Jun. 11, 1976.

30. Laura Foreman, "Mrs. Carter Leaves on Latin Tour Today," *New York Times*, May 30, 1977.

31. Linda Charlton, "Mrs. Carter's Model is Very Much Her Own: Mrs. F.D.R.," *New York Times*, Jun. 5, 1977.

32. Susanna McBee, "Mrs. Carter's Trip Carefully Crafted to Make Policy Points," *Washington Post*, May 29, 1977.

33. David Vidal, "Ambassador Rosalynn Carter: First Lady Confounds the Skeptics and Makes a Striking Success of Her Latin American Tour," *New York Times*, Jun. 14, 1977.

34. Kandy Stroud, "Rosalynn's Agenda in the White House," *New York Times Magazine*, Mar. 20, 1977: 20.

35. Meg Greenfield, "Mrs. President," *Washington Post*, Jun. 15, 1977.

36. Matthews, *Rise of Public Woman*, 4.

37. "Rosalynn Carter Elected," *New York Times*, Jun. 15, 1977.

38. Meg Greenfield, "Mrs. President."

39. "Women of the Year 1976," *Ladies' Home Journal*, May 1976: 73-4.

40. "Mrs. Ford Scored on Equality Plan," *New York Times*, Feb. 21 1975.

41. Myra MacPherson, "Blooming of Betty Ford," 124.

42. Paula G. Edwards, "Indiana Ratifies ERA—With Rosalynn Carter's Aid," *Washington Post*, Jan. 19, 1977.

43. Paula G. Edwards, "Rosalynn Carter Seeks Virginia Votes for ERA," *Washington Post*, Jan. 29, 1977.

44. Myra MacPherson, "Blooming of Betty Ford," 124.

45. "Mrs. Ford Scored."

46. Myra MacPherson, "Blooming of Betty Ford," 124.

47. Candice Bergen, "An Intimate Look at the Fords," *Ladies' Home Journal*, May 1975, 75.

48. "Anti-ERA Protests Aimed at First Lady," *Washington Post*, Feb. 5, 1977.

49. Kandy Stroud, "Rosalynn's Agenda in the White House," *New York Times Magazine,* Mar. 20, 1977, 20.

50. Susan J. Douglas, *Where the Girls Are: Growing Up Female With the Mass Media* (New York: Times Books, 1995), 221.

51. Karlyn Kohrs Campbell, "The Rhetorical Presidency: A Two-Person Career," in *Beyond the Rhetorical Presidency*, ed. Martin J. Medhurst (College Station: Texas A&M University Press, 1996), 181.

52. Barbara Ryan, *Feminism and the Women's Movement*, 54–55.

53. Susan Faludi, *Backlash: The Undeclared War Against American Women* (New York: Crown, 1991), xviii.

54. Bonnie J. Dow, *Prime-Time Feminism: Television, Media Culture, and the Women's Movement Since 1970* (Philadelphia: University of Pennsylvania Press, 1996), 87.

55. Thomas L. Friedman, "Hillary Clinton to Head Panel on Health Care," *New York Times*, Jan. 26, 1993.

56. Robert Pear, "Settling in: First Lady Hillary Clinton Gets Policy Job and New Office," *New York Times*, Jan. 22, 1993.

57. Michael Kelly, "Hillary Clinton Visits Capitol in Vivid Display of Her Clout," *New York Times*, Feb. 5, 1993.

58. Meg Greenfield, "Did She Take the Hill?" *New York Times*, Oct. 4, 1993.

59. Gwen Ifill, "Clinton's Health Plan; Role in Health Care Expands Hillary Clinton's Power," *New York Times*, Sept. 22, 1993.

60. Blaine Harden, "Finely Tailored Roles; Candidates' Wives Display Distinct Campaign Styles," *Washington Post*, Oct. 1, 1996.

61. Mary B. W. Tabor, "Meet Hillary Clinton, the Traditional First Lady," *New York Times*, Apr. 22, 1995.

62. Adam Clymer, "Hillary Clinton Says Administration Was Misunderstood on Health Care," *New York Times*, Oct. 3, 1994.

63. Marian Burros, "Hillary Clinton Asks Help in Finding a Softer Image," *New York Times*, Jan. 10, 1995.

64. Peter Baker, "First Lady Remains Vital Force in White House; Recognizing the Power of Her Voice and the Contours of Her Limitations," *Washington Post*, Jan. 20, 1997.

65. Linda Witt, Karen M. Paget, and Glenna Matthews, *Running as a Woman: Gender and Power in American Politics* (New York: The Free Press, 1995), 182.

12

GENDER BIAS AND MAINTENANCE

Press Coverage of Senator Hillary Clinton's Announcement to Seek the White House

Erika Falk

Since 1872 when the first woman sought the Oval Office most press coverage of women presidential candidates has been different from the press coverage of equivalent men running in the same races.[1] Women have gotten less coverage overall and had less printed about their issue positions. Their bodies and appearance have been more likely to be mentioned, and they have been more likely to be depicted as emotional. The surprising trend about these patterns is how little they have changed over time. Despite tremendous changes in the social and political role of women in the United States since the nineteenth century there has been little improvement in many of the objective and measurable variables of what constitutes fair coverage.

In January 2007, Senator Hillary Clinton declared her intention to seek the White House and, in doing so, became the first woman to enter the race as a front runner for the Democratic Party nomination. A December 2006 national poll by the Gallup Organization reported that respondents named Senator Clinton most often as their choice for president (33 percent). Senator Barack Obama, who entered the race four days before Clinton, was the second most likely person to be named (20 percent). In this chapter I examine the press coverage of the announcements by Senators Clinton and Obama to see if patterns of sexism and sex roles found in previous races were evident in the coverage of their entrance into the presidential race.

Examination of the first month of the Clinton campaign represents an interesting opportunity for exploring the portrayal of a woman running for president. This is true, first, because the coverage during the announcement sets the stage for the campaign and formally introduces the candidate to the electorate. Because most people never meet the presidential candidates in person, the way the media portray the candidates at the beginning of the campaign is particularly important to how the electorate form their first impressions. Second, the first month of the Clinton and Obama campaigns represents an unusual opportunity to compare how the press portrayed a front runner who was a woman. Never before had the top-polling candidate for a major party been a woman. Later in the campaign, Obama matched Clinton in polls, but in this early phase Clinton commanded a decisive lead.

Not only are press accounts important in constructing our ideas about candidates but also in creating our cultural understanding about gender and women. Judith Butler is well known for theorizing about how gender is misconstrued in the dominant American culture. She argued in *Gender Trouble* that gender difference is often mistakenly understood as the behavioral differences that result from biological sex. Instead she argued that both sex and gender are created and maintained through actions that are learned through cultural narratives, language, and performative acts. In other words, women are created by the very discourses that describe them.[2]

In the reporting about women who seek the Oval Office, the press has the opportunity to play a role in gender manipulation or traditional gender maintenance. These press narratives about women who run for office are part of the social dialogue by which the public learns about the appropriate roles for men and women and thereby construct the image of political women. Because press accounts are widely disseminated, they can play a greater role in image construction than any single conversation. Women who seek higher political office are not conforming to the traditional, domestic role for women in society; as a result, it is interesting to examine press accounts with thought to noticing whether the press treats men and women differently, thereby maintaining or promoting traditional sex and gender dichotomies.

THE CLINTON AND OBAMA RACES

In addition to the fact that Clinton and Obama were the first and second most frequently cited candidates for the Democratic nomination in the announcement phase of the campaign, they had other characteristics in common. Both were sitting in the U.S. Senate. Clinton was elected to that office in 2000 and reelected in 2006. Obama, elected in 2004, was in his first term. Both also had earned a JD from an Ivy League university (Clinton from Yale and Obama from Harvard). Their other political experience diverged from there. Clinton had served as first lady. Obama had served two terms in the Illinois State Senate.

To examine if the candidates were treated differently, I conducted a content analysis of the top six circulating newspapers in the United States (*USA Today*, *Wall Street Journal*, *New York Times*, *Los Angeles Times*, *Denver Post*, and *Chicago Tribune*) according to the Audit Bureau of Circulation.[3] Obama announced the formation of his exploratory committee on January 16, 2007, and Clinton announced four days later on January 20. To capture representative press coverage of these events, electronic databases were used to search for articles that contained the words "Clinton" or "Obama" in the headlines from January 1, 2007, to January 31, 2007. Once the data were collected and a codebook established, the author conducted a reliability test on 10 percent of the dataset randomly selected. All variables but one were higher than .80 for Scott's Pi. Assessments of Clinton's positive viability was the lowest with a Scott's Pi of .74. This is just below the typical minimum of .75 and thus these results should be treated with some caution.[4]

Amount of Coverage

Historically, analyses of press coverage of women candidates have found that women running for office get less coverage than do men. For example, political scientist Kim F. Kahn conducted a content analysis of press coverage of twenty-six U.S. Senate races between 1982 and 1986 and found that the women candidates received less news coverage than did their men counterparts. Approximately ninety-five paragraphs a week were written about male Senate candidates, but only seventy-nine paragraphs a week were written about female Senate candidates.[5] Such a disparity between men and women has also been found in coverage of international heads of state,[6] state officials,[7] and even women in newspapers in general.[8]

Studies that look specifically at women running for the presidency show a similar pattern. Falk, who examined the press coverage of eight women who ran for president between 1872 and 2004 and compared it to that of the most equivalent man running in the same race, found that on average men had twice as many articles written about them as did the women. Moreover, the articles that focused on men were, on average, 7 percent longer.[9] Heldman, Carroll, and Olsen,[10] in examining Elizabeth Dole's

2004 presidential race, came to the same conclusion. They determined that despite her strong second-place showing in the polls (after George Bush) she was mentioned less frequently in the press than was John McCain, who polled considerably worse.

The Clinton and Obama data from January 2007 was consistent with these past findings. The six newspapers examined ran more stories with Obama in the headline than Clinton. There were fifty-nine stories headlined with the word Obama and just thirty-six with Clinton. Obama was also more likely to be mentioned in stories about the campaign than was Clinton. Eighty-four stories mentioned Obama whereas just fifty-five mentioned Clinton. In fact only nine stories mentioned Clinton without mentioning Obama whereas thirty-eight stories mentioned Obama without mentioning Clinton. Finally, more paragraphs were written about Obama than Clinton (934 to 631). This trend is consistent with past research that showed that in seven of the eight previous races for president studied men had more coverage than equivalent women in the same races.[11]

It was also true that the articles that mentioned Obama but not Clinton were longer than the articles that mentioned Clinton but not Obama, although the difference was minimal. The articles exclusively about Obama averaged about 529 words, while those exclusively about Clinton averaged about 525 words. However, this finding should be treated with some caution as there were very few articles that mentioned only Clinton. Forty-six articles mentioned both candidates; thirty-eight mentioned Obama without mentioning Clinton, and just nine mentioned Clinton without mentioning Obama.

Substance of Coverage

Not only have women candidates historically received less press coverage than their male counterparts, they have also tended to have fewer of their issues covered by the press. In Falk's analysis of press coverage of women candidates for president, she found that reporters tended to write more about the policy positions of men candidates than women candidates. Over the eight races she examined, about 27 percent of the paragraphs written about the men candidates concerned issues, compared to just 16 percent of those about women candidates.[12] A study by Aday and Devitt that looked at Elizabeth Dole's presidential campaign found similar results. They concluded that "compared to her male opponents, Dole received less coverage on her positions on the issues."[13]

Whereas Obama may have had an advantage in overall coverage, at least according to these search criteria, reporters were not more likely to cover his policy positions than Clinton's. Twenty-two percent of the issue paragraphs written about Clinton were predominantly about issues whereas just 5 percent of those about Obama were. This finding, however, should be treated with caution. Several political pundits who followed the race between Clinton and Obama have noted that particularly in the early part of the campaign, Obama's speeches rarely touched on public policy specifics. The press coverage did report heavily that Obama was calling for "hope" and "change." However, because the reports did not link these ideas to specific policy positions, they were not coded as issues in this study.

It is also true that if the Clinton and Obama results are examined in historical context, it appears that Clinton did have more issue coverage than women who preceeded her but still had less issue coverage than a typical man. Falk found that over eight races on average about 16 percent of paragraphs about women candidates were predominantly about issues and 27 percent of paragraphs about equivalent men were about issues, while for Clinton it was 22 percent.[14]

Viability

Not only have women's issue positions been less likely to draw press attention, but the same also applies to positive assessments of their viability. In a 1994 study of media coverage of women running in forty-seven statewide campaigns, Kahn found the press was more likely to characterize women's candidacies as less viable and more likely to emphasize "their unlikely chances of victory" than competing men.[15] Falk similarly found that even when comparing men and women who ran for president who were equally likely to lose, the men had three times the positive viability statements printed about them in the press compared with the women.[16]

There was no evidence of this pattern in the coverage of the announcements of Obama and Clinton. Clinton received twenty-one positive viability mentions to Obama's seven, possibly because of Clinton's frontrunner status and Obama's relative obscurity. Sexism does not appear to have overcome this advantage for Clinton. Whether sexism mitigated the amount of positive viability assessments can not be ascertained from these data.

Physical Descriptions

Whereas issue positions have been in short supply in press coverage of women candidates, there has been an abundance of reporting on their physical attributes.[17] This pattern has been sustained for women running for president. For example, Heldman, Carroll, and Olson found when they compared the coverage of Elizabeth Dole's presidential campaign with the coverage of the other (male) candidates in the race that "her appearance was mentioned significantly more often than that of any of the other candidates."[18] In Falk's analysis of the press coverage of eight presidential campaigns she found that the female candidates were more than three times as likely as the men to have their physical appearance mentioned.[19]

This pattern, however, was not manifest in the Clinton and Obama comparison. Forty percent of articles about Obama included some physical description of him whereas just 29 percent of articles about Clinton did so. However, virtually all of the physical descriptions about Obama were of his skin color, a novel aspect of his campaign and his viability as a candidate.

When comparing Clinton to previous data on women candidates the percent of articles that described her physically was well below the average for women in eight previous races (41 percent). However, it was still a little higher than the average for eight white men in previous races (14 percent).[20] This suggests that as a woman she still may be more subject to physical descriptions than a white man, but also that Obama's race was more salient to reports than was Clinton's gender.

Other Differences

Falk also found several other ways in which the press treated male and female candidates differently. For example, women who had held elected office were more likely to have their titles (such as senator and representative) dropped and be referred to as "Ms." or "Mrs." than were men to be referred to by "Mr." rather their titles. Women were also more likely than men to be referred to by their first names. The gender of the candidate's supporters were more likely to be mentioned when women were running than were men, suggesting that women lacked broad voter appeal. Women were demonstrated to have one advantage in Falk's analysis. They were more likely to be quoted.[21] This may been because the women actually were more articulate or better at speaking in sound bites, or it may have been because expectations for women were lower, thus, what they said seemed to be more quote worthy.

These observations followed through for the Clinton and Obama early primary race. Hillary Clinton was more likely than Barack Obama to have her title dropped. She was referred to as Mrs. Clinton instead of Senator Clinton in 29 percent of her mentions whereas Obama was referred to as Mr. Obama in just 14 percent of his mentions. Clinton was also more likely to be referred to by her first name. Almost 5 percent of her references were to Hillary whereas just about 2 percent of Obama's were to Barack. Though it is possible that the Clinton campaign decision to refer to Clinton as "Hillary" on her yard signs and other promotional material (perhaps to distinguish her from Bill Clinton) may have contributed to this pattern, it is also true that both of these patterns are very consistent with those found in previous races in which the women did not refer to themselves by their first names.[22]

Reporters were also more likely to mention the gender of Clinton's supporters compared with Obama's. The sex of Clinton's supporters was mentioned in 13 percent of the stories about her, whereas Obama's were mentioned in just 1 percent. This is consistent with past research, which found that, on average, the gender of male candidate's supporters are mentioned in 1 percent of stories whereas women's are mentioned in 16 percent of stories.[23] One reason for this may be because women candidates (who are assumed to be gendered in our culture) are also assumed by reporters to be representatives of a select special interest (women).[24] In contrast, men candidates (who are assumed to transcend gender in political contexts) are free to be representatives of the electorate.

Also consistent with past patterns, Clinton was quoted more than Obama. Clinton had overall more words quoted than did Obama. Clinton had more than 2,400 words quoted, whereas Obama had closer to 1,600. When calculated on a per word basis, that translates to about 540 words per 10,000 words written about her for Clinton and 260 words for Obama. This pattern is consistent with past trends that show women candidates for president tend to be quoted more than men.[25]

The Novelty Frame

Though Falk, in her study, did not gather quantitative data on the "novelty" or "first" frame she did note that throughout the 130-year history of women running for president women were persistently framed as though each one was a "first."[26] Although not an overwhelming trend in these data, this frame was present. For example, the *New York Times* wrote, "If successful, Mrs. Clinton, 59, would be the first female nominee of a major

American political party."[27] The *Los Angeles Times* cast her as a different kind of first, "Sen. Hillary Rodham Clinton made her long-anticipated entrance Saturday into the 2008 presidential race, aiming to make history as the first woman elected to the White House after an audacious and turbulent political journey from first lady to a New York Senate seat."[28] It was the *Chicago Tribune* that invoked the most common version of the first frame when it penned, "She is the first woman to run for president who is considered credible enough to win."[29] What is worrisome about the persistence of the first or novelty frame is that it may make women seem riskier as candidates and reinforces the idea that women are unnatural in the political sphere.

Good News and Bad News

Given the history of press bias against women candidates for president there were both some promising surprises and some disappointingly familiar trends in the press coverage of Hillary Clinton's announcement. The most striking finding was that, given search terms and data set employed, Clinton got substantially less press coverage in the six circulating newspapers examined than did a man who polled less than she did. Several previous analyses have found that women candidates do get less coverage than men, and previous research has found that women candidates for president were mentioned on average in about half as many articles as equivalent men were.[30] Clinton did not do quite that poorly, but the disparity was still rather striking. Some of the disparity may be due to the fact that Obama was relatively unknown, while Clinton had been a major presence on the political scene for sixteen years.

Given that Clinton entered the race as a front runner and was considered by many to have had a more substantive political resume and experience, it is hard to imagine that anything but sexism could account for the disparities in press coverage outlined here. Traditional notions of news norms suggest that editors apply consistent standards in determining newsworthiness. Among those consistently named are prominence, topicality, human interest, conflict, timeliness, and unusualness. This finding in the context of previous similar findings appears to substantiate the idea that traditional news norms or notions of newsworthiness are mediated by sexism.

There were other troubling findings in these data that suggest that not only how much coverage candidates receive is affected by sexism but also the type of coverage as well. Clinton was more likely to have her title dropped and be referred to by her first name. Both results suggest subtle ways in which the press may have cued less prestige, respect, and honor for her.

The press was also more likely to mention the gender of her supporters compared to Obama's. This is a curious pattern found in previous races as well. Reporting the gender of supporters for women candidates may frame women as special interest candidates and therefore not effective representatives of the entire electorate. It is also another way to make the gender of the candidate salient.

Also consistent with previous research was the fact that Clinton was quoted more than was Obama. Why this consistently appears to be the case is not clear. One hypothesis is that if the reporters expect less of women, they would be surprised by their articulateness and therefore more likely to quote them. It is also possible that women candidates may simply be better at talking in quotable sound bites.

Despite these patterns that reflect ones found in earlier races, there were other findings that ran counter to expectations. For example, Clinton got more issue coverage than did Obama. Twenty-two percent of her paragraphs were about issues while just 5 percent of Obama's were. This disparity may be due to the fact that Clinton had been planning her run for so much longer than Obama and therefore may have been more likely to have more policy positions worked out at the time of her announcement, or it may reflect the absence of concrete issues in Obama's addresses at the onset of his campaign. However, it is still interesting to note that Clinton got less issue coverage than the average of eight men in previous races.[31]

Also contrary to expectations was the fact that Obama had more physical descriptions printed about him than did Clinton. This comparison is complicated by the fact that Obama's father was from Africa, making his race a frequent subject of comment in press accounts. However, the percent of articles that included a physical description for Clinton was well below the average for women found for eight previous races (29 percent versus 40 percent).[32] This may suggest one way in which the press may be normalizing the reporting about women candidates or it may suggest that frontrunner status may mitigate traditional associations with women. It is also possible that because Clinton was so well known to the public after having served two terms as first lady that her appearance was no longer deemed worthy of comment by most reporters.

There was a third way in which the coverage of Clinton departed from that of previous women candidates. She was described with positive viability more frequently than her male opponent. Of course, during this period she had a substantial lead in the polls. Whether the magnitude of that advantage was mitigated by sexism is not clear from these data.

FRAMING THE CANDIDATES

The idea that stories in the press may consistently take the same angle or approach to a topic has been called "framing" in communication literature. Studies have shown that by slightly altering word choice or selecting some information to make it salient while downplaying other aspects of a story, frames can effect how people perceive issues.[33]

These last three findings (more issue coverage, fewer physical descriptions, and more positive viability statements) suggest that Clinton was treated differently (at least in the announcement of her race) than previous women who have run for president. One theory that could explain this pattern is that reporters and editors approach women candidates with different frames in mind. The first frame is the "woman" frame. In this mindset the candidate is viewed as a symbolic candidate. That is to say, that the essence of the story is about a woman doing something unusual—for a woman. If reporters approach a story with the idea that the story is about a woman, they may be more likely to think and write about ideas that they associate with women. For example, if culture typically associates women with their beauty and appearance, how the candidate looks may be more likely to seem relevant and important to the story. Similarly, if the story is fundamentally about a woman and not about a candidate, policy positions are less likely to be considered relevant, and positive viability statements are less likely to be made.

A contrasting frame would be the "candidate" frame. If reporters fundamentally view the woman as a candidate then they will be more likely to write about her issue stands, less likely to write about how she looks, and more likely to talk about her positive viability. Clinton represents an interesting case in this context. Her status as frontrunner may have forced more reporters to look at her through a candidate lens than a woman lens and thereby focus more coverage on issues and less on physical appearance, and reporters may have been more likely to include the idea that she might win the race. This may have been possible because Clinton was unusual in that she entered the race as the most viable candidate. As more women put themselves forward as presidential candidates and do better in the polls we are likely to see a shift from the "woman" frame to the "candidate" frame in press coverage of their campaigns.

What is interesting in these data, however, is that despite the apparent movement from a woman frame to a more serious candidate frame this movement did not appear to impact the total amount of coverage. The fundamental question of newsworthiness still seems to have been impacted significantly by Clinton's gender. The fact that she was more likely to have her title dropped, and be referred to by her first name, and that she was regularly framed as a "first" and novelty also suggest that she was not completely viewed as a "candidate," but that the reporters approached her, at least in part, as a "woman," a symbolic representative of other women. While the coverage of Clinton's announcement does demonstrate some movement toward fairer coverage for women candidates for president, clearly there is still some way to go.

It is also interesting to note that there is ample evidence in the text that the mass media treats gender subjectively. The media treat men and women in different ways and in doing so reanimate, reinforce, and reassert traditional gender norms. Women who engage in non-stereotypical activities such as running for higher office, receive less exposure overall than men engaging in stereotypical activities. Thus stereotypical behaviors are highlighted while counter-stereotypical behaviors are diminished. Similarly, by framing women as novelties the press reasserts and highlights the fact that women who run for office are outside their "natural" sphere. By commenting on the gender and appearance of women running for office the press reminds the culture women should be judged on their appearance. Collectively these patterns suggest that gender is articulated and constructed through narratives present in the mass media.

NOTES

1. Erika Falk, *Women for President: Media Bias in Eight Campaigns* (Champaign: University of Illinois, 2008).

2. Judith Butler, *Gender Trouble: Feminism and the Subversion of Identity*, (New York: Routledge, 1990).

3. Audit Bureau of Circulation. (2006). *Top 200 Newspapers by Largest Reported Circulation.* Retrieved on February 5, 2007, from http://www.accessabc.com/products/top200.htm

4. Rodger Wimmer and Joseph Dominick, *Mass Media Research* (Belmont, Calif.: Wadsworth, 2000).

5. Kim Fridkin Kahn, "The Distorted Mirror: Press Coverage of Women Candidates for Statewide Office," *The Journal of Politics* 56, no. 1 (Winter 1994): 154–73. See also the following works for similar results: Kim Fridkin Kahn, *The Political*

Consequences of Being A Woman: How Stereotypes Influence the Conduct and Consequences of Political Campaigns, (New York: Columbia University, 1996); Kim Fridkin Kahn, and Eddie Goldenberg, "Women Candidates in the News: An Examination of Gender Differences in U.S. Senate Campaign Coverage," *Public Opinion Quarterly* 55, no. 2 (Summer 1991): 180–99, Martha Kropf and John Boiney, "The Electoral Glass Ceiling: How The News Affects The Viability Of Female Candidates" (paper presented at the annual meeting of the Midwest Political Science Association in Chicago, Illinois, April 1996).

6. Pippa Norris, "Women Leaders Worldwide: A Splash of Color in the Photo Op." In *Women, Media, and Politics* (New York: Oxford University, 1997), 149–65.

7. Diane Silver, "A Comparison of Newspapers Coverage of Male and Female Officials in Michigan," *Journalism Quarterly* 63, no. 1 (Spring 1986): 144–49.

8. Junetta Davis, "Sexist Bias in Eight Newspapers," *Journalism Quarterly* 59, no. 3 (Autumn 1982): 456–60.

9. Erika Falk, *Women for President.*

10. Caroline Heldman, Susan Carroll, and Stephanie Olson, "'She Brought Only a Skirt': Print Media Coverage of Elizabeth Dole's Bid for the Republican Presidential Nomination," *Political Communication* 22, no. 3 (July-Sept. 2005): 315–35.

11. Erika Falk, *Women for President.*

12. Falk, *Women for President.*

13. Sean Aday and James Devitt, "Style over Substance: Newspaper Coverage of Elizabeth Dole's Presidential Bid," *Harvard Journal of Press/Politics* 6, no. 2 (Spring 2001): 52. For similar results in the context of a gubernatorial race, see also Shirley Serini, Angela Powers, and Susan Johnson, "Of Horse Race and Policy Issues: A Study of Gender Coverage of a Gubernatorial Election by Two Major Metropolitan Newspapers," *Journalism and Mass Communication Quarterly* 75, no. 1 (Spring 1998): 194–204.

14. Erika Falk, *Women for President.*

15. Kim Fridkin Kahn, "The Distorted Mirror," 154.

16. Erika Falk, *Women for President.*

17. Maria Braden, *Politicians and the Media* (Lexington: University Press of Kentucky, 1996); James Devitt, "Framing Gender on the Campaign Trail: Female Gubernatorial Candidates and the Press," *Journalism and Mass Media Quarterly* 79, no. 2 (Spring 2002): 445–63; Diane Heith, "The Lipstick Watch: Media Cverage, Gender, and Presidential Campaigns," in *Anticipating Madam President*, ed. Robert P. Watson and Ann Gordon (Boulder, Colo.: Lynne Rienner, 2003): 123–30; Pippa Norris, "Women Leaders Worldwide: A Splash of Color in the Photo Op." in *Women, Media, and Politics* (New York: Oxford University, 1997), 149–65; Daniella Schonker-Schreck, "Political Marketing and the Media: Women in the 1996 Israeli Elections—A Case Study," *Israel Affairs* 10, no. 3 (2004): 159–77.

18. Caroline Heldman, Susan Carroll, and Stephanie Olson, "She Brought Only a Skirt," 324.

19. Erika Falk, *Women for President.*

20. Falk, *Women for President.*

21. Falk, *Women for President.*

22. Falk, *Women for President.*

23. Falk, *Women for President.*

24. Research indicates that there is little difference between men and women in their level of support for women candidates.

25. Erika Falk, *Women for President.*

26. Falk, *Women for President.*

27. Patrick Healy and Jeff Zeleny, "Clinton Enters the '08 Field, Fueling Race for Money," *New York Times,* January 21, 2007.

28. Stephen Braun and Janet Hook, "Clinton Joins 2008 Race for President; The N.Y. Senator Has Fame, Big Money and a Command of the Issues, but Obstacles Linger," *Los Angeles Times,* January 21, 2007.

29. Jill Zuckerman, "Clinton: 'I'm in to Win': Senator Launches Historic Bid for the White House," *Chicago Tribune,* January 21, 2007.

30. Erika Falk, *Women for President.*

31. Falk, *Women for President.*

32. Falk, *Women for President.*

33. Daniel Kahneman and Amos Tversky, "Choices, Values, and Frames," *American Psychologist* 39, no. 4 (April 1984): 107–28; Shanto Iyengar, *Is Anyone Responsible? How Television Frames Political Issues* (Chicago: University of Chicago Press, 1991).

⓭

VISUALIZING PRESIDENTIAL IMPERATIVES

Masculinity as an Interpretive Frame in Editorial Cartoons, 1988–2008

Janis L. Edwards

During the 2000 presidential campaign primaries, editorial cartoonists had a field day when an advisor to Al Gore suggested he assume the role of the alpha male in order to appeal to female voters. Although the ensuing, exaggerated images of Caveman Al were a response to Gore's specific situation, cartoons that make associations between candidates and masculinity have been prevalent in other campaigns and applied to other candidates. In editorial cartons that have referenced presidential campaigns in recent decades, masculinity has regularly been employed as a *topos,* or rhetorical framing device, by which cartoonists rendered judgment about a candidate's image, character, and qualifications for office. The particular visual method of address employed by cartoonists facilitate the presentation of the cultural imaginary in ways more obvious than other forms of political discourse found in the mainstream news media. As parodic television presents social definitions of masculinity as an operative framework in culture,[1] editorial cartoon parodies expose the construction of masculinity as a viable, if submerged and evolving, component of the rhetorical construction of political leadership.

Jeffords identifies visibility as the key mode of national identity formulation. "It is how citizens *see* themselves and how they *see* those against whom they define themselves that determines national self-perception,"[2] she argues. The literal visualization of actors in the political process in editorial cartoons offers significant evidence of the symbolic constructions that

constitute American expectations of political leadership and aspirants'
promises in fulfillment of those expectations. Similarly, Parry-Giles and
Parry-Giles have identified evidence of masculine imperatives in the visualized medium of presidential campaign films, arguing that, through their images and other content features, these films assert patriarchal value systems
that expose presidential politics as predicated on "traditionally 'masculine'
myths, icons, and character traits derived from participation in male-based
institutions."[3] In this chapter I conduct a cluster analysis of references
to masculinity employed as *topoi* in presidential campaign cartoons from
1988 to 2008.[4] In these cartoons, idealizations of masculinity are deployed
to create a perspective by incongruity[5] that implicitly equates presidential
candidates' fitness for office with their attributes (or lack thereof) of culturally sanctioned definitions of "manliness."

POLITICS AND GENDER

American political leadership has always been bound up with masculine
ideals in the embodiment of the person who occupies, or aspires to occupy,
the Oval Office, even though those associations are not always obvious. As
Heldman has observed, "The masculine bias of the presidency is such a
normalized part of American politics and culture that it is virtually invisible."[6] The presidential office is distinguished, in Heldman's argument, by
its emphasis on masculinity, compared to other offices, an assertion demonstrated by the nation's history. Thus far, the presidential office has been
a space profoundly gendered by the exclusion of women. Our democratic
government has long been marked by the inequity of women and men as
participants in that democracy. Despite attempted excursions by women
into presidential contests, the Oval Office remains a "bastion of maleness,"[7]
infused with messages about masculinity that appear during the campaign
for, and performance of, the office.[8] The power and achievement inherent in
being president resonates with societal messages men get about being male,
with candidates routinely recalling their exploits in the masculine arenas of
the battlefield and the athletic field, and journalists evaluating machismo
as a component of a candidate's character.[9] The historic occupation of the
nation's highest office by males has calcified gender-based imperatives of
ideal leadership, and made masculinity a viable theme for candidate messages, ranging from athletic displays to invocations of wartime experience,
from assertions of authority to embodiments of manly archetypes. Many
of these archetypes involve robust physicality. Hedley Donovan implicitly

masculinizes the criteria for those elected to the Oval Office in noting that the job requires physical, as well as moral, courage.[10] Kann further identifies the "grammar of manhood"[11] as central to the creation of democracy. The heroic ideal of leadership desired in the conceptualization of a president provided a model of manhood that improved and unified other men,[12] encouraging "them to strive for male maturity" through "a sense of fraternal solidarity and national pride."[13]

If themes of masculine identity pervade candidate messages, we can derive a more complete picture of the role of gender imperatives in presidential campaigns by examining how gendered themes are promulgated by the media. Hanke, for one, identifies the importance of media representations in producing and reproducing masculinity as a "cultural category."[14] Teasing out the nature of masculinity embedded in media messages forces us to confront two complications. One is that masculinity is traditionally considered to be invisible and unmarked, taken as the normative, universal human experience.[15] As such, the *masculine* is empowered by its hegemonic and universal nature, while disempowering Others who fall outside of these (perceived) normative parameters. As Dyer notes, "The claim to power is the claim to speak for the commonality of humanity." [16] Second, what we might define as "maleness" may find forms and expression outside of hegemonic conformance, and these forms shift over time. In other words, only certain attributes of masculinity are hegemonic, while other attributes that men may possess—homosexuality, emotional tenderness, physical disability— fall outside the normative boundaries of dominant masculinity. Thus, we more correctly speak of masculinities as variously defined gendered identities. In the political realm, however, I am interested in how culturally dominant forms of masculinity are implicitly invoked in visual commentaries directed at recent presidential candidates and what those depictions may signal about our perceptions of gender as it relates to the nation's highest leadership. As Malin notes, "Assumptions about masculinity have real consequences for people living in (a given) place and time."[17]

EDITORIAL CARTOONS AND THE RHETORIC OF MASCULINITY

Editorial cartoonists occupy a liminal space between the outsider function of the satirist and the insider status of the journalist. Cartoonists pull together the shared references and symbols of society to make judgments and observations on public actors, employing such rhetorical tools as metaphors, ideographs, stereotypes, and terministic screens to construct visible meaning. As a result, political cartoons offer a potent means by which societal attitudes about gender expectations and their role in legitimizing presidential candidates are delineated and amplified. As a growing body of research indicates, editorial cartoons articulate the significant symbols and mythic elements of a culture.[18] In doing so, cartoons become windows into the social realities to which a culture adheres. Political cartoons, rooted in the art of caricature, utilize observable features of their subjects in concert with the condensed meanings in stereotypes to create recognizable stock figurations. Gender, as an observable feature of most public personas, is a common framework used by cartoonists to stereotype their subjects, holding them up in comparison with the norms and ideals of societal prescriptions about gender-appropriate behaviors and displays. However small the actual numbers of working cartoonists (about one hundred), the widespread syndication and visibility of their work, and their association with elite and alternative media formats, enhances the impact of their capacity to communicate social, cultural, and political norms. Cartoonists addressed questions of gendering and the masculine as they relate to presidential candidates in three ways. First, cartoonists invoked comparisons between the candidates and symbols of hypermasculine heroism. Second, metaphorical representations of candidates were developed consonant with the parameters of hegemonic masculinity. Third, cartoonists reified masculinity in opposition to femininity by depicting candidate marriages as a zero-sum game.

Campaigns as Heroic Quests

A political campaign may be likened to a heroic journey and mirrors arenas in which masculine-identified constructs are valorized. For example, campaigns are frequently characterized in metaphorical terms as a conflict, drawing upon the experiences of sport and war, the most common cluster of metaphors that constitute political discourse.[19] The connection with sport and war is sometimes actual as well as metaphorical. A sports background is beneficial to the image of a candidate because it provides a "model for excellence," while military service has long been regarded as the "appropriate apprenticeship for leadership."[20] These traditional male preserves have served as proving grounds for heroic action from ancient times to twentieth-century American experiences.

Campaigns "perpetuate the mythic and heroic demands of the Presidential office."[21] Candidates not only link themselves to established political heroes, Americans long to see in their presidents the heroic qualities of wisdom and omnipotence. Thus, the presidential campaign reflects the master myth of masculinity: The Hero who sets out on a vision quest to perform a selfless deed and is tested by a series of personal trials in service to society[22] or to achieve a personal goal.[23] Columnist Maureen Dowd has identified the completion of the "hero-task" as a set campaign ritual.[24] The legendary hero revitalizes the tradition[25] and encompasses the romantic ideal of manhood; his image is "rhetorically efficacious in a time of distress or uncertainty."[26] We cultivate our heroes and project upon them our highest hopes and aims. In this sense the hero-president-candidate embodies the national persona: "He . . . is born collectively as our own myth."[27]

The valorization of traditionally male-defined activities such as sports and war in the presidential campaign scenario (particularly as strategic components of campaign ads and biographies) serves to define the candidate in predominantly male terms, through the enactment of a role set. A role set is a relatively stable cluster of behavioral relationships linked to one's position that provides general guidelines and expectations for behavior. Denton affirms the role set aspect of the American presidency:

> To know that a person is president is to know in a very general way how that person is likely to behave and how others will behave towards the individual. The title not only provides a means for anticipating a range of behaviors, but also confines the range of behaviors possible.[28]

The selection of a president fundamentally involves a response to the role set as articulated in "basic, holistic . . . image types"[29] or prototypes[30] that are conflated with personal character. Candidates incorporate these role expectations into their campaign messages, and the media measures candidates, in part, by their successes or failures at embodying gendered roles, even if the expectations are masked as normal demands of leadership, rather than presented as masculine ideals. Because cartoonists use shorthand visualizations and stereotypes, the gendered aspects of leader expectations are more evident than in many other forms of mediated discourse relating to political campaigns. This is particularly the case when cartoonists invoke hypermasculine versions of the Hero drawn from popular culture.

Man and Superman as Hero

Cartoonists may signal the masculinized expectations of political leadership by casting the candidates against familiar versions of hypermasculine heroes such as Rambo, Robocop, and Superman. The popularity of films featuring action or romantic heroes emphasizes such iterations of masculinity in political cartoons as broadly drawn exaggerations of the romantic hero archetype. Romantic heroism is a "highly prized model for male achievement."[31] Whether the hero is a film persona or a stock character, such as the soldier or cowboy, as an embodiment and defender of a strong code of behavior, the hero's task is to conquer a threat to weaker beings. The western novel or film provides a central case. Referring to the novel *The Virginian*, George Will wrote:

> There is an American hankering, found in many western novels, for someone who will lay down the law and then throw down the tin star and move on. (The hero) has to make the town safe for womenfolk and young'uns.[32]

As with the cowboy hero who rides off into the sunset, there is a danger in letting the heroic president remain in office permanently. Presidents are compelled to ride off into the political sunset, at least insofar as occupation of the White House is concerned, giving way to new heroes who will face new national and political challenges.

Derivations of the western hero provide repeating metaphors in presidential campaign cartoons. Although the references may take on a literal cast in the case of candidates who hail from western states, as did Texans Ross Perot and George W. Bush, or who adopt western modalities to define their personas, as did Bush, allusions to the cowboy hero are also widely present in cartoons in a more generic sense. In the cartoons examined, candidates were regularly tested by engaging in shootouts or by riding bucking broncos (or donkeys). Since satire's chief function is ridicule, cartoonists often present an incongruity between the western's heroic ideal and a presidential contender. In a 1988 cartoon by Steve Benson, for example, Sheriff Michael Dukakis (the Democratic nominee) bravely stares down a menacing Soviet tank, but he does so astride a toy horse.

All three candidates in 1992—Perot, Bush, and Clinton—were depicted as would-be outlaws who encounter a "Not Wanted" poster featuring their images (King 1992).

Cartoons that employed comic book versions of manly power, such as Superman, were also vivid in their characterizations, perhaps because Superman is regarded by some as "the quintessential male role model."[33] But the candidates, more often than not, fail to fit the role. After a while on the campaign trail, Ross Perot is nearly swallowed up in his Superman costume that "was a perfect fit just a few months back."[34] Perot shouldn't feel too bad because, according to a cartoon by Dick Locher, the entire 1992 primary field of candidates *together* could not fill Superman's costume, even if they flexed their muscles. Campaign strategists might prefer to promote their candidate in the image of superman, as some cartoons suggested, but the image usually falls short of reality. George H. W. Bush dressed as Superman but couldn't open the phone booth door, in a Paul Conrad cartoon, accentuating the media's conferral of "wimp" on Bush's persona. Similarly, Bush-as-Superman failed in his attempts to fly vigorously into the campaign in two different cartoons. While at least one cartoonist saw Bush as an authentic Superman, to Walt Handlesman the pose of strength was simply a Hollywood illusion. Bush looked strong, but he was really only "Superwimp," as Clyde Wells tagged him. Illusion was also a factor for Bill Clinton's 1992 triumphant Superman, whose costume is a perfect fit, but whose convention flight is assisted by wires.

Superman's equation to the president is clear. Superman is known for his physical strength and superhuman powers, effected in the cause of patriotism. He embodies the "machismo qualities of power, control, goodness, and competence,"[35] combining physical force with intelligence to outwit opponents in the cause of justice, offering effective solutions to create a reassuring world where good triumphs over evil. However, the equation between Superman and presidential power faltered after the 1990s and was absent during the campaign cartoons of George W. Bush. Perhaps the stakes were too high for a cartoon version of presidential heroics. Interestingly, when the Superman image returned to 2008 cartoons, it corresponded to "super delegates," a controversial set of figures in the hotly contested Democratic primary.

Hegemonic Masculinity and its Metaphors

The concept of hegemony "refers to the cultural dynamic by which a group claims and sustains a leading position in social life."[36] The power of hegemony is such that its aspects remain unnoticed because society regards them as natural. As Hanke notes, hegemonic beliefs about masculinity "become common sense that may be uncritically absorbed or spontaneously consented to, but that . . . (shape) consciousness (and) norms of conduct."[37] Through its pervasiveness and social acceptance, hegemonic masculinity underscores its own legitimacy. Hegemonic masculinity is validated through a series of representations and references that mirror its constitutive components. Trujillo, for example, argues that hegemonic masculinity is evidenced when power is defined through physical force and occupational achievement, when it is symbolized by the daring frontiersman

or outdoorsman, and when it is defined according to heterosexual and familial patriarchy.[38]

Political cartoon metaphors of the 1988 and 2008 presidential campaigns
mirrored the elements of hegemonic masculinity, which is defined in opposition to femininity, equates power with physical force and achievement,
reflects the tradition of the romantic hero, and celebrates heterosexuality
and familial patriarchy. Society implicitly translates the constitutive elements of hegemonic masculinity into thematic directives. Following from
Doty, Trujillo, and James Doyle,[39] I propose the following four directives
that define the appropriate role set for the American man and, by extension, the American president:

Don't be female
Be a warrior (be aggressive and successful)
Be a hero (be self-reliant, but be someone on whom others can rely)
Be (hetero)sexual (contained by the nuclear family relationship)

Most metaphors used by editorial cartoonists in the group of cartoons under
study reflect one or more of these four directives, offering representations
that continually reinforce and reconstitute hegemonic masculinity and its
applications to those who seek to occupy the Oval Office. An examination of
each directive, in turn, illustrates how cartoonists build a world of sex role
expectations for presidential candidates.

Don't Be Female Hegemonic masculinity demands a sex role performance that excludes other versions of gender. In particular, masculinity is
set in a binary relationship to femininity, so that masculinity is circularly
reasoned as the polar opposite of everything feminine. Feminizing a candidate works as a powerful strategy of debunking and ridicule. In this, cartoonists follow a burlesque tradition based on the reduced status of women
and its meaning for feminized men. Or, as one cartoonist opined when he
was asked why female politicians are rarely "masculinized" in the same way
male politicians are "feminized," women aren't as bothered by such ridicule
as men.

In cartoons, presidential candidates have been illustrated as familiar
female characters (e.g., brides) or dressed in women's clothing or they
enact female roles, even when an alternative male version is available.
For example, some cartoonists depicted George H. W. Bush in a female
cheerleader's costume—the skirt being the tell-tale marker—in relation to
his supportive roles in Iran Contra and antidrug campaigns. Similarly, Tom
Meyer presented Al Gore in a girl's cheerleader skirt to suggest he was

not capable of taking the football handoff from Clinton. Portraying these candidates as a cheerleader (a common female role) in a skirt (an exclusive female garment) rather than a more realistically gendered portrayal underscores ridicule through a direct attack on the authenticity of their manhood. Bush and Gore were especially vulnerable to such depictions because of their secondary status as vice presidents to popular incumbents. Bush additionally suffered from the "wimp" appellation that became attached to him in the 1988 campaign. Patrick Oliphant, one of America's most widely syndicated cartoonists, summed up Bush's image problem in a cartoon that compared the public relations image of Bush with the public perception. In the first frame he is a proud and vigorous war hero wearing his rugged flight jacket. In the second frame, Bush resembles a southern belle, with a party frock, picture hat, and purse. Oliphant continued to use a purse, with or without additional female costumes, as a metaphorical motif to feminize George H. W. Bush throughout his campaign and presidency.

Tom Toles presented an especially vivid version of Bush's perceived lack of appropriate masculinity by portraying him at a carnival hammer game, where his strength would indicate his level of masculine identity. The lower bars of the pole read like a laundry list of feminizing epithets: Wimp, Nebbish, Pixie, Cream Puff, Librarian. The goal, of course, is to strike the bell at the top of the pole, the one labeled "Regular Guy."

Others used a feminized Bush to accentuate wider contextual metaphors. Toles responded to the prevailing "Seven Dwarfs" metaphor of the 1988 campaign by imaging Bush as Snow White, while Bush became Snow White's evil (and female) nemesis in a Bush reelection campaign cartoon by Kevin Siers. Other cartoonists depicted Bush as Alice in Wonderland and Dorothy on the Yellow Brick Road long after Bush had presumably shed the wimp label. The feminization of Bush also took the form of prissy and sissified versions of male role performances, as when Bush's Little Lord Fauntleroy presence was contrasted with the tough guy manner of Bob Dole. Bush prompts the renaming of Bourbon Street in New Orleans to "Warm Milk Street" and presides over "Chez George," located next to Reagan's Country Western Irish Pub (where, presumably, the *real* men gather.)

While George H. W. Bush attracted many of the feminized characterizations in cartoons, other depicted candidates have also imaginatively broken the "Don't Be Female" dictate. For example, early Democratic contender Paul Tsongas was pictured as the incompetent Prissy (from *Gone With the Wind*) when faced with the challenge of Super Tuesday in 1992. Jerry Brown and Bill Clinton joined Tsongas as giggling maidens vying for the glass slipper held by the electorate.

The implicit critical stance in these representations—that a man's resemblance to anything female or feminine disqualifies him as a valid and believable presidential candidate—is reinforced by images that naturalize or extol aggressive behavior. In the cartoon universe Bush "goes a long way toward defusing his image problem"[40] when he turns a GOP debate into a bat-swinging free-for-all. Rather than a characterization applied uniquely to Bush, aggression permeates the visual discourse about presidential candidates.

Be a Warrior   Campaigns are routinely framed by metaphors of sport, conflict, and war,[41] so much so that it is often difficult to find alternate ways of describing common campaign terms such as "race," "dark horse," and "spar." Sport and war metaphors express a similar typology of aggression and conflict, with the proving grounds of the battlefield transposed to the playing field. Conflict metaphors also translate easily to the visual frame of cartoons, as debates and other campaign rituals take place on baseball fields, the basketball court, and the boxing ring. In editorial cartoons, presidential campaign battles were waged on land, sea, and air, imagined in contexts ranging from prehistoric times to the nuclear age. Whether it's the 1992 candidates shooting it out at Fort Deficit, stepping up to the baseball plate, or claiming credit for a debate performance that's a touchdown or a slam dunk, cartoonists place candidates in traditional male territory. Nowhere was the masculine nature of these metaphors more evident than in the oft-depicted boxing arena. Although the boxing metaphor was frequently applied to debates, it also had wider utility, with, for example, a diminutive Dukakis jabbing ineffectively at Bush's knees, or a weakened Bush cowering before a bout with Clinton in 1992. The viability of the boxing metaphor attests to a view of political discourse as oppositional, because boxing clearly pits one individual against one opponent, even though there have been some prominent third-party candidates in the 1988–2008 races.

The boxing metaphor also highlights the fact that cartoons emphasized the most stereotypically masculine sporting endeavors. And while some cartoons made literal references to a candidates' past military experience (Bush in 1988 and McCain in 2008), battlefield depictions transcended the war records and stances of the candidates. War was sometimes generalized as a metaphor by setting a campaign scene in a historical context, such as the Civil War or medieval times. Casting war metaphors in past history further accentuates the exclusivity of war as male territory by recalling historical fact.

In 2004, many of these kinds of metaphors were co-opted by the ramped-up masculinity of George W. Bush's decisive commander-in-chief image, cultivated through photo opportunities, his 2004 convention film, and his demeanor. Bush's warrior image was matched by John Kerry, who offered himself as an authentic war hero, an image that was eventually undercut by the opposition's feminizing discourse of European elitism that mirrored cartoon depictions of an overly elite George H. W. Bush in 1988 and 1992. The typologies of strength expressed in the warrior metaphors helped shape the presidential prescription of the heroic ideal.

Be a Hero   Earlier in this chapter I outlined the way in which editorial cartoonists emphasized gendered presidential requirements by invoking the hypermasculine image of the hero. Even in more everyday settings and characterizations in cartoons, expectations for presidential candidates are infused with the ideals of romantic heroism patterned after archetypes visible in fiction and film. Specific cartoons cast candidates as potential heroes to the voting public, embodied in familiar characters from literature, such as Don Quixote and Rhett Butler, or the chivalry of a skater (Bush in 1988) who guides wary voters (in the form of a young lady) around the cracks in the thin ice of Reaganomics.

Cartoonists were even more apt to translate romantic heroism into mere romantic impulse, as they portrayed presidential candidates as romantic suitors of their parties or the voters. No mainstream candidate was spared this characterization, although the romantic overtures were usually ineffective. Democrats wooing the Democratic donkey or Republicans trying to pick up an elephant in a bar were common enough through the years, but not many had to literally drag the intended bride (the Democratic party) to the altar by her heels, as did Clinton in one 1992 cartoon. Meanwhile, parties were also seeking worthy candidates, as in two cartoons that showed the Democratic prospective lover disregarding momentary 1988 frontrunner Jesse Jackson to pine for an elusive Mario Cuomo.

Although candidates sometimes "got the girl" there was usually a question about whether this was a match made in heaven. Even as Dukakis, following significant primary victories, stood at the altar with his "bride" the Democrats at the wedding continued to speculate on the prospects for other, more charismatic bridegrooms. Even when Dole and G. W. Bush were more accepted as their party's frontrunners, their ability to "woo the elephant" was dubious, according to some cartoons. By linking the metaphor of the romantic suitor with indications of ineffectuality or failure, cartoonists shaped the opportunity to demean political candidates by demeaning their masculinity. Perceptions about a candidate's virility and appeal played into some characterizations, as when a weary and cynical donkey who paid ten cents a dance to peruse the crowded 1988 field says to candidate Paul Simon, "Yeah, yeah . . . you dance divinely . . . yeah, you're my prince . . . yeah, yeah, yeah . . . ." The admonition of hegemonic masculinity to be a romantic hero also reflected, in these instances, the prescription to be heterosexual.

Be Heterosexual   Hegemonic masculinity's admonition to be sexual is constrained by sexual orientation. Cartoonists who depicted candidates as pursuing metaphorical romantic relationships with party members or voters always feminized the objects of the pursuit. When candidates are depicted in common roles that accentuate maleness—as a bridegroom or chivalrous person—it implicitly reinforces the hegemonic requirement that sexuality be expressed as heterosexuality. The cartoons that employ the metaphors of heterosexuality always place the candidate opposite the female. So, for example, when two candidates attempt to attract the support of California voters by displays of manly muscularity on the beach, as in a Dennis Renault cartoon published in the *Sacramento Bee*, the voters are gendered as women. For the masculine to be a unified concept "it must be masculine all the way through and so the feminine will always appear as something other or different."[42] The dynamic of opposition is especially configured in the relationship between the president-candidate and his real-world significant other—his wife.

Marriage as a Zero-Sum Game

Sexual orientation is not a passive state in the structure of hegemonic masculinity but actively coincides with paternal and familial norms. For presidential candidates, this means that wives and other family members often serves as props in campaign messages and appearances, authenticating the candidate's status in the patriarchy.[43] Candidate wives also increasingly function as surrogates for their husbands on the campaign trail, along with other adult family members. Spouses and female family members are perceived as attractions for women voters, an important demographic in recent campaigns. For example, in the Bush campaigns of 2000 and 2004, Laura and Barbara Bush, the candidate's wife and mother, were fixtures at "W Stands for Women" events. In 2008, Michelle Obama conducted special events appealing to working women and spoke on behalf of her husband at numerous rallies. In 1996 Elizabeth Dole was cited as a more effective campaigner than her husband, the candidate.[44] One commentator proposed a debate in 1996 between the two prospective first ladies, reflecting the increased media and public attention to the relative merits of the candidates' spouses,[45] but the spousal rite that has been a fixture of the presidential campaign season is a "cookie bake-off" sponsored by a woman's magazine.[46]

Few cartoons during the period under study depicted candidate wives until Clinton's run for office in 1992. Once a candidate is elected, his wife may be depicted on occasion, but these depictions are most likely when the wife's actions influence the public sphere. As Edwards and Chen have shown, first ladies gain attention in cartoons when they are most transgressive.[47]

As Edwards and Chen note, transgression was the theme of cartoon depictions of Hillary, following Bill Clinton's admiring promise that his candidacy offered "two for the price of one." But in the zero-sum game of political marriage, only one partner can be strong.[48] The other must be weak, reflecting the binary of masculinity and its opposite, femininity. Hillary was routinely depicted as exercising, or attempting to exercise, control over Bill and greater power in the White House. Her chair in the Oval Office was higher than Bill's, her new office in the White House larger than Bill's, and so forth. Several cartoonists were especially negative toward Hillary at the end of the 1992 campaign by showing her grabbing power or inserting herself during the presidential swearing-in, much to the consternation of her husband. Similarly, in 2004, a candid and outspoken Teresa Heinz Kerry was "disciplined" in cartoons, often accompanied by an image of her disapproving husband, although John Kerry had been supportive of his wife during the real life of the campaign.

MASCULINITY AS A TOPOS IN EVOLUTION

Editorial cartoons depicting presidential candidates regularly used masculinity as a commonplace, or rhetorical, topos, by which to indicate a candidate's suitability for office. Given the debunking function of graphic satire, most of these comparisons demeaned or lampooned the candidates' masculine identity. The application of various iterations of masculine reference was not even over the period from 1988 to 2008. Cartoons that referenced the campaign through the warrior metaphor, showing candidates engaged in sports and other conflicts, remained common throughout. But other aspects, such as hypermasculinity and other hegemonic metaphors, have received varied attention and grew relatively absent from 2000 on, superseded by other topoi.

Some might suggest that the personal factors of candidate identities dictated these depictions, but, although some personal references were clear (GHW Bush's "wimp" problem, Bill Bradley's former basketball career), similar appropriations and applications of masculinity were broadly deployed among the candidates.

It is possible, though, that other exigencies affect the function of masculinity as an appropriate topos in editorial cartoons. A number of authors have suggested that masculinity has been under cultural evolution and renovation in the post–Vietnam War,[49] Reagan,[50] Clinton,[51] and post-9/11[52] eras, the time frame of these cartoons. Yet there was a dramatic reduction in direct masculinity references in the campaigns of 2000 and beyond.

One reason for this phenomenon may be Bush's persona. While Gore was savaged for his attempt to personify the alpha male, Bush's persona was entwined with the image of the rugged cowboy and a "recovered masculinity" occasioned by the terrorist acts of September 11, 2001.[53] As Ducat argues, the aftermath of the WTC bombing resulted in "the revivification of 'heroic' manhood through the heraldry of the rescue workers,"[54] and effectively appropriated by President Bush and the social zeitgeist. His assertion of the commander-in-chief role in the 2004 campaign, and in photo-ops preceding the campaign, offset Kerry's attempt to claim the authenticity of the war hero identity. Thus, for both Kerry and Bush, masculinity and war heroism were actual assumed identities rather than metaphors.

In addition, women have run for president in the past three campaign seasons. Although Carol Moseley Braun and Elizabeth Dole did not enjoy Hillary Clinton's prominence as candidates, the incursion of women into the campaign may be leading to a more neutralized depiction of gender in cartoons.[55] While Clinton still received some stereotypical treatment in 2008, the topos of masculinity was almost completely absent from depictions of candidates McCain and Obama,[56] except for conflict metaphors.

Although it remains to be seen whether masculinity is revived as a dominant topos in subsequent campaigns, the prominence of women on the presidential campaign stage in 2008 suggests that the masculinity frame may become obsolete in politics. But its uses in the late twentieth century reflect the role of masculinity in national leadership and possibly indicate why women have not broken through that important glass ceiling as of this writing.

NOTES

1. Brenton J. Malin, *American Masculinity Under Clinton: Popular Media and the Nineties "Crisis of Masculinity"* (New York: Peter Lang, 2005), 65–77.

2. Susan Jeffords, *Hard Bodies: Hollywood Masculinity in the Reagan Era* (New Brunswick, N.J.: Rutgers University Press, 1994), 6.

3. Shawn J. Parry-Giles and Trevor Parry-Giles, "Gendered Politics and Presidential Image Construction: A Reassessment of the 'Feminine Style,'" *Communication Monographs* 63, no. 1 (December 1996): 350.

4. The cartoons were collected over time from a variety of sources. Other than available newspapers, cartoons published from 1986 to 1996 were collected from *Political Pix, Bull's Eye, Valley Comic News, Comic Press News, and the National Gallery (National Forum) of Editorial Cartoons.* Cartoons published from 2000 to 2008 were collected primarily from the internet site www.cagle.com. Approximately two thousand cartoons were viewed, with 1988 campaign cartoons comprising almost half of the total collected.

5. For background on the concept of perspective by incongruity in cartoons, see Denise M. Bostdorff, "Making Light of James Watt: A Burkean Approach to the Form and Attitude of Political Cartoons," *Quarterly Journal of Speech* 73, no. 1 (February 1987): 43–59.

6. Caroline Heldman, "Cultural Barriers to a Female President in the United States," in Lori Cox Han and Caroline Heldman, eds., *Rethinking Madame President: Are We Ready for a Woman in the White House?* (Boulder, Colo.: Lynne Reinner Publishers, Inc., 2007), 20.

7. Marcia Lynn Whicker and Hedy Leonie Issacs, "The Maleness of the American Presidency," in *Women in Politics: Outsiders or Insiders?* ed. Lois Duke Whitaker (Upper Saddle River, N.J.: Prentice Hall, 1991), 221.

8. For relevant discussions of masculinity and the presidential office, see Bruce Curtis, "The Wimp Factor," *American Heritage*, 40 (November 1989): 40–50; Walter R. Fisher, "Romantic Democracy, Ronald Reagan, and Presidential Heroes," *The Western Journal of Speech Communication* 46, no. 3 (Summer 1982): 299–310; and Bruce Gronbeck, "Mythic Portraiture in the 1988 Presidential Caucus Bio-Ads," *American Behavioral Scientist* 32, no. 4 (March/April 1989): 351–64;

9. Stephen J. Ducat, *The Wimp Factor: Gender Gaps, Holy Wars, and the Politics of Anxious Masculinity* (Boston: Beacon Press, 2004). Journalists have expressed this theme by commenting positively or negatively on the physical prowess and athletic abilities and pursuits of politicians.

10. Hedley Donovan, "Job Specs for the Oval Office: A Memorial Essay," *Presidential Studies Quarterly* 21, no. 1 (Winter 1991): 142.

11. See Mark E. Kann, *A Republic of Men: The American Founders, Gendered Languages, and Patriarchal Politics* (New York: New York University Press, 1998).

12. Georgia Duerst-Lahti, "Masculinity on the Campaign Trail," in Han and Heldman, eds., *Rethinking Madame President*, 97.

13. Mark E. Kann, *A Republic of Men*, 134.

14. Robert Hanke, "Theorizing Masculinity With/In the Media," *Communication Theory* 8, no. 2 (May 1988): 187.

15. Brenton J. Malin, *American Masculinity*, 9; Michael S. Kimmel, "Invisible Masculinity," *Society* (Sept./Oct. 1993): 28–35.

16. Richard Dyer. *White*. (London: Routledge, 1997): 2.

17. Brenton J. Malin, *American Masculinity*, 7.

18. Joan L. Conners, "Popular Culture in Political Cartoons: Analyzing the Cartoonist Approaches," *PS Political Science & Politics* XL, no. 2 (April 2007): 261–65; Michael DeSousa and Martin J. Medhurst, "Political Cartoons and American Culture: Significant Symbols of Campaign 1980," *Studies in Visual Communication* 8, no. 1 (1982): 84–97; Janis L. Edwards, *Political Cartoons in the 1988 Presidential Campaign: Image, Metaphor, and Narrative* (New York: Garland Press, 1997); Janis L. Edwards, "Visualized Narratives: Cartoonists Respond to 9/11," *Iowa Journal of Communication* 35, no. 2 (Fall 2003): 19–34; E. H. Gombrich, *The Uses of Images: Studies in the Social Function of Art and Visual Communication* (London: Phaidon, 1999).

19. Jane Blankenship, "The Search for the 1972 Democratic Nomination: A Metaphorical Perspective," in *Rhetoric and Communication*, ed. Jane Blankenship and Hermann G. Stelzner (Urbana: University of Illinois Press, 1972): 236–60.

20. Sheila Tobias, "Shifting Heroisms: The Use of Military Service in Politics," in *Women, Militarism, and War: Essays in History, Politics, and Social Theory*, ed. Jean Bethke Elshtain and Sheila Tobias (Savage, Md.: Rowman & Littlefield, 1990): 163–86. However, military service as a presidential imperative seems to be waning in the discourse since 1993.

21. Robert E. Denton Jr., *The Symbolic Dimensions of the American Presidency: Description and Analysis* (Prospect Heights, Ill.:Waveland Press, 1982): 61.

22. Joseph Campbell, *The Power of Myth*, ed. Betty Sue Flowers (New York: Doubleday, 1988).

23. William G. Doty, *Myths of Masculinity* (New York Crossroad Press, 1993).

24. Maureen Dowd. "Candidates Locked in Subliminal Battle to Become America's Hero," *Palm Beach Post*, 11 October 1992, 21(A).

25. Joseph Campbell, *Power of Myth*.

26. Bruce Gronbeck. "Mythic Portraiture," 357.

27. Rollo May, *The Cry for Myth*, (New York: W.W. Norton & Company, 1991): 58.

28. Robert E. Denton Jr., *Symbolic* Dimensions, 48.

29. Robert L. Savage, "Creating the Eye of the Beholder," in *Candidates Images in Presidential Elections*, ed. Kenneth L. Hacker (Westport, Conn.: Praeger, 1995):45.

30. Dan Nimmo, "The Formation of Candidate Images During Presidential Campaigns," in *Candidate Images in Presidential Elections*, ed. Kenneth L. Hacker, (Westport, Conn.: Praeger, 1995): 57.

31. Peter Tatham, *The Makings of Maleness: Men, Women, and the Flight of Daedelus* (New York: New York University Press, 1992): 3.

32. George F. Will, *The Leveling Wind: Politics, Culture, and Other News 1990-1994* (New York: Viking, 1994): 296.

33. Norma Pecora. "Superman/Superboys/Supermen: The Comic Book Hero as Socializing Agent," in *Men, Masculinity, and the Media*, ed. Steve Craig, (Newbury Park, Calif.: SAGE Publications, 1992): 63.

34. Henry Payne, "Cartoon," *National Forum of Editorial Cartoons* (date unknown, npage).

35. Norma Pecora, "Superman/.Superboys/Supermen," 67.

36. Robert W. Connell, *Masculinities* (Berkeley: University of California Press, 1995).

37. Robert Hanke, "Theorizing Masculinity," 185.

38. Nick Trujillo, "Hegemonic Masculinity on the Mound: Media Representations of Nolan Ryan and the American Sports Culture," *Critical Studies of Mass Communication* 8, no. 3 (September 1991): 290–308.

39. James A. Doyle, *The Male Experience* (Dubuque, Iowa: William C. Brown, 1989).

40. Jack Ohman, "Cartoon," *National Gallery of Cartoons*, 29 March 1992, 9.

41. Jane Blankenship, "Search for the 1972 Democratic Nomination."

42. Peter Middleton, *The Inward Gaze: Masculinity and Subjectivity in Modern Culture* (London: Routledge, 1992):138.

43. Notably, in 2008, readers may recall Cindy McCain's nearly ubiquitous presence standing onstage behind John McCain at political rallies. Conversely, Howard Dean's wife, Marilyn, was criticized in 2000 for not accompanying her husband on the campaign trail. John Edwards's wife and children often accompanied him on the vice presidential campaign trail in 2000, very much part of Edwards's image. The candidate wives have played a more visible role in recent conventions.

44. The Dole claim was made by Leslie Stahl in a CBS interview (date unknown) and substantiated by Bob Dole in the same televised segment.

45. Laura Blumenfeld, "And One of Them Shall Be First: Elizabeth Dole and Hillary Clinton Offer Conflicting Visions," *Washington Post Weekly Edition*, 8–14 September 1996, 6–7; Nancy Gibbs and Michael Duffy, "Just Heartbeats Away," *TIME*, 1 July 1996, 25–28.

46. It should be noted that candidate wives have been symbolically co-joined with their husbands' candidacies in campaign paraphernalia dating back at least to the early twentieth century. Much of the increased attention to political wives arguably stems from the movement of women away from exclusively domestic spheres into work and public life.

47. Janis L. Edwards and Huey Rong Chen, "The First Lady/First Wife in Editorial Cartoons: Rhetorical Visions Through Gendered Lenses," *Women's Studies in Communication* 23, no. 3 (Fall 2000): 367–91.

48. Kathleen Hall Jamieson outlines the parameters of the zero-sum political marriage in her book *Beyond the Double Bind: Women and Leadership* (New York: Oxford University Press, 1995).

49. Susan Jeffords, *The Remasculinization of America: Gender and the Vietnam War* (Bloomington: Indiana University Press, 1989).

50. Susan Jeffords, *Hard Bodies*.

51. Brenton J. Malin, *American Masculinity Under Clinton*.

52. Stephen Ducat, *Wimp Factor*.

53. Ducat, *Wimp Factor*, 227-230.

54. Ducat, *Wimp Factor*, 227.

55. Janis L. Edwards, "Drawing Politics in Pink and Blue," *PS Political Science and Politics* XL, no. 2 (April 2007): 249–53.

56. The factor of race in the 2008 may have complicated the application of hegemonic masculine references.

14

GENDERED BODIES

Considering the Sexual in Political Communication

Jimmie Manning and Cady Short-Thompson

Whether we speak of studies of media representations and discourses, movement rhetoric centered upon feminist ideals and practices, or inquiries into the various roles women play in politics, the majority of scholarly political communication studies place sex and gender into either differential or causal paradigms. Differential approaches to sex and gender tend to focus upon how female candidates differ from male candidates with the causal studies frequently examining how females entering political forums affect those forums. While such studies are productive in extracting gendered understandings of communication, continuing to expand the lenses through which scholars study gender could allow for new and diverse views of how sex and gender play into political understandings. Asking provocative questions about sex and gender is key to expanding and refining bodies of knowledge about gender and politics. One example of a strong and stimulating question about sex and gender in political rhetoric was offered by Nathan Stormer in his essay "A Vexing Relationship: Gender and Contemporary Rhetorical Theory." Here Stormer asks a provocative and potentially fruitful question with no easy answer: "What if we take the body as a rhetorical situation? What happens to gender and rhetorical theory then?"[1] Academic inquiries attempting to answer this question likely hold the potential to both enrich and complicate understandings of the intersections between gender and rhetorical theory; perhaps nowhere will this be more exciting or stimulating than in academic explorations into political communication.

In the spirit of Stormer's work, then, this essay expands notions of gender in the political-rhetorical realm and explores how political situations can be better understood through a lens where the body is considered as a rhetorical situation—one that is not only read in terms of sex or gender, but also in terms of sexuality. To this end, we pose questions as to whether the differences between sex and gender have been over- or underemphasized in understanding political rhetoric. The communication discipline clearly distinguishes between the notions of sex (biology) and gender (culture); but beyond this simple articulation of their difference, the two are often treated as interchangeable. This essay explores why this practice can be both liberating and constricting and considers how the oft-missing elements of sexuality[2] can intersect sex and gender to allow for sophisticated understandings of gendered impact upon political communication. In examining sexuality, we hope to provoke questions by contesting the much-stated (false) dichotomy of sex and gender, exploring the differences between sexuality and sex acts, and examining the implications reconceptualizing gendered political rhetoric has upon readings of bodies. Given the continuing dialogue we enter with this essay, we suspect we may raise as many questions as we answer.

SEXING THE SEX-GENDER DICHOTOMY IN POLITICAL COMMUNICATION

An enduring trend in academic conversations about *sex* and *gender* (and something much trumpeted in textbooks) is that the two terms are quite different. The difference in terms often is oversimplified as *sex* representing the biological aspects of an individual and *gender* representing psychological aspects of a person's being. *Sex*, then, represents the body while *gender* represents the mind that is controlling the body with the former being expressed as male or female and the latter with masculinity or femininity. While this draws an understandable (and occasionally contested) academic distinction, it ignores the practical understanding so much gender research seeks to utilize. To be certain, people do not talk about others in terms of the *masculines* and the *feminines*—they look at males and the females, and they read men and women as being synonymous with those two terms. Even in scholarly research, where the distinction between sex and gender is often recognized, both terms are often conflated. In post-positivist research, for example, gender is sometimes measured by asking participants for their biological sexes and then making gendered assumptions based on the sex demographic.[3] In interpretive and humanistic research, gender is often explored in terms of sex as well, with assumptions inherently placing feminine expectations upon females and masculine expectations upon males. And, regardless of methodological paradigm, scholars tend to treat gender (and, by default, sex) as something static and not open to continuous change.

To be fair, scholars have acknowledged some of the fluid possibilities of gender. Jamieson acknowledged changing gendered expectations twenty years ago when she concluded that gendered aesthetics govern visual representations and that political communication scholars must explore the nuances created through this change.[4] Specifically, she examined how men in political situations, because of the limitations of most political speakers being seen via the surface of a screen, were required to enact a sort of pseudo-intimacy causing them to be, on some level, effeminate, or feminized. As Campbell and Keremidchieva assert, this "queers" the notion of men's public address, creating a space where "the male body performs the discursive demands of the medium in drag"[5]—in other words, the masculine male is visual(ized) while the feminine is enacted. While we understand the spirit of the comment and understand how one might place evolving gendered understandings into a queer paradigm, such an assertion—at least within the context of communication—belies the nature of queerness. To "queer" something is to destabilize it—to remove its essential notion of identity. That is, for something to be queer it cannot fit into an institutional structure because it has not been accepted. While male politicians may very well be "enacting drag" by softening their dominant masculine traits to appease an audience, they are playing into an institution as opposed to defying it. They are stabilizing what constitutes accepted masculinity within a given context and within a given culture. They are stabilizing, in part, the connection between sex and gender in political communication.

Dominant notions of the masculine and feminine, then, are queered *by* political communication (as opposed to being queered *through* it) since political cultures have their own unique sets of masculine and feminine experiences. To define which political experiences can be deemed *masculine* and *feminine* in political campaign communication, however, is an aim fraught with its own complications, controversies, stereotypical tendencies, and intergenerational conflict. But to do so could be necessary and fruitful for political and gender scholars. It is to be expected, given the history of women being "othered," that what is masculine in political communication is often defined as what is not feminine. Karlyn Kohrs Campbell popularized the term *feminine style*[6] to describe a gendered difference in public address separated from an existing masculine norm; much of the feminine is explored by looking at the masculine comparatively. Masculine rhetorical experiences are rational, educated, aggressive, experienced, expert, ambitious, competitive, and authoritative.[7] Scholars have described the political experience as advantaging male candidates, since men possessed desired attributes associated with political leaders, such as military experience, advantages of incumbency, knowledge of foreign affairs, and expertise in economic and financial matters. Indeed, political leadership as an ideal has been shaped historically by masculine imperatives—but this is only made evident by comparison with the feminine. The feminine political experiences are typified by preoccupations with appearance, nurturance and sensitivity to others' needs, compassion, affection, family centeredness, and an absence of assertiveness (especially avoiding harsh language).[8] These attributes are also the product of centuries-old biases and stereotypes, but that does not disqualify the existence of generalized differences. Empirical studies have found that at least sixteen communication differences exist between men and women in political rhetoric,[9] with women using intensive adverbs, more relational talk, conciliatory rhetoric, and different nonverbal indicators (excessive smiling, frequent gestures, greater sensitivity to others' nonverbal cues) leading to what Mulac defines as a female style that is "indirect, elaborate, and effective."[10] While conclusions in published research on sex-gender differences of male and female candidates may slightly differ, most concede that "sex role stereotypes continue to help shape expectations regarding what is appropriate."[11] Such gender norms can lead to women being rated higher than men on sociointellectual status (social status, literacy) and aesthetic quality (nice, beautiful) while men are rated higher on dynamicism (strength, aggression).[12]

While it may be easy to dismiss the socially constructed rules of feminine or female styles in politics as potentially limiting (or even patriarchal), it is important to also consider the strengths of such attributes and how they are rooted in the long-held notion that equates the personal with the political. As scholar and cultural critic Catharine Mackinnon explains, "Women's distinctive experience as women occurs within that sphere that has been socially lived as the personal—private, emotional, interiorized, particular, individuated, intimate—so that what it is to know the politics of woman's situation is to know women's personal lives."[13] As Campbell,[14] Dow and Wood,[15] and other prominent scholars have noted, the "personal as political" is deeply rooted in female political rhetoric because of early social movements seeking women's rights.[16] Additionally, not all male and female political figures have been exclusively limited to stereotypically masculine or feminine rhetorical strategies, nor have they all demonstrated stylistic differences. Following three decades of mixed results from gendered studies in political campaign communication, several researchers reject strict gendered norms, calling for the recognition of an androgynous political experience.

The research of Mayhead and Marshall has examined the rhetoric of twenty-first-century contemporary women candidates, finding evidence of an evolution from a long-assumed feminine style and content to gender-neutral discursive practices occupying an androgynous "in-between space."[17] Androgynous stretching is a "morphing of . . . rhetorical approaches into a discourse shaped from the language of old but with potential for a new 'presencing' [which] provides for a more effective and more realistic way to examine the public argument of these elected officials."[18] The view advanced by Mayhead and Marshall asserts that women's political rhetoric is far more complex than a singular focus on women's issues or the usage of a prescribed set of feminine-styled rhetorical elements. This movement of women's rhetoric into an in-between space demonstrates speakers who value a variety of issues (whether or not they can be categorized as "women's" issues) with broad appeal and application. Moving toward the androgynous, this style rejects strict gender roles and, in a nonessentialist[19] way, privileges both men and women who may have more opportunity to speak on a wider variety of issues. Questions regarding androgynous stretching—or, as we call it, *gendered possibility*—are raised later in this essay.

MASCULINE AND FEMININE LANGUAGE, MASCULINE AND FEMININE BODILY ACTION

Before unpacking the notion of gendered possibilities, it is important to consider an element often missing from analysis of political rhetoric: the body. In considering the masculine and feminine in rhetoric, nonverbal elements such as the body have often been sidelined. While the body could be considered through a variety of valuable lenses, for the scope of this essay we begin with considering the social constructions of sex, gender, and sexuality as they pertain to the bodies of those in politics. It is easy to forget that it is bodies creating and delivering political discourses—and the gender of these bodies is important in our interpretations of appropriate or effective behaviors. For instance, if a man sheds a tear when talking about lost heroes, it may be taken as a reflection on his patriotism and his humanity as a leader. It shows that the stern disposition he usually carries is supplemented by compassion. For a woman to express the same emotions, however, may play into the commonplace notion that women are weak and cannot handle the pressures of political situations; her body is a woman's body, and it is frail and unable to handle the emotional stress. Where the tears soften the masculine body and temper the strength it has the potential to represent, the tears only make the weak feminine body weaker. Yet this example should not be considered a hard and fast rule for reading bodies, as different political situations bring about different possibilities for how gender is read and what agency it allows.[20] In 2008, the sight of Democratic presidential candidate Hillary Rodham Clinton tearing up during an intense and pressure-filled post-Iowa caucus campaign event was particularly scrutinized on numerous news networks and blog sites, falling in line with the expected negative critique of a female candidate's tears. Not falling in line with these expectations, however, is that many accused Clinton of employing tears as a tool of manipulation. In a surprising turn that defied the usual gendered interpretations, Clinton's emotional display was eventually seen as positive after the New Hampshire voters surprised the nation by upending Senator Barack Obama's bounce from his unpredicted Iowa caucus win.

Some attribute Clinton's ability to avoid ruin in this situation to her masculine style of speaking. Masculine style depends more on how words are said as opposed to the actual words themselves.[21] While paralinguistic features of language likely play heavily into the impact of words, so too do the actions of the body—and, undoubtedly, the look of the body, also. Intriguing questions can be raised regarding bodies and the qualities they must possess in order to be successful in political situations—what makes a body attractive in the minds of the voters? Language studies have supported the idea that, while men have latitude in showing emotion in political situations, these emotions must not be indicative of sadness, insecurity, or weakness. Does the sadness, insecurity, or the weakness of a body affect the perceptions of voters? While weakness may defined in different ways (such as illness) we turn our focus toward the possibilities of interpreted weakness in bodies that are performatively constructed as queer. How might political rhetoric, especially in consideration of gendered possibilities, be affected by queerness?

QUEERING LANGUAGE, QUEERING THE BODY

The term *sex* has two commonly understood meanings: It can refer to a so-cially constructed biological attribution of the body or it can refer to an act involving the body. The definitions we offer for the two different meanings of *sex* are likely be contested by many reading this essay, but regardless of how one sees either definition, we would hope they could agree that sex (the act) is often not associated with sex (the body) in political studies. The act of sex often only comes to public attention when a scandal emerges re-garding improper sexual conduct or when a politician whose sexual identity is nonheterosexual makes strides in gaining political traction. Moreover, we contend nonheterosexual identities are often limited in political research to only those who are gay, lesbian, bisexual, or transgender (GLBT). To extend understandings of these assertions, it is helpful to consider com-municative attributes regarding transgender, lesbian, gay, or bisexual per-sons and to consider how sexual identity categories beyond gender can be queered within political realms.

To begin, we acknowledge some research regarding sexual identity and attributions. For instance, lesbian women may be more likely to use traditionally masculine language than other women.[22] Moreover, even though some individuals are threatened by lesbian women using masculine language, a masculine lesbian may be less threatening to others than a masculine heterosexual woman—illustrating gendered expectations of what is expected from the body. When a body as read as lesbian, what it does is given different expectations than a nonlesbian body. These expectations are certainly fluid and culture dependent. Gay male talk, seen by many as "feminine" in style, has found wider social acceptance—largely through programs such as *Queer Eye for the Straight Guy* where a feminine edge is portrayed as sophisticated, chic, and helpful to males.[23] These representa-tions can be problematic, but they indicate how lines between masculinity and femininity are blurred or variable and how they are being accepted in conjunction with the queer bodies that perform them. Just as bodies can change how language is understood and how the delivery of language is accepted, language can also change how bodies are read. For instance, the language codes that are emerging regarding *trans* bodies have the potential to shatter gender expectations. Words such as *ze* or *hir* serve as pronouns for persons who may not consider themselves to be either masculine or feminine,[24] and so the he/she or him/her dichotomy does not appropriately fit the particular transgender identity. Creating new language to refer to *trans* bodies also allows for the understanding of those bodies to be shaped in new, fluid, and progressive ways.

While the brief and cursory considerations outlined in this section may seem irrelevant in a political context where gender is portrayed as a dichotomy and where gender roles are presumed to have static contextual meaning, the ideas explained here help to illustrate how little attention has been paid to sexuality or sexual orientation in political research. A cursory examination of American politics is indicative of many of the attitudes voters and politicians carry about sexuality: Other than instances of infidelity, the sexuality of a candidate is often only deemed relevant when a nonheterosexual identity is presented, because "sexiness" is downplayed in public representation. Typically then, candidates are scrutinized and attacked when their actions pose a threat to the idealized image of the American family, whether it be through heterosexual, extramarital affairs, nonheterosexual relationships, or public stances of support for sexually liberal policies.

We argue that it is time to consider the deeper connections between sex(iness) and gender in political culture—and, moreover, to consider sexuality as part of political identity as well as personal identity. Until scholars understand the reflexivity between candidate image and the sexual identities they directly or indirectly represent, situations that involve gay rights may continue to be quagmired and provoke unnecessary questions about the sexuality of supporters and opponents. Greater understandings of sexuality's role in political personae could lead to a more accepting political landscape in terms of gender and sexuality. While political figures are probably not going to be employing words such as *ze* or *hir* anytime soon, cultural change will interact with political understandings to create new and continuously evolving understandings of how bodies are sexed, gendered, and sexualized in political rhetoric. Political communication scholars should take special care to explicate these changes as they evolve.

FEMALE SEXUALITY: QUEER IN POLITICS?

For political communication scholars to continue unpacking gendered and sexualized bodies in politics, a fuller integration of sexuality and gender is in order. To begin this process, we seek to open dialogues regarding heterosexual privilege as well as masculine privilege. An easy place to begin this is in the patriarchal spaces created by political systems that control the sexuality of women. Ultimately, societal expectations for sexual desires and actions are centered on heterosexuality. Heteronormativity affects the sex roles, sex characteristics, and gendered performances of all individuals, queer or straight. In an ideal world, human relationships would not be controlled or idealized; and all would be predicated on equal terms with consensual subjectivity. But this is not an ideal world, and social control is exerted upon relationships in ways that allow patriarchal norms to dominate. Political systems display little interest in changing these structures; moreover, they seem to be content with constituting these structures in the policies they make and the behaviors they enact. This is most notable in the way that women are not allowed to be sexual as political figures. The situation between men and women in this regard is imbalanced in many ways because women's bodies are often automatically considered to be sites of sexual pleasure. Women are positioned, in terms of heterosexual relationships, as being the objects of men. The ongoing idea that a woman's body is representation of her sexuality leads to the notion that her very being is one that is sexual. Public punishment of men for their sexuality must stem from illicit affairs, whether heterosexual or homosexual. But for women, the potential grounds for sexual impropriety can be much thinner. For example, in 2007, as Senator Clinton campaigned for the presidency, she wore a garment that revealed a glimpse of cleavage. *Washington Post* reporter Robin Givhan commented on the Clinton situation, noting

> The cleavage registered after only a quick glance. No scrunch-faced scrutiny was necessary. There wasn't an unseemly amount of cleavage showing, but there it was. Undeniable. It was startling to see that small acknowledgement of sexuality and femininity peeking out of the conservative—aesthetically speaking—environment of Congress. After all, it wasn't until the early nineties that women were even allowed to wear pants on the Senate floor . . . . The last time Clinton wore anything that was remotely sexy in a public setting surely must have been more than a decade ago, during Bill Clinton's first term in office.[25]

While reporters have often discussed women candidates' clothing and appearance more than that of their male counterparts,[26] women candidates have typically been attired in businesslike clothing that flattered but desexualized their bodies, and conformed to the masculinized political realm. We normally ignore the sexuality of political women, particularly older women, based on societal attitudes. The image of Sarah Palin during her vice presidential candidacy highlights the notion of political representations reflecting societal demands. Those who cheered for her often did so by praising her virtues as a faithful and sexy wife who also serves as a good mother.[27] Unlike Clinton, who was publicly imagined to nag her husband Bill, Palin was celebrated as subservient and domestic while still being able to play with the boys. So, in addition to hunting the moose, she could dress it and serve it to her husband and children. As Gloria Steinem noted,[28] this played into societal expectations for the role Palin was assumed to play as vice president in the McCain administration: the compliant woman who gladly supports what the male figure (in this case John McCain) asserts and represents. That Sarah Palin is sexy is a bonus, but this sexiness supports her role as a metaphorical trophy wife or even as a mother, as the term "MILF"[29] was used to describe her in blogs and news stories. Palin's mediated representation is in direct opposition to feminist understandings of relationships, both the political and the interpersonal; it minimizes women's sexuality as a viable entity in its own right and makes it privy to (heterosexual) male dominance and control. We assert, then, that political campaigns and rhetoric encourage the forgetting of the sexual, particularly nonmale and nonheterosexual individuals.

HETERONORMATIVITY, HOMOSEXUALITY, AND FORGETTING THE BISEXUAL

While homosexuality or female sexuality is often silenced or scrutinized in political rhetoric, bisexuality is almost completely ignored or forgotten.[30] As a general rule, individuals are often perceived as either lesbian-gay or heterosexual.[31] Further, "most people will self-identify in homosexual categories (gay, lesbian) or as heterosexual (straight) even when they harbor attractions to the same sex."[32] In a society where fluidity is often eschewed in favor of rigidity, it is hard to consider that hetero-homo dichotomies may not exist, but that a hetero-homo continuum may be in play. In addition to being uncomfortable to think about, the idea of a person as bisexual has a direct effect on that person's credibility. Those who self-identify as bisexual are seen as less trustworthy than those labeled as heterosexual. Additionally, bisexual individuals are often stereotyped as fickle or being undecided or ambivalent about their sexuality.[33] People do not seem to like ambivalence toward issues in their candidates, suggesting that ambivalence about one's personal life is also a negative. Questions about what truly constitutes a bisexual identity also makes political considerations surrounding bisexuality particularly intriguing. Rumors persist that Hillary Clinton may actually be a lesbian but is married to Bill Clinton in order to gain political capital.[34] Would this alleged marriage of convenience represent bisexuality? While the answer is likely "no" in this situation, one could turn to the recent scandal involving Senator Larry Craig and wonder if the media, policymakers, and their constituents have missed one of the true questions emerging from the situation. After being caught in a public restroom known for same sex male couplings, the question often asked by the media was whether or not he was gay or straight. Craig defended himself by speaking of his love for his wife, and, while he denied the encounters and a gay sexuality, he never denied a bisexuality. Could it be his sexuality is not an either/or, but rather a both/and? These questions were never asked because of the dichotomous tendency to place sexuality into straight-gay frames not only in political communication but also in cultures. So, while bisexuality tends to remain invisible on the political stage, its absence still allows for potential misunderstandings or limited analysis of political situations. It also constitutes an unconsidered middle space for the reading of bodies.

GENDERED POLITICAL SITUATIONS ACROSS TIME

If the review and discussion offered in this essay already confuses the notion of gendered possibilities and sex roles in political rhetoric, even more problematic is how gender, sex roles, and sexuality continue to change throughout time in relation to political campaigns and politics in general. Perhaps the one aspect political communication scholars can agree upon regarding discourses centered upon the relationship between gender and politics is that gender continues to become more diverse and less defined as women play more prominent roles in political systems, men continue to embrace new forms of political rhetoric that some would consider feminized,[35] second-wave feminism's effects upon U.S. institutions continue to be felt, tolerant and affirmative attitudes regarding sexualities and gender identities continue to develop, and mass-mediated representations of gender continue to expand (even if the expansion of gender templates is often problematic). With the development of Internet technologies and more television news sources available than ever before, people can also access the kind of news they want and when they want it—often allowing them to focus on the political messages that are most palatable. This translates into the fragmentation of once-dominant cultural knowledge[36] and fragmented understandings of gender[37] and is problematic, as social scientists and rhetorical scholars continue to examine gender in the nonfragmented context of sex roles or identity politics[38] and do not seek fragmented, multi-contextualized understandings.

We should also consider how the elements of sex, gender, and sexuality come together to offer a notion of where political communication research and the study of political rhetoric are located at this point in communication scholarship. Social scientific approaches remain largely centered in the campaign model where different political discourses are considered through different political campaigns.[39] Gender, in this particular line of research, largely means a focus on women (although the study of masculinity in politics is becoming more prevalent). Perception, judgment, and interpretation are largely examined through a sex-differences worldview, one that assumes men constitute the normative standard. The research also explores media representations of women or feminist issues. Rhetorical research in political communication also tends to be centered in campaigns, but it might include the study of gendered movements and interactions between politics and culture. While Beasley[40] notes both perspectives have been valuable and generative (and we concur), both perspectives have almost exclusively focused on sex or gender through a biological sex frame—gender and sexuality have largely been ignored in the research. We dedicate the remainder of this essay to a line of scholarly thinking that could alleviate this concern. What if political scholars in the communication discipline considered the body as situation and effect in political rhetoric? And, given that different bodies are read in different ways across time and within a given context and situation, what if we read gendered bodies as possibilities?

THE BODY AS SITUATION AND EFFECT IN POLITICAL RHETORIC

Stormer clearly outlines complex considerations regarding the body as situation in political rhetoric,[41] taking into account Butler's theory of performativity,[42] alternative understandings of materiality, and relationships between theory and gender. Butler's theory of performativity examines the notion that sexuality is strongly tied to the nature of an individual. Sexual nature, then, becomes the cause of gender—yet, at the same time, is seen as an effect of gender. This makes reflexive lived experience a rhetoric of sorts. The body, as a sexed entity with expectations created from interactions with other sexed bodies (or subjected to discourses about sexed bodies), inherently performs gender while not necessarily performing a true gender at all. Sex, while not necessarily determining gender, does have a considerable historical weight that interrelates with gender through culture. Bodies, then, have sets of possibilities that are both willful (performed) and arbitrary (culturally related). The question then becomes how this reflexive nature of gender ties into reflexive notions of the body; and how that inter-relates with theoretical understandings of both gender and rhetoric.

As Foss, Foss, and Griffin eloquently state, "Understanding how rhetoric functions allows us to make conscious choices about the kinds of worlds we want to create, who and how we want to be in those worlds, and the values we want those worlds to embody. The study of rhetoric, then, enables us to understand and articulate the various ways individuals create and enact the worlds in which they choose to live."[43] We wholeheartedly agree with this assertion and believe it to be the key to also understanding gender and communication. Rhetorical studies do not offer a simple X = Y formula. Instead, the X in rhetoric leads to a possibility of Ys, and inversely the consideration of possible Ys can lead to the development of Xs. Simply put, one cannot look to a rhetorical situation and assert that the rhetorical situation has a certain solution because all rhetorical situations are dynamic with respect to their place, time, and other exigencies.

In political rhetoric, gender is especially categorized and often accepted within dominant-gendered expectations, but this impulse loses sight of history, allows for the dominant view to overcomes possible realities of gender in situation, and carves an unnecessary space between gender and theory. It is the job of the scholar to think deeper, to explore connections between existence and history, to avoid simple assessments of how the subject is created, and move beyond what Condit calls the "tedious predictability" of once again finding how men and women talk differently.[44] To limit the study of political rhetoric to language differences, or even to consid-erations of performance, limits the idea that the body, and its material performances, is always there. It is being read, it is being understood, and regardless of an individual's (or the person surrounding that individual's) best attempts to change the body, to prompt the body, to establish how the body will be—the body is always there, with its implied understandings of how to read it. And this understanding will change, over time, creating an exigency for the political communication scholar to understand the pos-sibilities the body brings with it for rhetorical understanding. Each body is different. Each body is carved with its own situation. Each body provides its own effect.

GENDERED POSSIBILITY AND THE POLITICAL BODY

This essay offers many considerations regarding gendered political bodies. First, it argues gender should be studied through political rhetoric, but not as a predetermined category with an already understood purpose. Our task is to allow *political rhetoric* to be theorized in respect to *gender theory* in a frame that does not require one to lead to the other in either direction. Political rhetoric is as dependent on understanding gender just as much as gender is dependent upon understanding political rhetoric. What is considered masculine and feminine in political arenas may change depending on differences in how bodies are read; and the differences will likely change over time. Second, the reflexive relationship between gender and political rhetoric ties into a larger understanding of how experience is not an exclusive phenomenon but rather a relational one. Instead of simple cause-and-effect logic, we affirm that readings of the body are polysemic. All meanings stand in relation to others' experiences. These experiences are ultimately what constitute readings of gendered political rhetoric. These experiences are the beginning to an understanding of gendered political bodies.

NOTES

1. Nathan Stormer, "A Vexing Relationship: Gender and Contemporary Rhetorical Theory," in *The SAGE Handbook of Gender and Communication*, eds. Bonnie J. Dow and Julia T. Wood (Thousand Oaks, Calif.: Sage, 2007), 258.

2. Perhaps a better term would be sexualities, as research examining the sexual nature of individuals tends to agree that many diverse and fluid sexualities can be found in a given culture. See Joseph Bristow, *Sexuality* (New York: Routledge).

3. Margrit Eichler, *Nonsexist Research Methods: A Practical Guide* (New York: Routledge, 1991).

4. Kathleen Hall Jamieson, *Beyond the Double Bind: Women and Leadership.* (New York: Oxford University, 1995).

5. Karlyn Kohrs Campbell and Zornitsa Keremidchieva, "Gender and Public Address," in *The SAGE Handbook of Gender and Communication*, 193.

6. Karlyn Korhs Campbell, *Man Cannot Speak for Her, Vol. 1* (New York: Greenwood, 1989).

7. Campbell, *Man Cannot Speak for Her*, 10.

8. Michael Z. Hackman and Craig E. Johnson, *Leadership: A Communication Perspective,* 4th ed. (Prospect Heights, Ill.: Waveland, 2004).

9. Judith A. Hall, "How Big are Nonverbal Sex Differences? The Case of Smiling and Sensitivity to Nonverbal Cues," in *Sex Differences and Similarities in Communication*, eds. Daniel J. Canary and Kathryn Dindia (Mahwah, N.J.: Erlbaum, 1998), 155–78.

10. Anthony Mulac, "The Gender-Linked Language Effect: Do Language Differences Really Make a Difference?" in *Sex Differences and Similarities,* 127–54.

11. Judith S. Trent and Robert V. Friedenberg, *Political Campaign Communication: Principles and Practices,* 6th ed. (Lanham, Md.: Rowman and Littlefield, 2008), 173.

12. Anthony Mulac, "The Gender-Linked Language Effect," 127–54.

13. Catharine A. MacKinnon, "Feminism, Marxism, Method, and the State: An Agenda for Theory," *Signs: Journal of Women in Culture and Society* 7, no. 3 (Spring 1982): 535.

14. Karlyn Kohrs Campbell, *Man Cannot Speak for Her.*

15. Bonnie J. Dow and Julia T. Wood, "The Evolution of Gender and Communication Research: Intersections of Theory, Politics, and Scholarship," in *The SAGE Handbook of Gender and Communication*, xix–xxiv.

16. This notion of personal as political, albeit in various different forms, seems to be an integral part of feminist political movements on a global level. See Dow and Wood, *The SAGE Handbook of Gender and Communication.*

17. Molly Mayhead and Brenda Devore Marshall,*Women's Political Discourse: A 21st-Century Perspective* (Lanham, Md.: Rowman and Littlefield, 2005), 18.

18. Mayhead and Marshall, *Women's Political Discourse*, 18.

19. As opposed to essentialism, or the idea that characteristics or qualities can be found in a given individual based on race, class, or sexual orientation, among other social categories. For a good discussion on sex, gender, and essentialism, see Monique Wittig, "The Category of Sex," *The Straight Mind and Other Essays* (Boston: Beacon Press, 1992), 1–8.

20. When Edmund Muskie famously teared up on the campaign trail in 1984, while defending his wife, he was derided for his emotional display.

21. Julia T. Wood, *Gendered Lives: Communication, Gender, and Culture*, 5th ed. (Belmont, Calif.: Wadsworth, 2003), 115–29.

22. Wood, *Gendered Lives*, 115–29.

23. Kylo-Patrick R. Hart, "We're Here, We're Queer, and We're Better Than You: The Representational Superiority of Gay Men to Heterosexuals on Queer Eye for the Straight Guy," *The Journal of Men's Studies* 12, no. 3 (Summer 2007): 241–53.

24. Jimmie Manning, "Inclusive Language Use," in *Handbook of Speaker-Audience Communication*, ed. Deb Ford (Belmont, Calif.: Wadsworth, 2004), 17.

25. Robin Givhan, "Hillary Clinton's Tentative Dip Into New Neckline Territory." *Washington Post*, 20 July 2007, C01.

26. For an overview and an interesting case study, see Caroline Heldman, Susan J. Carroll, and Stephanie Olson, "'She Brought Only a Skirt': Print Media Coverage of Elizabeth Dole's Bid for the Republican Presidential Nomination," *Political Communication* 22, no. 3 (July-Sept. 2005), 315–35.

27. We understand that Palin's "sexiness" did begin to enter the voter and media discourse during her campaign, but we contend it was overshadowed by reference to her female virtues.

28. Gloria Steinem, "Palin: Wrong Woman, Wrong Message," *Los Angeles Times*, Sept. 4, 2008, retrieved from http://www.latimes.com/news/printedition/opinion/la-oe-steinem4-2008sep04,0,1290251.story

29. MILF, or "Mother I would like to fuck" is scatological slang, popularized among adolescents by the film, *American Pie*.

30. By forgotten, it is not suggested that people literally forget someone is bisexual; rather, they forget about the possibility of a person being bisexual.

31. Jimmie Manning, "Heterosexuality," in *Encyclopedia of Gender and Society* (Thousand Oaks, Calif.: Sage, 2008).

32. Manning, "Heterosexuality."

33. Joseph Istvan, "Effects of Sexual Orientation on Interpersonal Judgement," in *Bisexuality in the United States*, ed. Paula C. Rodriguez Rust (New York: Columbia University Press, 1999), 499.

34. For one example, see the discussion on the political blog *Inside Politics* at http://www.insidepolitics.org/heard/heard062205.html

35. Men's adoption of feminine style in disourse is one illustrative example.

36. David Weinberger, *Small Pieces Loosely Joined: A Unified Theory of the Web* (Cambridge, Mass.: Perseus, 2002).

37. Victoria Pruin DeFrancisco and Catherine Helen Palczewski, *Communicating Gender Diversity: A Critical Approach* (Thousand Oaks, Calif.: Sage).

38. Victoria DeFrancisco and Catherine Helen Palczewski, *Communicating Gender Diversity*.

39. Vanessa B. Beasley, "Gender in Political Communication Research: The Problem with Having No Name," in *The SAGE Handbook of Gender and Communication*, 201–14.

40. Beasley, "Gender in Political Communication Research," 201–14.

41. Nathan Stormer, "A Vexing Relationship: Gender and Contemporary Rhetorical Theory," 247–62.

42. Judith Butler, *Bodies That Matter*.

43. Karen A. Foss, Sonja K. Foss, and Cindy L. Griffin, *Readings in Feminist Rheotrical Theory* (Thousand Oaks, Calif.: Sage, 2004), 7.

44. Celeste M. Condit, "In Praise of Eloquent Diversity: Gender and Rhetoric as Public Persuasion," *Women's Studies in Communication* 20, no. 3 (Fall 1997): 112.

AN EPISTOLARY EPILOGUE

Learning from Sarah Palin's Vice Presidential Campaign

Mary L. Kahl and Janis L. Edwards

Gender issues infused the 2008 presidential campaign, particularly with regard to Senator Hillary Clinton's historic near-miss as the first woman to occupy the White House. While race was at issue for the eventual winner, Paul Achter and Teresa Bergman, in their essays for this volume, demonstrate how gender and race may be substantially intertwined in creating political identities. But lessons in gender and politics must also be derived from the surprise nomination of Governor Sarah Palin for the second spot on the 2008 GOP ticket.[1]

Palin's selection by the Republican presidential nominee, Senator John McCain, proved more controversial than other choices might have been.[2] A relatively new and inexperienced governor of Alaska, she was an unknown on the national stage, and her apparent oratorical talents contrasted sharply with her nonsensical prolixity in the rare media interviews she granted. As one scholar put it in October, "We have seen more parodies of Palin than we have seen the actual Palin."[3] Writing in the *Wall Street Journal* following election day, Mark Lilla, former editor of the *Public Interest*, expressed the widespread derision of Palin found in mediated and public discourse. "The Palin farce is already the stuff of legend," he proclaimed. "For a generation at least it is sure to keep presidential historians and late-night comedians in gainful employment, which is no small thing."[4] In fact, the controversy over Palin continued for some weeks following election day, as she made high-profile appearances at political gatherings, campaigned on behalf of the Republican senatorial candidate in a run-off election in Georgia, and gave a glib pre-Thanksgiving television interview backed by a graphic turkey slaughter. Palin did not shuffle off into obscurity after the resounding defeat of the GOP ticket. Indeed, demonstrating an indefatigable taste for campaigning and what the *Washington Post* described as "manic good cheer,"[5] she has indicated her ambition for a political future well beyond the remote confines of the forty-ninth state. Whether or not that future materializes, however, Palin's position in the 2008 race is instructive.

Palin's selection for the second spot on the Republican ticket was viewed through a gendered lens from the moment that McCain announced his decision. Those in the press and in academe suggested that Palin's selection was a calculated risk; a tactical move designed to attract the votes of women who may have been disaffected, first by Hillary Clinton's loss of the presidential nomination and, second, by her exclusion from the Obama ticket. It was a tactic that ultimately failed to find traction, for although Palin was popular at many Republican campaign rallies, her candidacy failed to resonate with Clinton supporters or even with certain significant segments of the GOP's female base. Yet the response to her candidacy highlighted Palin's identity as a woman in other ways. Politics is full of symbolic overtones, and Palin's selection as the first woman on a Republican presidential ticket heightened her perception as a "symbolic woman." Drawing on Murray Edelman's emphasis on the symbolic aspects of political communication,[6] Virginia Shapiro identifies symbolic womanhood as a phenomenon that stems from women's relatively novel position in American politics (as with Palin's status as a "first"). As Shapiro observes, women "are interpreted through a narrow set of culturally embedded symbols"[7] which are attached to political women. "When we analyze the meaning of women in politics," Shapiro instructs, "we would be wise to understand that in an important sense we are not talking about real women at all, but symbolic women, representatives of their gender as well as many other things."[8] While some of the contributors to this volume make the case that the cultural expectations associated with masculinity temper the public interpretations of men who aspire to political leadership, that effect is heightened for women, because the applications of a cultural frame of gender is more pronounced and far more evident for women than for men. Masculinity in political campaigns, by comparison, "hides right in front of us."[9] In Palin's case, her persona was filtered through a typical set of gendered stereotypes, even as she resisted characterization by certain others.

Deliberative research on Palin will surely be forthcoming. But we suggest that even an initial examination of America's self-styled "pit bull with lipstick" provides three provocative lessons of interest to scholars of gender and political communication, lessons that function as an appropriate coda to this book.

LESSON 1: SOME THINGS STILL HAVEN'T CHANGED

Early research suggests that media and other voices responded to Palin much as they have responded to other women in American electoral politics. One scholar summarized the usual elements of stereotyped discourse: "When we talk of Palin we cannot seem to stop talking about her gender—her procreative abilities, her reproduction choices, her mothering, her children, and, of course, her appearance."[10] The questions raised about Palin's ability to assume the role of vice president while caring for a young family, including an infant with a disability and an unmarried, pregnant teen daughter, echo scholarship which shows that the media focus on family issues as relevant to women candidates far more than they do with respect to men candidates.[11] Wendy Atkins-Sayre's essay in this volume, on Governor Jane Swift's pregnancy and childbirth, suggests that stereotypical beliefs about women's domestic roles as impediments to active public lives continue to be salient in the culture. Moreover, the essay provides noteworthy parallels to the critiques of Palin that occurred in the blogosphere. Family issues may provoke legitimate questions, but they become stereotypical when these concerns are applied to women and not to men in similar circumstances.

Physical appearance and clothing is another area of critique commonly applied to women, but uncommonly to men.[12] The issue of Palin's clothing was complicated by the news that a Republican Party operative underwrote an extensive shopping spree for an updated campaign wardrobe for Palin.[13] The ensuing controversy over such stagecraft focused attention away from the content of the candidate's stump speeches toward far less cerebral discussions of her new duds and the popularity of her designer glasses. But Palin's appearance was dissected in another respect. As a former beauty queen, Palin was described not merely as attractive, but as a forty-four-year-old "hottie," an image that became repeatedly entangled with her political appeal in the remarks of voters, media, and other commentators. As one scholar put it, "Intoxicatingly presented, persuasively offered as saying something important about female accomplishment, her image is embedded in . . . dominant norms defining the feminine self, her body (slender, attractive, youthful—and not forgetting that trademark smile) . . . . Never mind those lurid headlines, or that she cannot help but polarize the U.S. electorate with her political beliefs, she looks perfect."[14] The sexualization of Palin's persona was further complicated by her own behaviors in a variety of campaign contexts. From her broad winks to the television camera during the vice presidential debate to her hands-on-hips stance during public rallies, Palin projected an image that, consciously or otherwise, encouraged such biased, gender-based scrutiny.

Perhaps more surprising, given the issues of experience and motive that surrounded McCain's selection of Palin, press response to the Alaska governor bore striking similarities to the response engendered by Representative Geraldine Ferraro's vice presidential candidacy twenty-four years earlier. In a comparative study of media frames in the two elections, Ohl found three frames consistently applied to both candidates, despite their ideological differences, the quarter-century time gap, and the disparity of circumstances between their campaigns.[15] Ohl found that each woman was critiqued for a lack of experience, her selection was perceived as a political stunt or tactic, and each candidacy represented a political gamble. Although some of these comparisons may appear to be based on concrete similarities, Ohl demonstrated their specific links to gender in media coverage of these two candidates.

LESSON 2: PALIN REDEFINED THE SYMBOLIC WOMAN

As our first lesson shows, Palin's status, and frequently her behavior, as a woman invited continued usage of the stereotypical frames commonly applied to female political candidates and leaders. But Palin was also a different sort of woman, one who sometimes embraced the term "feminist," but one who did not embody feminism in its more common liberal iterations. To be sure, not all women who have been presidential candidates, much less candidates for other elected positions, have been "liberals," particularly on core "women's" issues, such as abortion rights. Senators Elizabeth Dole and Margaret Chase Smith are two Republicans who were celebrated as iconic women in the pantheon of political diversity, perhaps because they were more liberal in many ways than the hard conservative wing of their party. Surely, women such as Maine senators Olympia Snowe and Susan Collins, two other possible picks for the 2008 Republican ticket, might be seen as similarly moderate. Even Barbara Bush, the wife of one Republican president and mother of another, has indicated her pro-choice sympathies. Palin, by contrast, is unapologetically conservative, particularly on abortion and birth control. Her embodiment of these political positions, through her proud declarations of her "choice" to proceed with a Down Syndrome pregnancy and her daughter's "choice" to give birth out of wedlock, contrasted with the prevailing liberal narrative on "women's issues" as a rationale for moving women into political office. Seemingly overnight, the political scenario changed from a pro-woman stance as a feminist counterpoint to the male-dominated political hierarchy to a more complex mix, where aspiring political women might also stand in contrast with liberal feminist ideals—a conservative backlash against liberal feminism. Indeed, the motive for Palin's selection was often rationalized as an effort to energize the conservative Republican base, and energize it she did, with particularly derisive and divisive rhetoric. Klien and Farrar, in their work in this volume, have paid attention to the influence of the politically conservative voice on gender issues. Even if Palin is unsuccessful in advancing her particular political fortunes, and even if liberalism assumes ascendancy over conservatism in the current political milieu, her appeal to many voters who would not ordinarily be considered a ready audience for the rhetoric of gender inclusion must be taken as a signal that the terrain of gendered politics is more complex than it has been previously assumed to be. Although the second-wave feminist movement has pushed for greater gender inclusion in politics, it is clear that liberal feminism no longer controls the predominant agenda of women in national politics.

Ironically, although Palin may have embodied opposition to the pro-choice agenda—long identified with political women—her mix of consistency and inconsistency with regard to the prevailing interpretations of symbolic womanhood may be at the root of her contestation of the liberal feminist narrative of women in politics. Anderson and Sheeler[16] have identified a series of metaphors that function as governing codes which inscribe political identity for women: pioneer, puppet, hostess/beauty queen, and unruly woman. They illustrate each metaphor using four separate case studies of prominent women in politics. Our examination[17] of Palin through these metaphoric clusters shows that, unsurprisingly, her representation and self-presentation are consistent with each. But the unique way in which she embodies them suggests her differences with the case studies observed by Anderson and Sheeler. For example, Palin was an actual beauty contest winner, but that fact about her personal past is given new currency in public and media commentary about her sexuality and physical attractiveness. Her embodiment of the "unruly woman" trope transcends the "reversal" of ideal femininity that Anderson and Sheeler attribute to the operation of this metaphor. Instead, Palin unapologetically capitalizes on her looks and her enactment of traditional domestic roles (her childbirthing and parenting choices) while also presenting a self that is unabashedly "unruly" in terms of liberal political correctness. Most prominently, she encouraged and embraced the image of a beauty queen who could also kill and field-dress a moose, and she invited discussion of her involvement in activities infused with machismo, such as hunting animals from small aircraft.

Thus, Palin embodies some aspects of the "unruly woman": She creates a spectacle of herself, she tries to dominate men (specifically McCain), she makes jokes and laughs at herself, is associated with some taboos[18] (while rejecting others), and she is not "excessive" in appearance. In fact, her greatest unruliness may be that she has the audacity to simultaneously conform to and challenge both traditional and feminist standards for femininity. Palin's persona combines the extremes of femininity (pretty, fertile, and youthful) with the extremes of masculinity (macho, fearless, self-sufficient). Her half-flirtatious, half-defiant style thus radically renovates the prevailing idea of what it means to be an iconic woman attempting to "break the glass ceiling." If it is true of populist and fundamentalist movements that they "appropriate symbols and signifiers from oppositional ideologies and articulate them to their own discourse"[19] Palin's masterful efforts suggest a third lesson.

LESSON 3: GENDER WORKS
IN CONCERT WITH OTHER FACTORS

As Lilla and others have observed, McCain's choice of a vice presidential running mate "was not a fluke, or a senior moment, or an act of desperation. It was the result of a long campaign by influential conservative intellectuals to find a young populist leader to whom they might hitch their wagons in the future"[20] The problem is that their choice came up lame, very lame." Palin's empty pronouncements against "Washington insiders" functioned as a substitute for sound argument and distracted the electorate in a time of national uncertainty, if not outright crisis.

Palin herself could not possibly have known that in 1976 Irving Kristol worried that "populist paranoia" was "subverting the very institutions and authorities that the democratic republic laboriously creates for the purpose of orderly self government."[21] Quite the opposite. Palin likely did not know that traditional conservatives were nearly always suspicious of populism. But no more. Palin's populist demagoguery during the campaign embodied nearly everything that older conservative thinkers once decried: it was anti-intellectual, angry, and uniformly disdainful of the educated classes. It was Sarah-of-Wasilla, beauty queen-huntress from the last frontier, hockey mom barracuda with the come-hither sailor wink, who apparently did not understand world geography, much less world politics.

What are we to make of Palin's brand of populism, or pseudo populism? And what of its rhetorical dimensions? For one thing, Palin's populism often seemed to transcend issues related to her gender, at least among those who were attracted to her persona. The implicitly desirable objective of a genderless society (one where social constructions of gender are effaced and stereotypes eliminated, at least in terms of political viability) is advanced when issues overcome image, at least when the image is closely derived from a candidate's sex. Even as gender remains a potent factor—as it clearly did in media coverage of Hillary Clinton's campaign—it cannot be completely separated from the ideologies and political issues articulated by a candidate. Neither Hillary's political failures, nor Sarah Palin's, can be wholly attributed to their identities as women. In a sense, Palin should not be viewed as primarily a female candidate, nor certainly as a feminist candidate, but as a nouveau populist candidate—an exemplar of populist chic (or chick). Therefore, we offer three concluding observations about Palin's rhetoric and her brand of populism. First, Palin's speech is peppered with colloquialisms that reinforce her status as an outsider and a standard bearer for the nonintellectual, "regular" people. As she asserted in her famously flat accent during the vice presidential debate, "I think we need a little bit of reality from Wasilla Main Street there, brought to Washington, D.C." [22] Palin's speech patterns violate nearly all the conventions of formal discourse. Again, in her vice presidential debate performance, for example, we find phrases such as "Say it ain't so, Joe" or, when speaking to both "Joe Sixpack" and Senator Joe Biden on her status as a maverick, we encounter Palin's garbled assertion of constructed-for-the camera populism:

> Oh, yeah, it's so obvious I'm a Washington outsider. And someone just not used to the way you guys operate. Because here you voted for the war and now you oppose the war. You're one who says, as so many politicians do, I was for it before I was against it or vice-versa. Americans are craving that straight talk and just want to know, hey, if you voted for it, tell us why you voted for it and it was a war resolution. [23]

Our second point is perhaps less obvious. Palin's discourse follows and exaggerates a line of Republican populist rhetoric that flows down from Ronald Reagan to George W. Bush. Her speech caricatures the populist tendency to substitute sincerity and earthiness for expertise and complexity of thought. This caricaturist quality of Palin's discourse is further under-scored by her nonverbal communication—by her broad winks, by her sometimes exaggerated beehive hairdo, by her frequently moistened lips, by the beauty queen-in-high-heels persona of her stump style. As she main-tained in her debate remarks, her primary qualification to succeed John McCain was her grasp of how "the average working class family is viewing bureaucracy in the federal government and Congress, and the inaction of Congress."[24] Palin claimed that her greatest asset was her ability to articu-late the thoughts of mainstream citizens:

> Just everyday, working-class Americans, saying, you know, government, just get out of my way. If you're going to do any harm and mandate more things on me and take more of my money and income tax and business taxes, you're going to have a choice in just a few weeks here on either supporting a ticket that wants to create jobs and bolster our economy and win the war or you're going to be supporting a ticket that wants to increase taxes, which ultimately kills jobs, and is going to hurt our economy.[25]

Palin's definition of mainstream citizens, or "real America" was, of course, limited to particular segments of the population and certain locales.

Third, as a populist candidate, the more Palin distanced herself from the mainstream media, the better. The more she could incite their deri-sion, the more she could cause incredulity in a Katie Couric, or claim that Charlie Gibson pressed her unfairly, the more she reinforced her status as "just plain folks." Palin carefully underscored this fact when she frequently invoked the familiar canard against the "liberal elite media" and when she steadfastly refused to play by the rules, as she did in her debate against Biden, claiming that she might "not answer the questions the way that ei-ther the moderator or you [Biden] want to hear."[26]

The three lessons of Sarah Palin we propose are not innovative, although some of the details may be surprising or noteworthy. Most scholars interested in the intersections of political communication and gender would recognize that media coverage consistently operates from gender stereotypes, that Palin was a far different sort of female-feminist candidate (if a feminist at all) than the iconic women we have recognized in the past three decades, and that Palin's conservative populism accounted for a substantial portion of her po-litical appeal. But we argue for renewed attention to these factors. Research in gender and politics fruitfully charts the continued presence of stereotypes. Such studies help explain why, with all the gains women have made in the po-litical sphere, there is still a great disparity between voter demographics and representation in the nation's elected leadership.[27] But research must also continue to reach beyond a recitation of "difference studies" and examine more carefully how gender relates to other candidate factors and issues, how gender is reconstituted over time by the examples of prominent candidates and political leaders, both male and female, and how these dynamics function on a broader cultural level. The complications to the prevailing liberal feminist narrative of women in politics presented by Palin also require recognition as a more ideologically diversified pool of women candidates inevitably develops in this new century. If Palin has "thrown the calculus out the window,"[28] we need to theorize a new rhetorical calculus that can accommodate varied definitions of feminism or multiple incarnations of "symbolic women." Considering Sapiro's observation that symbolic womanhood operates through a "a very limited set of symbols with apparently limited ranges of meaning and significance"[29] that hamper women unfairly, a new rhetorical calculus is certainly required. It would assist scholars in investigating the meaning of women (and gender) in politics from a stance that sees female political symbols as "much more varied than standard feminist analysis allows."[30]

NOTES

1. Portions of this essay were originally presented by Mary L. Kahl at the 2008 meeting of the National Communication Association in San Diego, California, as "Sarah Palin, Nouveau Populism, and Nonsensical Prolixity."

2. Palin was reportedly seen as less controversial, however, than was McCain's first choice for a running mate, Senator Joe Lieberman. The senior senator from Connecticut had been Al Gore's vice presidential running mate on the 2000 Democratic ticket.

3. Ann McKinnon, "Even Mud Has the Illusion of Depth: A McLuhanesque Reading of Sarah Palin," *FlowTV* 8, no. 10 (October 2008).

4. Mark Lilla, "The Perils of Populist Chic," *Wall Street Journal*, November 7, 2008.

5. Richard Cohen, "This Debate's Biggest Loser," *The Washington Post*, October 7, 2008, A21.

6. A summary of Edelman's position may be found in his early book, *The Symbolic Uses of Politics* (Urbana: University of Illinois Press, 1964).

7. Virginia Sapiro, "The Political Uses of Symbolic Women: An Essay in Honor of Murray Edelman," *Political Communication*, 10, no. 2 (April–June 1993): 142.

8. Sapiro, "Symbolic Women," 142–43.

9. Georgia Duerst-Lahti, "Masculinity on the Campaign Trail," in Lori Cox Han and Caroline Heldman, eds. *Rethinking Madam President: Are We Ready for a Woman in the White House?* (Boulder, Colo.: Lynne Reinner Publishers, 2007), 87.

10. Janet McCabe, "In the Feminine Ideal, We Trust," *FlowTV* 8, no. 10 (October 2008).

11. See, for example, Susan Gluck Mezy, "Does Sex Make a Difference? A Case Study of Women in Politics," *Western Political Quarterly* 31, no. 4 (December 1978): 492–501.

12. See, for example, Diane J. Heath, "Footwear, Lipstick, and an Orthodox Sabbath: Media Coverage of Nontraditional Candidates," *White House Studies* 1, no. 3 (Fall 2001): 335–47; Caroline Heldman, Susan J. Carroll, and Stephanie Olson, "She Brought Only a Skirt: Print Media Coverage of Elizabeth Dole's Bid for Republican Presidential Nomination," *Political Communication* 22, no. 3 (July-September 2005): 315–35; and Erika Falk, *Women for President: Media Bias in Eight Campaigns* (Chicago: University of Illinois Press, 2008).

13. Clothing is not just as issue for female candidates for public office. When Nancy Pelosi ascended to the position of Speaker of the House, putting her closer to the presidency than any woman before her, attention to her fashion choices was immediate and prominent in the media.

14. Janet McCabe, "In the Feminine Ideal, We Trust."

15. Jessy Ohl, "Media Frames for Female Vice-Presidential Candidates: Issues of Experience, Tactics, and Gambles," unpublished paper, presented at the University of Alabama, 2008.

16. Karrin Vasby Anderson and Kristina Horn Sheeler, *Governing Codes: Gender, Metaphor, and Political Identity* (Lanham, Md.: Lexington Books, 2005).

17. Specifically, we refer to the work of the "Palin Watch," a project assumed by Janis Edwards and her graduate students at the University of Alabama in the fall of 2008, as well as the prior presentation by Kahl.

18. Here, Anderson and Sheeler reference the work of Kathleen Rowe, *The Unruly Woman: Gender and the Genres of Laughter* (Austin: University of Texas Press, 1995).

19. Maria Komninos, online comments in response to McCabe, "In the Feminine Ideal We Trust."

20. Mark Lilla, "Perils of Populist Chic." See also Jane Mayer, "The Insiders," *The New Yorker*, October 27, 2008.

21. Lilla, "Perils of Populist Chic."

22. Commission on Presidential Debates, Debate Transcript: The Biden-Palin Vice Presidential Debate, October 2, 2008, 1-32.

23. Commission on Presidential Debates, Debate Transcript.

24. Commission on Presidential Debates, Debate Transcript.

25. Commission on Presidential Debates, Debate Transcript.

26. Commission on Presidential Debates, Debate Transcript.

27. The rather small-minded criticisms of Caroline Kennedy's interest in Hillary Clinton's Senate seat come to mind, given the country's embrace of new kinds of leaders in the 2008 presidential election.

28. Lois Roman, "Ideology Aside, This Has Been the Year of the Woman," *Washington Post*, October 24, 2008, http://mobile.washingtonpost.com/detail.jsp?key=300514&rc=to&p=1&all=1.

29. Virginia Sapiro, "Symbolic Women," 149.

30. Sapiro, "Symbolic Women," 149.

SELECTED BIBLIOGRAPHY

Ackerly, Brooke A., and Jacqui True. "Studying the Struggles and Wishes of the Age: Feminist Theoretical Methodology and Feminist Theoretical Methods." Pp. 241–59 in *Feminist Methodologies for International Relations*, edited by Brooke A Ackerly, Maria Stern, Jacqui True. Cambridge: Cambridge University Press, 2006.

Aday, Sean, and James Devitt. "Style over Substance: Newspaper Coverage of Elizabeth Dole's Presidential Bid." *Harvard Journal of Press/Politics* 6, no. 2 (Spring 2001): 52–73.

Andersen, Christopher. *Bill and Hillary: The Marriage*. New York: Morrow, 1999.

Anderson, Karrin Vasby. "The First Lady: A Site of 'American Womanhood.'" Pp. 17– 30 in *Inventing a Voice: The Rhetoric of American First Ladies of the Twentieth Century*, edited by Molly Meijer Wertheimer. Lanham, Md.: Rowman & Littlefield, 2004.

———. "From Spouses to Candidates: Hillary Rodham Clinton, Elizabeth Dole, and the Gendered Office of U.S. President." *Rhetoric and Public Affairs* 5, no.1 (Spring 2002): 105–32.

———. "Hillary Rodham Clinton as 'Madonna:' The Role of Metaphor and Oxymoron in Image Restoration." *Women's Studies in Communication* 25, no.1 (March 2002): 1–24.

———. "'Rhymes With Rich': 'Bitch' as a Tool of Containment in Contemporary American Politics." *Rhetoric and Public Affairs* 2, no.4 (Winter 1999): 599–623.

Anderson, Karrin Vasby, and Kristina Horn Sheeler, *Governing Codes: Gender, Metaphor, and Political Identity*. Lanham, Md.: Rowman & Littlefield, 2005.

Anthony, Carl Sferrazza. "Hillary's Hidden Power." *George* (November 1999): 108–40.

Austin, Curtis J. *Up against the Wall: Violence in the Making and Unmaking of the Black Panther Party.* Fayetteville: University of Arkansas Press, 2008.

Banks, Adam, Vorris Nunley, Howard Rambsy, and Keith Gilyard. "Just Another Angry Black Man?" *Black Issues in Higher Education* (April 11, 2002): 68.

Barry, L. M. "A Report of the General Investigator on Woman's Work and Wages to the Knights of Labor, 1888." Pp. 336–38 in *Public Women, Public Words: A Documentary History of American Feminism*, Vol. 1, edited by Dawn Keetley and John Pettegrew. Madison, Wisc: Madison House, 1997.

Baxter, Leslie, and Barbara Montgomery. *Relating: Dialogues and Dialectics.* New York: Guilford Press 1996.

Barthes, Roland. *Image—Music—Text.* Translated by Stephen Heath. New York: Hill and Wang, 1977.

Beasley, Maurine H. *First Ladies and the Press: The Unfinished Partnership of the Media Age.* Evanston, Ill.: Northwestern University Press, 2005.

Beasley, Vanessa, "Gender in Political Communication Research: The Problem with Having No Name." Pp. 201–14 in *The SAGE Handbook of Gender and Communication*, edited by Bonnie J. Dow and Julia T. Wood. Thousand Oaks, Calif.: SAGE Publications, 2006.

Belton, Don. *Speak My Name.* Boston: Beacon Press, 1995.

Bem, Sandra Lipsitz. *The Lenses of Gender: Transforming the Debate on Sexual Inequality.* New Haven, Conn.: Yale University Press, 1993.

Benoit, William L. "Acclaiming, Attacking, and Defending in Presidential Nominating Acceptance Addresses 1960–1996." *Quarterly Journal of Speech* 85, no. 3 (August 1999): 247–67.

Benson, Thomas W., and Brian J. Snee. "New Political Documentary: Rhetoric, Propaganda, and the Civic Prospect." Pp. 1–23 in *The Rhetoric of the New Political Documentary*, edited by Thomas W. Benson and Brian J. Snee. Carbondale: Southern Illinois University Press, 2008.

Blankenship, Jane. "The Search for the 1972 Democratic Nomination: A Metaphorical Perspective." Pp. 236–60 in *Rhetoric and Communication*, edited by Jane Blankenship and Hermann G. Stelzner. Urbana: University of Illinois Press, 1972.

Blankenship, Jane, and Deborah A. Robson. "The 'Feminine Style' in Political Discourse: An Exploratory Essay." *Communication Quarterly* 43, no. 3 (Summer 1995): 353–66.

Blatch, Harriett Stanton. "Educated Suffrage a Fetich [sic]., 1897." Pp. 266–68 in *Public Women, Public Words: A Documentary History of American Feminism*, Vol. 2, edited by Dawn Keetley and John Pettegrew. Madison, Wisc.: Madison House, 1997.

Borda, Jennifer L. "The Woman Suffrage Parades of 1910–1913: Possibilities and Limitations of an Early Feminist Rhetorical Strategy." *Western Journal of Communication* 66, no. 1 (Winter 2002): 25–52.

Bordo, Susan. *Unbearable weight: Feminism, Western Culture, and the Body.* Berkeley: University of California Press, 1993.

Bostdorff, Denise M. "Hillary Rodham Clinton and Elizabeth Doles as Running 'Mates' in the 1996 Campaign: Parallels in the Rhetorical Constraints of First Ladies and Vice Presidents." Pp. 199–227 in *The 1996 Presidential Campaign: A Communication Perspective*, edited by Robert E. Denton Jr. Westport, Conn.: Praeger, 1998.

———."Making Light of James Watt: A Burkean Approach to the Form and Attitude of Political Cartoons," *Quarterly Journal of Speech* 73, no. 1 (February 1987): 43–59.

———. "Vice-Presidential Comedy and the Traditional Female Role: An Examination of the Rhetorical Characteristics of the Vice Presidency." *Western Journal of Speech Communication* 55, no. 1 (Winter 1991): 1–27.

Boydston, Jeanne. *Home and Work: Housework, Wages, and the Ideology of Labor in the Early Republic.* New York: Oxford University Press, 1990.

Braden, Maria. *Women Politicians and the Media.* Lexington: University Press of Kentucky, 1996.

Brown, Sterling A. *Negro in American Fiction.* Washington, D.C.: The Associates in Negro Education, 1937.

Burchill, Scott. "Introduction." Pp. 1–27 in *Theories of International Relations,* edited by Scott Burchill and Andrew Linklater. New York: St. Martin's Press, New York, 1996.

Burns, Lisa M. "First Ladies as Political Women: Press Framing of Presidential Wives, 1900 2001." Diss. University of Maryland, College Park, 2004. Ann Arbor, Mich.: UMI, 2004.

———."A Forgotten First Lady: A Rhetorical Reassessment of Ellen Axson Wilson." Pp. 79–102 in *Inventing a Voice: The Rhetoric of American First Ladies of the Twentieth Century*, edited by Molly Meijer Werthheimer. Lanham, Md.: Rowman & Littlefield, 2004.

Burrell, Barbara. *Public Opinion, the First Ladyship, and Hillary Rodham Clinton* New York: Routledge Press, 2001.

Butler, Judith. *Gender Trouble: Feminism and the Subversion of Identity.* New York: Routledge, 1990.

Bystrom, Dianne G. "Women as Political Communication Sources and Audiences." Pp. 435–62 in *Handbook of Political Communication Research*, edited by Lynda Lee Kaid. Mahwah, N.J.: Lawrence Erlbaum Associates, 2004.

Bystrom, Dianne G., Mary Christine Banwart, Lynda Lee Kaid, and Terry A. Robertson. *Gender and Candidate Communication: Videostyle, Webstyle, Newstyle.* New York: Routledge, 2004.

Bystrom, Dianne G., Lori Melton McKinnon, and Carole Chaney, "First Ladies and the Fourth Estate: Media Coverage of Hillary Clinton and Elizabeth Dole in the 1996 Presidential Campaign." Pp. 81–95 in the *Electronic Election: Perspectives on the 1996 Campaign Communication*, edited by Lynda Lee Kaid and Dianne G. Bystrom. Mahwah, N.J.: Lawrence Erlbaum Associates, 1999).

Campbell, Joseph. *The Power of Myth*. Edited by Betty Sue Flowers. New York: Doubleday, 1988.

Campbell, Karlyn Kohrs. "The Discursive Performance of Femininity: Hating Hillary." *Rhetoric and Public Affairs* 1, no. 1 (Spring 1998):1–19.

———. "Femininity and Feminism: To Be or Not to Be a Woman." *Communication Quarterly* 31, no. 2 (Spring 1983): 101–8.

———. "Gender and Genre: Loci of Invention and Contradiction in the Earliest Speeches by U.S. Women." *Quarterly Journal of Speech* 81, no. 4 (November 1995): 475–95.

———. *Man Cannot Speak for Her: A Critical Study of Early Feminist Rhetoric*. Westport, Conn.: Praeger, 1989.

———. *Man Cannot Speak for Her: Key Texts of the Early Feminists*. Westport, Conn.: Praeger 1989.

———. "The Rhetoric of Women's Liberation: An Oxymoron." *Quarterly Journal of Speech,* 59, no. 1 (February 1973): 74–86.

———. "The Rhetorical Presidency: A Two-Person Career." Pp. 179–95 in *Beyond the Rhetorical Presidency*, edited by Martin J. Medhurst. College Station: Texas A&M University Press, 1996.

———. "Style and Content in the Rhetoric of Early Afro-American Feminists." *Quarterly Journal of Speech* 72, no. 4 (November 1986): 434–45.

———. *Women Public Speakers in the United States, 1800–1925: A Bio-Critical Sourcebook*. Westport, Conn.: Greenwood Press, 1993.

———. *Women Public Speakers in the United States, 1925–1993: A Bio-Critical Sourcebook*. Westport, Conn.: Greenwood Press, 1994.

Campbell, Karlyn Kohrs, and Claire E. Jerry. "Woman and Speaker: A Conflict in Roles." Pp. 123–33 in *Seeing Female: Social Roles and Personal Lives*, edited by Sharon Brehm. Westport, Conn.: Greenwood Press, 1988.

Campbell, Karlyn Kohrs, and Zornitsa Keremidchieva. "Gender and Public Address." Pp. 185–200 in *The SAGE Handbook of Gender and Communication*, edited by Bonnie J. Dow and Julia T. Wood. Thousand Oaks, Calif.: Sage, 2007.

Canada, Geoffrey. *Reaching Up for Manhood: Transforming the Lives of Boys in America*. Boston: Beacon Press, 1998.

Caroli, Betty Boyd. *First Ladies*. New York: Oxford University Press, 1995.

Carpenter, Liz. *Ruffles and Flourishes*. Garden City, New York: Doubleday & Company, 1970.

Childs, Sarah, and Mona Lena Krook. "Gender and Politics: The State of the Art," *Politics* 26, no. 1 (February 2006): 18–28.

Clatterbaugh, Kenneth. *Contemporary Perspectives on Masculinity: Men, Women, and Politics in Modern Society*. Boulder, Colo.: Westview Press, 1997.

Clinton, Hillary. *Living History*. New York: Simon & Schuster, 2003.

Cohn, Carol. "Slick 'Ems, Glick 'Ems, Christmas Trees and Cookie Cutters: Nuclear Language and How We Learned to Pat the Bomb." *Bulletin of the Atomic Scientists* 43 (June 1987): 17–24.

Cohn, Carol. "'Clean Bombs' and Clean Language." Pp. 33–55, in *Women, Militarism and War*, edited by Jean Bethke Elshtain and Sheila Tobias. Lanham, Md.: Rowman & Littlefield, 1990.

Cohn, Carol. "Wars, Wimps, and Women: Talking Gender and Thinking War." Pp. 227–46 in *Gendering War Talk*, eds. Miriam Cooke and Angela Woollacott. Princeton, N.J.: Princeton University Press, 1993.

Cohn, Carol. "A Conversation with Cynthia Enloe: Feminists Look at Masculinity and the Men Who Wage War." *Signs* 28, no. 4 (Summer 2003): 1187–1207.

Collins, Gail. *America's Women: 400 Years of Dolls, Drudges, Helpmates, and Heroines*. New York: HarperCollins, 2003.

Condit, Celeste M. "In Praise of Eloquent Diversity: Gender and Rhetoric as Public Persuasion." *Women's Studies in Communication* 20, no. 3 (Fall 1997): 91–116.

———. "Opposites in an Oppositional Practice: Rhetorical Criticism and Feminism." Pg. 205–30 in *Transforming Visions: Feminist Critiques in Communication Studies*, edited by Sheryl Perlmutter Bowen and Nancy Watt. Cresskill, N.J.: Hampton Press, 1993.

Connell, Robert W. *Gender and Power: Society, the Person and Sexual Politics*. Stanford, California, University Press. 1987.

———. *The Men and the Boys*. Berkeley: University of California Press, 2000.

———. *Masculinities*. Berkeley: University of California Press, 2005, 1995.

Conners, Joan. "Popular Culture in Political Cartoons: Analyzing the Cartoonist Approach." *PS Political Science and Politics* XL, no. 2 (April 2007): 261–65.

Cott, Nancy F. *The Grounding of Modern Feminism*. New Haven, Conn.: Yale University Press,1987.

Curtis, Bruce. "The Wimp Factor." *American Heritage* 40 (November 1989): 40–50.

Davis, Angela Y. *Women, Race, and Class*. New York: Random House, 1981.

Davis, Junetta. "Sexist Bias in Eight Newspapers," *Journalism Quarterly* 59, no. 3 (Autumn 1982): 456–60.

Dates, Janette Lake, and William Barlow. *Split Image: African Americans in the Mass Media*. Washington, D.C.: Howard University Press, 1993.

Dates, Janette Lake, and Oscar Gandy Jr. "How Ideological Constraints Affected Coverage of the Jesse Jackson Campaign." *Journalism Quarterly* 62, no. 3 (Autumn 1985): 595–600, 625.

Deem, Melissa. "From Bobbitt to SCUM: Re-memberment, Scatological Rhetorics, and Feminist Strategies in the Contemporary United States." *Public Culture* 8, no. 3 (Spring 1996): 511–37.

Deem, Melissa. "Stranger Sociability, Public Hope, and the Limits of Political Transformation." *Quarterly Journal of Speech* 88, no. 4 (November 2002): 444–54.

Denton, Robert E., Jr. *The Symbolic Dimensions of the American Presidency: Description and Analysis*. Prospect Heights, Ill.: Waveland Press, 1982.

Devitt, James. "Framing Gender on the Campaign Trail: Female Gubernatorial Candidates and the Press." *Journalism and Mass Media Quarterly* 79, no. 2 (Spring 2002): 445–63.

DeFrancisco, Victoria Priun, and Catherine Helen Palczewski. *Communicating Gender Diversity: A Critical Approach*. Los Angeles, Calif.: SAGE Publications, 2007.

DeSousa, Michael, and Martin J. Medhurst. "Political Cartoons and American Culture: Significant Symbols of Campaign 1980." *Studies in Visual Communication* 8, no.1 (Spring 1982), 84–97.

Dickinson, Anna. "Work and Wages, 1869." Pp. 352–54 in *Public Women, Public Words: A Documentary History of American Feminism*, Vol 1, edited by Dawn Keetley and John Pettegrew. Madison, Wisc.: Madison House, 1997.

Dillard, Angela D. "Adventures in Conservative Feminism." *Society* 42, no. 3 (March/April 2005): 25–27.

DiQuinzio, Patrice. "Love and Reason in the Public Sphere: Maternalist Civic Engagement and the Dilemma of Difference." Pp. 227–46 in *Women and Children First: Feminism, Rhetoric, and Public Policy*, eds. Sharon M. Meagher and Patrice DiQuinzio. Albany, N.Y.: SUNY Press, 2005.

Dodge, Grace. "Working and Saving, 1891." Pp. 344–45, in *Public Women, Public Words: A Documentary History of American Feminism*, Vol. 1, edited by Dawn Keetley and John Pettegrew. Madison, Wisc.: Madison House, 1997.

Donovan, Hedley. "Job Specs for the Oval Office: A Memorial Essay." *Presidential Studies Quarterly* 21, no. 1 (Winter 1991), 141–46.

Doty, William G. *Myths of Masculinity*. New York: Crossroad, 1993.

Douglas, Susan J. *Where the Girls Are: Growing Up Female With the Mass Media*. New York: Times Books, 1995.

Douglas, Susan J, and Meredith W. Michaels, *The Mommy Myth: The Idealization of Motherhood and How it Has Undermined all Women* New York: Free Press, 2004.

Dow, Bonnie. "Feminism, Difference(s), and Rhetorical Studies." *Communication Studies* 46, no. 2/3 (Spring/Summer 1995): 106–17.

———. *Prime-Time Feminism: Television, Media Culture, and the Women's Movement Since 1970*. Philadelphia: University of Pennsylvania Press, 1996.

———. "The 'Womanhood' Rationale in the Woman Suffrage Rhetoric of Frances E. Willard." *Southern Communication Journal* 56, no. 4 (Summer 2001): 298–307.

Dow, Bonnie J. and Mari Bohr Tonn. "Feminine Style and Political Judgment in the Rhetoric of Ann Richards." *Quarterly Journal of Speech* 79, no. 3 (August 1993): 286–303.

Dow, Bonnie J., and Julia T. Wood. "The Evolution of Gender and Communication Research: Intersections of Theory, Politics, and Scholarship." Pp. ix–xxiv in *The SAGE Handbook of Gender and Communication*, edited by Bonnie J. Dow and Julia T. Wood. Thousand Oaks, Calif.: Sage Publications.

Doyle, James A. *The Male Experience*. Dubuque, Iowa: William C. Brown, 1989.

Dubois, Ellen Carol. "Working Women, Class Relations, and Suffrage Militance: Harriott Stanton Blatch and the New York Woman Suffrage Movement, 1894–1909." Pp. 221–44 in *One Woman, One Vote*, edited by Majorie Spruill Wheeler. Troutdale, Ore.: New Sage Press, 1995.

Doyle, James A. *The Male Experience*. Dubuque, Iowa: William C. Brown, 1989.

Ducat, Stephen. *The Wimp Factor: Gender Gap, Holy Wars, and the Politics of Anxious Masculinity*. Boston, Mass.: Beacon Press, 2004.

Duerst-Lahti, Georgia. "Masculinity on the Campaign Trail." Pp. 87–112 in *Rethinking Madame President: Are We Ready for a Woman in the White House?* edited by Lori Cox Han and Caroline Heldman. Boulder, Colo.: Lynne Reinner Publishers, 2007.

Dye, Nancy. *As Equals and As Sisters: Feminism, the Labor Movement, and the Women's Trade Union League of New York*. Columbia: University of Missouri Press, 1980.

Dyson, Michael Eric. *Reflecting Black: African-American Cultural Criticism*. Minneapolis: University of Minnesota Press, 1993.

———. *Race Rules: Navigating the Color Line*. Reading, Mass.: Addison Wesley Publishing Company, 1996.

Edelman, Murray. *The Symbolic Uses of Politics*. Urbana: University of Illinois Press, 1964.

Edwards, Janis L. "Drawing Politics in Pink and Blue." *PS Political Science and Politics* XL, no. 2 (April 2007): 249–53.

———. *Political Cartoons in the 1988 Presidential Campaign: Image, Metaphor, and Narrative*. New York: Garland Press, 1997.

———. "Presidential Campaign Films in a Televisual Convention Environment: The Example of 2004." Pp. 75–92 in *The 2004 Presidential Campaign: A Communication Perspective*, edited by Robert E. Denton Jr. Lanham, Md.: Rowman & Littlefield, 2005.

———. "Visualized Narratives: Cartoonists Respond to 9/11." *Iowa Journal of Communication* 35, no. 2 (Fall 2003): 19–34.

Edwards, Janis L., and Huey Rong Chen. "The First Lady/First Wife in Editorial Cartoons: Rhetorical Visions Through Gendered Lenses." *Women's Studies in Communication* 23, no. 4 (Fall 2000): 367–91.

Edwards, Janis L., and Stacey Smith. "Mythic Images in Campaign 2000 Presidential Bio-Films." Pp. 17–25 in *The Millennium Election: Communication in the 2000 Campaign*, edited by Lynda Lee Kaid, John C. Tedesco, Dianne Bystrom, and Mitchell S. McKinney. Lanham, Md.: Rowman & Littlefield, 2003.

Eichler, Margrit. *Nonsexist Research Methods: A Practical Guide* New York: Routledge, 1991.

Elshtain, Jean Bethke. *Democracy on Trial*. New York: Basic Books, 1995.

Entman, Robert. "Modern Racism and the Images of Blacks in Local Television News." *Critical Studies in Mass Communication* 7, no. 4 (December 1990): 332–45.

Fabj, Valeria. "Motherhood as Political Voice: The Rhetoric of the Mothers of the Plaza de Mayo." *Communication Studies* 44, no. 1 (Winter 1993): 1–18.

Falk, Erika. *Women for President: Media Bias in Eight Campaigns*. Urbana/Champaign: University of Illinois Press, 2007.

Faludi, Susan. *Backlash: The Undeclared War Against American Women*. New York: Crown, 1991.

Farrar, Margaret E., and Jamie L. Warner. "Rah-Rah-Radical: The Radical Cheerleaders' Challenge to the Public Sphere." *Politics & Gender* 2, no. 3 (September 2006): 281–302.

Ferguson, Michaele L., and Lori Jo Marso. *W Stands for Women: How the George W. Bush Presidency Shaped a New Politics of Gender*. Durham, N.C.: Duke University Press, 2007.

Fisher, Walter R. "Narration as a Human Communication Paradigm: The Case of Public Moral Argument." *Communication Monographs* 51, no. 1 (March 1984): 1–22.

———. "Romantic Democracy, Ronald Reagan, and Presidential Heroes." *The Western Journal of Speech Communication* 46, no. 3 (Summer 1982): 299–310.

Flexner, Eleanor. *Century of Struggle: The Woman's Rights Movement in the United States*. Cambridge, Mass: The Belknap Press of the University of Harvard Press, 1959.

Foss, Karen A., Sonja K. Foss, and Cindy L. Griffin. *Readings in Feminist Rhetorical Theory*. Thousand Oaks, Calif.: Sage, 2004.

Foss, Sonja K. "Judy Chicago's *Dinner Party*: Empowerment of Women's Voice in Visual Art." Pp. 9–26 in *Women Communicating: Studies of Women's Talk*, edited by Barbara Bate and Anita Taylor. Norwood, N.J.: Ablex, 1988.

Frady, Marshall. *Jesse: The Life and Pilgrimage of Jesse Jackson*. New York: Random House, 1996.

Freeman, Sally A., Stephen W. Littlejohn, and W. Barnett Pearce. "Communication and Moral Conflict." *Western Journal of Communication* 56, no. 4 (Fall 1992): 311–29.

Gallagher, Julie. "Waging 'The Good Fight': The Political Career of Shirley Chisholm, 1953–1982." *Journal of African American History* 92, no. 1 (Winter 2007): 393–416.

Gilmore, David D. *Manhood in the Making: Cultural Concepts of Masculinity*. New Haven and London: Yale University Press, 1990.

Gilligan, Carol. *In a Different Voice: Psychological Theory and Women's Development*. Cambridge, Mass.: Harvard University Press, 1993.

Gluck-Mezy, Susan. "Does Sex Make a Difference? A Case Study of Women in Politics," *Western Political Quarterly* 31, no. 4 (December 1978): 492–501.

Goldzwig, Steve R. "Civil Rights in the Postmodern Era: An Introduction." *Rhetoric and Public Affairs* 2, no. 2 (Summer 1999): 171–76.

Golebiowska, Ewa A. "Group Stereotypes and Political Evaluation." *American Political Research* 29, no. 6 (Nov. 2001): 535–65.

Gombrich, E. H. "Magic, Myth, and Metaphor: Reflections on Pictorial Satire." *The Uses Of Images: Studies in the Social Function of Art and Visual Communication.* London: Phaidon, 1999.

Gould, Lewis L. *American First Ladies: Their Lives and Legacies.* New York: Garland Publishing, 1996.

Gronbeck, Bruce. "Mythic Portraiture in the 1988 Presidential Caucus Bio-Ads." *American Behavioral Scientist* 32, no. 4 (March/April 1989): 351–64.

Gray, Herman. "Television, Black Americans and the American Dream." Pp. 223–90 in *Critical Perspectives in Media and Society,* edited by Robert K. Avery and David Eason. New York: Guilford Press, 1991.

Amy E. Grim, "Citizens Deliberate the 'Good Death': The Vernacular Rhetoric of Euthanasia." Ph.D. dissertation, University of Colorado, 2005.

Gutgold, Nichola D. "Just Like 'Azaleas in the Spring': Elizabeth Dole as a Daughter of the South." Pp. 95–107 in *Telling Political Lives: The Rhetorical Autobiographies of Women Leaders in the United States,* edited by Brenda DeVore Marshall and Molly A. Mayhead. Lanham, Md.: Lexington Books, 2008.

———. *Paving the Way for Madam President.* Lanham, Md.: Lexington Books, 2006.

Gutin, Myra. *The President's Partner: The First Lady in the Twentieth Century.* New York: Greenwood Press, 1989.

Habermas, Jurgen. "The Public Sphere: An Encyclopedia Article (1964)." *New German Critique* 3 (1974): 49–55.

———. *The Structural Transformation of the Public Sphere: An Inquiry into a Category of Bourgeois Society.* Cambridge, Mass: Polity, 1989.

Hackman, Michael Z., and Craig. E. Johnson. *Leadership: A Communication Perspective,* 4th ed. Prospect Heights, N.Y.: Waveland, 2004.

Hall, Judith A. "How Big are Nonverbal Sex Differences? The Case of Smiling and Sensitivity to Nonverbal Cues." Pp. 155–78 in *Sex Differences and Similarities in Communication*, edited by Daniel J. Canary and Kathryn Dindia. Mahwah, N.J.: Erlbaum, 1998.

Hall, Stuart. "The Spectacle of the 'Other.'" Pp. 223–90 in *Representation: Cultural Representations and Signifying Practices*, edited by Stuart Hall. Thousand Oaks, Calif.: Sage Publications, 1991.

———. "The Whites of their Eyes: Racist Ideologies and the Media." Pp. 88–93 in *Gender, Race, and Class in Media: A Text Reader*, edited by Gail Dines and Jean M. Humez. Thousand Oaks, Calif: Sage, 1991.

Halley, Patrick S. *On the Road with Hillary: A Behind-the-Scenes Look at the Journey From Arkansas to the U.S. Senate.* New York: Viking, 2002.

Hancock, Brenda Robinson. "Affirmation by Negation in the Women's Liberation Movement." *Quarterly Journal of Speech* 58, no. 3 (October 1972): 264–71.

Hanke, Robert. "Theorizing Masculinity With/In the Media." *Communication Theory* 8, no. 2 (May 1998): 183–202.

Harper, Philip Brian. *Are We Not Men? Masculine Anxiety and the Problem of African-American Identity*. New York: Oxford University Press, 1996.

Hardman, M. J. "Gender Through the Levels." *Women and Language* 16, no. 2 (Fall 1993): 42–49.

———. "Derivational Thinking, or, Why is Equality So Difficult?" Pp. 250–63 in *SeekingUnderstanding of Communication, Language, and Gender*, edited by Carol Ann Valentine. Ft. Worth, Tex.: CyberSpace Publishing Corporation, 1993.

———. "The Sexist Circuits of English." *The Humanist*. March/April 1996: 25–32.

Hariman, Robert. *Political Style: The Artistry of Power*. Chicago: University of Chicago Press, 1995.

Hariman, Robert, and John Louis Lucaites. *No Caption Needed: Photography, Public Culture, and Liberal Democracy*, Chicago: University of Chicago Press, 2007.

———. "Performing Civic Identity: The Photograph of the Flag Raising at Iwo Jima." *Quarterly Journal of Speech* 88, no. 4 (November 2002): 363–92.

Hart, Kylo-Patrick R. "We're Here, We're Queer, and We're Better Than You: The Representational Superiority of Gay Men to Heterosexuals on Queer Eye for the Straight Guy." *The Journal of Men's Studies* 12, no. 3 (Summer 2007): 241–53.

Hauser, Gerard A. *Vernacular Voices: The Rhetoric of Publics and Public Spheres* Columbia: University of South Carolina Press, 1999.

Hayden, Sara. "Negotiating Femininity and Power in the Early Twentieth Century West: Domestic Ideology and Feminine Style in Jeannette Rankin's Suffrage Rhetoric." *Communication Studies* 50, no. 2 (April–June 1999): 83–102.

Hayden, Sara. "Family Metaphors and the Nation: Promoting a Politics of Care Through the Million Mom March." *Quarterly Journal of Speech* 89, no. 4 (August 2003):196–215.

Hays, Sharon. *The Cultural Contradictions of Motherhood*. New Haven, Conn.: Yale University Press, 1996.

Heath, Diane J. "Footwear, Lipstick, and an Orthodox Sabbath: Media Coverage of Nontraditional Candidates." *White House Studies* 1 (2001): 335–47.

———. "The Lipstick Watch: Media Coverage, Gender, and Presidential Campaigns." Pp. 123–30 in *Anticipating Madam President*, edited by Robert P. Watson and Ann Gordon. Boulder, Colo.: Lynne Rienner, 2003.

Heldman, Caroline. "Cultural Barriers to a Female President in the United States." Pp. 17–42 in *Rethinking Madam President: Are We Ready for a Woman in the White House?* edited by Lori Cox Han and Caroline Heldman. Boulder, Colo.: Lynne Reinner Publishers, 2007.

Heldman, Caroline, Susan Carroll, and Stephanie Olson. "'She Brought Only a Skirt': Print Media Coverage of Elizabeth Dole's Bid for the Republican Presidential Nomination." *Political Communication* 22, no. 3 (July–Sept. 2005): 315–35.

Herrick, Rebekah and Sue Thomas. "Gays and Lesbians in Local Races: A Study of Electoral Viability." *The Journal of Homosexuality* 42, no. 1 (March 2001): 103–26.

Herrnson, Paul S., J. Celeste Lay, and Atiya Kai Stokes. "Women Running 'as Women': Candidate Gender, Campaign Issues, and Voter-Targeting Strategies." *The Journal of Politics* 65, no. 1 (February 2003): 244–55.

Hilliard, David, ed. *The Black Panther Party: Service to the People Programs*. The Dr. Huey P. Newton Foundation. Albuquerque: University of New Mexico, 2008.

Hoberman, John. *Darwin's Athletes: How Sport has Damaged Black America and Preserved the Myth of Race*. Boston, Mass.: Houghton Mifflin, 1997.

hooks, bell. "Postmodern Blackness." *Postmodern Culture* 1, no. 1 (September 1990). http://muse.jhu.edu/journals/postmodern_culture/toc/pmc1.1.

Iyengar, Shanto, *Is Anyone Responsible? How Television Frames Political Issues*. Chicago: University of Chicago Press, 1991.

Iyengar, Shanto, and Donald R. Kinder. *News That Matters: Television and American Opinion*. Chicago: University of Chicago Press, 1993.

Jamieson, Kathleen Hall. *Beyond the Double Bind: Women and Leadership*. New York: Oxford University Press, 1995.

———. *Eloquence in An Electronic Age*. New York: Oxford University Press, 1988.

———. *Everything You Think You Know About Politics: And Why You're Wrong*. New York: Basic Books, 2000.

Jamieson, Kathleen Hall, and Paul Waldman. *The Press Effect: Politicians, Journalists, and the Stories That Shape the Political World*. New York: Oxford University Press, 2003.

Japp, Phillis M. "Esther or Isaiah? The Abolitionist-Feminist Rhetoric of Angelina Grimke." *Quarterly Journal of Speech* 71, no. 3 (August 1985): 335–48.

Jeffries, Judson R., ed. *Black Power in the Belly of the Beast*. Champaign: University of Illinois Press, 2006.

Jeffords, Susan. *Hard Bodies: Hollywood Masculinity in the Reagan Era*. Brunswick, N.J.: Rutgers University Press, 1994.

———. *The Remasculinization of America: Gender and the Vietnam War*. Bloomington: Indiana University Press, 1989.

Jetter, Alexis, Annelise Orleck, and Diana Taylor. *The Politics of Motherhood: Activist Voices from Left to Right*. Hanover, N.H.: University Press of New England, 1997.

Johnson, Allan G. *The Gender Knot: Unraveling Our Patriarchal Legacy*. Philadelphia: Temple University Press, 2005.

Jordanova, Ludmilla, "Medicine and Genres of Display." Pp. 202–17 in *Visual Display: Culture Beyond Appearances*, edited by Lynne Cooke and Peter Wollen. New York: Free Press, 1995.

Joshi, S. T. *The Angry Right: Why Conservatives Keep Getting It Wrong*. New York: Prometheus Books, 2006.

Kaid, Lynda Lee, ed. *Handbook of Political Communication Research*. Mahwah, N.J.: Lawrence Erlbaum Associates, 2004.

Kahn, Kim Fridkin. "The Distorted Mirror: Press Coverage of Women Candidates for Statewide Office." *The Journal of Politics* 56, no. 1 (Winter 1994):154–73.

———. *The Political Consequences of Being A Woman: How Stereotypes Influence the Conduct and Consequences of Political Campaigns*. New York: Columbia University Press, 1996.

Kahn, Kim Fridkin, and Eddie Goldenberg. "Women Candidates in the News: An Examination of Gender Differences in U.S. Senate Campaign Coverage." *Public Opinion Quarterly* 55, no. 2 (Summer 1991): 180–99.

Kahneman, Daniel, and Amos Tversky. "Choices, Values, and Frames." *American Psychologist* 39, no. 4 (April 1984): 107–28.

Kann, Mark E. *The Gendering of American Politics: Founding Mothers, Founding Fathers, and Political Patriarchy*. Westport, Conn.: Praeger, 1999.

———. *A Republic of Men: The American Founders, Gendered Language, and Patriarchal Politics* New York: New York University Press, 1998.

Karsten, Margaret Foegen. Managerial Women: Yesterday and Today." *Management and Gender: Issues and Attitudes*. Westport, Conn.: Praeger, 1994.

Kerber, Linda K. "Separate Spheres, Female Worlds, Women's Place: The Rhetoric of Women's History." *Journal of American History* 75, no. 1 (June 1988): 9–39.

Kessler-Harris, Alice. *Out to Work: A History of Wage-Earning Women in the United States*. Oxford: Oxford University Press, 1982.

Kessler, Suzanne J., and Wendy McKenna. *Gender: An Ethnomethodological Approach*. Chicago: University of Chicago Press, 1978.

Keyssar, Alexander. *The Right to Vote*. New York: Basic Books, 2000.

Kimmel, Michael S. *The Gendered Society*, 2nd ed. New York: Oxford University Press, 2004.

———. "Invisible Masculinity." *Society* (Sept./Oct. 1993): 28–35.

———. *Manhood in America: A Cultural History*. New York: The Free Press,1996.

Kintz, Linda. "Performing Virtual Whiteness: George Gilder's Techno-Theocracy." *Cultural Studies* 16, no. 5 (September 2002): 735–73.

Kitch, Carolyn. *The Girl on the Magazine Cover: The Origins of Visual Stereotypes in American Mass Media*. Chapel Hill: The University of North Carolina Press, 2001.

Kraditor, Aileen S. *Ideas of the Woman Suffrage Movement, 1890–1920.* New York: Columbia University Press, 1965.

———. *Up from the Pedestal: Selected Writings in the History of American Feminism*. New York: The New York Times Book Company, 1975.

Kropf, Martha, and John Boiney. "The Electoral Glass Ceiling: How The News Affects The Viability Of Female Candidates." Paper presented at the annual meeting of the Midwest Political Science Association, Chicago, April 1996.

Krolokke, Charlotte, and Anne Scott Sorensen. *Gender Communication Theories & Analyses.* Thousand Oaks, Calif.: Sage Publications, 2006.

Kuhr, Fred. "First in Their Houses" *Advocate* (November 7, 2006): 37.

Lake Dates, Jannette, and William Barlow. *Split Image: African Americans in the Mass Media.* Washington, D.C.: Howard University Press, 1993.

Lake Dates, Jannette, and Oscar H. Gandy Jr. "How Ideological Constraints Affected Coverage of the Jesse Jackson Campaign." *Journalism Quarterly* 62 (1985): 595–600.

Lakoff, Robin Tolmach. *Talking Power: The Politics of Language.* New York: Basic Books, 1990.

Landes, Joan B. "The Public and Private Sphere." Pp. 91–116 in *Feminists Read Habermas: Gendering the Subject of Discourse*, edited by Johanna Meehan. New York: Routledge, 1995.

———. *Feminism, the Public, and the Private.* New York: Oxford University Press, 1998.

Langellier, Kristen M. "Personal Narratives: Perspective on Theory and Research." *Text and Performance Quarterly* 9, no. 3 (October 1989): 243–76.

Langellier, Kristen M., Kathryn Carter and Darlene Hantzis. "Performing Differences: Feminism and Performance Studies." Pp. 87–124 in *Transforming Visions: Feminist Critiques in Communication Studies,* edited by Sheryl Perlmutter Bowen and Nancy Wyatt. Cresskill, N.J.: Hampton Press, 1993.

Lehrer, Susan. *The Origins of Protective Labor Legislation for Women, 1905–1925.* New York: State University of New York Press, 1987.

Lemons, J. Stanley. *The Woman Citizen: Social Feminism in the 1920s.* Urbana: University of llinois Press, 1973.

Livermore, Mary. "Superfluous Women." Pp. 340–42 in *Public Women, Public Words: A Documentary History of American Feminism*, Vol. 1, edited by Dawn Keetley and John Pettegrew. Madison, Wisc.: Madison House, 1997.

Longhurst, Robyn. *Bodies: Exploring Fluid Boundaries.* London: Routledge, 2001.

Lorber, Judith. *Gender Inequality: Feminist Theories and Politics.* Los Angeles, Calif.: Roxbury, 1998.

———. *Paradoxes of Gender.* New Haven, Conn.: Yale University Press, 1994.

Lublin, Daniel, and Sarah E. Brewer, "The Continuing Dominance of Traditional Gender Roles in Southern Elections." *Social Science Quarterly* 84 (June 2003): 379–96.

Luker, Kristin. *Abortion and the Politics of Motherhood.* Berkeley: University of California Press, 1984.

Mackay, Francis. "Gender and Political Representation in the UK: The State of the Discipline." *British Journal of Politics & International Relations* 6, no. 1 (Winter 2004): 99–120.

MacKinnon, Catharine A. "Feminism, Marxism, Method, and the State: An Agenda for Theory." *Signs: Journal of Women in Culture and Society* 7, no. 3 (Spring 1982): 515–44.

Maguire, Joe. *Brainless: The Lies and Lunacies of Ann Coulter.* New York: William Morrow, 2006.

Majors, Richard, and Janet Mancini Billson. *Cool Pose: The Dilemmas of Black Manhood in America.* Lanham, Md.: Lexington Books, 1992.

Malin, Brenton J. *American Masculinity Under Clinton: Popular Media and the Nineties "Crisis of Masculinity."* New York: Peter Lang, 2005.

Manning, Jimmie. "Heterosexuality." Pp. 684–89 in *Encyclopedia of Gender and Society*, edited by Jodi A. O'Brien. Thousand Oaks, Calif.: Sage, 2008.

———. "Inclusive Language Use." Pp. 56–63 in *Handbook of Speaker-Audience Communication*, edited by Deb Ford. Belmont, Calif.: Wadsworth, 2004.

Marshall, David. *Celebrity and Power: Fame in Contemporary Culture.* Minneapolis: University of Minnesota Press, 1997.

Marshall, Marguerite Mooers. "Newspaper Woman Protest Against 'Maternal Legislation.'" *Life and Labor* 10, no. 30 (1920): 84.

Marton, Kati. *Hidden Power: Presidential Marriages That Shaped Our Recent History.* New York: Pantheon Books, 2001.

Matlin, Margaret. *The Psychology of Women* 3rd edition. Ft. Worth, Tex.: Harcourt Brace, 1996.

Matthews, Glenna. *The Rise of Public Woman: Woman's Power and Place in the United States, 1630–1970.* New York: Oxford University Press, 1992.

Matthews, Sandra, and Laura Wexler. *Pregnant Pictures.* New York: Routledge, 2000.

Mattina, Anne F. "Hillary Rodham Clinton: Using Her Vital Voice." Pp. 417–33 in *Inventing a Voice: The Rhetoric of American First Ladies of the Twentieth Century*, edited by Molly Meijer Wertheimer. Lanham, Md.: Rowman & Littlefield, 2004.

May, Rollo. *The Cry for Myth.* New York: W.W. Norton & Co., 1991.

Mayer, Jane, "The Insiders," *The New Yorker*, October 27, 2008.

Mayhead, Molly A., and Brenda DeVore Marshall. *Women's Political Discourse: A Twentieth Century Perspective.* Lanham, Md.: Rowman & Littlefield, 2005.

McCabe, Janet. "In the Feminine Ideal, We Trust." *FlowTV* 8, no.10 (October 2008).

McClain, Paula D., Niambi M. Carter, and Michael C. Brady. "Gender and Black Presidential Politics: From Chisholm to Moseley Braun." *Journal of Women, Politics and Policy* 27, no. 1:2 (Winter/Spring 2005): 51–68.

McGee, Michael Calvin. "The 'Ideograph': A Link between Rhetoric and Ideology." *Quarterly Journal of Speech* 66, no. 1 (February 1980): 141–59.

McDonald-Valesh, Eva. "Woman and Labor, 1896." Pp. 338–40 in *Public Women, Public Words: A Documentary History of American Feminism*, Vol. 1, edited by Dawn Keetley and John Pettegrew. Madison, Wisc.: Madison House, 1997.

McKinnon, Ann, "Even Mud Has the Illusion of Depth: A McLuhanesque Reading of Sarah Palin." *FlowTV* 8, no. 10 (October 2008).

Middleton, Peter. *The Inward Gaze: Masculinity and Subjectivity in Modern Culture*. London: Routledge, 1992.

Milton, Joyce. *The First Partner: Hillary Rodham Clinton*. New York: Wm. Morrow, 1999.

Min-ha, Trinh T. "The Totalizing Quest of Meaning." Pp. 90–107 in *Theorizing Documentary*, edited by Michael Renov. New York: Routledge, 1993.

Joanne Morreale. *The Presidential Campaign Film: A Critical History*. Westport, Conn.: Praeger, 1996.

Morris, Roger. *Partners in Power: The Clintons & Their America*. New York: Henry Holt, 1996.

Mulac, Anthony. "The Gender-Linked Language Effect: Do Language Differences Really Make a Difference?" Pp. 127–54 in *Sex Differences and Similarities in Communication*, edited by Daniel J. Canary and Kathryn Dindia. Mahwah, N.J.: Erlbaum, 1998.

Muir, Janette Kenner, and Lisa Benitez. "Redefining the Role of the First Lady: The Rhetoric of Hillary Rodham Clinton." Pp. 139–58 in *The Clinton Presidency: Images, Issues, and Communication Strategies*, edited by Robert E. Denton Jr. and Rachel Holloway. New York: Praeger, 1996.

Nakayama, Thomas K. and Robert L. Krizek. "Whiteness: A Strategic Rhetoric." *Quarterly Journal of Speech* 81, no. 3 (August 1995): 291–310.

Nichols, Bill. *Introduction to Documentary*. Bloomington: Indiana University Press, 2001.

———. *Representing Reality*. Bloomington: Indiana University Press, 1991.

Nichols, John. "Will Any Woman Do? The Candidacy of Elizabeth Dole." *The Progressive*, 63 (July 1999): 31–33.

Nimmo, Dan. "The Formation of Candidate Images During Presidential Campaigns," *Candidate Images in Presidential Elections*. Edited by Kenneth L. Hacker. Westport, Conn.: Praeger, 1995.

Novkov, Julie. *Constituting Workers, Protecting Women: Gender, Law and Labor in the Progressive Era and New Deal Years*. Ann Arbor: University of Michigan Press, 2001.

Norris, Pippa. "Women Leaders Worldwide: A Splash of Color in the Photo Op." Pp. 149–65 in *Women, Media, and Politics*, edited by Pippa Norris. New York: Oxford University, 1997.

———. *Women, Media, and Politics*. New York: Oxford University Press, 1997.

Ohl, Jessy. "Media Frames for Female Vice-Presidential Candidates: Issues of Experience, Tactics, and Gambles." Paper presented at the University of Alabama Gender and Political Communication Student Colloquium, Tuscaloosa, Alabama, December, 2008.

Orbe, Mark. "Constructions of Reality on MTV's 'The Real World': An Analysis of the Restrictive Coding of Black Masculinity." *Southern Journal of Communication* 64, no. 1 (Fall 1998): 32–47.

Orleck, Annelise. "Tradition Unbound: Radical Mothers in International Perspective." Pp. 3–21 in *The Politics of Motherhood: Activist Voices From the Left to Right*, edited by Alexis Jetter, Annelise Orleck, and Diana Taylor. Hanover, N.H.: University Press of New England 1997.

Parry-Giles, Shawn J., and Diane M. Blair. "The Rise of the Rhetorical First Lady: Politics, Gender Ideology, and Women's Voice, 1789–2002." *Rhetoric and Public Affairs* 5, no. 4 (Winter 2002): 565–600.

Parry-Giles, Shawn J., and Trevor Parry-Giles. *Constructing Clinton: Hyperreality & Presidential Image-Making in Postmodern Politics*. New York: Peter Lang, 2002.

———. "Gendered Politics and Presidential Image Construction: A Reassessment of the 'Feminine Style.'" *Communication Monographs* 63, no. 1 (December 1996): 337–53.

Parry-Giles, Trevor, and Shawn J. Parry-Giles. "Political Scopophilia, Presidential Campaigning, and the Intimacy of American Politics." *Communication Studies* 47, no. 3 (Fall 1996): 191–205.

Pearce, W. Barnett, Stephen W. Littlejohn, and Alison Alexander. "The New Christian Right and the Humanist Response: Reciprocated Diatribe." *Communication Quarterly* 35, no. 2 (Spring 1987): 171–92.

Pecora, Norma. "Superman/Superboys/Supermen: The Comic Book Hero as Socializing Agent." Pp. 61–77 in *Men, Masculinity, and the Media*, edited by Steve Craig. Newbury Park, Calif.: SAGE Publications, 1992.

Peiss, Kathy. *Cheap Amusements*. Philadelphia: Temple University Press, 1986.

Perelman, Chaim, "Choice, Presence, and Presentation," in *The Realm of Rhetoric*. Notre Dame, Ind.: University of Notre Dame Press, 1982.

Plato. "Gorgias." Pg. 61–112 in *The Rhetorical Tradition*, edited by Patricia Bizzell and Bruce Herzberg. Boston, Mass.: Bedford Books, 1990.

Porter, Kathy. *A History of Suffrage in the United States*. New York: AMS Press, 1971.

Prelli, Lawrence, "Rhetorics of Display: An Introduction." Pp, 1–38 in *Rhetorics of Display*, edited by Lawrence J. Prelli. Columbia: University of South Carolina Press, 2006.

Procter, David. E., Roger C. Aden, and Phyllis Japp. "Gender/Issue Interaction in Political Identity Making: Nebraska's Woman vs. Woman Gubernatorial Campaign." *Central States Speech Journal* 39, no. 3:4 (Fall/Winter 1988): 90–203.

Ramsey, E. Michele, Paul Achter, and Celeste Condit. "Genetics, Race, and Crime: An Audience Study Exploring the Effects of *The Bell Curve* and Book Reviews." *Critical Studies in Media Communication*, 18, no. 4 (December 2001): 1–22.

Renov, Michael. *The Subject of Documentary*. Minneapoli: University of Minnesota Press, 2004.

———. ed. *Theorizing Documentary*. New York: Routledge, 1993.

Richards, Kate. "How I Became a Socialist Agitator." Pp. 349–52 in *Public Women, Public Words: A Documentary History of American Feminism*, Vol. 1, edited by Dawn Keetley and John Pettegrew. Madison, Wisc.: Madison House, 1997.

Rosen, Christine. "The Future of Women and Conservatism." *Society* 42 (2005): 32–35.

Rowe, Kathleen, *The Unruly Woman: Gender and the Genres of Laughter.* Austin: University of Texas Press, 1995.

Ruddick, Sarah. "From Maternal Thinking to Peace Politics." Pp. 141–55 in *Exploration in Feminist Ethics: Theory and Practice,* edited by Eve Browning Cole and Susan C. Coultrap-McQuin. Bloomington: Indiana University Press, 1992.

Ryan, Barbara. *Feminism and the Women's Movement: Dynamics of Change in Social Movement Ideology and Activism.* New York: Routledge, 1992.

Sanders, Lynn. "Against Deliberation." *Political Theory* 25, no. 2 (June 1997): 347–76.

Sapiro, Virginia. "The Political Uses of Symbolic Women: An Essay in Honor of Murray Edelman." *Political Communication* 10, no. 2 (April–June 1993): 141–54.

Sarkela, Sandra J., Susan Mallon Ross, and Margaret A. Lowe. *From Megaphones to Microphones: Speeches of American Women, 1920–1960.* Westport, Conn.: Praeger, 2003.

Savage, Robert L. "Creating the Eye of the Beholder." Pp. 37–50 in *Candidate Images in Presidential Elections,* edited by Kenneth L. Hacker. Westport, Conn.: Praeger, 1995.

Schonker-Schreck, Daniella. "Political Marketing and the Media: Women in the 1996 Israeli Elections—A Case Study." *Israel Affairs* 10, no. 3 (July 2004): 159–77.

Schram, Sanford. "The Post-Modern Presidency and the Grammar of Electronic Engineering." *Critical Studies in Mass Communication* 8, no. 2 (June 1991): 210–16.

Schudson, Michael. *The Good Citizen: A History of American Civic Life.* New York: The Free Press, 1998.

Serini, Shirley, Angela Powers, and Susan Johnson. "Of Horse Race and Policy Issues: A Study of Gender Coverage of a Gubernatorial Election by Two Major Metropolitan Newspapers." *Journalism and Mass Communication Quarterly* 75, no. 1 (Spring 1998): 194–204.

Silver, Diane. "A Comparison of Newspapers Coverage of Male and Female Officials in Michigan." *Journalism Quarterly* 63, no. 1 (Spring 1986): 144–49.

Simons, Herbert, *Persuasion in Society.* Thousand Oaks, Calif.: Sage, 2001.

Smith, Sally Bedell. *For Love of Politics: Bill and Hillary Clinton—The White House Years.* New York: Random House, 2007.

Sparks, Holloway. "Dissident Citizenship: Democratic Theory, Political Courage and Activist Women." *Hypatia* 12, no. 4 (Fall 1997): 74–110.

Spindel, Barbara. "Conservatism as the 'Sensible Middle': The Independent Women's Forum, Politics, and the Media." *Social Text* 77 (2003): 99–125.

———. "'Human Beings First, Women Second': Antifeminism and the Independent Women's Forum." Ann Arbor, Mich.: UMI, 2004.

Sreberny, Anabelle, and Liesbet van Zoonen. *Gender, Politics, and Communication* Cresskill, N.J.: Hampton Press, 1996.

Staples, Robert. *Black Masculinity: The Black Male's Role in American Society.* San Francisco: The Black Scholar Press, 1982.

Steans, Jill. *Gender and International Relations: An Introduction.* New Brunswick, N.J.: Rutgers University Press, 1998.

———. *Gender and International Relations: Issues, Debates, and Future Directions.* Cambridge: Polity Press, 2006.

Steinem, Gloria. "Shirley Chisholm: Front–Runner." *New York Magazine,* January 10, 2005.

Stokes, Ashley Quesinberry. "First Ladies in Waiting: The Fight for Rhetorical Legitimacy on the 2004 Campaign Trail." Pp. 167–94 in *The 2004 Presidential Campaign: A Communication Perspective,* edited by Robert E. Denton Jr. Lanham, Md.: Rowman & Littlefield, 2005.

Stormer, Nathan. "A Vexing Relationship: Gender and Contemporary Rhetorical Theory," Pp. 247–62 in *The SAGE Handbook of Gender and Communication,* edited by Bonnie J. Dow and Julia T. Wood. Thousand Oaks, Calif.: Sage, 2007.

Strachan, J. Cherie, and Kathleen E. Kendall, "Political Candidates' Convention Films: Finding the Perfect Image—An Overview of Political Image Making," Pp 135–54 in *Defining Visual Rhetorics,* edited by Charles A. Hill and Marguerite Helmers. Mahwah, N.J.: Lawrence Erlbaum, 2004.

Sturken, Marita, and Lisa Cartwright. *Practices of Looking: An Introduction to Visual Culture.* Oxford: Oxford University Press, 2001.

Sullivan, Patricia A. "Signification and African American Rhetoric: A Case Study of Jesse Jackson's 'Common Ground and Common Sense' Speech." *Communication Quarterly* 41, no. 1 (Winter 1993): 1–15.

Sullivan, Patricia A., and Lynn H. Turner. *From the Margins to the Center: Contemporary Women and Political Communication.* Westport, Conn.: Praeger, 1996.

Sylvester, Christine. *Feminist Theory and International Relations in a Postmodern Era.* Gateshead, Tyne & Wear, UK: Althenaeum Press Ltd., 1994.

Tannen, Deborah. *The Argument Culture: Changing the Way We Argue and Debate.* London: Virago Press, 1998.

Tatham, Peter. *The Makings of Maleness: Men, Women, and the Flight of Daedelus.* New York: New York University Press, 1992.

Taylor, Anita, and M. J. Hardman. "War, Language and Gender, What New Can Be Said? Framing the Issues." *Women and Language* 27, no. 2 (Fall 2004): 3–19.

Taylor, Charles. "The Politics of Recognition." Pp. 25–74 in *Multiculturalism,* edited by Amy Gutman. Princeton, N.J.: Princeton University Press, 1994.

Taylor, Jacqueline. "On Being an Exemplary Lesbian: My Life as a Role Model." *Text and Performance Quarterly* 20 no. 1 (January 2000): 58–73.

Taymor, Betty. *Running Against the Wind: The Struggle of Massachusetts Women in Politics.* Boston, Mass.: Northeastern University Press, 2000.

Tickner, J. Ann. *Gender in International Relations: Feminist Perspectives on Achieving Global Security.* New York, Columbia University Press: 1992.

——. "Hans Morgenthou's Principles of Political Realism: A Feminist Reformulation (1988)." Pp. 53–71 in *International Theory: Critical Investigations*, edited by James Der Derian. New York: New York University Press, 1995.

Tien, Charles, Regan Checchio, and Arthur H. Miller. "The Impact of First Wives on Presidential Campaigns and Elections." Pp. 149–168 in *Women in Politics: Outsiders or Insiders?* 3rd ed., edited by Lois Duke Whitaker. Upper Saddle River, N.J.: Prentice Hall, 1999.

Tobias, Sheila. "Shifting Heroisms: The Use of Military Service in Politics." Pp. 163–86 in *Women, Militarism and War: Essays in History, Politics, and Social Theory*, edited by Jean Bethke Elshtain and Sheila Tobias. Savage, Md.: Rowman & Littlefield, 1999.

Todorov, Tzvetan. *Theories of the Symbol.* Translated by Catherine Porter. *Théories du Symbole.* Ithaca: Cornell University Press, 1982.

Tonn, Mari Boor. "Militant Motherhood: Labor's Mary Harris 'Mother' Jones." *Quarterly Journal of Speech* 82, no. 1 (February 1996): 1–21.

Trent, Judith S. and Robert V. Friedenberg. *Political Campaign Communication: Principles and Practices*, 1st ed. New York: Praeger, 1983.

——. *Political Campaign Communication: Principles and Practices*, Third edition. Lanham, Md.: Rowan & Littlefield, 2004.

True, Jacqui. "Feminism." Pp. 210–251 in *Theories of International Relations*, edited by Scott Burchill and Andrew Linklater. St. Martin's Press: New York, 1996.

Trujillo, Nick. "Hegemonic Masculinity on the Mound: Media Representations of Nolan Ryan and American Sports Culture." *Critical Studies in Mass Communication* 8, no. 3 (September 1991): 290–309.

Wahl-Jorgensen, Karin. "Constructed Masculinities in U.S. Presidential Campaigns: The Case of 1992." Pp. 53–75 in *Gender, Politics, and Communication*, edited by Annabelle Sreberny and Liesbet van Zoonen. Cresskill, N.J.: Hampton Press Inc, 1996.

Walker, Nancy A. *Shaping Our Mothers' World: American Women's Magazines.* Jackson: University Press of Mississippi, 2000.

Watson, Robert P. "Introduction." Pp. 1–16 in *The Presidential Companion: Readings on the First Ladies*, edited by Robert P. Watson and Anthony J. Eksterowicz. Columbia: University of South Carolina Press, 2003.

——. "First Ladies and Their Influence on Politics, Policy, and the Presidency." Pp. 210–25 in *Women in Politics: Outsiders or Insiders?* 4th ed., edited by Lois Duke Whitaker Upper Saddle River, N.J.: Pearson/Prentice Hall, 2006.

——. *The Presidents' Wives: Reassessing the Office of First Lady.* Boulder, Colo.: Lynne Reinner Publishers, 2000.

Watson, Robert P., and Ann Gordon, eds. *Anticipating Madame President.* Boulder, Colo.: Lynne Reinner, 2003.

Watson, Robert P., and Anthony J. Eksterowicz, eds., *The Presidential Companion: Readings on the First Ladies*. Columbia, S.C.: University of South Carolina Press, 2003).

Weinberger, David. *Small Pieces Loosely Joined: A Unified Theory of the Web*. Cambridge, Mass.: Perseus, 2002.

Weitz, Rose. "A History of Women's Bodies." Pp. 3–11 in *The Politics of Women's Bodies: Sexuality, Appearance, and Behavior*, 2nd ed., edited by Rose Weitz. New York: Oxford University Press, 2003.

Welter, Barbara. "The Cult of True Womanhood: 1820–1860." *American Quarterly* 18, no. 2 (Summer 1966): 151–74.

Wertheimer, Molly, ed. *Inventing a Voice: The Rhetoric of First Ladies of the Twentieth Century*. Lanham, Md.: Rowman & Littlefield, 2004.

White Joseph L., and James H. Cones III. *Black Man Emerging*. New York: Routledge, 1999.

Whicker, Marcia Lynn, and Hedy Leonie Isaacs. "Gendering the Political Executive's Space: The Changing Landscape?" Pp. 201–09 in *Women in Politics: Outsiders or Insiders?* 4th ed., edited by Lois Duke Whitaker. Upper Saddle River, N.J.: Pearson/Prentice Hall, 2006.

———. "The Maleness of the American Presidency." Pp 221–32 in *Women in Politics: Outsiders or Insiders?* edited by Lois Duke Whitaker. Upper Saddle River, N.J.: Prentice Hall, 1999.

Will, George F. *The Leveling Wind: Politics, Culture, and Other News 1990–1994*. New York: Viking, 1994.

Wimmer, Rodger, and Joseph Dominick. *Mass Media Research*. Belmont, Calif.: Wadsworth, 2000.

Winfield, Betty Houchin. "The First Lady, Political Power, and the Media: Who Elected Her Anyway?" Pp. 166–80 in *Women, Media, and Politics*, edited by Pippa Norris. New York: Oxford University Press, 1997.

Winston, Brian. *Claiming the Real: The Documentary Film Revisited*. London: British Film Institute, 1995.

Witt, Andrew. *The Black Panthers in the Midwest: The Community Programs and Services of the Black Panther Party in Milwaukee, 1966–1977*. London: Routledge, 2007.

Witt, Linda, Karen M. Paget, and Glenna Matthews. *Running as a Woman: Gender and Power in American Politics*. New York: The Free Press, 1995.

Woloch, Nancy. *Women and the American Experience, A Concise History*. Boston, Mass.: McGraw Hill, 2000.

Wood, Julia T. *Gendered Lives: Communication, Gender, and Culture*, 5th ed. Belmont, Calif.: Wadsworth, 2003.

Zaeske, Susan. The "Promiscuous Audience: Controversy and the Emergence of the Early Woman's Rights Movement." *Quarterly Journal of Speech* 81, no. 2 (May 1995): 191–207.

Zaeske, Sue. *Signatures of Citizenship: Petitioning, AntiSlavery, and Women's Political Identity*. Chapel Hill: University of North Carolina Press, 2003.

Zelizer, Barbie. *Remembering to Forget: Holocaust Memory through the Camera's Eye*. Chicago: University of Chicago Press, 1998.

Zulick, Margaret. "The Agon of Jeremiah: On the Dialogic Invention of Prophetic Ethos." *Quarterly Journal of Speech* 78, no. 2 (May 1992): 521–23.

INDEX

ABOUT THE CONTRIBUTORS

Paul J. Achter (PhD, University of Georgia) is an assistant professor of rhetoric at the University of Richmond. His articles have appeared in journals such as the *Quarterly Journal of Speech*, *Critical Studies in Media Communication*, *Southern Communication Journal*, and *Politics and the Life Sciences*. An award-winning teacher, Achter's courses focus on rhetorical theory, practice, and criticism. His current projects include an analysis of the rhetoric of Iraq war veterans, a study of the influence of comedy and news parody in public life, and an interdisciplinary course and research program called Critical Confederacy Studies,

Wendy Atkins-Sayre (PhD, University of Georgia) is an assistant professor of speech communication and director of the Speaking Center at the University of Southern Mississippi. Her research interests center on issues of identity as shaped by discourse in the areas of gender and social change. Her research has appeared in *Women and Language* and her reviews have appeared in *Women's Studies in Communication*, *Southern Communication Journal*, and *Quarterly Journal of Speech*.

Heather Aldridge Bart, (PhD, University of Kansas) is an associate professor of communication studies at Augustana College in Sioux Falls, South Dakota. Her work is in the area of rhetoric and argumentation, primarily in the context of political communication. She is the coauthor of "Rap on

Violence: A Rhetorical Analysis of Rapper KRS-One," which was published in *Communication Studies*. She works with undergraduates in developing research projects to prepare them for graduate study.

Teresa Bergman (PhD, University of California, Davis) is an associate professor at the University of the Pacific and a former documentary film-maker. She teaches courses in the rhetoric of documentary film, communication criticism, and mass communication. Her research explores the evolving representation of nationalism and citizenship in orientation films at U.S. national parks and memorials, and she has appeared in *Rhetoric and Public Address* and the *Western Journal of Communication*. She is currently working on a book on this topic.

Lisa M. Burns (PhD, University of Maryland, College Park) is an associate professor of media studies at Quinnipiac University. Her research focuses on media coverage of U.S. first ladies and presidents. She is the author of *First Ladies and the Fourth Estate: Press Framing of Presidential Wives*. Her articles on first lady press coverage have appeared in *Rhetoric and Public Affairs* and the *White House Studies Journal*. She teaches classes in political communication, media history, and media influence.

Janis L. Edwards (PhD, University of Massachusetts, Amherst) is an associate professor of communication studies at the University of Alabama. Her research interests include the rhetorical dimensions of media in political contexts and the intersection of visual rhetorics, place, and memory studies. She is the author of *Political Cartoons in the 1988 Presidential Campaign: Image, Metaphor, and Narrative*, and her research has appeared in such journals as *Quarterly Journal of Speech*, *Communication Quarterly*, and *PS Political Science and Politics*. She is a contributing author to *Inventing a Voice: American First Ladies of the Twentieth Century*, *Defining Visual Rhetorics*, and *Visual Rhetoric: A Reader in Communication and American Culture*.

Erika Falk (PhD, University of Pennsylvania) is the associate program chair of the MA in communication at Johns Hopkins University. She is the author of *Women for President: Media Bias in Eight Campaigns* and several articles about women and the American presidency. She is also a contributing author to *Anticipating Madame President*.

Margaret E. Farrar (PhD, Pennsylvania State University) is associate professor and chair of political science at Augustana College in Rock Island, Illinois. Her previously published work includes *Building the Body Politic: Power and Urban Space in Washington, D.C.*, from the University of Illinois Press, and "Rah-Rah Radical: The Radical Cheerleader's Challenge to the Public Sphere" with Jamie Warner in the journal *Politics and Gender*.

Heidi Hamilton (PhD, University of Iowa) is an assistant professor of communication at Emporia State University in Emporia, Kansas. Her work is primarily in the areas of gender, foreign policy rhetoric, and political communication. Her work on political activism and celebrity has appeared in the *American Communication Journal*, and she is past chair of the feminist and women's studies division of the National Communication Association.

Mary L. Kahl (PhD, Indiana University) is an associate professor of communication and media at the State University of New York at New Paltz. Her research focusing on political discourse, gendered communication, and the rhetorics of place has been published in *Quarterly Journal of Speech*, *Western Journal of Communication*, *Qualitative Research Reports*, and other journals . She is a past president of the Eastern Communication Association and serves on the editorial boards of several regional and national communication journals.

Shereé Keith (PhD, University of Iowa) is an assistant professor in the humanities department at Macon State College. Her research centers on how the discussion of gender roles is shaped by theoretical notions such as the "feminine communication style" outlined by Karlyn Kohrs Campbell, Bonnie Dow, and others. Her article on gender, social change, and metaphors appears in the *Texas Journal of Communication*.

Stephen A. Klien (PhD, University of Illinois, Urbana-Champaign) is an associate professor of communication studies and chair of the fine and performing arts division at Augustana College in Rock Island, Illinois. His previously published work includes "Public Character and the Simulacrum: The Construction of the Soldier Patriot and Citizen Agency in *Black Hawk Down*" in *Critical Studies in Media Communication*.

Jimmie Manning (PhD, University of Kansas) is assistant professor and graduate program director for communication at Northern Kentucky University. His research largely explores relationships and communication, including relational support and control; internal and external definitions of relationships; relational representations; and legal-political discourses shaping relationships. He has published a variety of journal articles and chapters on these topics and has received eight top paper–panel awards from regional and national conferences.

Janette Kenner Muir (PhD, University of Massachusetts, Amherst) is an associate professor of Interdisciplinary and Integrative Studies and an affiliate member of the communication and women's studies departments, George Mason University. Her research focuses on political campaigns and civic engagement. She is coeditor of *Readings on Political Communication* and a contributing author to *Inventing a Voice: The Rhetoric of American First Ladies of the Twentieth Century*. She currently serves as editor of the journal *Communication Quarterly*.

Kimberly S. Reiser (MA, University of Montana) is an adjunct assistant professor of communication studies in the College of Technology at the University of Montana, Missoula, where she also coordinates the first year experience. As a former forensics competitor and coach, her special interests are in public address and political communication, focusing on gender. Her interest in children's communication stems from her background as a high school teacher, as well as one of the most important people in her life—her two-year-old son. She has received top paper awards for her presentations at the Western States Communication Association.

Cady Short-Thompson (PhD, University of Cincinnati) is professor and chair of communication at Northern Kentucky University. Political campaign research has been her main focus, including longitudinal, survey research conducted prior to the New Hampshire primary each presidential election year, as well as in-depth analysis of women candidates' campaign communication at all levels of elective politics.

Christina Standerfer (PhD, University of Colorado) is an assistant professor at the University of Arkansas Clinton School of Public Service. Her research centers on the investigation of the rhetorical construction of civic engagement, public issues, public opinion, and the practical import of communication theory to public service work. She currently serves on the editorial board of *Women's Studies in Communication*.

Anita Taylor (PhD, University of Missouri) is professor emerita in communication and women's studies at George Mason University. Professor Taylor is executive editor of the research periodical, *Women and Language*. Her most recent books are *Hearing Many Voices*, coedited with M. J. Hardman; *Conflict and Gender*, coedited with Judi Beinstein Miller; and *Women Communicating*, with Barbara Bate. She has also written about Studio D, the feminist film studio at the National Film Board of Canada. She serves on the executive board of the Organization for the Study of Communication, Language, and Gender, and, with M. J. Hardman, has coedited a special issue of *Women and Language* on language, gender, and war.